BIRD

OF

NEW ZEALAND

—

LOCALITY GUIDE

BY STUART CHAMBERS

ARUN BOOKS
SOUTH AUCKLAND

BIRDS

OF

NEW ZEALAND

—

LOCALITY GUIDE

First published 1989
This updated edition 2000
Published by ARUN BOOKS, Clarks Beach, South Auckland, New Zealand
Email: as_chambers@xtra.co.nz
www.kiwiculture.com

ISBN 0-473-07327-7

Typeset by Arun Books and Rice Printers
Printed by Rice Printers, 102 Rostrevor Street, Hamilton, New Zealand

ACKNOWLEDGMENTS

The second edition of this book wholeheartedly supports the acknowledgments recorded in the first edition.

I would, though, like to acknowledge the work of Hamish Spencer who read the whole text, made necessary comments about each bird locality, and provided important South Island locations unknown to the author.

My thanks also go to Roger Chorlton for his scrutiny of the original text. Richard Chambers, Hugh Clifford, Paul Cuming, Morag Fordham, Simon Fordham, John Gale, David Helliar, Tony Habraken, David Lawrie, Brian Parkinson, Gwenda Pulham, Adrian Riegen, John Rowe, Stella Rowe, Ian Southey, Betty Seddon, Roger Sutton, Michael Taylor, Bev Woolley, Barbara Walter and Keith Woodley helped with new localities in this edition.

I also wish to thank Tracey Borgfeldt and Richard Chambers for their help with editorial ideas, layout and typesetting, and Robert and Andrew Chambers for their work with the photographs and illustrations. Brian Chudleigh has again provided world class photographs. Jim Hague and David Stonex have provided encouragement and been most helpful with additional photographs.

Selwyn Dephoff, Katherine Hay and Bevan Parker have greatly assisted the final text and layout.

I also wish to thank Alison Chambers for her help and tolerance in putting up with this project and all those who purchased the first edition. Their support has allowed this edition to proceed.

Stuart Chambers
Clarks Beach
2000

Front Cover Photographs: Bush scene - Rafael Valentino.
Little Spotted Kiwi - Simon Fordham,

CONTENTS

PLACES

BIRDS OF NEW ZEALAND - LOCALITY GUIDE

FOREWORD

One of the really exciting things to have occurred in recent years is the enormous growth in the number of people who literally follow their hobbies and interests to the very ends of the earth. Birding, possibly more than any other specialist activity, lends itself splendidly to this fairly recent development, and New Zealand is experiencing constant reminders that it is very much a "must visit" destination for birders from all over the world.

Whilst native New Zealand bird species have declined over a number of years there is still much to interest both local and overseas birders and the ready availability of camper vans, camping grounds and clean, reasonably priced motel and bunk-bed accommodation makes this a first rate country in which to see birds. Another great attraction is that many of our native birds can still be seen in natural bush, forest, mountain, wilderness and wetland areas.

In my capacity, first as resident warden at the Miranda Naturalists' Trust's Visitors' Centre on the Firth of Thames, only a pleasant one hour's drive from Auckland, and subsequently as the Trust's chairman, I have enjoyed meeting many hundreds of visitors from all over the world. Birders, very much like the birds they seek so avidly, come in a great variety of shapes and sizes. They range from the jet-setting ornithophile to the young family from the city who wish their children to share with them the thrill of saying farewell to the many godwits and knots gathered on the shellbanks before they depart on their epic journey to the breeding grounds amongst the Arctic tundra of far away Siberia and Alaska.

Likewise, the variety of books available to both the expert and newly converted bird-watcher is staggering. Glossy publications with marvellous photographs vie in bookshops with learned treatise which cover every aspect of birds and birding. Some moderately priced books try to cover in one volume a

7

world-wide range of species which is clearly an essay into the impossible.

Much more useful to travelling birders are books which set out to cover a reasonable range of birds within a given area or specific country. There are some excellent field guides available but even these can be frustrating to travellers who have spent the long evenings of the American or European winter gaining a wide ranging knowledge of the particular birds they wish to add to their "life" lists. Armed with this painstakingly acquired background they arrive at their birding destinations only to be confronted with the fact that they have no idea where to start looking for the birds, and surprised to discover that the country which looked so small on the world atlas is going to present real logistical problems if it is to be adequately covered in the few weeks at their disposal.

I believe that Stuart Chambers in his second and revised edition of "Birds of New Zealand - Locality Guide", has again solved the problem. A greatly respected naturalist with a deep knowledge of New Zealand and of its natural history and geography, he has managed to bring together in one book a very comprehensive guide to the various species and where they are most likely to be found. This is equally satisfactory to the expert ornithologist or to the birding beginner. No mean feat.

I have met many visitors who found the first edition of immense use to them whilst in New Zealand. This included one who actually covered the whole of New Zealand from Stewart Island to Cape Reinga with no other map or reference book of any kind. I therefore feel qualified on the grounds of these often repeated and by no means solicited testimonials to Stuart Chambers' book, to write this "foreword" to this new revised edition. This I know is even more informative than the first. I am also greatly honoured.

John Gale
Immediate Past Chairman
Miranda Naturalists' Trust
Auckland
December 2000

ABOUT THIS BOOK

This book is written for all bird-watchers. It is valuable for those New Zealand bird-watchers who have difficulty in identifying birds and knowing where to find them. It is also valuable for overseas birders and includes notes to make their visits to New Zealand easier.

Note: This book does not attempt a complete coverage of New Zealand birds or places. Rather, it is selective, introducing people to birds they have a chance of seeing, and only taking them to places which are easy to get to and which promise results.

This book supports the notion that birds are less endangered and better protected if the public is knowledgeable and educated about them. It is especially suitable for the following people -

- **Listers:** People who want to know the birds around them and to make lists of them.
- **Tickers and twitchers:** People who have a competitive desire to see as many birds as possible, usually on a world-wide basis.
- **Family gatherers:** People who have a desire to see all the bird families of the world.
- **Ornithologists:** People who make scientific studies of birds.
- **Bird-watchers:** People who just like looking at birds.
- **Out-door people and nature lovers:** People who enjoys the out of doors and the places where birds live.

The lay-out of this book: The birds are assembled in the evolutionary order of the **"Checklist Of The Birds Of New Zealand" (1990)**.

Excursions: This book contains choices of seven-day excursions which could be useful for overseas' visitors.

How to use: Should you want to first get to know New Zealand's own endemic families study the articles on Kiwi, Rifleman, Rock Wren, Saddleback and Kokako and then plan accordingly.

Status: Birds are classified as to endemic, native, migrant, introduced, vagrant, circumpolar.

Bird size: Measurements are from bill to tail. The House Sparrow, for example is 145mm, and is used in the text as the base-line for bird size.

Maps: These can be purchased in any good book shop and used in conjunction with the written text instructions.

Other reading:

"The Field Guide To The Birds Of New Zealand" by Barrie D Heather and Hugh A Robertson. Viking (1996).

"Collins Handguide to The Birds of New Zealand" by Chloe Talbot Kelly. Collins (1982).

ABOUT NEW ZEALAND

Location of New Zealand: New Zealand is a South Pacific country lying to the east of Australia and to the south of the tropical islands of Fiji. It lies between the 34th and 48th latitudes and on a world basis is diametrically opposite the country of Spain in the northern hemisphere. It is a three hour flight from Auckland, New Zealand's largest city, to Sydney in Australia, and a similar time to Nadi in Fiji or to Invercargill in the south of New Zealand.

Landscape: New Zealand is generally of hilly and mountainous terrain but with substantial areas of fertile agricultural and pastoral land. Farm products make up a large proportion of New Zealand's exports.

Landscape diversity: A major feature of the New Zealand landscape is its diversity within very small areas. A short drive can produce coastal scenery, forests, pastoral scenes or mountains. Hence, a short drive can produce a number of bird habitats.

Climate: The climate is termed temperate. The North Island experiences hot summers suitable for swimming and boating activities. Yachting is a major sport. In the South Island, summers inland are hot but southern coastal areas are cool. Winters in the south are cold. On Stewart Island the temperature remains much the same throughout the year at between 12° - 16° Celsius. Summer temperatures, in the main islands average around 22° C or 72° Fahrenheit. Winter temperatures are between 10° C and 15° C in the north and between 5° C and 15° C in the south. Wind can be a problem during any season especially in the equinoctial months of late September and late March.

Forests: These are of several varieties. In the north they contain mixes of kauri (*Agathis australis*) and podocarp species, (Podocarpaceae). In coastal northern areas, mixes of taraire (*Beilschmiedia tarairi*), tawa (*B.tawa*), puriri (*Vitex lucens*) and kohekohe (*Dysoxylum spectabile*), are common. In central North Island, and the west coast of the South Island mixes of podocarps, tawa, mangeao (*Litsea calicaris*) and rata (*Metrosideros robusta*) are common. In the colder mountainous areas, and the Fiordland area, forests of beech (*Nothofagus spp.*) are found. Most forests have been modified by man, browsing animals such as deer and possums, and by the introduction of exotic vegetation species.

Birdlife: The arrival of humans in New Zealand has had an effect on the populations of native birds with the decline of many species and the extinction of some. A bird population, which evolved in a predator-free environment and which in many instances became ground-feeding, slow moving and slow breeding, became severely depleted upon the introduction of mustelids (*Mustela spp.*), rats (*Rattus spp.*), feral cats (*Felis catus*) and the harmful effects of people upon the environment.

The result today is a severely depleted avi-fauna. Forests away from the predator-free, off-shore islands, no longer contain the richness of bird-life which they used to and which a visit to an off-shore island illustrates.

There is evidence, though, that many native species are learning to adjust to the new environment and birds such as the Bellbird, which W L Buller (1873) suggested would eventually die out, have made remarkable recoveries and are on the increase. The Whitehead, Tomtit and North Island Robin are other good examples of bird species on the increase.

Law and order: New Zealand is governed by a parliament elected every three years. Police have a low profile in New Zealand but are readily available if needed. Crime is not a big problem but cars and hotel rooms should be kept locked. Cars left at birding spots, no matter how isolated, should be locked. Valuables, cameras, lens and telescopes should be left in the car boot (trunk) and out of sight. New Zealand could be termed a safe country but normal precautions should be taken.

Driving: Cars travel on the left hand side of the road. Roads are generally tarmac even in the best birding spots, but metal roads (gravel) are always encountered somewhere on one's travels. The open road speed limit is 100 kms per hour. In towns it is 50 kms per hour. Road signs are written in English and are similar to those encountered overseas.

Rental Cars: These are readily available at all the bigger airports. There is a wide range of vehicles from mini-buses to 1300cc cars and sometimes smaller. There is also a wide range of campervans available. You can hire in one town and drop off in another.

Hospitals: Hospitals are of a high standard. Visitors should possess travel insurance but should they have an accident while in New Zealand, medical fees are paid by the New Zealand Accident Compensation Corporation.

Hotels and Motels: These are of a high standard. For cheapest rates stay at hotels in small towns and keep away from the giant tourist complexes. Motels have kitchens where meals can be prepared. The water in all hotels and motels is drinkable.

Language: English is the main language.

Money: Money is dollars and cents. Eftpos is now widespread and credit cards are accepted almost everywhere. Most used cards are Visa, Bankcard, Diners and American Express.

Tipping: Tipping is seldom encountered in New Zealand, so forget about it.

Clothing and dress: Generally New Zealand people of both sexes wear shorts for summer birding. However, long trousers are often required in the South Island, especially in Fiordland where biting insects called sandflies (Simuliidae spp.) can cause bother. Always have a raincoat and an extra jacket. Don't bring large quantities of clothes.

Population density: Population is highest in the Auckland area. Here the pace of life is faster but once away from the city and away from the motorways (freeways) the pace slows.

Birding in New Zealand: Birding in New Zealand is undertaken mainly for enjoyment, scientific and conservation purposes. "Twitchers" are seldom encountered. Overseas birders should therefore not become upset by New Zealanders' low-key attitudes to finding rare and difficult species.

BROWN KIWI

Brian Chudleigh

Family: Apterygidae   **Common name:** Brown Kiwi
Species: *Apteryx australis*   **Status:** Endemic
Size: 500 mm (cf sparrow 145 mm, domestic hen 500 mm)

Discussion: The Brown Kiwi is New Zealand's most unique bird. It is also its most ancient. The fact that it is flightless, having only rudimentary wings and no tail, suggests arrival here prior to the separation of the ancient landmass of Gondwanaland. The Brown Kiwi is a member of the ratite family of birds which include the extinct New Zealand Moa, Ostrich, Emu, Cassowary and Rhea. It varies from these birds by way of its much smaller size, its long extended bill with nostrils at the end, and by having four toes rather than either two toes or three toes as in the other species. Further, it is a nocturnal species.

Species and subspecies: The Brown Kiwi is divided by ornithologists into three subspecies, the North Island subspecies (*A. a. mantelli*), the South Island subspecies (*A. a. australis*) and the Stewart Island subspecies (*A. a. lawryi*). There are also two other distinct species of kiwi, the Little Spotted Kiwi (*Apteryx owenii*) and the Great Spotted Kiwi (*A. haastii*).

The name "Kiwi": Many, in the past, have considered the Maori named the kiwi after its call. Its call, though, does not closely resemble the word kiwi. This has caused people to look for other explanations and some now believe that its name arose from its similarity to night calling birds with which the early Maori had become accustomed to in their original Polynesian homelands.

One such night-calling bird from the Pacific island homeland is the Bristle-thighed Curlew (*Numenius tahitiensis*), known as Kivi to the islanders of Tahiti and Rarotonga. This bird calls loudly in the night - a long drawn out "krreep" sound. The early Maori, upon arrival in New Zealand, could have likened this call to the night calling Kiwi. The night calling Bush Thick-knee (*Burhinus grallarius*) of Australia, also calls "kivi" but it is not known from the islands

12

of the Pacific.

Habitat: Birds are found in forests both native and exotic, secondary forests and scrublands.

Range: North Island, South Island and Stewart Island. Also on Moturoa Island, Kawau Island, Little Barrier Island, Ponui Island and Kapiti Island.

Description:

Upperparts: Brown, streaked with dark brown. Feathers are unique with hair-like qualities, being basically shaftless and barbless. **Under-parts:** Similar colouring to upperparts. **Bill:** Grey.

Conspicuous characteristics:

- The kiwi is nocturnal.
- When feeding it often sit on its haunches. In this position it can look like a mound of brown dirt or even a hedgehog.
- When running away, it has a waddling, side to side, swaying gait.
- At night, when startled by a torch, it tends to extend its head and hold its beaks in a horizontal position before running off.
- Feeding Brown Kiwi regularly make heavy breathing-like, snuffle sounds.

Calls: Brown Kiwi start calling about 40 minutes after sundown and continue to call intermittently throughout the night with a noisy period before dawn. The call of the male bird is a shrill *"ah-el, ah-el"*, uttered several times. The female has a quieter and hoarser call *"aarh, aarh aarh"* or *"ah-eh, ah-eh"*. (Description; Colbourne 1981.)

Nest and breeding season: Female Brown Kiwi are unique in the size of the egg they lay which can be equivalent to a quarter of the female's body weight. Usually two white eggs are laid in burrows, cavities, or under vegetation and trees. These can be incubated by both sexes but more often, especially with North Island birds, by the male bird, which will also care for the young within the burrow in the early stages. Prior to nesting, male birds are known to be strongly territorial about their nesting area. Birds are thought to breed throughout the year with the July to February months being the most common. Male birds are vocal during late winter which indicates mating and the start of breeding.

Best calling months: June, July and August are considered the best months but it can be heard during any month of the year. Northland birds are noisy during November and December.

Best viewing hours: Birds can be located by their calls just after sundown but also at any time during the night. Should a Brown Kiwi be missed in early evening, try again in the early morning hours. Remember that a calling bird in bush is almost impossible to locate. The only real chance of seeing one is on an open track, beach or pastureland.

Evidence of Brown Kiwi:

Calls: Calls indicate their presence. Also, their snuffle sounds and sometimes the sounds of breaking vegetation, caused as they push through the undergrowth.

Footprints: Footprints in mud, on tracks or on sand often indicate their presence. Brown Kiwi footprints are bold and bigger than those of a domestic hen. Usually only three toes are showing, unless the bird has been walking through deep and soft sand. Then the hind toe might be seen.

Dung: White, pungent smelling dung on a trail or around a forest burrow can suggest its presence. Note that there will be no cobwebs across the entrance of a recently used burrow.

Probe marks: Feeding Brown Kiwi leave probe marks or small holes in the ground, usually with a circular whirl at the entrance. These are good indicators of their presence. In the pine forests the pine needles become whirled in this circular manner.

Equipment needed: Binoculars, other than night vision ones, are of little use when looking for Brown Kiwi in the dark. Take a good torch or spotlight.

Where to find - North Island:

Northland - Bay of Islands - Aroha Island, Kerikeri: This small island is linked to the mainland by a causeway. It has been developed by its owners the Queen Elizabeth II National Trust, as an ecological centre with an emphasis on Brown Kiwi conservation. It has a small population of this bird, and in the adjoining Rangitane Scenic Reserve. (See "Places" in back of book.)

Northland - Bay of Islands: The Waitangi Forest, owned by Rayonier NZ Ltd, not far from the coastal town of Paihia, is known for its large populations of Brown Kiwi. This forest is of exotic pines (*Pinus radiata*) and other species. (See "Places" in back of book.)

Northland - Trounson Park: This forest is located north of Dargaville and has a very good population of Brown Kiwi. Night time excursions into it can be arranged. It gives an 80% chance of a sighting. (See "Places" in back of book.)

North Auckland - Little Barrier Island: This small island is free of introduced predators and so has kiwis. (See "Places" in back of Book.)

Bay of Plenty - Mount Otanewainuku: This forested area is in the Tauranga district. It is approached either through Oropi or up No 2 Road, Te Puke. If approached via Oropi, turn off Highway 29 past the Pyes Pa round-about. It is an indigenous forest and a track leads to the summit from a well signposted carpark. The walk is rich in bush birds and Brown Kiwi are known from it. Walk up the mountain in daylight hours and return at dusk, listening for calling birds. Brown Kiwi sometimes use walking tracks as probing sites and for easy access to other parts of their territories. (See "Places" in back of book.)

Lake Okataina near Rotorua: If staying near Rotorua the access road to this lake is worth a try at night. It is forested for its entire length. It is signposted off Highway 30.

Where to find - South Island:

Fiordland - Eglinton Valley: Birds can be expected from the forests around Lake Gunn. The Lake Gunn walk is signposted just past Cascade Creek on the Eglinton Road. (See "Places" in back of book.)

Westland - Paparoa Forest near Westport: Brown Kiwi and Great Spotted Kiwi are in these forests. Visit these forests when looking for Westland Black Petrel. (See "Places" in back of book.)

Where to find - Stewart Island:

Stewart Island: Stewart Island provides an excellent chance of seeing Brown Kiwi. There is a commercial tourist operator on the island who runs evening excursions when the weather is good. (See "Places" in back of book.)

Mason Bay: There is a walking track to Mason Bay. This leaves from Oban town leading off the road to the airstrip. Enquire from the Department of Conservation about this walk.

Ocean Beach: Ocean Beach is on the peninsula on the south side of Paterson Inlet. The commercial tourist operator visits this locality.

Ackers Point walking track: This track is on the southern arm of Half Moon Bay.

Ulva Island: Kiwi have been released here but their status is unknown.

Other excursions for birds while in the area: While on Stewart Island take a sea trip for seabirds.

Kiwi Houses: If you miss the Brown Kiwi in the wild, visit a "Kiwi House". There are many of these and some are listed in "Places" in back of book.

General: Aroha Island near Kerikeri in Northland, Trounson Park north of Dargaville and the commercial tourist operation on Stewart Island offer the best chances for seeing kiwi in New Zealand.

References:

Sturmer AT; Grant A D 1989. Female Kiwi Incubating. Notornis 35: P 193.
Colbourne R 1981. Why is the Kiwi so called? Notornis 28: P 216.

LITTLE SPOTTED KIWI

Brian Chudleigh

Family: Apterygidae **Common name:** Little Spotted Kiwi
Species: *Apteryx owenii* **Status:** Endemic
Size: 400 mm (cf sparrow 145 mm, Brown Kiwi 500 mm)
Discussion: This kiwi is smaller than the Brown Kiwi and has different

colouration, being brownish grey, finely mottled and banded with white. Other features, such as bill and body proportions, are similar.

Range: The largest population of about 1000 birds is on Kapiti Island. These birds were released there in the 1920s probably from the diminishing population found at that time in the Paparoa Ranges on the west coast of the South Island. In 1980 several pairs were liberated on Red Mercury Island off the Coromandel coast and in 1988 several pairs were liberated by the Department of Conservation on Hen Island off the Northland coast. Since then birds have been placed on Tiri Tiri Island and Motuara (Long) Island in Queen Charlotte Sound where they have been reported breeding.

Where to find:
Tiri Tiri Island, Kapiti Island and Motuara Island: These are the only places to see this bird. (See "Places" in back of book.)

GREAT SPOTTED KIWI

Brian Chudleigh

Family: Apterygidae   **Common name:** Great Spotted Kiwi, Roa (Maori)
Species: *Apteryx haastii*   **Status:** Endemic
Size: 500 mm (cf sparrow 145 mm, Brown Kiwi 500 mm)

Discussion: The Great Spotted Kiwi is about the size of the Brown Kiwi. It has similar colouring as the Little Spotted Kiwi but with denser mottling and lateral speckling.

Range: Found down the west coast of the South Island to Franz Josef Glacier, with biggest populations in the Paparoa Ranges south of Westport where they are sustaining themselves well. Also recorded in Arthurs Pass National Park.

Where to find - South Island:

Westland - Paparoa Ranges: These ranges are steep, bush clad slopes above the main Westland highway between Westport and Greymouth. In many places the forests come right down to the road edge. Records of Great Spotted Kiwi come from both the coastal forests and the steeper ridges.

Westland - Bullock Creek: At Punakaiki, on Highway 6, access into the bush is possible at Bullock Creek. This road is 1 km north of Punakaiki Motor Camp. Travel along this road for 6.2 kms to a locked gate. To the right of the gate is a rough camping site. Walk into the forest from the gate and turn right at the first junction and follow to pool. From the pool turn left and start listening for kiwi. When in the forests in this area at night, beware of holes in the ground which might be entrances to caving systems.

Westland: Any roadside bush in the Westport to Greymouth area, could contain Great Spotted Kiwi. Brown Kiwi are also in this area.

Westland - Lake Brunner: This lake is found due east of Greymouth. It can be approached either from the Arthurs Pass road, Highway 73, at Kumara or from the Greymouth to Reefton road, Highway 7, at Stillwater. At the picnic, motor camp area at the north end of the lake near the Arnold River, kiwi are often heard, and also in the wider area. (See "Places" in back of book.)

Westland - Arthurs Pass: Great Spotted Kiwi are sometimes heard from the Arthurs Pass village and in the Rough Creek area nearby. There are motels in the village from which a kiwi excursion could be planned. Enquire at the Department of Conservation office here.

General: Try the Lake Brunner camp-site first, before moving on to other areas.

Charles A Fleming

**Little Spotted Kiwi - Brown Kiwi - Great Spotted Kiwi
Showing size differentiation**

DABCHICK

Brian Chudleigh

Family: Podicipedidae **Common name:** Dabchick
Species: *Podiceps rufopectus* **Status:** Endemic
Size: 280 mm (cf sparrow 145 mm)

Discussion: The New Zealand Dabchick belongs to the worldwide family of Podicipedidae of which there are 19 species. The closest relation of the New Zealand species is the Australian Hoary-headed Grebe (*P. poliocephalus*) but this species differs around the head.

Habitat: The Dabchick is generally a bird of deep and clean lakes although sometimes found on shallower farm ponds and sand dune lakes.

Range: North Island only. Grebes seen on South Island lakes are either the Southern Crested Grebe (*P. cristatus*), Hoary-headed Grebe (*P. poliocephalus*) or Little Grebe (*Tachybaptus novaehollandiae*).

Description:

Head and neck: Blackish, finely streaked with silver. **Upperparts:** Blackish-brown. **Upper breast and foreneck:** Dark chestnut. **Lower breast:** Brown. **Wing:** Greyish-brown with white secondary feathers. **Abdomen and undertail:** Silvery with brownish flanks. **Bill:** Black. **Eye:** Pale yellow iris with black pupil. **Legs and toes:** Blackish, with flat lobed toes.

Conspicuous features:

- The button-like eye, when viewed through the telescope, appears as a ring of pale yellow around a black pupil.
- The dark chestnut breast is noticeable.
- White of wings on upper secondary feathers is noticeable on birds in flight.

Conspicuous characteristics:

- Dabchicks are often viewed alongside Scaup. Note that they sit lower in the water than Scaup and have longer and more slender necks. They also

18

lack the longer tail of the Scaup.
- Dabchicks constantly dive often surfacing some distance away.
- Dabchicks bring up food and feed their young above the water.

Description chicks:

Upperparts: Horizontally "zebra" striped in black and white. **Underparts:** White.

Call: Usually silent, except during the breeding season when calls can be heard.

Nest: A pile of rushes floating on water but anchored. Up to 3 white eggs are laid.

How to locate: Dabchicks spend much time underwater. This means they could be missed on the first scan of the lake so patience is needed.

Where to find - North Island:

Northland - Awanui: Lake Ohia off Inland Road, Lake Ngatu off Coast Road, Lake Waiparera off Highway 1 and Lake Waikaramu off Kaimaumau Road are all worth a try. Australian Little Grebe are also known from these lakes.

Northland - Bay of Islands: Lake Owhareiti and Lake Omapere have occasional Dabchick and Australian Little Grebe. Lake Owhareiti can be viewed from Lubrook Road, which runs west from Highway 1 at Pakaraka. Lake Omapere can be viewed from Lake Road or Te Pua Road. A telescope is needed. (See Australian Little Grebe article.) (See "Places" in back of book.)

North Auckland - Waiwera: Strakas Refuge occasionally has Dabchick. Travel 1.8 kms along Puhoi Valley Road from Highway 1. The refuge is on the left scarcely visible from the road.

North Auckland - Lake Kereta: This sand-dune lake is north of Muriwai and the Muriwai Gannet colony, off South Head Road. Take Wilson Road, just past the Shelley Beach turn-off and travel to end. It has Dabchick and sometimes Australian Little Grebe.

South Auckland - Wattle Farm Reserve: This reserve is the site of the old Manurewa sewage ponds. It has two lakes of modest size with numerous waterfowl, including Dabchick. Also Black-billed Gulls. From the Great South Road at the south end of Manurewa, travel down Mahia Road and left into Coxhead Road. Then turn into Wattle Farm Road.

Bay of Plenty - Matata Lagoon: These roadside lagoons, right at Matata town usually have a pair of Dabchicks. (See "Places" in back of book.)

Bay of Plenty - the Rotorua lakes: Most of the lakes in the Rotorua district have Dabchick. The easiest location is on Lake Rotorua behind the Rotorua gardens and the Bath House. Travel along Arawa Street to the gardens and then past the Bath House and alongside the golf course to the end of the road. (See "Places" in back of book.)

Bay of Plenty - Lake Okareka: Many Dabchicks can be found here. It is accessed from Tarawera Lake Road, from Lynmore. (See Scaup article.)

Lake Taupo: Dabchick and other waterfowl can be viewed at the Turangi end of Lake Taupo near Waihi Village. From Highway 1 travel down Highway 41 towards Tokaanu and look for roads which lead to the lake.

Central Plateau - Lake Kario, Ohakune: This lake is 14 kms south of Ohakune on Highway 49. It is signposted on the left when travelling south. It has many waterfowl including up to six Dabchicks.

Wellington - Waikanae: Look for it at Waimeha Lagoon. (See Shoveler article.)

AUSTRALIAN LITTLE GREBE

Brian Chudleigh

Family: Podicipedidae   **Common name:** Little Grebe
Species: *Tachybaptus novaehollandiae*   **Status:** Native
Size: 250 mm (cf sparrow 145, Dabchick 280 mm)

Discussion: This bird is a recent arrival to New Zealand from Australia and is now breeding in some locations.

Habitat: Clean water lakes and sand-dune lakes.
Range: Found in limited areas in both North and South Islands.

Description - breeding:
    Head and neck: Black. **Face and sides of fore-neck:** Chestnut, with yellow tear-drop in front of eye and sloping to bill. **Upperparts:** Blackish, with flanks browner. **Breast:** Rufous over brown. **Wings:** Greyish-brown with white on secondary feathers. **Underparts:** Silvery-white. **Eye:** Light yellow iris with black pupil. **Bill:** Black.
Description - non-breeding:
    Crown, hindneck and upperparts: Dark olive-brown. **Sides of face and neck:** Light brown. **Underparts:** Pale grey. **Eye and tear drop:** Pale yellow.
Conspicuous features:
- Slightly smaller than the Dabchick.
- Look for the yellow tear drop of naked skin just in front of eye.
- Look for the chestnut face and neck markings.
- Note that the bill is shorter than the Dabchick.

Conspicuous characteristics: As for Dabchick.

Where to find - North Island:
Northland - Karikari: Try Lake Waiporohita on the corner of Inland Road and

Rangiputa Road. Inland Road is off Highway 10, west of Coopers Beach.

Northland - Awanui: Regularly seen on Lake Waiparera near Waiharara, 10 kms north of Awanui. Lake Waiparera is signposted from Highway 1.

Northland - Awanui: Good numbers are on Lake Rotokawau which lies alongside Rotokawau Road, off Highway 1 at Waipapakauri, about 5 kms north of Awanui. It is a small lake which can be viewed from the road through trees. Do not enter the private land surrounding the lake.

Northland - Awanui: Lake Ngatu, on West Coast Road, is a large sand hill lake not far from Lake Rotokawau. It sometimes has Little Grebe.

Northland - Lake Omapere: This is a large lake north of the town of Kaikohe. From just east of Kaikohe take Te Pua Road off Highway 10 and then left into Lake Road. The lake can also be viewed from a roadside parking area off Highway 1 just west of Ohaeawai. The lake is distant and a telescope is required. (See Dabchick article.)

Northland - Lake Owhareiti: Regularly seen here. (See Dabchick article and "Places" in back of book.)

Northland - Kaiiwi Lakes: These lakes lie 25 kms north of Dargaville. They are well signposted. Follow Highway 12 from Dargaville and then turn left into Omamari Road and right into Kaiiwi Road. A small side road leads into the lakes running between Lake Kaiiwi and Lake Taharoa. Examine Lake Kaiiwi (the southern lake) first for both Dabchick and Australian Little Grebe. The larger lake, Lake Taharoa, is used extensively for recreation and so bird life tends to be sparse.

North Auckland - Lake Kereta: This is worth a try. (See "Places" in back of book.)

Where to find - South Island:

Marlborough - Lake Elterwater: This lake lies just south of Lake Grassmere on Highway 1 about 15 kms from Seddon. It is worth a try and is good for other waterfowl. (See "Places" in back of book.)

North Canterbury - St Annes Lagoon: This small lake is 4.5 kms north of Cheviot. It is well signposted from Highway 1, and is on the west side of the road. It is worth a try. (See "Places" in back of book.)

South Canterbury - Timaru: Gravel pits on Falveys Road off Highway 1, north of the town of Timaru near Levels, occasionally have two pairs. They are known to have bred here. Look at the ponds on the south side of the road. These are partly obscured from the road. This is near the Timaru aerodrome.

HOARY-HEADED GREBE

Family: Podicipedidae   **Common name:** Hoary-headed Grebe
Species: *Podiceps poliocephalus*   **Status:** Native
Size: 280 mm (cf sparrow 145 mm, Dabchick 280 mm)

Discussion: This bird is a recent arrival to New Zealand which has bred here but there have been no records over recent years.

Habitat: Deep water lakes. In Australia, also a species of coastal waters.
Range: In limited locations in both North and South Islands.

Description - breeding:
  Head: Brownish, horizontally streaked with silver feathers. **Upper-parts:**
  Greyish-brown. **Breast:** Buff coloured. **Wings:** Greyish-brown. **Underwings:**
  White, with dark grey tips to primary feathers. **Underparts:** Silvery-white.
  Bill: Black, with white tip. **Legs:** Greenish. **Eye:** Iris brown, pupil black.
Description - non-breeding:
Crown: Brown to below eye and down hind-neck. **Wings:** Dark grey.
  Underparts: Pale grey.

K. Stepnell - NPIAW

Hoary-headed Grebe

Conspicuous features:
  • Look for the silver-streaked head.
  • If in flight look for the wide, white wing-patches.

Differences between Hoary-headed Grebe and Dabchick:
  • The Hoary-headed has a bigger and more elongated head.
  • Its head is adorned with brushed-back type silver feathering in the
    breeding   season. These feathers are distinctive.
  • Its breast lacks the dark chestnut colouring of the Dabchick, being of a
    light buff colouring instead.
  • The Hoary-headed has a more conspicuous white wing bar which is
    noticeable on the resting or diving bird.

Where to find - North Island:
Northland - Awanui: Try all the lakes in the Awanui area. (See Dabchick and
  Australian Little Grebe articles.) Especially, try Lake Waikaramu. From
  Highway 1, about 15 kms north of Awanui, turn right into Kaimaumau Road.
  Turn left at the next junction and follow to end. The lake is on the left and

difficult to see. Also try Lake Waiparera on the left of Highway 1, at the Kaimaumau Road junction. From this area that sightings have been confirmed.

Where to find - South Island:
Marlborough - Lake Elterwater: (See "Places" in back of book.) (See Australian Little Grebe article.)
South Island Lakes: Reports of sightings have come from Lake Ohau, Lake Tekapo and Lake Te Anau but the current status of the species is unknown.

AUSTRALASIAN CRESTED GREBE

Brian Chudleigh

Family: Podicipedidae
Common name: Crested Grebe, (sometimes Great Crested Grebe or Southern Crested Grebe)
Species: *Podiceps cristatus*
Status: Native
Size: 500 mm (cf sparrow 145 mm, Dabchick 280 mm)

Discussion: The Crested Grebe is a bird which is found almost worldwide in temperate zones. In New Zealand it is scarce and shy when compared with its close relatives in Europe and Africa. The New Zealand species closely resembles the Australian species in colour and habitat.

Habitat: It is a bird of inland lakes always in secluded areas. In recent years many of these lakes have been invaded by holiday-makers, a fact which appears to have hastened its decline.
Range: Confined to specific areas in the South Island. Largest populations are in the mid-Canterbury lakes district. There is also a Westland population.

Description:

Crown: Brown with ornate tufts projecting upwards on the back of head. **Face:** White. **Neck:** A frill of rufous feathers hangs from under the cheeks when in breeding plumage. **Foreneck:** white. **Upperparts:** Brown. **Underparts:** Silky white. **Bill:** Brown and finely pointed. **Feet:** Greenish with flat-lobed toes.

Description chicks:

Upperparts: "Zebra-striped" with black and white horizontal markings. **Underparts:** White.

Conspicuous features:

- Sits low in the water and reveals a long thin neck.
- Look for the head which is held at a right angle to the neck.
- Look for the long white neck.
- Look for noticeable white on forewing and primaries.

Conspicuous characteristics:

- A bird which is constantly diving and bobbing to the surface.
- In flight its long neck is held straight and slightly below body line.
- Flies very close to the water.
- Usually seen in pairs.
- In the breeding season it is sometimes seen with its young riding among its folded wings.
- Usually seen feeding near the rush line where it can be hard to detect.

Where to find - South Island:

North Canterbury - St Annes Lagoon: This small lake has had odd reports of grebes from time to time. It is worth checking.

Canterbury - Lake Forsyth: Good numbers can be found here. From Christchurch take Highway 75 to Akaroa on Banks Peninsula. After Kaituna Lagoon on the northern edge of Lake Ellesmere, watch for Lake Forsyth on the right. The Kaituna Lagoon area also has sightings from time to time.

Canterbury - Arthurs Pass: Lake Pearson and Lake Grasmere each have good numbers of birds. Follow Highway 73 from Christchurch. Both lakes can be easily viewed from the road. (See "Places" in back of book.)

Canterbury - Lake Clearwater: From Ashburton take Highway 77 to Ashburton Forks and then to Mount Somers. Then take Ashburton Gorge Road to Hakatere and on to Lake Clearwater and Lake Camp.

Canterbury - Lake Heron: Instead of travelling into Lake Clearwater turn right at Hakatere and travel up to Lake Heron where there is a campground. Grebes are known to nest around this lake.

South Canterbury - Lake Alexandrina: This lake is to the west of Lake Tekapo. From Tekapo drive south on Highway 8 and turn right (west) at the first road. This leads to Lake Alexandrina and to Lake McGregor. Take first turn to left and follow in to the lake. Crested Grebes are usually seen here. A telescope may be necessary. Further up the road visit Lake McGregor which is also a good waterfowl lake. Travel on to the Cass River and look for Black Stilt and Wrybill if it is spring.

Westland - Lake Kaniere: This lake is due east of Hokitika and is worth a detour when travelling down the west coast. It is a good waterfowl lake and also good for Spotless Crake, Marsh Crake and Fernbird. Falcon is also reliably seen in this area.

Westland - Lake Ianthe: This lake is south of Hokitika. Birds can be seen here but usually near the distant shores for which a telescope is needed.

Westland - Lake Mapourika: Often a pair is seen near the wharf.

Westland - Lake Paringa: This lake is further south of Lake Ianthe and has Crested Grebe as does Lake Moeraki further south again and before Haast.

Southland - Lake Hayes: Lake Hayes is north of Queenstown on Highway 6 on route to Arrowtown. It is signposted from the main road and located up a small side road. Grebe are occasionally seen here along with other waterfowl.

Southland - Eglinton Valley: Lake Gunn and Lake Fergus, near Cascade Creek, occasionally have birds but no recent sightings have come from here.

Southland - Lake Manapouri: Breeds along the western shores in areas not suitable for viewing without a boat. There are walking tracks into Shallow Bay on Lake Manapouri. Cross the Waiau River at the carpark just south of Horseshoe Bend on the Manapouri to Te Anau Road and walk in. The chances are slim but it is a pleasant walk.

ALBATROSSES

The "Checklist of the birds of New Zealand" Third Edition 1990, lists 20 species and subspecies of albatross for New Zealand waters. Ten of these species and subspecies are likely to be seen if the time of year is right for that species. This makes New Zealand an important seabird venue.

Note about names: In New Zealand, the two species of albatross which have white backs, the Wandering Albatross and the Royal Albatross are called albatrosses. The other species and subspecies in the genus *Diomedea,* all with black upperwings and black backs, are called mollymawks. The Sooty and Light-mantled Sooty Albatrosses, in the genus *Phoebetria,* retain the name albatross.

Mainland nesting sites: Only one species of albatross, the Northern Royal Albatross (*Diomedea epomophora*), nests on mainland New Zealand. All the other species nest on off-shore islands from the Chatham Islands south to the Campbell Islands.

Beach "wrecked" birds: Birds collected by members from the Ornithological Society of New Zealand, over many years, clearly indicate that all the albatrosses listed here are found in waters right around New Zealand from time to time. Auckland west coast beaches, for example, have provided dead birds of all listed species.

Although these birds range widely they are only in northern waters during the winter months. Generally they do not come close to the shoreline but during rough weather, Wandering Albatrosses have been known to enter Auckland Harbour near Rangitoto Island, and occasionally are recorded in Wellington Harbour. The southern waters, from Cook Strait south, provide the best opportunities to view these birds as they are closer to the breeding grounds.

Note: Permission is required from the Department of Conservation to visit most of the seabird nesting islands.

Seabird places and excursions ideas: Seabird excursions and land-based seabird sighting place are recorded in the back of the book.

References: Powlesland R G 1985. Seabirds found dead on New Zealand beaches in 1983 and a review of Albatross recoveries since 1960. Notornis 32: 23-41.

WANDERING ALBATROSS

Brian Chudleigh

Family: Diomedeidae   **Species:** *Diomedea exulans*
Common name: Wandering Albatross   **Status:** Circumpolar
Size: 750 - 1200 mm (cf sparrow 145 mm)

Subspecies: Two subspecies are recognised - the Wandering Albatross (*D. e. exulans*) and the Snowy Albatross (*D . e. chionoptera*). The Snowy Albatross is a bird found from the Macquarie Islands, south.
Breeding islands close to New Zealand: Antipodes Island, Auckland Island, Macquarie Island and Campbell Island.
Breeding months: Starts in January and young birds leave the nest one year later. The parental pair then have one year's rest before commencing egg laying again.
Range worldwide: The southern oceans north to the Tropic of Capricorn, occasionally straggling further north.
New Zealand range: Around New Zealand but more common in New Zealand waters in winter months.

Description - mature bird:
 Head: White. **Upperwing:** White, darkening to black on secondaries and primaries. **Underwing:** White, with black trailing edges and tips to primaries, and a thin black line from wing tip to carpal joint on leading edges. **Upperparts:** White. **Underparts:** White, with grey darkening on neck. **Tail:** White, usually tipped with black on both under and upper edges. (Sometimes the black is absent.) **Bill:** Pink, with a faint yellow tip.
Description - immature bird:
 Note: Birds vary with maturity but range from -
 Face: White.
 Upperparts: Pure black.

Underwing: White, with primaries on trailing edges lined with black.
Underparts: Black.
Tail: White, tipped with various amounts of black.
- to variations of black upperparts and underparts with the black slowly being replaced by white in stages.

Differences between Wandering and Royal Albatrosses:
It is difficult to separate adult Wanderings from adult Royals at sea. The Northern Royal is the easiest to separate but the Southern Royal and the Wandering can nevertheless be identified. Pointers to aid separation are -
- Wandering Albatrosses usually show some breast darkening.
- Royals (Northern and Southern) have totally white breasts and abdomen.
- Wandering Albatrosses have black tips to undertail feathers.
- Royal (Northern) has some black undertail markings.
- Royal (Southern) has no black undertail markings.
- Wandering Albatrosses have black tips to uppertail.
- Royals have no black uppertail tips.
- Wandering Albatrosses have some white on primary and secondary upperwings feathers. This is similar to the Southern Royal. However Northern Royals have totally black upperwings.
- Northern Royals have very dark leading edges to the underwing with the black extending heavily from end of wing to carpal joint.

Juvenile Wandering Albatrosses are usually birds with -
- large amounts of upper black markings.
- traces of black around the head and upper back.
- blotchy black and white upperwing markings.

Where to find:
This wide ranging bird can be seen off the New Zealand coast and should be watched for on any seabird excursion.

Charles A Fleming

Royal Albatross and Light-mantled Sooty Albatross

Charles A Fleming

Immature stages of Wandering Albatrosses

Charles A Fleming

Semi-mature stages of Wandering Albatrosses

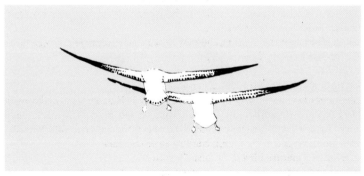

Charles A Fleming

Wandering Albatross and Royal Albatross (Southern)

ROYAL ALBATROSS

Charles A Fleming

Family: Diomedeidae   **Species:** *Diomedea epomophora*
Common name: Royal Albatross   **Status:** Endemic
Other names: Northern Royal Albatross and Southern Royal Albatross.
Size: 1120 - 1300 mm (cf sparrow 145 mm)

Subspecies: Two subspecies are recognised. They are the Northern Royal (*D. e. sandfordi*) and the Southern Royal (*D. e. epomophora*).

Breeding islands close to New Zealand: Islands off the Chatham Islands, Auckland Islands, Enderby Island, Campbell Island, and on the South Island of New Zealand at Taiaroa Heads on the Otago Peninsula.
Breeding months: October to September. Breeding season commences about two months earlier than the Wandering Albatross.
Range worldwide: Probably similar to the Wandering Albatross but does not wander as far north into the tropics.
New Zealand range: Ranges around New Zealand but more regularly seen from the Stewart Island coast to Cook Strait.

Description - mature bird (Northern Royal):
Upper and underparts: White. **Upperwings:** Black. **Underwings:** White, with black leading edges from carpal joint to wing tip and black along the trailing edge. **Tail:** White, but sometimes black dotted on the undertail. **Bill:** Pinkish, with cream tip and black cutting-edge to upper mandible.
Description - mature bird (Southern Royal):
Upper and underparts: White. **Upperwings:** Black, but with broad areas of white on inner leading edges. **Underwings:** White with black leading edges from carpal joint to wing tip and black along the trailing edge. **Tail:** White. **Bill:** Pinkish, with cream tip and black cutting-edge to upper mandible.

Note: Similar to the Wandering Albatross.

Description - immature bird:
Generally Royal Albatross immatures have traces of black on head, back and uppertail which are otherwise white. Northern Royals have more black markings than Southern Royals.

Differences between Northern and Southern Royal Albatrosses:
- The Northern Royal adult has an all black upperwing.
- The Southern Royal adult has a black upperwing with broad areas of inner white on the leading edge and across the back.

Differences between Royal and Wandering Albatrosses: (See "Wandering Albatross" article.)

Differences between Albatrosses and Mollymawks:
- Albatross species are white-backed, Mollymawks black-backed.

Where to find - North Island: (See also "Albatross Excursions".)

Auckland - Hauraki Gulf: An excursion in winter into deep waters to the north of the gulf could locate a Royal Albatross. In stormy weather birds sometime enter the Auckland Harbour where they can be observed from the Waiheke Island ferry.

Bay of Plenty - White Island: Often recorded on the voyage from Whakatane to White Island in winter.

Wellington - Cook Strait: Watch for them from the inter-island ferry. In stormy conditions birds are known to enter Wellington Harbour where they can be observed from outer harbour coastal verges. A telescope may be required for positive identification.

Where to find - South Island: (See also "Albatross Excursions".)

North Canterbury - Kaikoura: Watch for them if on an "Ocean Wings" excursion from Kaikoura township.

Canterbury - Akaroa: A deep water excursion might locate albatrosses.

Otago Peninsula - Taiaroa Heads: The Northern Royal Albatross nests on Taiaroa Heads near Dunedin. This is the only mainland breeding colony of Royal Albatrosses in New Zealand. Visit this general area, especially when windy, from the month of November onwards until the fledgling chicks leave the colony the following September. (See "Places" in back of book.) Sometimes Southern Royals will also be seen in the area along with Bullers Mollymawk and Sooty Shearwaters.

Otago Peninsula - Cape Saunders: When travelling towards Taiaroa, take a right turn at Portebello where signposting will lead you to Hoopers Inlet and Cape Saunders. Do not enter private property but view the general area from road.

Southland - Curio Bay: This bay is well known for its petrified coastal forest and is signposted from Tokanui on the alternative Invercargill to Balclutha route via the Catlins Forest Park. A telescope mounted above the coastline could reveal many seabirds. (See Sooty Shearwater article.)

Southland - Bluff: Try Stirling Point at Bluff when weather is rough.

Where to find - Stewart Island:
Seen in the waters of Foveaux Strait and further out from Half Moon Bay.

BLACK-BROWED MOLLYMAWK

Charles A Fleming

Family: Diomedeidae   **Species:** *Diomedea melanophrys*
Common name: Black-browed Mollymawk
Status: Black-browed Mollymawk (*D.m.melanophrys*) - circumpolar
  New Zealand Black-browed Mollymawk (*D.m.impavida*) - endemic
Size: 750 - 900 mm (cf sparrow 145 mm)

Subspecies: Two subspecies are recognised. They are the Black-browed
  Mollymawk (*D. m. melanophrys*) and the New Zealand Black-browed
  Mollymawk (*D. m. impavida*).

Breeding islands close to New Zealand: Antipodes, Campbell Island and
  Macquarie Island.
Breeding months: August until April.
Range worldwide: Through the southern oceans to the Tropic of Capricorn.

New Zealand range: Ranges in all waters around New Zealand. Seen in northern
  waters such as the Hauraki Gulf and coastal Northland, in winter months.
  Usually keeps well out to sea for most of the time.

Description - mature bird:
  Head: White, with a black triangle in front of and around eye. **Upperwings
  and back:** Black. **Neck and rump:** White. **Underwings:** White, with a heavy
  black leading edge, wing tips and a lesser black trailing edge. **Underparts:**
  White. **Tail:** Grey with black tip. **Bill:** Bright yellow with pink tip. **Eye:** Honey-
  coloured with surround of elongated black.
Description - immature bird:
  This has a variety of feather patterns often showing black on the neck and
  wider areas of black under the wings.

Conspicuous feature of Black-browed Mollymawks:
- The Black-browed Mollymawk (*D. m. melanophrys*) has about 50% of the white underwing edged heavily with black.
- The New Zealand Black-browed Mollymawk (*D. m. impavida*) has about 60% of the white underwing edged heavily with black.

Where to find - North Island:
North Auckland - Kawau Island: Look for it in the deeper waters.
Tauranga: Winter sea trips in the Bay of Plenty could find a bird.
Wellington - Cook Strait: Watch for it while crossing between islands.

Where to find - South Island:
North Canterbury - Kaikoura: Look for it from a whale-watch excursion.

Where to find - Stewart Island:
Foveaux Strait: Look for it here and into deeper waters.

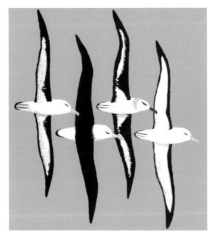

Charles A Fleming

Left - (1 & 2): **New Zealand Black-browed Mollymawk** (*D. m. impavida*)
Middle - (3): **Immature - underwing** (*D. m. impavida*)
Right - (4): **Black-browed Mollymawk - underwing** (*D. m. melanophrys*)

GREY-HEADED MOLLYMAWK

Family: Diomedeidae
Common name: Grey-headed Mollymawk
Size: 800 - 900 mm (cf sparrow 145 mm)

Species: *Diomedea chrysostoma*
Status: Circumpolar

Breeding islands close to New Zealand: Campbell and Macquarie Islands.
Breeding months: September to May.
Range worldwide: Ranges around the southern oceans to about the 30th parallel which equals the north of New Zealand's North Island.
New Zealand range: Regarded as a bird of open waters but can be seen in coastal waters around New Zealand in winter months.

Description - mature bird:
Head: Grey. **Upperwings and back:** Black. **Rump:** White. **Underparts:** White. **Tail:** Grey and black tipped. **Bill:** Black, edged with bright yellow above and below, and tipped with pink.

Conspicuous features:
- Dark grey head is noticeable. Head is similar to Bullers Mollymawk but lacks its white crown. Shy Mollymawks have a range of slightly grey-headed birds. This means that bills must be closely checked.
- Underwing shows more white than Black-browed but less than Bullers. The leading underwing edge shows a wider belt of black than the trailing black edge which is fairly narrow.

Where to find - North Island:
Wellington - Cook Strait: Sometimes seen here in winter. Can be mistaken here for Bullers Mollymawk and Salvins Mollymawk.

Where to find - Stewart Island:
Foveaux Strait: Birds range through Foveaux Strait in summer months.

Charles A Fleming

**Grey-headed Mollymawks (left) Grey-headed Mollymawk (above)
Bullers Mollymawk (below)**

YELLOW-NOSED MOLLYMAWK

Paul M Sagar

Family: Diomedeidae   **Species:** *Diomedea chlororhynchus*
Common name: Yellow-nosed Mollymawk
Status: Circumpolar - uncommon
Size: 700 mm - 750 mm (cf sparrow 145 mm, a small mollymawk)

Breeding islands close to New Zealand: Breeds on islands to the south of the
Atlantic and Indian Oceans. Does not breed close to New Zealand.
Breeding months: September to April.

34

Range worldwide: From north of the Tropic of Capricorn to about 55° south around New Zealand's southern islands.

New Zealand range: A winter visitor to New Zealand waters appearing regularly off the east coast of the North Island from East Cape to North Cape.

Description - mature bird:
   Head: White. **Upperwings and back:** Black. **Rump:** White. **Underparts:** White. **Underwing:** Mainly white, with wing edges and wing tips black. **Tail:** Dark grey upper and under, tipped with black. **Bill:** Black, with upper edge of yellow, and orange tipped.

Conspicuous features:
   - Underwing white, finely edged with black.
   - Smaller than both Grey-headed and Bullers Mollymawks.
   - Bill is the most distinctive feature being black with a yellow top edge. Bullers and Grey-headed have black-sided bills but with top ridges and bottom edges, yellow.

Where to find - North Island:
North Auckland - Kawau Island: Waters beyond Kawau Island in winter.
Coromandel - Whitianga: The Mercury Islands area on the eastern side of the Coromandel Peninsula often have Yellow-nosed quite close in to shore.
Bay of Plenty - Tauranga: In winter out from Tauranga Harbour.
Bay of Plenty - White Island: Often in these waters. Take an eco-tour from Whakatane. Enquire at the Department of Conservation in Whakatane.

General: Records show that only a few birds reach the Tasman Sea, the Hauraki Gulf and the Bay of Plenty over winter months. To find one of these birds is therefore a bonus.

Charles A Fleming (illustration left), Stella Rowe (photo right),

Yellow-nosed Mollymawk

BULLERS MOLLYMAWK

Dennis Buurman

Family: Diomedeidae   **Species:** *Diomedea bulleri*
Common name: Bullers Mollymawk   **Status:** Endemic
Size: 750 mm - 800 mm (cf sparrow 145 mm, larger than Yellow-nosed and smaller than Shy Mollymawk)

Subspecies: Two subspecies are recognised. They are Northern Bullers Mollymawk (*D. b. platei)* and Southern Bullers Mollymawk (*D. b. bulleri).*

Breeding islands close to New Zealand: Northern Bullers Mollymawk - Three Kings Islands and Chatham Islands. Southern Bullers Mollymawk - Snares Island and Solander Island.
Breeding months: Northern Bullers Mollymawk - October to June. Southern Bullers Mollymawk - January to October.
Range worldwide: Restricted to seas from around New Zealand to South America.
New Zealand range: Out of the breeding season it is seen right around New Zealand. In particular it is seen around Stewart Island and Foveaux Strait and up the east coast to Hawke Bay. Often seen quite close to land.

Description - mature bird:
Head: Grey, with a silvery grey cap on Northern Bullers and silvery white cap on Southern Bullers. Has a dark patch through upper eye. **Upperwings and back:** Black wings connecting a blackish grey back. **Rump:** White. **Underwings:** White, with a cleanly defined thickish black leading edge and a thin black trailing edge. **Underparts:** White. **Tail:** White, with broad dark grey tip. **Bill:** Black-sided with bright yellow edges to top and bottom. The bill of Northern Bullers Mollymawk is slightly heavier.

Conspicuous features:
- A handsome bird when sitting on the water.
- Smaller on the water when compared with the Grey-headed and the Shy.
- Bill similar to Grey-headed with bright yellow edges and black sides.
- Generally similar to the Grey-headed Mollymawk but has the distinctive silvery white or silvery grey crown.

Where to find - South Island:

Wellington - Cook Strait: Sometimes seen from the Cook Strait ferry. Grey headed birds seen here are probably Bullers and not Grey-headed.

North Canterbury - Kaikoura: Look for it if on a whale-watch excursion.

Otago Peninsula - Taiaroa: Seen from Taiaroa Heads in rough weather.

Otago Peninsula - Cape Saunders: Often seen from land here.

Southland - Bluff: Regularly seen out to sea after January.

Southland - Curio Bay: Sometimes seen from land through a telescope.

Where to find - Stewart Island:

Foveaux Strait: Regularly seen out from Half Moon Bay in deeper water but seldom before January.

Ackers Point: A telescope set up here in windy weather can spot both Bullers and Shy Mollymawks. Watch for the birds behind incoming fishing boats.

Charles A Fleming

Black-browed Mollymawk (above), Yellow-nosed Mollymawk (below)
Bullers Mollymawks (left)

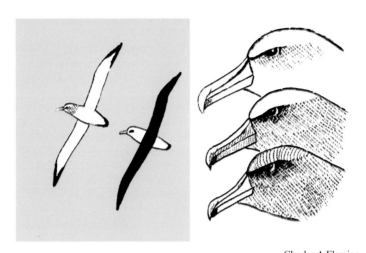

Charles A Fleming

**Salvins (left) Black-browed (right) in flight
Shy Mollymawk (above) Salvins (middle) Chatham Islands (lower)**

SHY MOLLYMAWK

Charles A Fleming

Family: Diomedeidae   **Species:** *Diomedea cauta*
Common name: Shy Mollymawk (a name it is said to have acquired because of
   its habit of being shy about gliding behind ships)
Other name: White-capped Mollymawk   **Status:** Endemic
Size: 900 mm - 1000 mm (cf sparrow 145 mm, smaller than a Royal Albatross
   but larger than Bullers Mollymawk)

Subspecies: These include the Shy Mollymawk (*D. c. cauta*), Salvins Mollymawk
   (*D. c. salvini*) and the Chatham Island Mollymawk (*D. c. erimita*).

Breeding islands close to New Zealand: Auckland Island group.
Breeding months: September to April.
Range worldwide: Ranges to South Africa between the 40th to the 55th parallel.
New Zealand range: From New Zealand west into the Indian Ocean.

Description - mature bird:
  Head: White, with a black shadow in front of eye. Sometimes grey mottling on cheeks. **Upperwing:** Black. **Back:** Grey-black back, merging into darker grey. **Underwings:** White, with thin black edging and black primary tips. **Neck and rump:** White. **Underparts:** White. **Tail:** White, tipped with a broad band of dark grey. **Bill:** Grey, with yellowish top and tip.
Conspicuous features:
  • Look for whitish head cap. (Some birds may have greyish cheeks.)
  • Underwing is clean white with narrow black edges.
Conspicuous characteristics:
  • Has a habit of coming in behind fishing boats and looking for fish scraps.
  • Will alight on the water and feed.

Where to find - North Island:
North Island: Recorded from beach "wrecks" along much of the coastline.
Bay of Plenty - Tauranga: Look for it in deeper water.

Where to find - South Island:
Wellington - Cook Strait: Look for it if on the Cook Strait ferry.
Otago Peninsula - Cape Saunders: Look for it out to sea.
Southland - Bluff: Sometimes seen from Stirling Hill near Bluff township.

Where to find - Stewart Island:
Foveaux Strait: A common species in these waters. It comes in close to Half Moon Bay on Stewart Island often following boats into the port. Good views can be had from Ackers Point on the south arm of Half Moon Bay.

Charles A Fleming

Shy, Salvins, and Chatham Islands Mollymawk

39

SALVINS MOLLYMAWK

Charles A Fleming

Family: Diomedeidae   **Species:** *Diomedea cauta salvini*
Common name: Salvins Mollymawk, Bounty Island Mollymawk
Status: Endemic
Size: 900 mm - 1000 mm (cf sparrow 145 mm)

Breeding islands close to New Zealand: Bounty Island and Snares Island.
Breeding months: September to April.
Range worldwide: Ranges to South America and the South Atlantic.
New Zealand range: Ranges around the New Zealand coast.

Description - mature bird:
    Head: Dark grey with black through eye and whitish cap. **Upperwings:** Black.
Back: Grey-black, merging into darker grey. **Rump and underparts:** White.
Underwings: White, with thin black edging and black primary tips. **Tail:**
White, tipped with a broad band of dark grey. **Bill:** Dark-grey sided, with
yellow edges top and bottom but the yellow on the bottom mandible giving
way to a black patch at the tip.
 Conspicuous features:
* Look for grey head and neck with a whitish cap.
* Bill differs from the Shy Mollymawk being dark-grey sided with a line
  of yellow under bottom mandible.

Where to find - North Island:
North Auckland - Kawau Island: Beyond Great Barrier Island in winter months.
Wellington - Cook Strait: Regularly seen from the Cook Strait ferry.

Where to find - South Island:
North Canterbury - Kaikoura: Seen from the "whale watch" excursions.
Foveaux Strait: Regularly seen in these waters along with Shy Mollymawk.

CHATHAM ISLAND MOLLYMAWK

Alan Tennyson

Family: Diomedeidae   **Species:** *Diomedea cauta erimita*
Common name: Chatham Island Mollymawk
Status: Endemic
Size: 900 mm - 1000 mm (cf sparrow 145 mm)

Breeding islands close to New Zealand: Pyramid Rock at Chatham Islands.
Breeding months: September to April.
Range worldwide: A sedentary species not thought to wander far from the waters
  of the Chatham Islands group.
New Zealand range: Around the Chatham Islands and westwards.

Description - mature bird:
  Head and neck: Dark grey with dark patch through eye. **Upperwings and
  back:** Grey-black back merging into darker black wings. **Rump:** White.
  Underparts: White. **Underwings:** White, thinly edged with black and with
  dark primary tips, showing more black than on either the Shy or Salvins. **Tail:**
  White, tipped with a broad band of dark grey. **Bill:** Bright yellow, with black
  patch at end of lower mandible.
Conspicuous features:
  - Head and neck are all over dark grey.
  - Bill is bright yellow with black tip to lower mandible and this separates
    it from both the Shy and Salvins.

Where to find:
Chatham Islands: Pyramid Rock and waters around the Chathams Islands.

LIGHT-MANTLED SOOTY ALBATROSS

Charles A Fleming

Family: Diomedeidae   **Species:** *Phoebetria palpebrata*
Common name: Light-mantled Sooty Albatross
Status: Circumpolar
Size: 800 mm - 900 mm (cf sparrow 145 mm)

Breeding islands close to New Zealand: Auckland Islands, Antipodes Island, Campbell Island and Macquarie Island.
Breeding months: October to June.
Range worldwide: The southern oceans from the south of New Zealand southwards.
New Zealand range: Not seen in northern New Zealand waters but occasionally seen in waters to the south of the South Island.

Description - mature bird:
 Head and throat: Sooty-brown. **Upperwings:** Dark grey. **Nape to rump:** Ash-grey. **Underwing:** Greyish-brown. **Underparts:** Greyish-brown. **Bill:** Black, with fleshy blue line on mandible groove. **Eye:** Semi-circle of white at rear of eye.
Conspicuous features:
 - Differs from the Sooty Albatross by its lighter tonings on mantle and back.
 - Its overall brownish colouring separates it from other albatross species.

Where to find:
Foveaux Strait: There is a slight chance of seeing one here.

General: Not common in New Zealand waters. Birders would have to travel well to the south of Stewart Island to see this very beautiful albatross. Sea "wrecks" on northern North Island beaches do indicate that it feeds in seas well to the north but birds are seldom seen in close to land.

Charles A Fleming

Light-mantled Sooty Albatrosses

FLESH-FOOTED SHEARWATER

Brian Chudleigh

Family: Procellariidae   **Species:** *Puffinus carneipes*
Common name: Flesh-footed Shearwater   **Status:** Native
Size: 440 mm (cf sparrow 145 mm, Black Petrel 460 mm)

Breeding islands close to New Zealand: Breeds on many off-shore islands from the Bay of Plenty northwards. Main colonies are on the Mercury Islands group and the Hen and Chicken Islands. It also breeds on islands in Cook Strait and off Taranaki on the Sugar Loafs. Also Lord Howe Island off Australia.
Breeding months: November to April. 1 white egg is laid in a burrow.
Range worldwide: New Zealand and Australian birds range north into the Pacific to Alaska and Siberia.
New Zealand range: Ranges from Cook Strait northward but more common in northern waters, especially in the Hauraki Gulf.

Description:
  Upperparts: Brownish-black. **Underparts:** Slightly paler than the upperparts.
  Bill: Pale yellow with top edge and tip dark grey. **Feet:** Flesh coloured.
Conspicuous features:
  • Of dark black plumage.
Conspicuous characteristic:
  • A slow wing-flapping shearwater.
  • Glides along waves with the occasional toss into the air.
    Often will alight and sit on water near fishing boats.

Differences between the Flesh-footed and the Sooty Shearwater:
  • The Flesh-footed Shearwater has darker plumage than the Sooty.
  • The Flesh-footed Shearwater lacks the silver underwing of the Sooty.
  • The Flesh-footed Shearwater has a yellowish bill, the Sooty Shearwater has a dark grey bill. (Bill colouring also separates it from Black Petrel, Westland Black Petrel and White-chinned Petrel.)
  • The Flesh-footed Shearwater has a pale yellow bill with a grey top edge, the Sooty Shearwater has a dark grey bill.
  • The Flesh-footed Shearwater has flesh coloured feet, the Sooty Shearwater has dark lilac-brown feet.

Note: The Flesh-footed Shearwater is easily confused with the Sooty (and with the Black Petrel, Westland Black Petrel, White-chinned Petrel).
Call: A wailing "ku-koo-wah", heard after dark above nesting burrows.

Where to find - North Island:
Bay of Islands: Regularly seen out from Paihia in deeper waters.
North Auckland - Kawau Island: Seen in deeper waters.
Coromandel - Mercury Islands: Regularly seen out from Whitianga.

Where to find - South Island:
Wellington - Cook Strait: Watch for them from the Cook Strait ferry.

BULLERS SHEARWATER

Rod Morris

Family: Procellariidae   **Species:** *Puffinus bulleri*
Common name: Bullers Shearwater   **Status:** Endemic
Size: 460 mm (cf sparrow 145 mm, Flesh-footed Shearwater 450 mm)

Discussion: This shearwater is generally easy to find and to identify. It ranges away from its breeding islands and comes in close to land to be seen from the coastline. It feeds in bays and into wider harbours. Since the removal of pigs from Poor Knights Islands in 1936 its numbers have increased remarkably.

Breeding island close to New Zealand: Poor Knights Islands of the east coast of Northland.
Breeding months: October to May. 1 white egg is laid in a burrow.
Range worldwide: To Australia and northwards into the northern Pacific and to the North American coast.
New Zealand range: From the northern South Island and around the North Island. It is especially common off the Northland coast.

Description:
  Head: Dark brown above the eye. Pure white under the eye. **Upperparts:** Light grey. **Upperwings:** Light grey with dark brown open M marking across wings and rump. Primaries are black. **Rump:** Dark brown. **Underwings:** Clean white, edged with black. **Underparts:** Pure white. **Tail:** Brown with a black tail tip. **Bill:** Bluish-grey. **Feet:** Bluish-grey.
Conspicuous features:
  • Slightly bigger in size than the Sooty Shearwater and the Flesh-footed Shearwater both of which are common in the same waters of Northland.
  • The clean white underparts are distinctive.
  • The brown open M marking on the wings and rump is very noticeable.

Conspicuous characteristics:

- Regularly comes in close to boats.
- Often seen in rafts with Fluttering Shearwaters.
- Will join up with feeding groups of Flesh-footed and Sooty Shearwaters.
- Soars along waves close to water.

Where to find - North Island:
Bay of Islands: A conspicuous shearwater regularly seen close to land.
Auckland - Tiri Tiri Island: Can be seen near Tiri Tiri Island and from Whangaparaoa Peninsula. Look for Fluttering Shearwaters here too.
Coromandel Peninsula: Can be seen from the coast north of Coromandel.
Wellington - Cook Strait: Not regularly seen here but possible.

SOOTY SHEARWATER

Dennis Buurman

Family: Procellariidae   **Species:** *Puffinus griseus*
Common name: Sooty Shearwater, Mutton-bird
Status: Native.
Size: 440 mm (cf sparrow 145 mm, Flesh-footed Shearwater 450 mm)

Discussion: The Sooty Shearwater is probably New Zealand's most common species of seabird of some several million birds.

Breeding islands close to New Zealand: Breeds on many islands from the Three Kings Islands to the north of the North Island, to the Campbell and Macquarie Islands to the far south of New Zealand. Very large populations breed on the islands around Stewart Islands.
Breeding months: November to May. 1 white egg is laid in a burrow, the first birds arriving back to the breeding colonies in late September.
Range worldwide: Undertakes a circular migration of the Pacific Ocean, moving into the northern hemisphere waters around the first week of May.

New Zealand range: Widely spread around all New Zealand waters. At times can be seen feeding close to land, especially when weather is rough.

Description:
  Upperparts: Black. **Underparts:** Greyish-brown. **Underwing:** Primary feathers black, with some silver streaking on the secondary feathers. **Bill:** Dark grey. **Legs and feet:** Brownish.
Conspicuous features:
  - Smaller than the Flesh-footed Shearwater and Bullers Shearwater both of which can be seen in the same waters.
  - The silver streaking on the underwing quickly separates this species from the Flesh-footed Shearwater, Grey-faced Petrel and Black Petrel.
  - Brownish coloured feet separate it from the conspicuous, flesh-coloured feet, of the Flesh-footed Shearwater.
  - Dark grey bill separates it from the pale yellow bill of the Flesh-footed Shearwater.

Conspicuous characteristic:
  - A fast flying shearwater with rather stiff wing action, which flaps and then glides for some distance along waves tops and in wave troughs.
Call: "Kuu - ah kuu - ah", heard from incoming birds over the breeding islands. Call can be hysterical in tone and deafening.

Where to find - North Island:
Bay of Islands: Both Sooty and Flesh-footed Shearwaters can be seen here.
North Auckland - Kawau Island: Usually seen well out from Kawau Island.
Coromandel - Mercury Islands: In the waters out from Whitianga.
Wellington - Cook Strait: Often seen from the Cook Strait ferry.

Where to find - South Island:
Marlborough Sounds: Look for them when leaving the sounds.
Otago Peninsula - Taiaroa Heads: Can often be seen well out to sea in thousands. Use a telescope here.
Southland coast: Sooty Shearwaters can be seen in hundreds from the Southland coast. A telescope mounted on the beach or on a cliff can reach feeding seabirds. Try the following places -
  - **Nugget Point:** Nugget Point is accessed from Balclutha. South of Balclutha on the Owaka Road, take the Otanomomo sign and follow south to Kaka Point and then Nugget Point. Check the sea for birds wherever it is visible in this area. At Nugget Point also look for Yellow-eyed Penguins. (See "Places" in back of book.)
  - **Curio Bay:** This place is 50 kms east of Invercargill on the south coast. It is known for its ancient fossilised forest exposed by the sea. In mid-summer seabirds feed off-shore in hundreds. A telescope can pick up a constant view of moving Sooty Shearwaters. While in this area visit nearby Porpoise Bay and drive on to the Chasland forests and look for bush birds.
  - **Bluff Hill:** The town of Bluff is south of Invercargill on a direct and easy road. After driving through the town to road's end, set your telescope up on Stirling Point.

- **Riverton:** This area is to the west of Invercargill. From either Riverton, or Colac Bay nearby, you will get unimpeded coastal views. While here you will also see both Spotted and Stewart Island Shags.

Note: Preferably try the Curio Bay area first. Either area could be as rewarding as chartering a boat for a sea trip.

Where to find - Stewart Island:

Stewart Island: Often the waters straight out from Half Moon Bay have fewer Sooty Shearwaters than those which can be seen from the coastline from Taiaroa Heads to Riverton. Try the mainland viewing first.

Foveaux Strait: The ferry crossing of Foveaux Strait can often provide good views of many seabirds and can save the birder having to charter a boat.

Note: Confusion with the Flesh-footed Shearwater will not be a problem in the waters around Stewart Island as these are beyond their range.

FLUTTERING SHEARWATER

Paul M Sagar

Family: Procellariidae   **Species:** *Puffinus gavia*
Common name: Fluttering Shearwater   **Status:** Endemic
Size: 330 mm (cf sparrow 145 mm, Sooty Shearwater 430 mm)

Discussion: Some authorities believe the Fluttering Shearwater (*P. gavia*), Huttons Shearwater (*P. huttoni*) and the Manx Shearwater (*P. puffinus*), of the northern hemisphere, to be the same species. At sea they all look very similar and are difficult to separate. New Zealand authorities, however, separate all three and regard Fluttering Shearwater and Huttons Shearwater as distinct species.

Breeding islands close to New Zealand: Breeds on islands from the Three Kings Islands in the north to islands in Cook Strait.
Breeding months: September to February. 1 white egg is laid in a burrow.

Range worldwide: Around New Zealand and to the south-west coast of Australia.

New Zealand range: Particularly common in northern waters.

Description:
  Upperparts: Dark brown. **Underparts:** White. **Bill:** Dark grey. **Feet:** Brownish marked with white.

Conspicuous features:
- A small shearwater.
- The very white underparts are noticeable.
- Look for the fine dark grey bill.
- Feet protrude slightly behind the tail in flight.

Conspicuous characteristics:
- Birds have a habit of rapidly fluttering their wings as they take off from the sea. Accompanying the wing beats, the feet also assist with take off.
- Through the months of mid-December, January and February, Fluttering Shearwaters come together in communal flocks and sit on the water in rafts. These rafts can be approached by small boats. Sometimes rafts will form just off the coastline.
- Flocks of Fluttering Shearwater will follow schooling fish and will join in the melee for these fish along with gannets, White-fronted Terns and gulls. Usually Arctic Skuas will also be close by. In such situations Fluttering Shearwaters often adopt the diving characteristics of Diving Petrels.
- The usual flight pattern of a Fluttering Shearwater is four to five wing beats and then a short glide.
- Occasionally Fluttering Shearwaters get caught on fishermen's hooks.

Call: Very noisy near their breeding colonies where they make a "ka-haa ka-haa kehek", type call.

Differences between Fluttering Shearwaters and Huttons Shearwaters:
- The Fluttering Shearwater is smaller in size than Huttons.
- The Fluttering Shearwater has a shorter bill by 4 mm, than Huttons.
- The Fluttering Shearwater has lighter feather colouration and is whiter under the wing.
- The Fluttering Shearwater has a different breeding habitat nesting on small predator-free islands from the Three Kings to Marlborough Sounds in the south. Most Fluttering Shearwater's burrows are at low altitudes.
- Huttons Shearwater breeds on the mainland of the South Island high in the Kaikoura Ranges above 1200 metres.
- The Fluttering Shearwater starts breeding in mid-September (egg dates late September and to mid-October).
- Huttons Shearwater starts breeding mid-October (egg dates November).
- Huttons Shearwater is a bird of the open seas rather than of the waters around sheltered off-shore islands and bays. However, in the breeding season it will flock to about 1 km off the shoreline at dusk.

Where to find:
Northland waters: Boat trips in the Bay of Island, to Kawau Island and to Tiri Tiri Island, will usually locate Fluttering Shearwaters. Over the summer months,

flocks can be seen from Northland and Coromandel beaches.

Auckland Harbour: Regularly seen from the Auckland to Waiheke Island ferry during summer months, usually not far from the Waiheke Island wharf.

Wellington - Cook Strait: Large flocks come into Wellington Harbour and sit in rafts. These can often be seen from the ferry. Huttons may also be in the waters beyond Wellington Harbour. Try and separate the two species.

Marlborough Sounds: Look for them near the Chetwode Islands.

HUTTONS SHEARWATER

Graeme Taylor

Family: Procellariidae   **Species:** *Puffinus huttoni*
Common name: Huttons Shearwater
Status: Endemic
Size: 360 mm (cf sparrow 145 mm, Fluttering Shearwater 330 mm)

Mainland breeding site: On the seaward Kaikoura Range in the northern part of the South Island of New Zealand, above 1200 metres above sea level.
Breeding months: August to April. 1 white egg is laid in a burrow.
Range worldwide: Around New Zealand and the southern half of Australia.
New Zealand range: Around the North Island but in the breeding season from Otago Peninsula to Cook Strait.

Description:
  Upperparts: Dark brown. **Underparts:** White. **Bill:** Dark grey. **Feet:** Brownish marked with white.
Conspicuous features:
  • Look for the dirtier underwing as opposed to the clean white underwing of the Fluttering Shearwater.
  • Look for the longer bill as compared with the Fluttering.
  • Look for a darker coloured bird as compared with the Fluttering.

Where to find:

South Island waters: The waters from Cook Strait to Otago Peninsula should have Huttons Shearwater rather than Fluttering Shearwater.

Marlborough - Tory Channel: If crossing Cook Strait on the ferry watch out for flocks of Huttons Shearwater near the entrance to Tory Channel.

North Canterbury - Kaikoura: This is by far the best place to see this bird and where the observer can be certain of accurate identification. As it generally feeds well out to sea, the best way to see it is to go on an Ocean Wings bird-watching excursion. These leave daily from Kaikoura if the weather is suitable.

North Canterbury - Kaikoura coast: Try from the coastal road either north or south of Kaikoura town, at dusk, using a telescope. Birds will be moving in from the deeper water prior to visiting the breeding colonies in the ranges. At times they rest momentarily, very close to the shoreline. As there are many kilometres of road right on the coast there is plenty of scope for viewing.

Canterbury - Banks Peninsula: Rafts of Huttons Shearwaters sit in the open bays of Banks Peninsula during summer.

LITTLE SHEARWATER

Rod Morris

Family: Procellariidae   **Species:** *Puffinus assimilis*
Common name: Little Shearwater, Allied Shearwater
Status: Endemic
Size: 300 mm (cf sparrow 145 mm, Fluttering Shearwater 330 mm)

Subspecies: Seven subspecies are recognised. Of these, the Kermadec Little Shearwater (*P. a. kermadecensis*), and the North Island Little Shearwater (*P. a. haurakiensis*), might be encountered by mainland New Zealand birders.

Breeding islands close to New Zealand: The Kermadec Little Shearwater breeds in the Kermadec Islands, while the North Island Little Shearwater breeds on many islands from the Cavalli Islands in the north to the Mercury Islands off Coromandel Peninsula in the south.

Breeding months: July to December. 1 white egg is laid in a burrow.

Range worldwide: The New Zealand subspecies are considered sedentary and not thought to range widely from their nesting islands.

New Zealand range: Around the north of the North Island.

Habitat: The Little Shearwater tends to keep well off-shore in northern New Zealand waters unlike the Fluttering Shearwater.

Description:
    Upperparts: Black. **Underparts:** White. **Face:** White to just above the eye. **Bill:** Dull lead-blue. **Feet:** Blue.

Conspicuous features:
- The Little Shearwater is the smallest shearwater in New Zealand waters. It is bigger, though, than the Diving Petrel and the White-faced Storm Petrel which might also be seen in the same waters.
- A small dark shearwater in appearance.
- Its blue feet are conspicuous.

Conspicuous characteristics:
- A fast flying bird.
- Flight pattern is of several fast wing beats followed by a short glide period.
- Will skip and skim the waves in rough weather.

Call: Heard usually just on dusk near the breeding colony, is a rapid "kakakakakaka...urr", sound.

Where to find - North Island:

Bay of Islands: Best locality for this species is to the north of Paihia in the waters near to the Cavalli Island group. These waters are an easy boat ride from Paihia or Kerikeri.

Northland - Hen and Chickens Islands: It nests on these islands in small numbers so is often seen from these waters.

North Auckland - Kawau Island: The waters beyond Kawau Island in the direction of Little Barrier Island are Little Shearwater territory.

Coromandel - Whitianga: A short excursion from the town into the waters of the Mercury Islands will take you into Little Shearwater territory. Fluttering Shearwaters, White-faced Storm Petrel and Diving Petrel will also be here.

COMMON DIVING PETREL

Family: Pelecanoididae   **Species:** *Pelecanoides urinatrix*
Common name: Diving Petrel   **Status:** Native
Size: 200 mm (cf sparrow 145 mm, Little Shearwater 300 mm)

Discussion: A commonly seen bird in all waters. Can be mixed with the South Georgian Diving Petrel (*Pelecanoides georgicus*) in waters off Stewart Island where the two species are almost inseparable at sea. Underwing and underparts are darker on the Common Diving Petrel than on the South Georgian.

Common Diving Petrel

Subspecies: Four subspecies are recognised of which only *P. u. urinatrix* is likely to be encountered by mainland New Zealand birders.

Breeding islands close to New Zealand: Breeds on many islands from Three Kings Islands to Stewart Island and the Chatham Islands. Also on Snares Island.
Breeding months: August to February. 1 white egg is laid in a burrow.
Range worldwide: Ranges around New Zealand and into the Tasman Sea towards Australia. Considered a sedentary species, many birds not moving far from their breeding islands and regularly visiting their nesting burrows at any time of year.
New Zealand range: Found in all New Zealand coastal waters.

Description:
  Upperparts: Black. **Face, neck and throat:** Sides of face, neck and throat mottled grey. **Chin:** White. **Underparts:** White. **Bill:** Black. **Legs and feet:** Blue.
Conspicuous features:
  • A small short-tailed bird similar in size to a storm-petrel.
  • Stump-tail is noticeable.
Conspicuous characteristics:
  • When sitting on the water it could at first be mistaken for a penguin.
  • Usually recognised by its fast flight.
  • Has a tendency to fly on a parallel plane straight into waves.
  • Stays under water for several seconds with each dive.
  • Because it is a very active bird it is difficult to get on to with binoculars.
Call: Very noisy near and at the breeding colony with "kuaka ka ka" type calls, the male and female calls being recognised by experts.

Differences between the Common Diving Petrel and the South Georgian Diving Petrel:

- South Georgian Diving Petrels are up to 20 mm shorter in length.
- South Georgian Diving Petrels have a longer and more slender bill.
- South Georgian Diving Petrels have a paler underwing and all white underparts.

Confusion between the Common Diving Petrel and the South Georgian Diving Petrel:

The Common Diving Petrel and the South Georgian Diving Petrel live in close proximity around Stewart Island with the South Georgian Diving Petrel, breeding in burrows on Codfish Island off the north-west coast of Stewart Island. It is estimated that less than 40 pairs breed here. Confusion arises with the two species overlapping.

Best time of year for viewing: Diving Petrel are known to revisit their old nesting burrows at any time of year. This suggests that some birds are always in New Zealand waters at any time. Generally the breeding months of August to February provide most chances.

Where to find - North Island:

Northland - Bay of Islands: Birds can be seen less than 5 kms from Paihia or Kerikeri in rough weather.

North Auckland - Kawau Island: Can be seen in the open seas around and beyond Kawau Island.

Auckland - Tiri Tiri Island: Sometimes seen on the trip to Tiri Tiri Island. In rough weather these birds will be seen to the entrance of the Waitemata Harbour and sometimes in the harbour.

Where to find - South Island:

Wellington - Cook Strait: Look for them from the Cook Strait ferry.

Marlborough - Pelorus Sound: Expect them in the sound and out in the deeper water.

Where to find - Stewart Island:

Whero Island: Beyond Whero Island Diving Petrels are seen in good numbers. Probably both species are here.

Note: Authorities say that the Common Diving Petrel and the South Georgian Diving Petrel can only be separated in the hand.

Reference: West J; Imber M J 1989. Survey of South Georgian Diving Petrels (*Pelecanoides georgicus*) on Codfish Island. Notornis 36: 157 - 158.

BLACK-COLOURED PETRELS AND SHEARWATERS

Black-coloured petrels and shearwaters ranging around New Zealand waters are always difficult to identify. These include the dark brownish coloured Sooty Shearwater (*Puffinus griseus*), the Flesh-footed Shearwater (*P. carneipes*), the White-chinned Petrel (*Procellaria aequinoctialis*), the Westland Black Petrel (*P. westlandica*) and the Black Petrel (*P. parkinsoni*).

In the deeper waters of the Hauraki Gulf, the Sooty Shearwater, Flesh-footed Shearwater, and the Black Petrel can be seen together and confusion can result. In waters such as Cook Strait all the above species might be seen.

Locality and breeding differences between the White-chinned Petrel (*Procellaria aequinoctialis*) the Westland Black Petrel (*P. westlandica*) and the Black Petrel (*P. parkinsoni*):

- The Westland Black Petrel is a winter breeder occupying its breeding colonies from February to December. The Black Petrel breeds from October through to July and the White-chinned breeds from November to May.
- The Westland Black Petrel is considered to be non-migratory in the true annual migration sense. It spreads across the Tasman towards Australia while the Black Petrel migrates north-east of New Zealand and above the equator. The White-chinned Petrel is truly circumpolar.
- The breeding colonies of the three species are widely separated with the Black Petrel breeding on Little Barrier Island and Great Barrier Island, the Westland Black Petrel nesting on the Paparoa Ranges of mainland South Island while the White-chinned Petrel nests well to the south of New Zealand on Auckland Island, Campbell Island and Antipodes Island as well as other islands around the southern oceans.

Diagnostic similarities and differences between Sooty Shearwater, Flesh-footed Shearwater, White-chinned Petrel, Westland Black Petrel and Black Petrel:

Bills and feet:
- Sooty Shearwater - bill dark grey. Legs and feet, lilac-brown.
- Flesh-footed Shearwater - bill pale yellowish, with top edge and tip, greyish. Legs and feet, flesh pink.
- White-chinned Petrel - bill yellowish with dark grey only at the end of the nasal tubes. Pale yellowish bill tip. Legs and feet, black.
- Westland Black Petrel - bill pale yellowish with black tip. Legs and feet, black.
- Black Petrel - bill pale yellowish with dark grey tip. Legs and feet - black.

General:
- Birds have either yellowish or dark grey coloured bills.
- Birds have either black or pinkish legs and feet.
- All birds are difficult to separate at sea.
- Although the Westland Black Petrel is slightly bigger than the Black Petrel and smaller than the White-chinned Petrel, this is not a useful identification feature when viewing birds at sea.

- The white chin of the White-chinned Petrel is not a good diagnostic feature as not all birds have it, but those with it are White-chinned Petrels.
- With the size of the population of Black Petrel being small, the chances of seeing this species at sea is reduced. Chances are better for the Westland Black Petrel which numbers around 1100 breeding pairs.
- All species are noted for their habit of circling the coasts off their breeding islands at dusk, and then at dark, coming in and falling through the shrub canopies to land, all the time making very noisy and vocal calls. After a brief respite around midnight the noise again starts as birds leave the burrows for their take-off points.

Graeme Taylor
Black Petrel
(Fledgling climbing a tree before its first take-off.)

BLACK PETREL

Family: Procellariidae   **Species:** *Procellaria parkinsoni*
Common name: Black Petrel   **Status:** Endemic
Size: 460 mm (cf sparrow 145 mm, Westland Black Petrel 480 mm, White-chinned Petrel 550 mm)

Discussion: The Black Petrel is thought to have originally nested in the higher ranges of the North Island and in the Heaphy Range near Nelson in the South Island. Predators introduced by European settlers helped to bring about its demise. Although the breeding colonies of this species must have overlapped with the Westland Black Petrel in the past, the species have evolved separately with different breeding seasons and migration patterns. It is considered a close relative of the White-chinned Petrel (*P. aequinoctialis*) which breeds to the south of New Zealand on the Auckland, Campbell and Antipodes Islands. This species is also a summer breeder.

Black Petrel

Breeding islands close to New Zealand: Little Barrier and Great Barrier Island. The Little Barrier Island colony near the summit, was in the past severely predated on by cats but with the eradication of these, numbers are said to be on the increase (7 pairs breeding in 1988, 100 pairs in 1999). Great Barrier Island currently has a population of 800 pairs.

Breeding months: November to July. 1 white egg is laid in a burrow.

Range worldwide: Eastwards from New Zealand into the tropical Pacific and across the Tasman to Australia.

New Zealand range: Around the North Island and north of the South Island.

Description:
  Upperparts: Black. **Underparts:** Black. **Bill:** Pale yellowish with dark grey tip. **Feet and legs:** Black.
Conspicuous features:
  • An all black petrel.
  • Pale yellowish bill with dark grey tip.
Conspicuous characteristics:
  • Wheels, glides, tosses and skids down waves in rough weather. A rather stiff-winged and continuous flier in calm weather.
Call: Staccato like clacks and dull moans.

Where to find:
Northland - Bay of Islands: Occasionally seen in these waters.
North Auckland - Kawau Island: Waters towards Little Barrier Island are the most reliable waters in which to see this species.
Coromandel - Mercury Islands: Expect to see them in these waters.

Where to find - South Island:
Wellington - Cook Strait: Occasionally seen from the Cook Strait ferry. Could be mixed with Westland Black or White-chinned Petrel in these waters.

WESTLAND BLACK PETREL

Dennis Buurman

Family: Procellariidae   **Species:** *Procellaria westlandica*
Common name: Westland Black Petrel   **Status:** Endemic
Size: 480 mm (cf sparrow 145 mm, Black Petrel 460 mm, White-chinned Petrel 550 mm)

Discussion: The Westland Black Petrel has a breeding population estimated to be around 9000 birds and increasing.

Breeding place: This is in the steep ranges in the Punakaiki district of Westland, in the South Island.
Breeding months: April to December. 1 white egg is laid in a burrow.
Range worldwide: Migrates from its breeding colonies mainly east of New Zealand beyond Chatham Island and into the Tasman Sea towards Australia.
New Zealand range: Around the northern waters of the South Island and up the west coast of the North Island. Storm wrecked birds have been collected from Auckland west coast beaches.

Description:
  Upper and underparts: Black. **Bill:** Pale yellowish with a black bill tip. **Feet and legs:** Black.
Conspicuous features:
- An overall black bird.
- Pale yellowish bill with dark bill tip.

Conspicuous characteristics:
- Has a steady and even wing beat when seen returning to its breeding colony in the evenings.
- On the water it has all the characteristics of typical petrel flight, wheeling, turning and skimming down waves.

Call: A silent bird when on its return to the breeding burrow but it makes a noisy guttural "coo-coo-rah" near its burrow.

Where to find - South Island:
Westland - Paparoa Ranges: The breeding colonies of this bird are in the Paparoa Ranges south of Westport on the west coast of the South Island. Breeding areas start at the Punakaiki River which is about 50 kms south of Westport. They extend south to Barrytown. Main concentrations of birds are in the Punakaiki River area and to the south. Birds can be seen returning to their burrows from the main highway.

Best area to see them: Try Scotchmans Creek 4 kms south of the Punakaiki River.
Time of year to see them: Between the months of late February and December with June onwards being when the colony is at its peak of activity.
Viewing times: 5 p.m. onwards in June. Some nights are better than others. See "Places" at back of book for the commercial operation in the area.

General: This locality is easily reached from Greymouth. While in the area look for Great Spotted Kiwi.

Reference: Best HA; Owen K L 1976. Distribution of breeding sites of the Westland Black Petrel. Notornis: 23, 233 - 242.

WHITE-CHINNED PETREL

Dennis Buurman

Family: Procellariidae   **Species:** *Procellaria aequinoctialis*
Common name: White-chinned Petrel   **Status:** Circumpolar
Size: 550 mm (cf sparrow 145 mm, Black Petrel 460 mm, Westland Black Petrel 480 mm)

Breeding islands close to New Zealand: Breeds on Auckland Island, Campbell Island, Antipode Island and their surrounding islands. Also breeding on many islands around the southern oceans.

Breeding months: November to May. 1 white egg is laid in a burrow.

Range worldwide: The southern oceans from the Antarctic to about 30°S, although ranging further north in winter around southern Australia, South America and South Africa.

New Zealand Range: North to the Northland coast in winter and to Cook Strait in summer. Most commonly seen off the south-east coast of the South Island, from Otago south in summer.

Description:
  Upper and underparts: Black. **Chin:** Variable amounts of white. **Bill:** Pale yellow with dark grey at the end of nasal tubes in front of nostrils and on the groove of lower mandible.

Conspicuous features:
  - The pale yellow bill lacks the dark tip of the Black Petrel and the Westland Black and also the dark top and tip of the bill of the Flesh-footed Shearwater.
  - The white chin is seldom seen on birds in New Zealand waters.

Conspicuous characteristics:
  - A slow and lazy flier.
  - Has a tendency to follow ships.
  - Has typical petrel-like flight in rough weather of tossing and wheeling.

Call: Near the burrow, it groans, squeals, clacks and clatters.

Where to find - North Island:

Wellington - Cook Strait: Birds are likely here during the New Zealand winter. Watch for them from the ferry.

Where to find - South Island:

Otago - south: Regularly in these waters during winter. This is probably the most common of the large black petrels to be seen in these waters, although the Westland Black is also known from them.

Otago Peninsula - Taiaroa and Cape Saunders: Sometimes seen from the Royal Albatross observatory from mid-March onwards.

Southland - Nugget Point: Often seen from near the Nugget Point lighthouse and from the Yellow-eyed Penguin look-out above Roaring Bay.

General: Should be looked for in deep water during winter excursions.

CAPE PIGEON

Family: Procellariidae   **Species:** *Daption capense*
Common name: Cape Pigeon   **Status:** Native
Other name: Cape Petrel, Pintado Petrel
Size: 400 mm (cf sparrow 145 mm)

Subspecies: Two subspecies are recognised, the Southern Cape Pigeon *(D. c.*

Brian Chudleigh

Cape Pigeon

capense) and the smaller Snares Cape Pigeon (*D. c. australe*). In winter and early spring both subspecies overlap in range and spread widely well to the north of New Zealand.

Breeding months: November to March. Birds are cliff nesters with 1 white egg being laid in a rough scrape. The subspecies *australe* breeds up to three weeks earlier than *capense*.

Breeding islands near New Zealand: The subspecies *australe* breeds on Chatham Island, Pyramid Rock, Snares Island, Antipodes Island, Bounty Island and Campbell Island. The subspecies *capense* breeds on the Antarctic coast.

Range worldwide: Southern hemisphere to latitude 18°.

New Zealand range: Right around the New Zealand coast.

Description:

Head and neck: Black. **Upperwings:** Black and lightly speckled with white, with two large white patches on the upper primary feathers of each wing. **Back and rump:** Mottled with black and white. **Underwings:** White, with black leading edges and thin black trailing edges. Primary wing-tip feathers, black. **Underparts:** White. **Tail:** Mottled with black and white, and tipped with broad black tail- band. **Bill and feet:** Black.

Conspicuous feature:

- In flight the four white wing patches are noticeable.

Conspicuous characteristics:

- Flies off the stern of boats and follows ships for some distance.

Where to find - North Island:

Bay of Islands: Not so common in these waters but usually seen in winter.

North Auckland - Kawau Island trip: Regularly seen at most seasons.

Bay of Plenty - Tauranga: Can be seen in outer waters.

Wellington - Cook Strait: Regularly flies in behind the inter-island ferry. Follows shipping into Wellington Harbour.

Where to find - South Island:
Marlborough - Pelorus Sound: Common in the outer waters.
North Canterbury - Kaikoura: Common from whale-watch excursions.
Otago: Common in waters around the Otago Peninsula.

Where to find - Stewart Island:
Foveaux Strait: Common from the Bluff to Stewart Island ferry.
Stewart Island: A common bird in these waters.

SOUTHERN GIANT PETREL

Jim Hague

Family: Procellariidae   **Species:** *Macronectes giganteus*
Common name: Southern Giant Petrel   **Status:** Native
Size: 800mm – 900 mm (cf sparrow 145 mm, Black-backed Gull 600mm)

Discussion: The Southern Giant Petrel, comes in variable plumages. There is a
   dark phase, which is similar to the Northern Giant Petrel except for bill colour.
   There are also white and variable phases showing marked differences.

Differences between Southern Giant and Northern Giant Petrel:
   • Southern has a whitish head and breast, or may be all white.
   • Southern has yellowish bill; Northern has yellowish bill tipped with tan.

Range: Around oceans of the southern hemisphere below latitude 18°.
Breeding islands close to New Zealand: Nearest is at the Macquarie Islands.

Where to find:
Otago, Southland Coast: Occasionally seen off-shore. Birds are occasionally
   found in beach "wrecks" around other New Zealand shores.

NORTHERN GIANT PETREL

Charles A Fleming

Family: Procellariidae
Common name: Giant Petrel, Nelly
Size: 800 mm - 900 mm (cf sparrow 145 mm)

Species: *Macronectes halli*
Status: Native

Breeding islands close to New Zealand: Chatham Islands, Stewart Island, Antipodes Island, Campbell Island, Auckland Island and Macquarie Island.

Breeding months: August to February. Birds tend to nest in small loose communities.

Range worldwide: New Zealand west to South Africa.

New Zealand range: Around New Zealand for much of the year. In rough conditions it will enter harbours and has been recorded in both Auckland and Wellington Harbours. Generally it prefers to keep to deeper waters but will scavenge behind fishing boats well into calm water.

Description - mature bird:
  Head: Forehead pale brown with sides of face and chin grey. **Upperparts:** Greyish-brown. **Underparts:** Tending to dark grey. **Underwings:** Brown, with variable areas of grey. **Bill:** Light tan with distinctive light brown tip. Has a prominent nasal tube. **Feet and legs:** Dark grey.

Description - immature birds:
  Upper and underparts: Varying from black to dark brown.

Conspicuous features:
  - The overall brownish grey, with lighter grey around the face, throat and upper breast, is noticeable.
  - Light tan bill with light brownish tip, separates this bird from the Southern Giant Petrel.
  - Heavy nasal tube is noticeable.

Conspicuous characteristics:
- Flight is often straight and direct.
- It often glides and wheels behind ships.
- Can glide motionless for some distance.

Where to find - North and South Islands:
North Auckland: Often in waters near Little Barrier Island.
Wellington - Cook Strait: Regularly seen from the Cook Strait ferry.
North Canterbury - Kaikoura: Regularly seen from both the Kaikoura coastline and from whale-watching excursions.

Where to find - Stewart Island:
Half Moon Bay: Regularly seen in waters around Half Moon Bay and to the entrance of Paterson Inlet.
General: Can be expected to be seen around New Zealand from any boat trip in deeper waters during winter months.

PRIONS

All six recognised species of prion are known from New Zealand waters. These are -
- The Fairy Prion (*Pachyptila turtur*), which is a true New Zealand species breeding on off-shore islands from the Poor Knights in the north to Stewart Island. Regularly seen at any season off the New Zealand coast.
- The Fulmar Prion (*Pachyptila crassirostris*), which breeds on Snares Island and other southern islands. Sometimes included with the Fairy Prion.
- The Thin-billed Prion (*Pachyptila belcheri*), which breeds from the Macquarie Islands (small colony only), east to the Indian Ocean. It occasionally strays into New Zealand waters.
- The Antarctic Prion (*Pachyptila desolata*), which breeds on the southern islands from the Auckland Islands eastwards. This species is a common winter visitor to the northern seas about New Zealand. Some authorities place this species with the Broad-billed Prion.
- Salvins Prion (*Pachyptila salvini*), a species which breeds on Indian Ocean islands but straggles to New Zealand and is sometimes collected from beach "wrecks". Placed with the Broad-billed Prion by some authorities.
- The Broad-billed Prion (*Pachyptila vittata*), which breeds in abundance around the Chatham Islands and Stewart Island. This species can be found in all New Zealand waters and especially those to the south.

Similarities: All species of prion are difficult to identify in normal sea conditions. They are all of blue-grey colouring with white underparts, apart from dark central tail feathers, and all have a dark brown open M mark across the wings and back. In New Zealand waters in summer, bird-watchers are likely to come across only Fairy Prion in northern waters and both Fairy and Broad-billed Prions in southern waters. In winter all species might be found in the same waters so reliable identification will be difficult.

Note: The Broad-billed and the Fairy Prion are considered true New Zealand species and so are individually discussed.

FAIRY PRION

Charles A Fleming

Family: Procellariidae   **Species:** *Pachyptila turtur*
Common name: Fairy Prion   **Status:** Circumpolar
Size: 230 mm (cf sparrow 145 mm)

Breeding islands close to New Zealand: Breeds on many islands around New Zealand from Poor Knights Island in the north, south to Snares Island. Also on Mangere Island in the Chatham Islands group.

Breeding months: November to February. 1 white egg is laid in a burrow.

Range worldwide: Found around southern oceans from New Zealand to South Africa up to latitude 19° S. Some adult birds do not move far from the breeding grounds as birds are known to make occasional visits back to their nesting sites in winter. Immatures probably range more widely.

New Zealand range: Found in all waters around New Zealand.

Description:
   Face: Grey with a faint whitish stripe above the eye. **Upperparts:** Bluish-grey. **Wings:** Bluish-grey with a black open M marking across wings and lower-back. **Underwing:** Distinctly white. **Underparts:** White. **Tail:** Grey, with half the tail being boldly tipped with black. **Bill:** Black.

Conspicuous features:
- Dark open M marking on upperwings is noticeable.

Conspicuous characteristics:
- A fast flying species.
- Birds toss and swerve in a jaunty manner above the wave tops.
- Birds alight on the water to feed.

Differences between the Fairy Prion and the Broad-billed Prion:
- Very white underwing and underparts of the Fairy Prion separates it from the Broad-billed Prion.
- The Fairy Prion lacks the dark under-eye marking of the Broad-billed Prion.
- The bold black tail tip of the Fairy Prion separates it from the Broad-billed which has a narrow black tip.

Where to find - North Island:

Bay of Islands: Can be sighted when about 2 kms out to sea. Throughout the year a common species in the outer waters of the Bay of Islands.

North Auckland - Kawau Island: Should be encountered on the eastern side of Kawau Island being in good numbers here during summer months.

Coromandel - Mercury Islands: Regularly seen off Whitianga in good numbers throughout the year.

Where to find - South Island:

Wellington - Cook Strait: Regularly seen here. Look for it if on a boat trip in Pelorus Sound or near Duffers Reef and Chetwode Island.

Where to find Stewart Island: Can be confused with Broad-billed Prion here.

BROAD-BILLED PRION

Brian Chudleigh

Family: Procellariidae   **Species:** *Pachyptila vittata*
Common name: Broad-billed Prion   **Status:** Native
Size: 280 mm (cf sparrow 145 mm)

Breeding islands close to New Zealand: Breeds on islands in Foveaux Strait, around Stewart Island, around the Chatham Islands and at Snares Island.
Breeding months: August to January. 1 white egg is laid in a burrow.
Range worldwide: Known from New Zealand west to South America and up to

latitude 19°S. Some adult birds remain close to its breeding grounds over winter months and occasionally make visits to their burrows.

New Zealand range: Found right around the coast but with greater numbers near the breeding islands in the south.

Description:

Face: Above eye, white. Under eye to behind eye, black. **Upperparts:** Bluish-grey. **Underparts:** White, except for tip of tail which is black. **Wings:** Distinctive dark primaries and scapulars create an black open M marking across wings when in flight. **Underwing:** White, with grey on secondary feathers and wing tips. **Bill:** Dark grey, tapering to a broad base at the gape.

Conspicuous features:
- The open M wing marking is distinctive.
- Has prominent high forehead.
- White stripe above the eye is prominent.

Conspicuous characteristics:
- Birds in fast flight reveal their white underwing to the sun.
- All prions are fast flying birds which can be seen singly or in flocks. In flocks they tend to fly erratically with frequent swerving from side to side.

Where to find - North Island:

Bay of Islands: In winter birds can be found beyond Cape Brett.

North Auckland - Kawau Island to Great Barrier: In winter birds can be found in deeper waters.

Coromandel -Mercury Islands: In winter birds can be seen in these waters. .

Where to find - South Island:

Southern waters: Look for it when crossing from Bluff to Stewart Island on the ferry. Should be found in the deep water off Paterson Inlet.

Note: Not likely in northern waters during the summer.

PYCROFTS PETREL

Family: Procellariidae   **Species:** *Pterodroma pycrofti*
Common name: Pycrofts Petrel   **Status:** Endemic
Size: 280 mm (cf sparrow 145 mm)

Discussion: Some authorities consider Pycrofts Petrel to be a race of Stejnegers Petrel (*Pterodroma longirostris*). Stejnegers Petrel, though, is a bird of the west coast of South America with a general northerly migration pattern. Pycrofts Petrel breeds on the opposite side of the Pacific and has a northerly migration into waters separated from Stejnegers. New Zealand authorities therefore have always treated Pycrofts as a distinct species. Records of Stejnegers Petrel have been found in beach "wrecks" on New Zealand beaches. These are thought to have been of non-breeding birds.

Breeding islands close to New Zealand: Hen and Chicken Islands, Poor Knights and Mercury Islands.

Don Merton

Pycrofts Petrel

Breeding months: November to April. Birds lay 1 white egg in isolated burrows often located in flat areas among the forest.

Range worldwide: Range is uncertain but it is known to move north from New Zealand into the Pacific Ocean at the end of the breeding season in a narrow belt to the Equator.

New Zealand range: Waters to the north of the Bay of Plenty.

Description:

Head: Dark grey crown with light forehead feather scalation. **Face, throat and around bill:** White with dark grey through the eye. **Upperparts:** Grey. **Upperwings:** Grey, with dark grey open M marking across wings and rump to wing-tips. **Underparts:** White. **Underwings:** White, with black edges and a small black tag at the leading wing joint. **Tail:** Grey with dark grey tip.

Conspicuous feature:

- Similar to Cooks Petrel but with more dark grey on wings and tail.

Differences between Pycrofts and Cooks Petrel:

- Cooks Petrel has a longer bill than Pycrofts. This feature is of little value when identifying birds at sea.
- Cooks Petrel has a more distinct M marking on the upperwing caused by the light grey of the secondary feathers extending well towards the leading edge of the wing.
- Pycrofts Petrel has a darker crown and darker wings.
- Pycrofts Petrel has shorter wings and a longer tail than Cooks. These features are not distinguishable at sea and are of little use to the observer.
- Pycrofts has a darker grey uppertail, a feature which may help to separate the species at sea.

Note: At sea Pycrofts Petrel and Cooks Petrel are almost inseparable.

Breeding habitat differences: Pycrofts Petrel tends to nest at lower altitudes and on different terrain from Cooks Petrel. Nests are found on flattish areas at low altitudes with rat-hole like burrows being dug into soft soils, unlike Cooks which digs its holes on the steep sides of banks and among old roots high up on its Little Barrier Island colony.

Call: This is a "Ti ti ti ti ti", higher-pitched than Cooks and more delicate. Calls commence about one hour after dark on the Hen and Chicken Islands.

Best viewing months: October through to March.

Where to find - North Island:

Northland - Bay of Islands: Birds can be found beyond Cape Brett and towards the Poor Knights Islands to the south of the cape near their breeding islands.

North Auckland - Kawau Island: A trip out from Sandspit to Kawau Island and beyond leads into Pycroft Petrel waters. There will also be Cooks Petrel in these waters so the problem of separating them will be difficult.

Coromandel - Mercury Islands: A short boat trip from Whitianga soon takes you into Pycroft Petrel waters. These islands are close to the mainland.

General: This is a difficult species to separate from Cooks Petrel at sea. There is an excellent chance though on a boat trip beyond Kawau Island of seeing petrels with nicely scalated crowns which will be either Pycrofts or Cooks Petrels but most likely Cooks due to their far greater numbers in these waters. In the Bay of Islands and around the Mercury Islands the chances are greater for Pycrofts.

Charles A Fleming
Cooks Petrel and Pycrofts Petrel

COOKS PETREL

Geoff Moon

Family: Procellariidae **Species:** *Pterodroma cookii*
Common name: Cooks Petrel, Titi **Status:** Endemic
Size: 300 mm (cf sparrow 145 mm)

Discussion: Cooks Petrel is confined to one major breeding population on Little Barrier Island with smaller colonies on nearby Great Barrier Island and on Codfish Island off the north-west coast of Stewart Island. The Little Barrier Island colony was for many years severely predated by cats before their eradication, but it is now expanding.

Breeding islands close to New Zealand: Little Barrier Island, Great Barrier Island and Codfish Island.
Breeding months: November to April. Codfish Island birds lay about one month later than Little Barrier Island birds. Birds lay 1 white egg in burrows high up on Little Barrier Island in close colonies.
Range worldwide: Central and eastern Pacific from latitude 19° north to Alaska.
New Zealand range: Around New Zealand. Most readily found in the Hauraki Gulf north of Auckland and around Stewart Island.

Description:
  Head: Dark grey crown with white forehead, leading to grey feather scalation before the crown. **Face, throat and around bill:** White, with dark grey stripe through eye. **Upperparts:** Light grey. **Upperwings:** A dark grey M marking extends across wings and rump. **Underparts:** White. **Underwings:** White, with dark grey edges and a dark tag at the leading edge wing-joint. **Tail:** Light grey with dark grey tip. **Bill:** Black.
Conspicuous features:
  • The grey scalation on the crown is distinctive.

70

- The open M wing markings on flying birds is very noticeable.
- Look for the black, slender and longish bill.

Conspicuous characteristics:
- Birds have a habit of sitting in small rafts on the sea.
- In flight, birds tip and toss and show their white underparts and their wing M markings almost consecutively.

Call: A distinctive "ti ti ti ti" which is heard after dark over Northland. These calls are made by birds returning to Little Barrier Island after feeding in the Tasman Sea.

Where to find - North Island:
North Auckland - Kawau Island: The best area for this bird is east of Kawau Island in the waters between the mainland and Little Barrier.

Where to find - Stewart Island:
Southern seas: Cooks Petrel can be heard over Oban and may be sighted over south-western coastal waters. There are also Mottled Petrels here.

BLACK-WINGED PETREL

Don Merton

Family: Procellariidae   **Species:** *Pterodroma nigripennis*
Common name: Black-winged Petrel   **Status:** Native
Size: 300 mm (cf sparrow 145 mm, Cooks Petrel 300 mm)

Discussion: The Black-winged Petrel is a conspicuous small petrel with a widening New Zealand range. In recent years this species has been picked up from beach "wrecks" on North Island west coast beaches.

Breeding islands: Kermadec Islands, Three Kings, Motuopao Island off Cape Maria Van Dieman, Poor Knights Islands, East and Portland Islands off

Gisborne, and South East Island off Chatham Island where the population is on the increase. Also attempting to breed on mainland New Zealand at Cape Maria Van Dieman although here it is being predated on by cats.

Breeding months: November to April. 1 white egg is laid in a burrow.
Range worldwide: Central Pacific from Chatham Islands to latitude 30° north.
New Zealand range: Now seen in waters around northern Northland but not common in other New Zealand waters away from the Chatham Islands.

Description:
Forehead: White, with pale grey feather scalation to pale grey crown. **Head:** Pale grey, the grey extending down the neck to the rump and forming an incomplete collar to the throat. Dark patch through eye. **Upperwings:** Grey with a dark grey open M marking across wings and rump from wing tip to wing tip. **Underparts:** White. **Underwings:** White with a heavy black incomplete V shaped mark on the leading edge with black wing tips and primary edges. **Tail:** Grey, with dark grey tip. **Undertail:** White, with dark grey tip. **Bill:** Black. **Feet:** Pink.

Conspicuous features:
- Look for the black underwing incomplete V marking. The very similar Chatham Island Petrel has a much bolder and wider incomplete underwing V marking.

Conspicuous characteristics:
- Birds have a habit of flying over their breeding colonies in day-light.
- Birds are attracted to shipping and will land on decks.

Call: "Ahhoo - wiwiwiwi" heard at dusk.

Where to find:
Northland - Cape Maria Van Dieman: From the Cape Reinga lighthouse search west with a telescope towards Cape Maria Van Dieman.
Bay of Islands: Sometimes seen from boating excursions out beyond Cape Brett. These birds are probably from the Poor Knight Islands breeding colony.
Chatham Island: Numbers are building up in these waters from the South East Island (Rangatira Island) colony.

CHATHAM ISLAND PETREL

Family: Procellariidae **Species:** *Pterodroma axillaris*
Common name: Chatham Island Petrel **Status:** Endemic
Size: 300 mm (cf sparrow 145 mm)

Discussion: An extremely rare petrel.

Breeding island: South East (Rangatira) Island near Chatham Island.
Breeding months: December to June. 1 white egg is laid in a deep burrow.
Range worldwide: A found only around the Chatham Islands.

Description:
Forehead: White, with pale grey feather scalation to pale grey crown. **Head:**

Charles A.Fleming

Chatham Island Petrel

Pale grey, the grey extending down the neck to the rump and forming an incomplete collar to the throat. Dark patch through eye. **Upperwings:** Grey with a dark grey open M marking. **Underparts:** White. **Underwings:** White, with a bold, heavy black leading edge from base of wings, black wing-tips and a lighter black trailing edge which encircles the white. **Tail:** Grey, with dark grey tip. **Undertail:** White, with dark grey tip. **Bill:** Black. **Feet:** Pink.

Differences between Chatham Island Petrel and Black-winged Petrel:
- Chatham Island Petrel has far greater areas of underwing black.

Call: "Chee chee chee chee", heard throughout the evening.

Charles A Fleming

Black-winged Petrel and Chatham Island Petrel

Where to find:

Chatham Islands - South East Island: This is the only island where this species can be found. Here they are now competing with Black-winged Petrels for breeding space on South East Island.

MOTTLED PETREL

Rod Morris

Family: Procellariidae
Common name: Mottled Petrel
Size: 340 mm (cf sparrow 145 mm)

Species: *Pterodroma inexpectata*
Status: Endemic

Breeding islands close to New Zealand: Breeds on Snares Island, the islands in Foveaux Strait and around Stewart Island including Big South Cape and Codfish Island. On Codfish Island a small colony of Cooks Petrel also breeds which can cause confusion when both species are viewed together at sea.

Breeding months: November to April. Birds lay 1 white egg in a burrow.

Range worldwide: Ranges north of New Zealand up the Pacific in a wide band to Alaska.

New Zealand range: Ranges around New Zealand near its breeding islands.

Description:

 Crown: Grey with dark grey feather scalation above bill. **Upperparts and upperwings:** Dark grey with black open M marking from wing tip, across rump, to wing tip. **Uppertail:** Grey. **Underparts:** White with prominent grey abdomen patch. **Underwings:** White with bold black incomplete V marking. **Tail:** Grey with a broad black tip.

 Call: A high-pitched "ti ti ti ti ti" is uttered by returning birds at night.

Differences between Mottled Petrel and Cooks Petrel:
- The Mottled Petrel is a bigger bird.
- The Mottled Petrel has a dark grey abdominal patch.
- The Mottled Petrel has a noticeable black V, underwing marking.
- The Mottled Petrel has an overall darker upperwing and a darker M marking on the upperwing than has Cooks Petrel.

Where to find - Stewart Island:
Foveaux Strait: Watch for it if crossing Foveaux Strait on the ferry.
Half Moon Bay: Known to feed well out to sea.

Charles A Fleming
Mottled Petrel (left) Bullers Shearwater (right)

GREY-FACED PETREL

Family: Procellariidae   **Species:** *Pterodroma macroptera*
Common name: Grey-faced Petrel, Great-winged Petrel (Australian)
Status: Endemic
Size: 410 mm (cf sparrow 145 mm)

Breeding islands close to New Zealand: Breeds on many off-shore islands from Gisborne northwards to the Three Kings Islands on the east coast of the North Island, and Taranaki north on the west coast. Major breeding islands are the Hen and Chicken Islands, Mokohinau Islands, Motuhora Island, Mercury Islands off Coromandel, Alderman Islands, Whale Island and White Island in the Bay of Plenty.
Breeding months: May to December. Birds return to the breeding grounds in late February. Birds lay 1 white egg in a burrow.

Brian Chudleigh

Grey-faced Petrel

Range worldwide: Ranges in the non-breeding months from New Zealand to South Africa northward to about latitude 20°.

New Zealand range: Common in northern New Zealand waters.

Description:
  Face and throat: Grey. **Upperparts and underparts:** Blackish-brown. **Bill and feet:** Black.
Conspicuous feature
  • Generally an all black bird.
  • Wings are long and narrow.
  • Look for the short dark bill.
  • Look for the grey face.
Conspicuous characteristics:
  • Look for the flight pattern. Birds toss into the air at a fast pace before plunging again down near the wave crest.
Call: A guttural "oi oi oi" is made by birds when near their burrows.

Differences between Grey-faced Petrels, Black Petrels, Sooty Shearwaters and Flesh-footed Shearwaters:
  • The Grey-faced Petrel has a short, almost stubby, black bill when compared with the long thin bills of the shearwaters.
  • Grey-faced Petrels have a black bill.
  • Black Petrels have a yellowish bill tipped with black.
  • Sooty Shearwaters have a dark grey bill.
  • Flesh-footed Shearwaters have a yellowish bill tipped with brown.
  • The Grey-faced Petrel, Black Petrel and Sooty Shearwater, have black legs and feet which separate them from the Flesh-footed Shearwater which has flesh coloured feet.
  • The Grey-faced Petrel has a grey face which is noticeable in good light.

- The Grey-faced Petrel is a fast flier tending to bounce up off the waves to a much higher altitude than Sooty and Flesh-footed Shearwaters, which are more wave skimmers.
- The Grey-faced Petrel lacks the silver underwing of the Sooty.

Note: In the Hauraki Gulf all four species of these black coloured petrels and shearwaters can be seen together.

Where to find - North Island:

Northland - Bay of Islands: Grey-faced Petrels range through these waters.

North Auckland - Kawau Island towards Hen and Chickens Islands: Grey-faced Petrel can be seen here during late winter, spring and early summer. Birds move away from their breeding grounds by January.

North Auckland - Goat Island Reserve: Try here from the headland not far from the marine reserve. (See "Places" in back of book.)

Coromandel - Mercury Islands: Always seen in these waters.

Bay of Plenty - Tauranga: Grey-faced Petrel can be found outside of the harbour. There is a breeding colony on Mount Maunganui and nearby Motuotau Island.

Bay of Plenty - Matata: Grey-faced Petrel can be seen off-shore at Matata.

General: A visit to a Grey-faced Petrel island is an exciting occasion once the petrels start returning to their burrows just after dusk. At this time the whole island comes to life with angry "oi oi oi" calls which carry on into the night. Birds fall down through the trees and scamper to their burrows.

CHATHAM ISLAND TAIKO

Stella Rowe

Family: Procellariidae   **Species:** *Pterodroma magentae*
Common name: Chatham Island Taiko, Magenta Petrel   **Status:** Endemic
Size: 380 mm (cf sparrow 145 mm)

Discussion: The Taiko was rediscovered in 1978 by David Crockett, a New Zealand ornithologist with a special interest in this species. Over the ensuing years, expeditions have been led to the Chatham Islands, by David Crockett, in an attempt to locate the breeding burrows. Radio telemetric tracking of birds, which previously had been captured and fitted with transmitters, led to the first nesting burrow of a Taiko being discovered in November 1987. Many Taiko have now been banded but the overall status of the species has not yet been fully established. It is regarded as one of the world's rarest seabirds.

Relationship with other petrels: Some authorities regard the Taiko as being a race of the tropical occurring Phoenix Petrel (*Pterodroma alba*). Differences exist in the plumage of this species, with the Taiko having some forehead scalation and cleaner white underparts. It is also a slightly bigger bird. Additional differences occur in breeding habits with the Taiko being a burrow nesting bird while the Phoenix Petrel nests above ground. The Phoenix Petrel also has no fixed breeding season whereas the Taiko is a summer breeder. The Taiko also shows similarities with the Tahitian Petrel (*Pseudobulweria rostrata*).

Breeding islands close to New Zealand: Chatham Island.
Breeding months: November to April.

Description:
  Forehead: Grey with variable light grey feather scalation. **Chin:** Grey. **Throat and upperbreast:** Dark sooty-grey. **Upperparts:** Dark sooty-grey. **Underparts:** White. **Underwings:** Sooty-grey. **Undertail:** White tipped with black.
Conspicuous feature:
  • The Taiko is of a similar size to the Fluttering Shearwater.

WHITE-FACED STORM PETREL

Family: Hydrobatidae   **Species:** *Pelagodroma marina*
Common name: White-faced Storm Petrel   **Status:** Endemic
Size: 200 mm (cf sparrow 145 mm, Fluttering Shearwater 300 mm)

Discussion: White-faced Storm Petrels are one of the more common seabirds around the New Zealand coast although preferring deeper and rougher waters.

Breeding islands close to New Zealand: Breeds on many islands from the Three Kings Islands to Stewart Island and the Chatham Islands. Also Auckland Island to the south of New Zealand.
Breeding months: October to March. Northern birds nest up to one month earlier than southern ones. 1 white egg is laid in a burrow.
Range worldwide: Migrates from New Zealand in a north-east direction into the Pacific towards central America.
New Zealand range: Found right around the coast.

White-faced Storm Petrel

Description:
  Face: White, with a grey bar through and under eye. **Upperparts:** Greyish-brown. **Upperwings:** Secondary feathers dark grey with black primaries. **Rump and tail:** Pale grey rump with black tail. **Underparts:** White. **Legs:** Black with yellow webs to feet.

Conspicuous features:
  - White face is noticeable.
  - Yellow webs of feet are sometimes visible.
  - Slightly forked tail can be observed.

Conspicuous characteristics:
  - The habit of appearing to walk on the water with feet touching the waves distinguishes this bird.
  - Usually unperturbed by nearby boats.
  - Appears more plentiful in rough weather.

Call: Cackle and twitter sounds near the breeding colonies.

Where to find - North Island:
Bay of Islands: Often seen around Cape Brett.
North Auckland - Kawau Island: Seen towards Little Barrier Island.
Auckland - Tiri Tiri Island: Occasionally seen around this island.

Where to find - South Island:
Wellington - Cook Strait: Seen from the ferry especially in rough weather.
Marlborough - Pelorus Sound: Seen in open water before the sound.

Where to find - Stewart Island:
Southern seas: A regular bird in deeper waters.

General: Note that the Grey-backed Storm Petrel (*Garrodia nereis*) ranges north from its breeding grounds at the Chatham Islands, Antipodes Islands and Auckland Islands and can overlap with White-faced Storm Petrels.

YELLOW-EYED PENGUIN

Rod Morris

Family: Spheniscidae　　　　　　**Species:** *Megadyptes antipodes*
Common name: Yellow-eyed Penguin　　　**Status:** Endemic
Size: 760 mm (cf sparrow 145 mm)

Discussion: The Yellow-eyed Penguin is a large endemic species with a declining population caused by its mainland nesting colonies being disturbed by people and predators. This species is sedentary, not usually straying far from its nesting location. It can therefore be found in the waters near these breeding areas over much of the year.

Habitat: A bird of coastal waters.
Range: Birds nest from Banks Peninsula right around the coastline to Fiordland. Also around Stewart Island and on Campbell and Auckland Islands.

Description:
　　Head: Yellowish, streaked with black. A broad yellow band passes through the eye and around the crown. **Upperparts:** Soft black. **Flippers:** Upper surface black, edged with white. **Underparts:** White. **Eye:** Yellow.
Conspicuous features:
- Considerably larger than the Fiordland Crested Penguin with which it often overlaps.
- The streaked yellow head and the yellow eye are very noticeable both on surfacing birds and birds on land.

Conspicuous characteristics:
- Birds come ashore to their breeding colonies from early afternoon.
- Upon landing on the beach they have the strange habit of standing for some time while gaining direction and their "land-legs".
- When on the water they surface regularly but only for short intervals.

- Comes ashore on sand rather than rocks.

Call: A "musical" trumpet, which can be heard from birds at the nesting sites.

Breeding season: Birds start visiting nesting sites in July with egg laying commencing in September. Fledglings leave the nests during the following April. They breed in loose colonies on vegetated dunes, with nests being built under vegetation and well spaced, but within calling distance of each other. During the breeding season birds return to the nests to relieve their mates or to feed their young, usually from early afternoon onwards. It should be noted that they will not come ashore at this time if humans are in the area.

Equipment needed: At the nesting colony use a telescope.

Where to find - South Island:

South Canterbury - Oamaru: There is a viewing hide at Bushy Beach south of the Oamaru Harbour breakwater. Take Tyne Street and then Bushy Beach Road. Afternoon or evening viewing gives the best chances. (See "Places" in back of book.)

Otago Peninsula Penguin Tours: These include -

- **Wild South -** which visits "Penguin Place Conservation Reserve" at Pipikaretu Beach. Here you get within close distance of the birds.
- **Southlight** - where you collect a key and enter a gate near the Taiaroa Heads. From here you drive to a viewing platform and watch the birds returning from the sea. Southlight does not require bookings. There is an entry charge. It is located just past Pakihau Road almost at the end of the peninsula and a short distance from the Royal Albatross colony at Taiaroa Heads. It is signposted. While here view the albatrosses and the Stewart Island Shag colony and visit Papanui and Hoopers Inlets for waterfowl and shorebirds.
- **Wings of Kotuku** - which tours to Sandfly Bay.
- **Morning Magic** - which tours to Sandfly Bay.

Otago Peninsula - Sandfly Bay: This locality is found a short distance from Dunedin at the end of Sealpoint Road on the east side of the Otago Peninsula. Find Highcliff Road, which runs adjacent to Portobello Road. Sealpoint Road leads from it and heads to the south coast. There is car parking at the end of the road. A sandhill walk leads to a viewing hide. Note here that birds will not come ashore if people are in sight. (See "Places" in back of book.)

South Otago - Nugget Point: This locality is south of the Otago Peninsula. From Balclutha take the sign to Owaka. Turn right to Otanomomo and follow on to Nugget Point. A track leads to the Roaring Bay hide before you get to the lighthouse carpark. This area is also a good seabird viewing place.

Southland - Hina Hina Cove: This locality is just south of Owaka. Turn eastward down Maitland Road and drive to Hina Hina Cove. It is a steep climb to the beach. Numbers here have dwindled over the years.

Fiordland - Milford Sound: Birds are often seen in the fiord from tourist boats.

Where to find Stewart Island:

Half Moon Bay: If travelling to Stewart Island by boat always watch for birds near the coastline.

Paterson Inlet: If crossing to Ulva Island or Ocean Beach watch for surfacing birds.

BLUE PENGUIN

Brian Chudleigh

Family: Spheniscidae   **Species:** *Eudyptula minor*
Common name: Blue Penguin, Little Blue   **Status:** Endemic
Size: 400 mm (cf sparrow 145 mm)

Discussion: The Blue Penguin is the smallest of the penguins. It is a common species which breeds on both the mainland and the off-shore islands.

Subspecies: Five subspecies, based on localities, are currently recognised. The most distinctive one is the White-flippered Penguin, found around Banks Peninsula.

Habitat: Outside of the moult and the breeding season, when they come to land, Blue Penguins are strictly sea living birds in coastal waters.

Range: Found right around the New Zealand coast. Also found around the south Australian coast and Tasmania.

Description:
    Upperparts: Blue. **Throat:** Grey. **Underparts:** White. **Flippers:** Blue, edged with white. Note that the White-flippered variety has very bold white leading edges to the flippers. **Bill:** Black.

Conspicuous features:
- The small size when compared with other penguins is noticeable.
- Look for the heavy bill.
- Look for the blue colouring.

Conspicuous characteristics:
- When on the surface of the sea only the head and the upperpart of the back is noticeable.
- At times birds will loaf on the water in rafts appearing quite unafraid.
- Birds will "porpoise" when swimming towards the shore.

Call: At sea a duck-like quack is often heard. At the nesting site, deep toned growls with some trumpeting and mewing sounds are made.

Breeding season: The breeding season is from August to February. Birds nest in burrows or rock cavities, sometimes high up on cliff faces. Burrows are usually isolated but within calling distance of each other (one Kapiti Island nest was recorded at 300 metres a.s.l.). Birds return to the burrows just after dark each evening, hopping from the water on to rocks.

The moult: The Blue Penguin moults after the breeding season during the months of December to March. To moult, the penguins come ashore and hide in caves, often close to the shoreline, where they stay for periods of up to two weeks. It is during this period that they become vulnerable to holidaymakers who often suspect the birds are sick and attempt to assist them unnecessarily. Also at this time domestic dogs on beaches often attack them.

Equipment needed: Take a torch for night viewing.

Where to find - North Island:

Northland - Bay of Islands: Common in these waters.

North Auckland - Kawau Island: Common here. Birds nest in large numbers on the Hen and Chicken Island group and on Little Barrier Island.

North Auckland - Tiri Tiri Island: Birds are regularly seen on the crossing from Whangaparaoa to Tiri Tiri Island. Nesting birds can also be seen on the island in special viewing nesting holes.

Wellington - Cook Strait: Usually seen from the inter-island ferry.

Where to find - South Island:

South Canterbury - Oamaru: Visit the hides in Oamaru Harbour at the base of the breakwater at the end of Waterfront Road. Viewing starts on dark. There is an entry charge. (See "Places" in back of book.)

Fiordland - Milford Sound: Usually seen from boating trips.

Charles A Fleming

Blue Penguin and White-flippered Penguin

Oban and Paterson Inlet: Birds can be seen coming ashore after dark on the Ackers Point walk, which leads out to the lighthouse on the south side of Half Moon Bay. Because of the long twilight here in summer, birds seldom start coming in to their burrows before 10 pm. Burrows usually give themselves away by their stench. The entrances are dung littered. Look for loafing rafts near Ackers Point.

WHITE-FLIPPERED PENGUIN

Rod Morris

Family: Spheniscidae   **Species:** *Eudyptula minor albosignata*
Common name: White-flippered Penguin   **Status:** Endemic
Size: 400 mm (cf sparrow 145 mm)

Discussion: This species of penguin is regarded by some as a distinct species and so birders try to find it and compare it with the Blue Penguin.

Range: Found around Banks Peninsula near Christchurch in the South Island.

Description:
   Flippers: The main difference, when compared with the Blue Penguin, is the heavy white leading edge to flipper, and the whiter underparts.

Where to find - South Island:
Banks Peninsula: From Christchurch take the Halswell - Banks Peninsula road to Akaroa. Eco-tours leave from the wharf. (See "Places" in back of book for a commercial tourist operator for this species.)

FIORDLAND CRESTED PENGUIN

Charles A Fleming

Family: Spheniscidae   **Species:** *Eudyptes pachyrhynchus*
Common name: Fiordland Crested Penguin   **Status:** Endemic
Size: 710 mm (cf sparrow 145 mm, Blue Penguin 400 mm)

Discussion: The Fiordland Crested Penguin is closely related to the other crested penguins of the southern New Zealand coastline and off-shore islands. These are the Erect-crested Penguin (*E. sclateri*) which breeds well to the south on the Bounty and Antipodes Islands, and the Snares Crested Penguin (*E. robustus*) which breeds on Snares Island. The Fiordland Crested Penguin is the mainland breeder of the three.

Habitat: Coastal waters of southern New Zealand.
Range: The Fiordland Crested Penguin is found along the south Westland coast, the Fiordland coast with concentrations in Dusky Sound, the western Southland coast and around Stewart Island.

Description:
 Head: Glossy black to under throat. **Eyebrow:** A yellow band goes from above the eye to back of head. **Crest:** Yellow, slightly drooping down the neck. **Upperparts:** Soft black. **Underparts:** White from throat down. **Flippers:** Soft black, with a faint white trailing edge. **Bill:** Reddish-brown.
Conspicuous features:
 • Yellow crest is noticeable. The head cannot be confused with the yellow-tinged head of the Yellow-eyed Penguin.
 • The all white underparts are conspicuous.
 • Note it lacks the fleshy coloured gape of the Snares Crested Penguin.
Conspicuous characteristics:
 • Birds sit on rocks in the sun, just on the vegetation line, during the day in the breeding season. Such birds are very visible.

- Birds also give themselves away with vocal displays of grunting, mewing and growling near the nesting sites, heard more during morning hours.

Call: A loud braying sound.

Breeding season: Birds return to nesting areas in July. Two white eggs are laid in early August and birds fledge at the end of November. Nests are in cavities and under vegetation near the shoreline. Birds are isolated nesters but nests are usually within calling distance of other pairs. Fiordland Crested Penguins nest about two months earlier than Snares Crested Penguins.

Moult: Birds return to their nesting grounds to moult over the months of January and February.

Differences between the Fiordland Crested Penguin, Erect-crested Penguin and Snares Crested Penguin:
- The Fiordland Crested lacks the more erect tufted-type crest of the other two species. Its crest is broad but not tufted.
- The Fiordland Crested lacks the fleshy gape marking which is noticeable on the Snares Crested.
- The Fiordland Crested tends to have a finer bill and head.
- The Fiordland Crested has slightly lighter cheek colouration when compared with the black of the other two species.

Charles A Fleming

Rockhopper Penguin, Fiordland Crested Penguin, Erect Crested Penguin, Snares Crested Penguin, Yellow-eyed Penguin

Where to find - South Island:

Westland - Lake Moeraki: Enquire at Lake Moeraki Lodge for directions to a Fiordland Crested Penguin breeding location near Knights Point. There are commercial operators in this area who will take you to see this species.

Fiordland: The coastlines and seas around Fiordland provide the best opportunities for views starting at Jacksons Bay.

Fiordland - Milford Sound: During the June to November breeding months, it can often be seen either on the rocks, sheltering in cavities, or resting among the vegetation of the coastline. From late December onwards birds are seldom seen along the coast. Note that both the Yellow-eyed Penguin and the Blue

Penguin are also found in Milford Sound. (See "Places" in back of book.)

Launch bookings: These can be made at Fiordland Travel Ltd in Te Anau town. Alternatively they can be arranged at the office at Milford Sound.

Where to find - Stewart Island:

Paterson Inlet: Look for this species when on a boat trip in Paterson Inlet. It is regularly seen here.

AUSTRALASIAN GANNET

Brian Chudleigh

Family: Sulidae   **Species:** *Morus serrator*
Common name: Australasian Gannet, Takapu   **Status:** Native
Size: 900 mm (cf sparrow 145 mm, Red-billed Gull 370 mm)

Discussion: The Australasian Gannet (*M. serrator*) is a close relative of the Northern Gannet (*M. bassana*), which is found along both sides of the north Atlantic Sea almost to the Arctic circle. It is also a very close relative of the Cape Gannet (*M. capensis*), which is found around the southern coasts of Africa. Main differences between the subspecies are associated with variations of the yellow head and blue eye colouring. Also the Australasian and Cape Gannets generally have more black on wings and tail and longer black underbill gular stripes, the Cape Gannet having the longest one. All three subspecies migrate to warmer climates over the colder months.

Habitat: A coastal species which feeds close in-shore but also in deeper waters some kilometres out to sea.

Breeding islands close to New Zealand: Nests on islands from the Three Kings in the north to Little Solander Island in Foveaux Strait in the south.

Mainland breeding colonies: Breeds at Muriwai Beach west of Auckland and at Cape Kidnappers south of Napier in the North Island, and Farewell Spit in the north of the South Island.

Breeding months: July to February.

Breeding: Birds nest in close proximity to each other with nest spacings of about one metre. 1 pale blue-green egg is laid in an open nest made of seaweed. Because of the wide egg laying season from mid-September to mid-December, the visitor to a gannet colony can usually witness a variety of breeding behaviour. Nesting gannets create geometric patterns of black and white.

Range worldwide: Ranges from New Zealand westward and around southern Australia and up the Queensland coast.

New Zealand range: Ranges from the south of the South Island northward. Juvenile New Zealand birds migrate to northern Queensland where they spend between three years to seven years before returning to New Zealand to breed.

Description:

Forehead: White, with black markings in front of eyes. **Head:** Yellow. **Upperparts and underparts:** White. **Wings:** Primary feathers black. Remainder white. **Tail:** Central tail feathers black. Remainder white. **Bill and bare skin of face:** Bluish-grey. Black line around gape. **Feet and legs:** Legs greyish, with feet striped with yellow.

Description - Immature birds: Immature birds vary from having all brown upperparts in the first year with white underparts, to various amounts of brown and black markings over white in succeeding years, until year four.

Conspicuous features:
- Yellow head on white body is noticeable.

Conspicuous characteristics:
- Birds feed by diving on to fish from considerable heights with wings folded back. If they catch a fish they usually bob to the surface and eat it before becoming airborne once again. Otherwise they take to the air promptly.
- Birds are regularly seen flying parallel to the coastline with heads down.

Call: Excited high-pitch chatter heard at the breeding colony.

Where to find - North Island:

Auckland - Muriwai Gannet Colony: This includes both an island colony and a mainland one located at Muriwai Beach, north-west of Auckland. It is signposted. There is an easy walking track from the carpark to the colony and there are well constructed viewing platforms from which to view the birds.

Coromandel - Coromandel Islands: The islands off the coast to the north of Coromandel township have nesting colonies which can be observed from the coast road or from a boat. Spotted Shags nest in close vicinity.

Hawkes Bay - Cape Kidnappers: This is New Zealand's most famous gannet colony. It is located on Cape Kidnappers at the southern end of Hawke Bay. Gannets have taken over the whole of the rocky outcrop which juts into the sea and over the years the colony has expanded to high on the promontory.

Note: While in the area look for Black-fronted Dotterel on the Tukituki River.

Where to find - South Island:

Marlborough - Farewell Spit: Commercial operators run to the Farewell Spit.
For further details: Phone: +64 3 524 8257 or fax +64 3 524 8939.

SHAGS

Groupings of New Zealand shags: New Zealand's shags tend to be placed into three subgenera by New Zealand ornithologists although international authorities tend to group them as the one genus, *Phalacrocorax*.

In New Zealand the three subgenera are -

Phalacrocorax - black-footed shags: These include the Black Shag (*Phalacrocorax carbo*), the Little Black Shag (*P. sulcirostris*), the Pied Shag (*P. varius*), and the Little Shag (*P. melanoleucos*). This group, apart from the Pied Shag which only occasionally ranges inland, are birds of both coastal waters and inland fresh water lakes and rivers. They are all tree-nesting birds although Black Shags will sometimes nest on rock ledges and sand banks.

Leucocarbo - pink-footed shags: This group includes the King Shag (*Leucocarbo carunculatus*), the Stewart Island Shag (*L. chalconotus*), the Bounty Island Shag (*L. ranfurlyi*), the Chatham Island Shag (*L. onslowi*), the Campbell Island Shag (*L. campbelli*), the Auckland Island Shag (*L. colensoi*) and the Emperor Shag (*L. atriceps*). The pink-footed group are strictly coastal birds which breed on rock ledges.

Stictocarbo - orange-footed shags: This group includes the Spotted Shag (*Stictocarbo punctatus*) and the Pitt Island Shag (*S. featherstoni*). They are strictly coastal in habitat and nest on rock ledges in inaccessible places.

Some authorities separate the slightly larger variety of Spotted Shag found on Stewart Island and call it the Blue Shag (*S. p. steadi*). This species has darker upper plumage and lacks the wide white facial and neck stripe of the spotted, this being reduced to a narrow band of white which does not extend in front of the eye.

Similarities: As a family, New Zealand shags share similar fishing habits and the after fishing habit of perching on a prominent place while holding their wings out to dry. This latter action is necessary to dry water-logged wings as shags have inadequate feather waterproofing, possessing grease glans which are not equipped to cater for long under-water fishing excursions. It is thought that the reason for this lack of waterproofing is in fact to hinder the flotation of swimming birds so enabling them to spend longer under the water.

All the New Zealand shags have similar flight patterns, usually flying low to the water with necks outstretched. At times, though, they will fly at quite high altitudes. Some also have the ability to raise a crest during the breeding season.

BLACK SHAG

Family: Phalacrocoracidae   **Species:** *Phalacrocorax carbo*
Common name: Black Shag, (Great Cormorant elsewhere)
Status: Native
Size: 880 mm (cf sparrow 145 mm)

Discussion: The Black Shag is a common species over most of New Zealand. It is also found in Australia and through much of the world from North America to Europe and through Africa, Asia and Micronesia. The New Zealand Black Shag tends to have far less white on the face and throat than does the African species which is white-throated. Some New Zealand birds lack the white altogether.

Habitat: A bird of muddy estuaries, tidal areas, and sand banks but also to be found inland along drains, canals and lakes in most fresh-water localities.
Range: Found throughout New Zealand.

Charles A Fleming
Black Shag
Description:
  Face: White. (On some birds only.) **Facial skin:** Yellow. **Upperparts and underparts:** Black. **Flank patches:** White. (On some birds only.) **Bill:** Grey.
Description - immature birds:
  Upperparts: Brownish-black. **Underparts:** Variable amounts of dirty white.
Conspicuous feature:
  • A heavy looking all black bird.
Conspicuous characteristics:
  • Often seen perched high up on trees, with wings extended.
  • Often seen sitting on sand banks in an upright position with a kinked neck bulge projected forward and noticeable.
  • Flight heavy and slow.
Nest: A colonial nester which makes a platform of sticks in a tree. Up to 4 bluish-green eggs are laid.
Call: Usually silent, but croaks and grunts are made at the nest.

Where to find - North Island:
Auckland - Manukau Harbour: Regularly seen from the Southern Motorway where it crosses the headwaters of the Manukau Harbour just past the Manurewa turnoff. Here, Black Shags sit in large numbers along the water's edge at low tide.
Auckland - Waitemata Harbour: Commonly seen in places such as Hobson

Bay and the Tamaki Estuary.

South Auckland - Miranda: Common here especially towards the southern end of Firth where the water appears the muddiest.

North Island generally: Found in most waterways and estuarine localities.

Where to find - South Island:

South Island generally: Any waterway, whether coastal or inland, should be examined for this bird. It is usually easy to find.

PIED SHAG

Brian Chudleigh

Family: Phalacrocoracidae **Species:** *Phalacrocorax varius*
Common name: Pied Shag **Status:** Native
Size: 810 mm (cf sparrow 145 mm, Black Shag 880 mm)

Discussion: The Pied Shag of New Zealand is closely related to Australian Pied Shag which is identical in appearance. The Australian bird, though, is a bird of inland waterways as well as of coastal habitat while the New Zealand bird generally inhabits the coastal margins and only occasionally travels inland. In northern New Zealand, where populations of this species are most common, the Pied Shag is an ever present part of the New Zealand summer. In these parts it can regularly be found roosting and nesting on cliff dwelling coastal pohutukawa trees (*Metrosideros excelsa).*

Habitat: A generally coastal bird which usually prefers clean water for fishing, unlike the Black Shag which readily fishes in muddy waters.

Range: Found around the New Zealand coast including Stewart Island with some gaps along the Westland coast and the Canterbury coast. Concentrations are found in Northland and the Bay of Plenty in the North Island, and the Marlborough Sounds and Fiordland in the South Island. There are several breeding colonies in Paterson Inlet on Stewart Island.

Description:

    Crown: Black. **Face and side of neck:** Pure white. **Eye-ring:** Blue.
    Facial skin: Yellow. **Upperparts:** Pure black. **Underparts:** Pure white. **Bill:**
    Grey. **Feet and legs:** Black.

Conspicuous feature:

- It is slightly smaller than the Black Shag but bigger than the Little Shag.

Conspicuous characteristics:

- A white mark in a coastal pohutukawa tree is usually a Pied Shag.
- Regularly sits on rocks and more commonly on those surrounded by water. Will sit in the company of other species and in particular the Spotted Shag and the Little Shag.
- Will sometimes sit in groups on sandy beaches in horizontal, duck-like, posture with tails cocked vertically above their backs.

Call: Grunts, croaks and squeals are heard at the nesting site.

Nest: A colonial nester making a twig nest in a tree. Up to 4 greenish eggs are laid.

Where to find - North Island:

Coastlines: Any coastal stretch of water can have Pied Shags.

Northland - Bay of Islands: Very common along the coastline.

North Auckland - Whangaparaoa: Regularly roosts in trees by the Weiti (Wade) River to the left of the wharf.

Auckland: A nesting colony can be found in old pines close to the main Panmure-Howick highway near the Panmure Basin.

South Auckland - Waiau Beach: A very large colony exists near Waiau Beach which can only be accessed by boat but is worth a visit. From Auckland's southern motorway, Highway 1, take the Papakura off-ramp and head west through Karaka, Kingseat and Waiau Pa. Follow the sign to Waiau Beach, rather than to Clarks Beach. There find the boat ramp. By boat head south along the coast to Waitete Point and then turn left up the Taihiki River for about 1 km. The colony is in trees on the north side of the inlet.

Coromandel Peninsula - Thames: A big nesting colony can be found above the roadside in old pine trees, 2 kms north of the Thames boundary. These birds spread along the western side of the Coromandel Peninsula where they can be seen on rocks or in pohutukawa trees.

Bay of Plenty - Kaituna River-mouth: About 30 pairs nest in old macrocarpa trees on the river's edge. View this if visiting Matata Lagoon. (See "Places" in back of book.)

Where to find - South Island and Stewart Island:

Marlborough Sounds: Common on both Queen Charlotte Sound and Pelorus Sound. At this location do not confuse with the King Shag.

Otago Peninsula - Taiaroa Heads: Usually absent from the Otago coast.

Paterson Inlet: A large nesting colony can be seen on Ulva Island close to the landing wharf. Little Shags nest alongside in the same trees.

LITTLE BLACK SHAG

Family: Phalacrocoracidae   **Species:** *Phalacrocorax sulcirostris*
Common name: Little Black Shag   **Status:** Native
Size: 610 mm (cf sparrow 145 mm, Black Shag 880 mm)

Discussion: The Little Black Shag is found throughout a number of countries from Borneo to Indonesia and the Philippines, to Australia and New Zealand.

Habitat: Found on harbours and estuaries, inland lakes and rivers and often near human habitation, such as at Orakei Basin in Auckland, along the Waikato River in Hamilton and in the bays of Lake Rotoiti close to cottages.
Range: Well-spread through Northland, the Waikato and the Bay of Plenty, but scattered populations exist in many other places in the North Island. Away from the Marlborough Sounds it is generally uncommon in the South Island.

Description:
   Upperparts: Black. **Underparts:** Black. **Bill:** Lead colour. **Feet and legs:** Black.
Description - immature bird: Black.
Conspicuous features:
  • Smaller than the Black Shag.
  • Of sleeker appearance than the Little Shag.
  • Bill is long, slender and lead coloured.
  • Tail is slightly shorter than that of the Little Shag.
Conspicuous characteristics:
  • Often seen swimming in packs. Sometimes up to 100 birds might be seen all bobbing up together and diving together.
  • A gregarious species which often roosts together in large numbers.
Call: Croaks and whistles, at the nest site only.
Nest: A colonial nester making a twig nest in a tree. Up to 4 greenish eggs.

Differences between immature Little Black Shags and Little Shags:

- Little Black Shags are sleeker and have more gloss to their plumage.
- Little Black Shags have longer and more slender bills than Little Shags.
- Little Black Shags have lead coloured bills. Little Shags have yellow bills.
- Little Black Shags lack the small head crest of Little Shags.

Where to find - North Island:
Northland: Easy to find around the coast and on wharfs and jetties.
Auckland: Often at Hobson Bay and Orakei Basin in Remuera.
South Auckland - Miranda: Sits on coastal rocks at Matingarahi.
Waikato - Waikato River: Found along the lower reaches in large numbers.
  Often seen fishing in packs in the Hamilton city stretch of river.
Rotorua - Lake Rotorua: Common on Rotorua Lake.
Wellington - Waikanae Estuary: Large numbers can be seen here.

Where to find - South Island:
Marlborough - Pelorus Sound: Often in Queen Charlotte Sound.

LITTLE SHAG

Brian Chudleigh

Family: Phalacrocoracidae   **Species:** *Phalacrocorax melanoleucos*
Common name: Little Shag
Other names: Little Pied Shag or White-throated Shag
Status: Native
Size: 560 mm (cf sparrow 145 mm, Pied Shag 810 mm)

Discussion: Little Shags are widely spread from East Borneo, Java, New Guinea,
  Australia and New Caledonia to New Zealand. The Australian and the New
  Caledonian birds are totally pied having all white underparts.

Phases: The Little Shag comes in four distinct plumage phases. These are - a white-faced phase, a white-faced plus a white-throated phase, a white-faced and totally white underparts phase and a white-faced and a smudgy underparts phase. To complicate this species further, the fledglings come in two phases. One phase is totally black, but separated from the Little Black Shag by a yellow bill. (Little Blacks have lead coloured bills.) The other fledgling phase has a smudgy white face and all white underparts. It also has a yellow bill.

Habitat: A bird of coastlines, estuaries, harbours, inland rivers and lakes.

Range: Well-spread throughout New Zealand, including Stewart Island.

Description:

Head: White face and throat is common on all phases. The white colouring extends up the face to the crown with only a narrow belt of black being visible on the top of the head. A very small crest separates black phase juvenile birds from Little Black Shags. **Upperparts:** Black. **Underparts:** (See various phases above.) **Bill:** Yellow. **Feet and legs:** Black.

Conspicuous characteristics:

- Sits in social groupings on harbour and lake jetties and on lake shorelines, often with all phases including the fledglings in the one group.
- Birds nest in loose colonies sometimes in large numbers. Egg laying is well spread over the months of August until March.
- Birds follow flight paths from breeding colonies to feeding grounds.
- Birds tend to feed singly and not in packs as does the Little Black Shag.
- Birds can spend up to 20 seconds under water in each dive for food.

Call: Guttural croaks and squeals at the nesting site only.

Nest: A colonial nester making a twig nest trees. Up to 4 bluish-green eggs are laid.

Where to find - North Island:

Auckland - Orakei Basin: A small colony of birds can be seen at Orakei Basin, near the Orakei bridge. Some nest alongside Pied Shags.

Rotorua - Okere Falls: A large nesting colony can be found on the banks of the Kaituna River, about 1 km up-stream from the foot bridge at the falls. This locality is at the west end of Lake Rotoiti. Follow Highway 30 out of Rotorua travelling north and then continue on into Highway 33. At Okere Falls turn left up a small side road and into a parking area. Walk across the bridge and turn right. Then follow the river for some distance until Little Shags show up in the riverside trees. This birds feed in both Lake Rotorua and Lake Rotoiti.

Coastlines and waterways: Can be found in most districts where there is water. Common around the coastline.

Where to find - Stewart Island:

Ulva Island: Little Shags nest alongside Pied Shags near the wharf.

KING SHAG

Don Hadden

Family: Phalacrocoracidae   **Species:** *Leucocarbo carunculatus*
Common name: King Shag, Rough-faced Shag   **Status:** Endemic
Size: 760 mm (cf sparrow 145 mm, Pied Shag 810 mm)

Discussion: This shag is a close relative of the Stewart Island Shag (*Leucocarbo chalconotus*). It is separated by its lack of a crest during the breeding season and by the fact that it comes only in a pied phase. The Stewart Island Shag is dimorphic as to plumage colouring coming in both a pied phase of all white underparts, and a dark phase of all black underparts which is known as the bronze phase. Breeding starts in April and continues to August. The Stewart Island Shag reaches its breeding peak in September - October. Overall numbers of the King Shag are small.

Habitat: A coastal species found around the rock stacks of off-shore islands.
Range: Confined to rocky stacks and small islands at the entrances of Pelorus and Queen Charlotte Sounds. This area is about 500 kms from the nearest colony of Stewart Island Shags at Taiaroa Heads.

Description:
    Head: Black. This distinguishes it from the Pied Shag which has a white face to just above the eye. **Eye-ring:** Blue. **Caruncles:** Yellow. (These are rough patches of flesh on the sides of the face at the base of the bill, also found on other pink-footed shags.) **Upperparts:** Black. **Wings:** Black, with a slash of white on the scapular feathers. **Underparts:** White. **Bill:** Grey. **Feet and legs:** Pink.
Conspicuous features:
- Lack of white on face is distinctive when compared with the Pied Shag.
- The blue eye-ring is distinctive.

Conspicuous characteristics:
- When in flight head is held lower than the Pied Shag.
- Flies close to the water.

Call: Usually silent unless displaying when grunts and croaks are made.

Nest: A colonial nester making a nest of seaweed and twigs on the ground. Up to 3 pale blue eggs are laid.

Where to find - South Island:

Marlborough - Queen Charlotte Sound: Birds nest on White Rocks, to the north-west of the tip of Arapawa Island. (See "Places" at back of book.)

Marlborough - Pelorus Sound: Nests on Chetwode Island, Sentinel Rock, Duffers Reef, and Trio Islands at the entrance of the Sound.

STEWART ISLAND SHAG

Stella Rowe

Family: Phalacrocoracidae   **Species:** *Leucocarbo chalconotus*
Common name: Stewart Island Shag   **Status:** Endemic
Size: 680 mm (cf sparrow 145 mm, King Shag 760 mm)

Discussion: The Stewart Island Shag has in common with the other species in the genus *Leucocarbo* the orange-yellow caruncles on the face, the blue eye-ring, the pink feet and in its pied phase the white scapular slash markings on the wings. It differs from the other species by being dimorphic as to feather colouring, coming in two phases - a pied phase and an all black phase known as the "bronze" phase. The name Bronze Shag was given to the black phase when at first it was considered to be a separate species. The name was derived from the green iridescent sheen which covers the black upper feathers of this bird. (See King Shag article.)

Habitat: It is strictly coastal in habitat and favours rocky coastlines.

Range: Found around the coast of the South Island from the Otago Peninsula to Stewart Island and into Fiordland.

Description - pied form:

Head: Black. **Eye-ring:** Blue. **Caruncles:** Orange-yellow, tending to more orange than the King Shag. **Upperparts:** Black. Feathering has a noticeable sheen when in breeding plumage. **Wings:** Black, with a slash of white on scapular feathers. **Underparts:** White from the throat down. **Bill:** Grey. **Feet and legs:** Pink.

Description - "bronze" form:

Upperparts and underparts: Black, with an iridescent green sheen to the feathering.

Description - intermediate phases:

Upperparts: Black. **Underparts:** White, in varying amounts.

Note: The intermediate phases can always be found in the larger colonies such as those at Taiaroa Heads and on Whero Island off Stewart Island.

Conspicuous features:

- All black head is conspicuous.
- Look for the blue eye-ring. A telescope is really needed for this.

Conspicuous characteristics:

- Often seen in groups on off-shore rocks.
- Usually seen feeding in deeper water than Pied Shags. This can help prevent confusion between the two species in some areas.
- A more confiding bird than the King Shag of the Marlborough Sounds.

Call: Silent, except when displaying at the colonies, when grunts are made.

Nest: It nests on the ground on rock ledges or among rock crevices where it builds a nest made of plant and vegetable material. 2 pale blue eggs are laid.

Where to find - South Island:

Otago Peninsula - Taiaroa Heads: Birds can be seen from the Royal Albatross observatory at Taiaroa Heads with a telescope. Here both Stewart Island Shags and Spotted Shags can be seen together.

Southland: Can be seen around the coast of Southland especially in the Tautuku Bay and Porpoise Bay areas in eastern Southland.

Southland - Riverton: Look for it in the Riverton, Colac Bay area west of Invercargill, where birds sometimes roost on the beach.

Where to find - Stewart Island:

Boat trip: A boat trip to Whero Island allows very good views of this bird in all its phases.

Ackers Point: Ackers Point is the eastern arm of Half Moon Bay on Stewart Island. Stewart Island Shags often roost on rocks and piles along the coast. Sometimes Pied Shag, Little Shag and Spotted Shag can be viewed together. (See Kiwi article.)

SPOTTED SHAG

Brian Chudleigh

Family: Phalacrocoracidae   **Species:** *Stictocarbo punctatus*
Common name: Spotted Shag   **Status:** Endemic
Size: 730 mm (cf sparrow 145 mm, Pied Shag 810 mm)

Discussion: The Spotted Shag is one of the orange-footed shags in the sub-genus of *Stictocarbo*. It is considered closely related to the Red-legged Shag (*Phalacrocorax gaimardi*) which is found along the west coast of South America. The slightly different Blue Shag (*S. p. steadi*), found in coastal Southland, Stewart Island and coastal Westland, is considered a subspecies of *S. punctatus*. The Spotted Shag is one of the most beautiful of shags and over the last 40 years has increased in numbers.

Habitat: A coastal species which roosts and nests on cliff ledges and in and around crevices and small rock caves.
Range: In the North Island most of the population is confined to the Hauraki Gulf, along the coast near the township of Coromandel and at Erangi Point at Bethells Beach (Te Henga), west of Auckland. Also around the Wellington coast. In the South Island the range is extensive with *S. punctatus* being found from Marlborough to Otago and *S. p. steadi* being found around eastern Southland and up the West Coast. It is absent from Fiordland.

Description:
    Head: Black, with a distinctive white head and neck stripe starting from above the eye then down the neck. **Naked skin around eye:** Greenish-blue. **Crest:** Black in breeding plumage birds. **Wings:** Greyish-brown with black spotting. **Breast:** Soft grey. **Underwings and undertail:** Black. **Bill:** Light brown. **Legs and feet:** Orange.
Conspicuous characteristics:
- Birds roost on coastal rocks with the incoming tide.

- Birds regularly feed up to 15 kms out to sea.
- Birds often congregate in giant feeding rafts on the water, by day, where food is plentiful.
- Birds congregate at breeding colony roosts at night and can be seen in late afternoon flying low over the water as they head towards these places.

Call: Usually silent but grunts and croaks can be heard when displaying.

Nest: A colonial breeder nesting on the ground on cliffs or rocks. Nests are made of grass and seaweed. Up to 3 pale blue eggs are laid. Nesting colonies can spread over steep cliff faces.

Differences between the Spotted Shag, Blue Shag and Pitt Island Shag:

Spotted Shag: This species is most colourful when in breeding plumage. It is distinguished by a broad white stripe which extends from above the eye and down the side of the neck. The black spotting on greyish-brown wings is clearly visible.

Blue Shag: The white head and neck stripe is much thinner and starts from behind the eye and not above it as in the Spotted Shag. This species has darker wings with the black spotting being barely noticeable.

Pitt Island Shag: The white head and neck stripe is missing on this species. Sometimes white freckling can be seen on the hind neck. The black spotting on the wings is less noticeable than with the Spotted Shag.

Where to find - North Island (Spotted Shag - *S. punctatus*):

West Auckland: From Titirangi take Scenic Drive and follow through to Te Henga Road and then Bethells Road. At Bethells Beach (Te Henga), cross the river and walk north to the first headland which is Erangi Point. Look for birds on the south side.

South Auckland - Firth of Thames: If approaching Miranda from the Clevedon-Kawakawa Bay route, start looking for Spotted Shags just past Matingarahi Beach. Birds roost on the rocks from about two hours before high tide. Note that the rocks cover with water at very high tides so plan the trip accordingly. Other species of shag will also be seen on these rocks.

Coromandel - Thames: About 4 kms north of the town of Thames, Spotted Shags can be seen on the rocks, prior to the high tide, from the coastal road.

Coromandel - Waiomu Beach: Waiomu Beach is about 15 kms north of Thames. 1 km further north is a large rock stack just off the coast which at high tide covers over with Spotted Shags. Parking is difficult here, as on most parts of this road, so be prepared to walk back to the stack. Take a telescope.

Coromandel Peninsula: Anywhere along the west coast of this peninsula Spotted Shags can be expected. They nest on the off-shore islands west and north of Coromandel township.

Wellington - Waikanae Estuary: Spotted Shags regularly roost on logs within Waikanae Estuary.

Wellington Harbour: Look for them around the wharf if taking the ferry to the South Island.

Where to find - South Island - (Spotted Shag - *S. punctatus*):

North Canterbury - Kaikoura: Spotted Shags are common along this coast. One spectacular viewing spot is at the Raramai tunnel about 8 kms south of

Kaikoura in the Goose Bay, Oara vicinity. Here hundreds of shags roost and nest on two prominent rock stacks close to the main road.

South Canterbury - Oamaru: Birds nest on the cliffs in the Oamaru Harbour in the same vicinity as where Blue Penguins can be seen.

Otago Peninsula - Taiaroa Heads: Birds can be seen roosting alongside the breeding Stewart Island Shags just below the albatross observatory. Take a telescope for the best view.

Where to find - South Island (Blue Shag - *S. p. punctatus*)

Westland - Perpendicular Point, north of Punakaiki: These cliffs are 4 kms north of the Punakaiki Rocks tourist attraction. Search the cliffs here from the viewing areas.

Westland - Motukiekie Rocks: These rocks are 13 kms north of Greymouth just north of Nine Mile Bluff. Blue Shags breed here, with a population of up to 300 birds.

Southland - Invercargill: Common along the rocky coast from the Otago Peninsula to Riverton west of Invercargill. Riverton Beach is an easy locality to find this species.

Where to find - Stewart Island (Blue Shag - *S. p. punctatus*):

Paterson Inlet: Common in Paterson Inlet and may overlap with *S. punctatus*, although the two subspecies are difficult to separate when not in breeding plumage. It is often seen roosting on rocks and cliffs on the north side of the inlet.

Whero Island: This rocky islet, just off the entrance to Paterson Inlet has good numbers.

Native Island: This island, which is just inside Paterson Inlet, always has good numbers around the more rugged coastal areas.

Ulva Island: This island, which is well inside Paterson Inlet, always has some birds around the coastline.

Brian Chudleigh

Pitt Island Shag

WHITE-FACED HERON

Brian Chudleigh

Family: Ardeidae
Common name: White-faced Heron
Size: 670 mm (cf sparrow 145 mm)

Species: *Ardea novaehollandiae*
Status: Native

Discussion: A relative newcomer to New Zealand from Australia, the White-faced Heron was confirmed breeding in 1941. Since the early 1960s it has made a dramatic colonisation. It is now the most common species of heron in New Zealand. At times White-faced Herons have been blamed for the decline in Reef Heron numbers but in some areas, such as the Bay of Islands, Reef Heron again seem to be increasing even though White-faced Heron numbers are high.

Habitat: Found along coastal estuaries, harbours and widely spread through inland swamps and over pasture. Note that Reef Herons seldom fly inland in New Zealand.

Range: Widely spread over both the main islands and Stewart Island and has reached many of the off-shore islands.

Description:
Head: Forehead, face and chin, white. **Upperparts:** Bluish-grey. Long pale grey plumes on back can be seen in the breeding season. **Wings:** Bluish-grey with dark grey primaries. **Underparts:** Light grey. **Bill:** Black. **Legs and feet:** Greenish-yellow.

Description - juveniles:
Face: Bluish-grey with a white chin. Juveniles lack the white face but retain a small amount of white on the chin. **Wings:** Bluish-grey, with almost black primaries both under and on top of the wings.

Conspicuous features:
- Face and forehead are distinctly white.
- Plumage is more bluish than the Reef Heron.

Conspicuous characteristics:
- Has a less hunched gait than the Reef Heron and appears slightly larger.
- Often seen sitting on the edges of farm water troughs.
- Often seen feeding on wet pastureland.
- Nests high in old conifers or eucalypt trees.
- Flight is slow and wafting. Head is usually tucked in, in a hunched position. Sometimes, though, it will fly with an extended neck.

Call: Makes a guttural croaking sound, especially when approaching the nest.
Nest: A bundle of sticks high in a tree. Up to 4 pale blue-green eggs are laid.
Flocking habit: In winter birds form loose feeding flocks of up to 150 birds.

Where to find:
All New Zealand: Common throughout pastureland and coastal localities.

WHITE HERON

Brian Chudleigh

Family: Ardeidae   **Species:** *Egretta alba*
Common name: White Heron, Kotuku, Great White Egret (Australia)
Status: Native
Size: 910 mm (cf sparrow 145 mm, White-faced Heron 670 mm)

Discussion: A cosmopolitan species found throughout much of the world including Australia where it is common. In New Zealand it is rare, so always regarded as something special. As well as the White Heron, New Zealand now has three other white coloured herons. These are the Little Egret (*E. garzetta*), the Plumed Egret (*E. intermedia*), and the Cattle Egret (*Bubulcus ibis*).

Habitat: In late summer, after breeding is over, birds spread to harbours and estuaries in ones and twos. It is in these habitats that they are most easily observed. Also encountered inland near lakes, waterways and wetlands.

Range: Throughout New Zealand.

Description:

Upper and underparts: White. **Bill:** Black in breeding birds but yellow in non-breeding birds. **Legs and feet:** Black. Yellowish-green above the knees in breeding birds. Juveniles have all black legs.

Conspicuous features:

- A large all-white heron. (The biggest of the white coloured egrets.)
- The strangely kinked neck, somewhere near the middle vertebrate, is noticeable.
- Yellow bill and black legs are conspicuous in non-breeding birds.
- White back plumes are noticeable in breeding plumaged birds.

Nest: A colonial nester making a nest of twigs in a tree. Up to 4 bluish-green eggs are laid.

Nesting site and population: The New Zealand population sustains its numbers from a small breeding population of around 50 pairs which nest in a forested area at the head of the Okarito Lagoon in south Westland in the South Island. This breeding site is inaccessible except by boat, which gives the birds good protection. Little Shags and Royal Spoonbills also nest here.

Where to find - North Island:

Northern estuaries: Any northern estuary might host a heron over winter.

South Auckland - Miranda: Often one or two here in winter.

Bay of Plenty - Matata Lagoon: Often one on the lagoon or at the Tarawera river-mouth.

Where to find - South Island:

Marlborough - Nelson area: Often seen in the estuaries of the Marlborough Sounds and at Motueka Estuary near the town.

Canterbury - Lake Ellesmere: A regular visitor to the area near Lakeside, east of Leeston. Find Timberyard Road and drive to the Aquatic Centre. Sometimes a Little Egret may be here too. (See Mute Swan article.)

Westland - Okarito Lagoon: Near the Okarito seaside resort a bird is sometimes seen feeding along the estuary edge.

Note: A tourist operation takes people to view the nesting area at the head of the Okarito Estuary. (See "Places" in back of book.)

General: This bird can turn up anywhere.

LITTLE EGRET

Brian Chudleigh

Family: Ardeidae   **Species:** *Egretta garzetta*
Common name: Little Egret   **Status:** Native vagrant
Size: 560 mm (cf sparrow 145 mm, White-faced Heron 670 mm)

Discussion: The Little Egret is a wide-ranging, cosmopolitan species which regularly straggles to New Zealand from Australia. In New Zealand it cannot be confused with the Reef Heron as the New Zealand Reef Heron, unlike those of the Pacific Islands, only comes in a dark grey phase.

Habitat: Found along estuaries.

Range: Found at such places as the Mangere Sewage Ponds, Miranda, Matata Lagoons, Whakaki Lagoon near Wairoa, Ahuriri Estuary near Napier, Waikanae Estuary near Wellington, Lake Ellesmere in Canterbury, Okarito Lagoon in Westland and the Invercargill Estuary.

Description:
  Upperparts and underparts: White. **Bill:** Black. **Legs:** Black. **Feet:** Yellow.
Conspicuous features:
- A small all-white heron.
- In breeding plumage it has two very distinctive long narrow plumes which fall from the nape and ornamental filamentous plumes on back and breast.

Conspicuous characteristic:
- Usually a solitary bird but sometimes it associates with the White Heron.
- When feeding it is very active, dashing in pursuit of prey.

Call: Harsh croaks.

Nest: A tree nester. It does not breed in New Zealand.

Where to find - North Island:
Shore-bird localities: Likely places are shore-bird localities such as Mangere Sewage Ponds, Miranda, Matata, Whakaki Lagoon and Waikanae Estuary.

Where to find - South Island:
Canterbury: Try Lake Ellesmere, in the Lakeside area.
Southland: Try the Waituna Lagoon, east if Invercargill, New River Estuary from Otatara, and Awarua Bay, accessed from Tiwai Road.
General: There is no certain location for this bird as so few are recorded in any one year. Watch for them in usual shore-bird localities.

REEF HERON

Brian Chudleigh

Family: Ardeidae **Species:** *Egretta sacra*
Common name: Reef Heron, Blue Heron, Matuku (Maori)
Size: 660 mm (cf sparrow 145 mm, White-faced Heron 670 mm)
Status: Native

Discussion: Ranges from India to Australia and New Zealand and through the Pacific Islands to Tahiti. The Reef Heron (*E. sacra*) appears very similar in colouring and character to the Reef Heron of Africa (*E. gularis*) which comes in both a white and grey phase and is very similar to *E. sacra*.

Phases: In the Pacific Islands it comes in both a white and grey phase with some blotchy intermediate types being observed from time to time especially in the Cook Islands. Australia also has both the grey and white phases with whites being more prevalent in the north. New Zealand has only the grey.
Habitat: Generally a coastal bird but sometimes it is found inland on the edges of lakes and wetlands which are not too distant from the head-waters of estuaries or harbours.

Range: Found around the coastline of both the North and South Islands and on Stewart Island. More often seen along the east coast of Northland than anywhere else.

Description:
Upperparts and underparts: Charcoal-grey. **Bill:** Yellowish-brown. The Pacific white phase has a yellow bill. **Legs:** Yellowish-green. **Eye:** Iris is yellow.

Conspicuous features:
- Birds are a darker grey than the more common White-faced Heron.

Conspicuous characteristics:
- Birds have a hunched gait and appear slightly smaller and heavier than the White-faced Heron.
- Birds when feeding often raise their wings to shade the water where they are fishing, so enhancing their water vision.

Call: A guttural croaking often indicates a bird about to land.

Nest: Solitary nesters making a nest of twigs and dried seaweed in caves or rock crevices on the ground. Up to 4 pale blue-green eggs are laid.

Where to find - North Island:
Northland - Bay of Islands: Try the Waitangi Estuary, just north of the town.

Northland - Aroha Island, Kerikeri: Usually one bird can always be seen around this island. Follow Aroha Island signs from Landing Road in Kerikeri. Aroha Island is off Kurapari Road. (See "Places" in back of book.)

North Auckland - Weiti River (Wade River): This locality lies along the western side of the Whangaparaoa Peninsula, north of Auckland city. Usually a bird can be found near the old Weiti River wharf. At Whangaparaoa shopping centre turn right (west) along Wade River Road and follow it down until the wharf is reached. Look across the river and search the sandspit coastline. Also New Zealand Dotterels here.

South Auckland - Miranda: The coastline just to the south of Matingarahi, on the coast of the Firth of Thames, frequently has a Reef Heron.

Waikato - Raglan Harbour: This harbour regularly has birds near the town by the foot-bridge over the estuary which leads to the Kopua camping ground. Also often seen south of the Raglan wharf.

Bay of Plenty - Kaituna Lagoon and Maketu Estuary: This area, west of the Matata lagoons, often has birds along its extensive coastline. Pukehina Beach, Maketu Estuary and Kaituna River-mouth are all good localities. Access to the Maketu Estuary is easiest via the western end of Pukehina Beach but a telescope is needed.

Bay of Plenty - Tarawera River-mouth: Reef Heron are often seen here.

Where to find - South Island:
Marlborough - Pelorus Sound to Golden Bay: Reef Herons are regularly seen in this area feeding along the tide line.

Marlborough - Motueka Estuary: Usually seen here with White-faced Herons and sometimes Royal Spoonbills.

Southland - Chaslands coast: Look for them where the road nears the sea.

Where to find - Stewart Island:
Paterson Inlet: Sometimes seen in Paterson Inlet.

CATTLE EGRET

Brian Chudleigh

Family: Ardeidae   **Species:** *Bubulcus ibis*
Common name: Cattle Egret   **Status:** Native
Size: 510 mm (cf sparrow 145 mm, White Heron 910 mm)

Discussion: The Cattle Egret first arrived in New Zealand in the 1960s. In the mid-1970s it arrived in larger numbers to winter on selected properties, mainly in the Rangiriri district, south of Auckland. It is now an annual visitor.

Habitat: Generally it is found on pastureland associated with dairy cattle. Occasionally found on coastal estuaries such as the salt-flats at Miranda.
Range: Found in many districts in both the main islands.

Description:
   Head and breast: White, rusty coloured when in breeding plumage. **Upper and underparts:** White, tending to rusty colour on back when in breeding plumage. **Bill:** Yellow. **Legs:** Dark grey.
Conspicuous features:
- A small white heron.
- Trailing dark grey legs are noticeable when birds are in flight.
- Rusty breeding plumage is conspicuous.

Conspicuous characteristics:
- Birds are gregarious usually being found in large flocks. The Rangiriri flock has consistently been comprised of over 200 birds.
- Birds are scary and cannot be easily approached.

Call: In New Zealand silent, but near the nest in Australia, the call is a "rick-rack rick-rack", or a "kraah".
Nesting habits: As yet Cattle Egrets have not been found breeding in New Zealand. Birds obtain breeding plumage and then return to Australia to breed where they nest in trees in colonies. 4 - 5 whitish, green-tinged eggs are laid.

Where to find - North Island:
Far North - Kerikeri: A dairy farm on Kapiro Road just west of the junction with Landing Road usually has birds among the cows and near the road.
South Auckland - Miranda: Birds visit "The Stilt Ponds" here.
North Waikato - Rangiriri: From Auckland follow Highway 1, south. At Rangiriri, turn right at the Waikato Bridge sign and turn right again into Churchill East Road. Scan the herds of cows along this road. Birds are also found near the end of Lumsden Road nearby. After the Rangiriri Hotel on Highway 1 turn left into Tahuna Road and then immediately left into Lumsden Road. They are also sometimes seen on Highway 1 just south Rangiriri.
Hauraki Plains - Pipiroa: From Highway 29, turn north into Shelly Beach Road instead of crossing the Piako River. Drive to the end of this road.

Where to find - South Island
Canterbury - Lake Ellesmere: From Leeston drive north and then right towards the lake at Doyleston. (See Mute Swan article.)
Otago - Momona: After Momona, when driving south from Dunedin, turn right into Marshall Road. Follow the second road on the left which is Bull Creek Road.

General: It is possible to chance a sighting of a Cattle Egret in many localities, usually among dairy cattle. Scan all herds in likely areas.

NANKEEN NIGHT HERON

Brian Chudleigh

Family: Ardeidae   **Species:** *Nycticorax caledonicus*
Common name: Nankeen Night Heron   **Status:** Native
Size: 560 mm (cf sparrow 145 mm, White-faced Heron 670 mm)

Discussion: The Nankeen Night Heron has now been recorded breeding near Pipiriki on the Whanganui River. A population of over 10 birds is now known to live in this locality. This species is widely spread from Indonesia to Australia and New Caledonia where it inhabits swamp areas, lake verges and river boundaries. It roosts by day and flies to feeding grounds at dusk but will venture out and start feeding before dark, especially when feeding young.

Habitat: In New Zealand it is only found along the Whanganui River, preferring this habitat when the willow trees are in leaf.

Range: Whanganui River only.

Description:
    Crown and nape: Blue-black. Two white plumes protrude from the nape on birds in breeding plumage. **Face:** Greenish in front of eye and white above and behind eye. **Back, neck and wings:** Chestnut-red. **Throat and neck:** White, with a pale chestnut wash on upper neck. **Underparts:** White. **Iris:** Yellow. **Bill:** Black with a short and stout appearance. **Legs:** Yellow.

Description - young birds: Brown, spotted with white.

Conspicuous features:
- The blue-black head is noticeable.
- Look for yellow eye and legs.
- Look for rather hunched appearance.

Conspicuous characteristics:
- The bird has a squat appearance when feeding.
- Regularly stands and then walks slowly.
- Stands hunched on branches in willow trees.

Call: Harsh croaks or quacks often heard when feeding. The young when in the nest have a noisy cackle.

Nest: A platform of loose sticks in a tree usually high up. Up to 4 pale greenish-blue eggs are laid.

Where to find - North Island:

Wanganui - Pipiriki: Sightings come from the Pipiriki Wharf on the Whanganui River and from the stretch of river between Pipiriki and down- stream to Jerusalem. To get to Pipiriki, if driving south, turn off Highway 4 at Raetihi and take the Pipiriki sign. Travel for about 21 kms.

Reference: Marsh N 1995. Nankeen Night Herons (*Nycticorax caledonicus*) on the Whanganui River. Notornis 42: P 282 - 283.

AUSTRALASIAN BITTERN

Brian Chudleigh

Family: Ardeidae   **Species:** *Botaurus poiciloptilus*
Common name: Australasian Bittern   **Status:** Native
Size: 710 mm (cf sparrow 145 mm, White-faced Heron 670 mm)

Discussion: A cosmopolitan species which has a range through Europe, Southern Africa, North and South America, Asia and Australasia. The Australasian race is found in south-east Australia, Tasmania, New Caledonia and New Zealand. In all countries it is a difficult species to find although it has a habit of turning up in unexpected places.

Habitat: A bird of wetlands and wetland verges with a preference for feeding along lakes, rivers and drain margins.

Range: An unobtrusive species which nevertheless has a wide range throughout New Zealand and which can be expected in wetlands anywhere in either the North or South Island. More likely to be encountered, though, in Northland, South Auckland and the Waikato.

Description:
 Upperparts and underparts: Brown made up of both buff shadings and dark brown shadings. **Throat:** Whitish. **Bill:** Upper mandible brown, lower mandible greenish. **Legs:** Green.

Conspicuous characteristics:
 - When feeding birds have a hunched posture and can spend many minutes motionless in this stance.
 - When alerted Bitterns have the habit of freezing and extending their bills skywards. When in this position their various shadings of brown feathering tend to line up in patterns similar to the surrounding reeds and rushes of the wetland in which they are feeding. This habit is termed a "surveillance

posture" as it extends the level of the birds' eyes upwards to allow better scanning. Birds will eventually hunch back into the rushes if danger is nigh (Whitehead 1989).

- Birds have a wafting flight of slow wing beats, with head tucked in and legs trailing.

Call: A strange vibrating booming sound like a distant fog horn is uttered throughout the breeding season. The female's reply is quieter. Note that booms are well spaced at between five to 20 minute intervals.

Nest: A platform of broken reeds among rushes or raupo. Up to 4 olive-brown eggs are laid.

Where to find - North Island:

Northland - Bay of Islands: Any wetland near Kerikeri or Paihia is worth investigating. Wetlands surrounded by grazed pasture, such as gully bottoms, are the easiest places to inspect and are often the most fruitful.

Northland - Bay of Islands – Waitangi area: Recorded in wetlands here often sharing the same haunts as Fernbird and Crake.

South Auckland - Miranda: Regularly seen along the Miranda coastal verge and sometimes at the lake at Miranda Naturalists' Trust Centre.

North Waikato - Meremere and Whangamarino Wetland: At Meremere power station on Highway 1, about 5 kms south of Mercer, turn left (east) at the signpost which says Island Block. This road leads into dense wetlands known as Whangamarino. Bitterns live here. Search anywhere along this road. At a closed gate, walk along the gravelled road until you reach Pylon 73. A small board walk extends into the swamp here and both Bitterns and Fernbirds have been seen from it. There are also Spotless Crakes here which could respond to the playing of a tape.

South Auckland - Finlayson Road, Maramarua: Extensive wetlands along this road are worth inspecting for Bitterns and waterfowl. At Meremere Power Station turn into Island Block Road and follow east until Falls Road is reached. Turn right here and follow along until Finlayson Road on the right is reached. Search the wet areas on the right and further along on the left. The most likely place is the first wetland.

Hauraki Plains - Lake Patetonga: This lake is found on the western edge of the Hauraki Plains, south of the Firth of Thames. Leave Highway 2 at the Mangatarata, Ngatea junction. Travel south on Highway 27 and over the Kaihere hill. At the Patetonga Service Station turn left and drive along a flat straight road right to the end. Park beside the Piako River and look for a sign on the left saying Patetonga Reserve. The lake is found after a walk of about 800 metres following the river in a northerly direction. Observe this area with a telescope from a distance so as not to disturb the waterfowl. Sometimes, once the waterfowl have been disturbed Bitterns will rise.

North Waikato - Huntly, Lake Waahi: South of Huntly, cross the Waikato River and drive west through two intersections until the Lake Waahi sign is encountered at Weavers Crossing Road. Drive along this road to the boat launching ramp and search with a telescope the lake verges for Bitterns.

North Waikato - Taupiri: From Highway 1, turn left into Gordonton Road at Taupiri, 8 kms south of Huntly. After 2 kms look for a wetland on the left (east). This can be viewed from the road or from a cemetery further south. On the south swamp verge, below the cemetery, Spotless Crake have been seen.

Bay of Plenty - Matata Lagoon area: These wetlands have Bittern near the Tarawera River. Here they are found in similar habitats as Fernbird.

Where to find - South Island:

North Canterbury - Cheviot, St Annes Lagoon: This small lagoon, 4.5 kms north of Cheviot, has the occasional Bittern. (See "Places" in back of book.)

Southland - Manapouri: Try any wetland area around Lake Manapouri and Lake Te Anau. The Blackmount Road has several areas of wetland which are worth inspection. There are also Spotless Crakes in this area.

Southland - Redcliff Wetland Reserve: This area, well along Blackmount Road, is worth a visit. Also look for Fernbirds in this area.

Southland - Awarua Bay: Bitterns and also Spotless Crake are found here.

Reference: Whiteside A J 1989. The Behaviour Of Bitterns And Their Use Of Habitat. Notornis 36: 89 - 95.

GLOSSY IBIS

Brian Chudleigh

Family: Plataleidae   **Species:** *Plegadis falcinellus*
Common name: Glossy Ibis   **Status:** Native
Size: 600mm (cf sparrow 145mm, White-faced Heron 670mm)

Discussion: The Glossy Ibis is now a regular visitor to New Zealand, probably from Australia. This bird is a cosmopolitan species breeding in a wide belt across the southern Mediterranean, through Afghanistan, northern India, Indonesia and Australia. It wanders into Africa, South America and in recent years has started a breeding population in eastern United States. Visits to New Zealand frequently occur in the month of November. They are probably of immature birds from the Australian populations. Occasionally autumn birds arrive with the Cattle Egret migration and winter over.

Habitat: Glossy Ibis are traditionally birds of shallow fresh-water areas such as the edges of lakes, rivers and swamps in inland situations.

Range: In New Zealand they can appear in any locality which has swamps or lakes. However in recent years they have most consistently turned up in the south Auckland area of Rangiriri and Whangamarino, and at Lake Patetonga on the Hauraki Plains.

Description:
   Upper and underparts: Reddish-brownish with a greenish gloss on the wings. **Bill:** Olive-brown and markedly curved downwards. **Legs and feet:** Olive-brown.

Conspicuous features:
- About Cattle Egret size.
- In-flight birds show long curved bill.
- Birds fly with neck and legs extended.

Conspicuous characteristics:
- Glossy Ibis tend to be very nervous. They should be approached stealthily.
- When feeding they tend to disappear into the grass and rushes.

Where to find - North Island:

South Auckland - Waiuku District: Birds regularly inhabit a farm on Forestry Road. From Waiuku follow Otaua Road then Hoods Landing Road and then Forestry Road. Birds are sometimes found on both the left and right of this road prior to the road climbing to the Maiora Sands lookout.

North Waikato - Rangiriri: During November watch for them in the Rangiriri, Whangamarino districts in any place where there are wetlands, lakes or water lying. The Cattle Egret flocks in the Churchill East Road should be checked. (See Cattle Egret article.)

Hauraki Plains - Lake Patetonga: Birds are often found here in the more secure environment at the back, western area of the lake. (See Bittern article.)

Where to find - South Island:

Canterbury - Lake Ellesmere: Try the Lakeside area out from Leeston. (See Mute Swan article.)

South Canterbury - Oamaru: Try All Day Bay Lagoon, south of Oamaru and along the coast south from Kakanui. (See "Places" in back of book.)

Southland - Waituna Lagoon: Regularly seen in this area.

ROYAL SPOONBILL

Family: Plataleidae   **Species:** *Platalea regia*
Common name: Royal Spoonbill   **Status:** Native
Size: 770 mm (cf sparrow 145 mm, White Heron 910 mm)

Discussion: A growing population of Royal Spoonbills is now breeding in New Zealand in several places. Some of these will have originated from the small breeding colony associated with the White Heron breeding colony on the Waitangi Taona River near Okarito Lagoon in south Westland.

Royal Spoonbill

Habitat: Feeds in estuaries and harbours usually near the water line.
Range: Throughout New Zealand in a variety of coastal habitats.

Description:
Face: Black skin to behind eye with a yellow patch above each eye and a red spot in centre of forehead. **Upperparts and underparts:** White. **Bill:** Black and spoon-shaped. **Legs:** Black.

Conspicuous features:
- A large white heron-like bird.
- Black spoon-shaped bill is noticeable.

Conspicuous characteristics:
- Flies with neck and legs outstretched.
- Bill shape is noticeable when in flight.
- Legs extend beyond body when in flight
- Birds are gregarious feeders.
- Birds when feeding are constantly on the move.
- Birds have a comical waddling gait when feeding caused by their feeding action of swinging the bill from side to side through water and soft mud.
- Birds have a habit of perching on prominent treetops or poles.

Call: Soft guttural grunts near the nest but usually silent. Sometimes soft bill chattering is heard.

Nest: Colonial nesters in tall trees making a platform nest of twigs. Up to 4 white, lightly-blotched brown eggs are laid. Breeding colonies are now established at such places as Parengarenga, Kapiti Island, Wairau Lagoon near Blenheim, Maukiekie Island near Moeraki, south of Oamaru and Green Island Nature Reserve, Dunedin.

Nest desertion: Royal Spoonbills are of a nervous temperament and easily desert their nests if disturbed. Hence they nest in isolated places.

Where to find - North Island:

Wintering localities: Wintering birds are found in many places throughout New Zealand and any estuary or harbour can expect to have birds. Likely places include Parengarenga Harbour, Whangarei Harbour, Manukau Harbour, Mangere Sewage Ponds, Miranda, Coromandel Harbour, Maketu Estuary, Matata Lagoon, Wairoa Lagoon, Ahuriri, Foxton Estuary, Waikanae Estuary, Farewell Spit, Wairau Lagoon, Avon Heathcote Estuary, Lake Ellesmere, Hawkesbury Lagoon, Brighton Estuary, Kaikorai Estuary and Invercargill Estuary.

Auckland - Mangere Sewage Ponds: See "Places" in back of book.

South Auckland - Miranda: See "Places" in back of book.

Bay of Plenty - Matata Lagoon: See "Places" in back of book.

Manawatu - Foxton Estuary: This estuary is found after driving through the Foxton township and taking the signs to the motor-camp. Park past the camp and walk to the estuary and then scan towards the south. There is usually a flock here towards the end of the breeding season from March onwards.

Wellington - Waikanae Estuary: From Highway 2 at Waikanae follow Te Moana Road and drive towards the coast. At the coastal road turn left and travel south until the estuary is reached. The Waikanae population of Royal Spoonbills are probably birds from a colony on Kapiti Island nearby.

Where to find - South Island:

Marlborough - Wairau Lagoon, Blenheim: From Blenheim head towards Riverlands on Highway 1. Then take Redwood Pass Road. Side roads from it lead to the Big Lagoon.

Marlborough - Motueka River-mouth: Drive to the coast past the golf course. The estuary here regularly has birds.

Christchurch: Try the wildlife refuge and oxidation ponds in the Avon-Heathcote Estuary.

Canterbury - Lake Ellesmere: Try Timberyard Road at Lakeside near Leeston. (See Mute Swan article.)

South Canterbury- All Day Bay: All Day Bay, about 13 kms south of Oamaru near Kakanui, has a waterfowl lagoon just opposite the beach carparking area. Royal Spoonbill can be seen here along with Shoveler, Grey Duck, Grey Teal and Mallards. If travelling north on Highway 1 follow Waianakarua Road. If travelling south there are various ways of finding the bay, but the coastal road from Oamaru is the easiest.

South Canterbury - Moeraki Point: Try this area which is south of Oamaru and near Hampden. Here a breeding colony has established on a small island off the coast which is not readily visible from the mainland.

Dunedin - Kaikorai Estuary: Try this area. (See "Places" in back of book.)

Westland - Okarito near Whataroa: Birds breed here with the White Herons.

Invercargill Estuary: Birds are frequent visitors here.

MUTE SWAN

Family: Anatidae   **Species:** *Cygnus olor*
Common name: Mute Swan   **Status:** Introduced
Size: 1500 mm (cf sparrow 145 mm, Black Swan 1200 mm)
Discussion: A bird which was introduced from Europe for ornamental purposes. Small collections are still being bred around the country. A feral population still survives on Lake Ellesmere.

Habitat: Fresh-water lakes and ponds.

Description:
   Face: Facial skin in front of eye is black. **Upperparts and underparts:** White.
   Bill: Orange, with black base and a black knob on the forehead. **Legs and feet:** Black.
Conspicuous features:
- Orange bill with black knob at base is noticeable.
- The long S curved neck separates it from a feral goose.

Conspicuous characteristics:
- Has a stately manner about it when sitting on the water.
- A bird of leisurely character.

Call: Usually silent but it occasionally trumpets and often hisses.
Nest: A mound of reeds, raupo and rushes, usually floating among the vegetation of the lake edge. Up to 7 white eggs are laid.

Where to find - North Island:
Hawkes Bay - Havelock North: Follow the road to Ocean and Waimarama Beaches. A roadside pond before Maraetotara Road has several pairs.
Wanganui - Virginia Lake: This park is located on the Wanganui, New Plymouth road and has maintained two pairs of birds for some years.

Palmerston North: Horowhitu Lagoon off Fitzherbert Avenue has birds.

Where to find - South Island:
North Canterbury - Cheviot, St Annes Lagoon: Often birds here.
Canterbury - Lake Ellesmere: From Highway 1, at Dunsandel turn left to Leeston then take the road to Lakeside. Before Lakeside turn left into Timberyard Road which leads to the Aquatic Centre.

BLACK SWAN

Brian Chudleigh

Family: Anatidae   **Species:** *Cygnus atratus*
Common name: Black Swan   **Status:** Introduced.
Size: 1200 mm (cf sparrow 145 mm, Mute Swan 1500mm)

Discussion: The Black Swan is an introduced Australian species which has multiplied rapidly and spread to most wetland areas of New Zealand. It is hunted during the shooting season in May and June, in many areas.

Habitat: A bird of inland lakes, tidal harbours and estuaries.
Range: Found throughout New Zealand on both the main islands and Stewart Island. Also on some of the off-shore islands.

Description:
   Upperparts and underparts: Black. **Wings:** Black, with white on primaries and some of the secondary feathers. **Bill:** Red, with a white band near the tip and a white tip. **Legs and feet:** Black.
Conspicuous features:
   • A large black Swan.
   • The "painted" white band across the upper mandible is noticeable.
   • White wing primaries are very noticeable when bird is in flight but not conspicuous when bird is on the water unless the bird flaps its wings.

Conspicuous characteristics:
- When on the water birds continually raise their wings and flap them.
- In flight, neck is outstretched.
- Song and wing whistle are regularly heard overhead at night.

Call: The Black Swan has a very musical song usually heard when birds are flying. Also, a musical whistle is uttered when birds are sitting on the water.

Nest: A mound of grass and rush stems near the shoreline and on the ground. Up to 6 pale green eggs are laid.

Where to find - North Island:

North Auckland - Waiwera: Strakas Refuge has a small population.

Auckland - Western Springs Lake: Good numbers can be found here.

North Waikato - Lake Whangape: Turn off Highway 1 at Rangiriri and follow the sign which says Glen Murray. Eventually you will come to the lake.

Hamilton Lake: Good numbers here and on surrounding Waikato lakes.

Rotorua - Lake Rotoma: This lake, in the Rotorua district, has a very large summer population. A resident population remains the year around.

Tauranga Harbour: Found here at the northern end close to the beaches near Katikati.

Bay of Plenty - Matata Lagoon: Always a large population here.

Where to find - South Island:

North Canterbury - Cheviot, St Annes Lagoon: Large numbers here.

Canterbury - Lake Ellesmere: Large populations can be found here.

CANADA GOOSE

Brian Chudleigh

Family: Anatidae   **Species:** *Branta canadensis*
Common name: Canada Goose   **Status:** Introduced
Size: 830 mm (cf sparrow 145 mm, Black Swan 1200 mm)

Discussion: Canada geese were introduced into New Zealand as game birds and have established large populations in the South Island where they breed in the seclusion of the high country and winter nearer the coast. In recent years they have established large populations in the North Island.

Habitat: A bird of lakes, wetlands and open countryside.
Range: Found throughout most of New Zealand except for Northland.

Description:
  Head and neck: Black. **Face:** Prominent white patch under eye to chin. **Upperparts:** Brownish. **Breast and underparts:** Greyish-brown barred with white. **Uppertail:** Black with white under. **Bill:** Black. **Legs and feet:** Dark grey.
Conspicuous features:
  - The contrasting black and white on the head is its main feature.
  - Note the greyish-brown breast barring.
Conspicuous characteristics:
  - Birds are scary and quickly take to the air if disturbed.
  - Birds rest on the water in large groups away from disturbance.
  - In-flight birds fly in scattered skeins.
Call: A musical double honk.
Nest: A solitary nester which makes a bowl of twigs and grass, lined with feathers, usually on a mound with good visibility. Up to 5 white eggs are laid.

Where to find - North Island:
Auckland - Lake Pupuke: This lake, near Takapuna is accessed at Sylvan Park off Kitchener Road. There are good numbers of waterfowl here.
Hauraki Plains - Lake Patetonga: There is a good population here towards the back of the lake. (See Bittern article.)
North Waikato - Lake Waikare: This lake is near Rangiriri. To get here drive east from Highway 2 to Te Kauwhata and then to on to Lake Road.
North Waikato - Lake Waahi: This lake near Huntly has a large population of over 250 birds, which is periodically controlled. (See Bittern article.)
Waikato - Hamilton Lake: This lake in the city has a small population.
Bay of Plenty - Matata Lagoon: Often seen here in small numbers.

Where to find - South Island:
Marlborough - Lake Elterwater: Usually has a small population.
North Canterbury - Cheviot, St Annes Lagoon: Good numbers here.
Canterbury - Lake Ellesmere: Large populations can be found here.

PARADISE SHELDUCK

Family: Anatidae   **Species:** *Tadorna variegata*
Common name: Paradise Shelduck, Paradise Duck or Parry
Status: Endemic
Size: 630 mm (cf sparrow 145, Mallard 580 mm)

Brian Chudleigh

Female

Discussion: The Paradise Shelduck is an endemic species closely related to the South African Shelduck and the Chestnut-breasted Shelduck of Australia. In recent years it has spread in large numbers over both the North and South Islands and is now a common species.

Habitat: Usually frequents ponds and dams but also found along rivers especially where they run through farmland. Sometimes seen along forest rivers in inaccessible places. Over the summer months Paradise Shelduck flock in large numbers on to large lakes, such as the Rotorua lakes in the North Island and places like Lake Alexandrina in the South Island. Here they seek sanctuary while they become temporarily flightless during their moult.

Range: Found throughout New Zealand.

Description - male:
Head and neck: Black, with a metallic greenish sheen. **Upper and underparts:** Black, lightly barred with white. **Wings:** Black, with prominent white wing-coverts upper and under the wings and a large green speculum. **Abdomen:** Reddish-brown. **Undertail:** Orange-chestnut. **Bill:** Black. **Legs and feet:** Black.

Description - female:
Head: White with black eye. **Breast and underparts:** Orange-chestnut, tending to brownish when not in breeding plumage. **Wings:** Black with prominent white wing-coverts upper and under the wings and a large green speculum. **Undertail:** Orange-chestnut. **Bill and legs:** Black.

Description - ducklings: Zebra-striped brown and white when first born. They have a habit of sitting in little pyramid-like heaps when very young, always within sight of the parent birds. If disturbed they quickly scatter.

Description - immature birds: Fledglings of both sexes resemble the male.

Conspicuous features:
- The white on the head of the female is very noticeable.
- The white on the wings of in-flight birds is easily seen.

Conspicuous characteristics:
- For much of the year this species is usually seen in pairs.
- After the breeding season family parties are encountered.
- When disturbed, birds usually take to the wing and circle while calling all the time in a duet manner.
- Generally a nervous bird ever alert for intruding people.

Call: Male - a deep "klonk klonk". Female - a high-pitched "ziz zik".

Nest: Usually nests in holes in the ground or in old rotting stumps or rock crevices but sometimes in holes in trees. Up to 9 white eggs are laid.

Brian Chudleigh

Paradise Shelduck family

Where to find - North Island:

South Auckland - Miranda: Found here in roadside ponds.

Hauraki Plains - Lake Patetonga: Here in good numbers.

Rotorua - Lake Rotoehu: A summer spectacle when birds flock in to moult on it over the summer months.

Bay of Plenty - Matata: Large populations here.

Waikanae Estuary: Good numbers here.

Where to find - South Island:

Marlborough - Lake Elterwater: Large numbers here.

North Canterbury - Cheviot, St Annes Lagoon: Large numbers here.

South Canterbury - Lake Alexandrina: This lake is also a spectacle over the summer. Other waterfowl and Australasian Crested Grebe are also here.

Otago - Hoopers Inlet: Usually a wintering flock here.

General: A very easy bird to find. Inhabits most wetlands and pasture areas.

CHESTNUT-BREASTED SHELDUCK

Simon Fordham

Family: Anatidae   **Species:** *Tadorna tadornoides*
Common name: Chestnut-breasted Shelduck   **Status:** Native
Size: 630 mm (cf sparrow 145 mm, Paradise Shelduck 630 mm)

Discussion: The Chestnut-breasted Shelduck is a relative newcomer to New Zealand, being regularly seen here since 1982 when it was first recorded on Lake Ellesmere. Since then it has been seen in several localities. It is considered a close relative of the Paradise Shelduck. Two records of breeding success have been confirmed from the South Island.

Habitat: A bird of coastal lagoons, coastal lakes, ponds, dams and open pastureland.
Range: Northern South Island appears to be the most regular habitat although isolated sightings have come from Southland and from South Auckland.

Description - male:
   Head and neck: Black, with a metallic green sheen and a white ring around the edge of the black at the base of the neck. **Upperback and breast:** Orange-chestnut. **Wings:** Black, with prominent white wing-coverts upper and under the wings, and a large green speculum. **Underparts:** Brown finely barred with white. **Bill:** Black with small white patch at base. **Legs and feet:** Dark grey.
Description - female: Similar to the male except for a white eye-ring and a larger amount of white around the base of the bill.
Conspicuous features:
   • Bright chestnut breast separates it from the male Paradise Shelduck.
   • White neck-ring and white ring around bill separates it from the male Paradise Shelduck.

- In flight, birds show large areas of white on both upper and underwing.

Conspicuous characteristic:
- Usually in pairs on pasture or near water. Sometimes in family groups.

Call: Male bird makes a "zizzing-zonk" sound while the female makes a high pitched two syllabic "ong-chank" sound. When put to flight both birds usually call in an agitated manner not unlike the Paradise Shelduck.

Nest: In a hole in a tree or stump. Up to 9 white eggs are laid.

Moult: In Australia birds congregate in large numbers on inland lakes where they seek the sanctuary of deep water during the moult and a period of flightlessness. This habit is similar to Paradise Shelduck behaviour in New Zealand. Moulting sites for New Zealand birds is unknown.

Where to find - North Island:

Auckland - Mangere Sewage Ponds: Records have come from this locality.

Hauraki Plains - Lake Patetonga: One record comes from this lake.

South Auckland - Lake Whangape: One record comes from this waterfowl habitat.

Where to find - South Island:

Marlborough - Lake Elterwater: This lake has been the only reliable location for some years. It is approximately 36 kms south of Blenheim, east of the main highway and can be viewed from a road layby or from grassland at the southern end of the lake. (See "Places" in back of book.)

Canterbury -Lake Ellesmere: Try the Timberyard Road locality at Lakeside.

Canterbury - Lake Grasmere: This lake on the Arthurs Pass Road is worth a try if in the area looking for Blue Ducks or Crested Grebe.

Westland - Lake Moeraki: This lake is found south of Fox Glacier and before Haast. It can be viewed from Highway 6. If in the area looking for Fiordland Crested Penguins or Crested Grebe examine it for Chestnut-breasted Shelducks at the same time.

Southland - Redcliff Wetland Reserve: Records come from here. From Manapouri drive east along Hillside Road and then right into Weir Road and into Blackmount Road. Travel for about 18 kms and look for sign.

Otago - Hawkesbury Lagoon, Dunedin: Records come from here. From Highway 1, north of Dunedin and just prior to Waikouaiti, take Beach Road and then Scotia Street. The embankments enclosing the lagoon are walkable.

General: This is a species which should be looked for and expected on waterways which contain large numbers of waterfowl.

BLUE DUCK

Family: Anatidae   **Species:** *Hymenolaimus malacorhynchus*
Common name: Blue Duck, Whio   **Status:** Endemic
Size: 530 mm (cf sparrow 145 mm, Mallard 580 mm)

Discussion: The Blue Duck is a unique New Zealand endemic river duck which has been placed in its own genus of *Hymenolaimus*. It has been separated from

Blue Duck

Brian Chudleigh

the "dabbling" ducks (*Anas spp.*) because of its special physical adaptations to the environments of high country rivers. These adaptations are associated with its bill shape, its feeding habits and its feet size. Fleming (1982) writes: "The Blue Duck may have originated as a mid-Tertiary segregate from early dabbling ducks, but its specialised features probably evolved as the mountains were generated in the late Tertiary and especially during the Quaternary".

The Blue Duck is a species which has adapted to living and feeding among the white waters of mountain rivers where it feeds on a soft diet of river insect larvae and under-stone algae. Its bill, which is soft and pliable, with upper mandible flaps which tend to protect the lower mandible, is adapted for the taking of food among rough rocks and turbulent waters. Captain Cook described this bill as: "soft and of a skinny or more properly cartilaginous substance". Blue Duck ducklings are born with disproportionately large feet to enable them to swim strongly in turbulent waters from birth.

Blue Ducks are a strongly territorial species living on set stretches of river from which they seldom move. Territories are about 1 km of river long. In time, young fledgling birds are driven from these territories by their parents. This act must cause considerable numbers to perish, as territories uninhabited by Blue Duck on suitable mountain rivers are a diminishing resource.

Habitat: Confined to clear water, forested, mountain rivers in secluded areas away from human interference. Birds will extend territories into river stretches which are bordered by pastureland but they never seem to venture for long away from the security of forested river-banks. Some birds, probably unmated juveniles, turn up on lakes and ponds away from mountain rivers, over winter.

Range: In the North Island, birds are confined to the forested rivers in the central North Island. South Island birds are confined to similar habitats on the western side of the Southern Alps and into eastern areas of Fiordland.

Description:

Upperparts: Grey. In good light a bluish tinge may be evident. Birds are generally the colour of the mountain rocks around which they live. **Breast:** Reddish spotting over grey. **Abdomen and undertail:** Grey. **Bill:** Off-white. **Eye:** Iris, yellow. **Legs and feet:** Brown.

Conspicuous features:

- Larger than a Shoveler.
- Pale bill stands out.
- Upper mandible flaps on tip of bill make it different from other ducks.
- Yellow eye is noticeable.

Conspicuous characteristics:

- Birds are always in pairs when on river territories. Single birds do turn up on ponds and lakes away from normal breeding habitats.
- Swimming birds often hold up tail.
- When feeding, birds are regularly seen with tails up and heads under the water. They also regularly stand and dabble.
- Birds are quiet by nature and prefer to swim away from disturbance rather than fly.
- Birds tend to venture out and feed in early morning and late afternoon, while hiding away among overhanging river vegetation by day. However, day time sightings are not uncommon.

Call: Male bird a loud whistle - "whio" (wh is f in Maori). Female birds answer with a harsh "craak craak". Usually they call at dusk or dawn.

Nest: A bowl of grass lined with down, under a log or in dense vegetation. Up to 6 cream eggs are laid.

Best viewing times: Birds are more active one hour before dawn or dusk but can be found during the middle of the day.

Where to find - North Island:

Eastland - Lake Waikaremoana: To get to Lake Waikaremoana, which is in the Urewera National Park, travel south to Rotorua. From Rotorua travel south on Highway 5, the Taupo road, and turn left at Rainbow Mountain towards Murupara on Highway 38. Travel on to Ruatahuna and finally reach the Urewera National Park. From Ruatahuna travel approximately 18 kms until you find the Hopuruahine Stream which crosses the road and is signposted. Stop here and walk down the stream looking for birds resting on rocks. These birds tend to blend in with the stones. Walk for at least 1 km before giving up. Chance of a bird here is 90%.

Eastland - Lake Waikareiti Track: This track leads into the bush near the Waikaremoana Park Headquarters approximately 10 kms further on from the Hopuruahine Stream location. A short walk along it gives a view into the stream. Ask at the headquarters about Blue Ducks if you fail to locate them. Chance of a bird here is about 90%. A bridge just before the headquarters, over the Aniwaniwa Stream, is another place to look.

King Country - Pureora Forest: Rivers in this forest have Blue Duck. None are easily accessible. Enquire at the Pureora Park Headquarters.

King Country - Ongarue River: The headwaters of this river are where the ducks live. Drive up Ongarue Stream Road, which leads in from Waimiha, to the end of the road which follows the river and then enter private land. Drive to the farmhouse and ask permission to look for Blue Duck.

Central Plateau - Waihaha River: This river is about 40 kms towards Turangi from Whakamaru. It is 10 kms on past the Tihoi Trading Post, a main road shop and petrol station. The road drops steeply down to the river and crosses the Waihaha over a small bridge. There is a parking area near the bridge (lock your car) on the left. The up-stream walk is along an easy track but it takes at least two hours to get into Blue Duck territory. A small river is crossed after a 35 minutes walk. The track then climbs quite steeply over a saddle and back to the river. Once the river is again reached Blue Duck might be found. Make this an all day excursion. Blue Duck also live downstream from the bridge but this is a difficult walk.

Tongariri National Park - Desert Road: Most of the roads which run east towards the Kaimanawa ranges, off the Desert Road, lead to the Tongariro River. All these localities sometimes have Blue Duck with Rangipo Intake Road being the most reliable. These include -

- Access Road 10 which leads into the Waikato Falls.
- Tree Trunk Gorge Road which leads into a gorge and the Pillars of Hercules.
- Rangipo Intake Road which leads into the river. A walking track from the end of this road leads up stream and back to the river and is worth a try.

Tongariro National Park - Whakapapa River: The Whakapapa River flows under Highway 47 not far from the Chateau, Tongariro. Follow it up to the Chateau and examine it especially near the Chateau.

Tongariro National Park - Whakapapa intake: The Whakapapa River flows under Highway 47 not far from the road up to the Chateau. From Highway 47, just east of the Whakapapa Village and The Chateau road, turn down Access Road (north) and travel to a carpark at the end. The water intake area above the dam and the buildings sometimes has Blue Ducks as do downstream areas. Before the carpark a track leads off on the right. This steeply descends over about 2 kms to a footbridge. This locality sometimes has birds too.

Tongariro - Raetihi: Drive north from Raetihi and turn left down Ohura Road. Travel for approximately 25 minutes until a large steel bridge over the Maunganui Ateao River is encountered. Try for Blue Duck here. Try again further along wherever the Maunganui Ateao comes into view.

Bay of Plenty - Waioeka Gorge: Travel south from Opotiki towards Gisborne. Once in the gorge examine the Waioeka River and the Manganuku Stream confluence where Redpath Road crosses the Waioeka River.

Where to find - South Island:

Westland - Arthurs Pass: After travelling through Arthurs Pass township, when travelling west from Canterbury, stop where the road meets the Otira River in the Otira Gorge at Pegleg Creek. Walk up-stream or down-stream.

Westland - Bullock Creek near Punakaiki: Regularly seen in the Bullock Creek gorge. Follow the track in from the gate at the end of the road.

Fiordland - Eglinton Valley: Try Wesney Creek just before Knobs Flat. Also try Smithy Creek and Lylle Creek just past Knobs Flat on the Eglinton Valley Road. Try Cascade Creek downstream from the road.

Fiordland - Hollyford River: Anywhere on this river could have a pair.

Fiordland - Falls Creek: This creek is the first after The Divide. Blue Duck are sometimes seen where it enters the Hollyford River.

Fiordland – Falls Creek: Following this creek up into the hills may give a view of a Blue Duck. It is a steep climb but birds have been seen here after a 15 minute walk.

General: Blue Ducks are hard to find, they being rare and generally with crepuscular feeding habits. Sometimes in wet weather though, they will feed freely in the open by day so don't discount bad weather as an inappropriate time for looking for them.

MALLARD

Brian Chudleigh

Family: Anatidae   **Species:** *Anas platyrhynchos*
Common name: Mallard   **Status:** Introduced
Size: 580 mm (cf sparrow 145 mm)

Discussion: The Mallard is New Zealand's most common duck. It was introduced for hunting and has spread widely throughout the country.

Habitat: Mallards can be found in both fresh-water and salt-water environments. They are at home on farm drains, forest rivers, fresh-water lakes and lagoons and along many tidal estuaries and coastal beaches.
Range: Found throughout New Zealand and on off-shore islands.

Description - male:
   Head and neck: Glossy green, with a white ring at base of green. **Back:** Brown. **Wings:** Grey, with blue speculum which has a thin black and white edge front and back. **Uppertail:** Black edged white and with two curled ornamental black feathers. **Undertail:** Black. **Breast:** Chestnut. **Underparts:** Pale grey. **Bill:** Yellow. **Legs and feet:** Orange.
Description - female:
   Head: Brown with dark brown eye-stripe. **Upper and underparts:** Streaked

128

and spotted brown and buff. **Wings and speculum:** As for male. **Bill:** Orange brown.

In moult: Male birds attain feather patterns similar to female birds.

Conspicuous features:
- Blue speculum separates the Mallard from the Grey Duck.
- Female Mallards, and hybrids between Mallard and Grey Duck, lack the yellow and black face markings of the Grey Duck.
- Mallards appear lighter in eclipse plumage than Grey Duck.

Conspicuous characteristics:
- Often found near human habitation such as on park lakes.
- Mallards usually take to the air quicker than Grey Ducks when disturbed.
- Head bobbing, neck stretching and circling of the male by the female, on the water, are noticeable behaviour as birds pair-bond after February.

Call: The male makes a high-pitched "quek quek" call or just a piping whistle and the female a raucous quack.

Nest: A solitary nest on the ground made of grass and sticks and lined with down. Up to 12 green eggs are laid.

Where to find: Common everywhere.

GREY DUCK

Brian Chudleigh

Family: Anatidae   **Species:** *Anas superciliosa*
Common name: Grey Duck, Black Duck (Australia)   **Status:** Native
Size: 580 mm (cf sparrow 145 mm, Mallard 580 mm)

Discussion: A widely spread species found in a belt from Indonesia, through Australia and New Zealand to the Pacific Islands, as far east as Tahiti. Originally this species was New Zealand's most common duck and was the main bird shot for sport. Today, though, its numbers have lessened. The introduction of the Mallard, which has competed for Grey Duck habitat and which has interbred with it may be a reason for the decline. The Grey Duck - Mallard hybrid birds are known in some areas.

Habitat: Generally found in secluded waterways in remote areas on lakes and rivers but some can be found in the headwaters of estuaries. Seldom seen in lowland wetlands where Mallards are common possibly because Mallards can take a wider range of food types.

Range: Found throughout the North, South, and Stewart Island. Also on the Chatham Islands and many off-shore islands.

Description:

Crown: Black. **Face and throat:** Pale yellow with a dark eye-stripe running through the eye from bill to back of head A similar but lesser dark stripe crosses the lower cheek. **Upperparts and underparts:** Brown, feathers being edged with a pale buff colouring. **Wings:** Brown, with a green speculum edged front and back with black. **Bill:** grey with dark tip. **Legs and feet:** Greenish-brown.

Conspicuous features:
- Look for the yellow face with black eye-stripe.
- Mallard size.
- In flight looks black.

Conspicuous characteristics:
- Usually found in pairs.
- Tends to skulk in rushes at the edge of lakes and ponds.
- Uncommon in parks and gardens unlike the Mallard.
- Rises slowly into the air when disturbed on a waterway.
- Odd lonely pairs in remote places are usually always Grey Ducks.

Call: Male bird has a high-pitched "quek quek quek" call, and often a piping whistle, while the female makes a raucous "quack quack".

Nest: A solitary nest on the ground made of grass and sticks and lined with down,. Up to 12 green eggs are laid.

Differences between Grey Ducks and Mallards:
- Yellow face with bold black stripe through the eye separates the Grey Duck from the female Mallard. Always look at the head first.
- The green speculum on the wing separates the Grey Duck from the Mallard. The Mallard has a blue speculum.
- The Mallard drake, when in breeding plumage, and not the eclipse plumage, is very different from the Grey Duck drake, being a colourful and more striking   bird. The Grey Duck drake, in comparison, is rather drab.
- Grey Ducks rise more slowly from the water than Mallards.
- Frequents more remote and higher altitude areas than Mallards.

Where to find - North Island:
Bay of Islands: Try Lake Owhareiti and Lake Omapere.

North Auckland - Waiwera: Regularly at Strakas Refuge at Waiwera.

North Auckland - Weiti (Wade) River: Occasionally here around the wharf.

Auckland - Tahuna Torea: This wetland in east Auckland always has some Grey Ducks, along with Mallards. (See "Places" in back of book.)

South Auckland - Miranda: Occasionally seen at Pukorokoro River-mouth.

Waikato - Huntly: Just north and east of the town centre of Huntly, and across the railway line, lies Lake Hakanoa. It can be viewed from several Huntly side roads but its reserve area is signposted from Highway 1. This lake has more Grey Ducks on it than Mallard. It also has other waterfowl.

Bay of Plenty - Matata: This is a reliable place to find Grey Duck. A flock of up to 50 birds can always be seen here.

Rotorua lakes: These all have Grey Ducks on them in their quiet corners.

Rotorua - Lake Okareka: This is a very good waterfowl lake. (See Scaup article.)

Rotorua - Lake Rotorua: Always some near the Centennial Gardens.

Central Plateau - Lake Kario, Ohakune: This lake is 14 kms south of Ohakune on Highway 49. It is signposted on the left when travelling south. It has many waterfowl including Grey Duck and Dabchicks.

Where to find - South Island:

Westland - Lake Kaniere: Visit Lake Kaniere which is located east of Hokitika and signposted.

Fiordland - Cascade Creek: Try Mirror Lakes about 10 kms south of Cascade Creek, on the Eglinton Valley road. These always have pure Grey Duck. Scaup live with them. Stop there and also enjoy the bush birds.

Lake Te Anau: Always some near the shoreline not far from the town.

General: Grey Ducks are becoming harder to find in most districts.

WATERFOWL COLLECTIONS

Escapes: Waterfowl straying from collections include Chestnut Teal (*Anas castanea*), Carolina Wood Ducks (*Aix sponsa*) and Mandarin Ducks (*Aix galericulata*).

Jim Hague

Carolina Wood Duck

Brian Chudleigh

Chestnut Teal

Brian Chudleigh

Carolina Wood Duck

Brian Chudleigh

Mandarin Duck

GREY TEAL

Brian Chudleigh

Family: Anatidae   **Species:** *Anas gracilis*
Common name: Grey Teal   **Status:** Native
Size: 430 mm (cf sparrow 145 mm, Mallard 580 mm)

Discussion: This bird is found in Indonesia, New Guinea, New Caledonia, Vanuatu and Australia where it is considered the most common of Australia's waterfowl. In New Zealand, though, it is less common. This might be the result of accidental shooting by duck-shooters as it is easily mistaken for the Grey Duck. As a species it is known to be particularly mobile and to fly long distances with relative ease, interchanging between the islands.

Habitat: A bird of both fresh-water lakes and lagoons and becoming increasingly common on tidal estuaries and in harbours.
Range: Found throughout New Zealand with concentrations in areas such as the Waikato, the Rotorua district, Otago and Southland.

Description:
    Head: Top of head is dark brown. **Face and under neck:** Pale yellow.
    Upperparts and underparts: Overall of grey-brown appearance with feathers having dark brown centres and buff edges. **Upperwings:** Brown, with a large black speculum which has a metallic green sheen and which is edged with white, the leading white edge being triangular in shape. **Underwing:** Brownish-grey. **Eye:** Iris red. **Bill:** Blue-grey upper mandible and yellowish lower mandible. **Legs and feet:** Greyish-brown.
Conspicuous features:
- Considerably smaller than the Mallard.
- Sexes are alike.
- The pale yellow face lacks the heavy black eye-stripe of the Grey Duck.
- The bird looks smaller, neater and softer in colouring than the Grey Duck.

- The white on upperwings is very visible on in-flight birds.

Conspicuous characteristics:
- Roosting birds sometimes show the white markings of their wings. This appears as a white flank marking.
- When flying in flocks they have an immaculate and coordinated group flight pattern with individual wing beats appearing to be in unison.
- The wing beats of Grey Teal are faster than either Mallard or Grey Duck.

Call: A rapid "cuck cuck cuck", and also a sharp whistle.

Nest: A bowl of grass lined with down, usually in clumps of rushes or tall grasses. Up to 7 cream coloured eggs are laid.

Artificial nest boxes: In recent years, a concerted effort by Ducks Unlimited, involving the placement of wooden nesting boxes along many waterways, has greatly increased the numbers of Grey Teal.

Where to find - North Island:

Northland - Bay of Islands: Lake Omapere and Lake Owhareiti sometimes have this bird.

North Auckland - Waiwera: Strakas Refuge sometimes has Grey Teal.

North Auckland - Weiti (Wade) River: Grey Teal sometimes can be seen along this estuary across from the wharf.

South Auckland - Miranda: Regularly seen in good sized flocks on the roadside ponds and near the Pukorokoro River at the edge of the mangroves. This is an easy locality to find this bird but it is usually dependent on a high tide. (See "Places" in back of book.)

Hauraki Plains - Lake Patetonga: Always birds here. (See Bittern article.)

Waikato - Ngaruawahia: From Ngaruawahia drive north on Highway 1 and before you cross the bridge over the railway line look down a small side road on the right where Grey Teal nest boxes have been constructed around a lake. Birds are often found here sitting on the nest boxes.

Bay of Plenty - Kaituna River-mouth: From Te Puke on Highway 2 turn left into Maketu Road and then left into Kaituna River Road and then right down Ford Road. Tumu Road also leads into this lagoon from Highway 2. Sometimes seen here in large numbers.

Bay of Plenty - Matata Lagoon: Always some here.

Rotorua lakes: These are always worth examining for Grey Teal.

Where to find - South Island:

North Canterbury - Lake Grasmere: This lake, along with nearby Lake Pearson, is on the road to Arthurs Pass. They are very obvious. There are always birds here. (See "Places" in back of book.)

North Canterbury - St Annes Lagoon, Cheviot: Always some birds here. (See "Places" in back of book.)

Otago - Hawksbury Lagoon: From Dunedin take Highway 1 north. Before Waikouaiti turn left down Beach Road and then right into Scotia Road. This is a reliable area.

Otago - Hoopers Inlet: If visiting the Royal Albatross nesting colony on Taiaroa Heads also visit Hoopers and Papanui Inlets. These are good for Grey Teal and other waterfowl and sometimes Brown Creeper and Rifleman are in roadside verge bush nearby.

Southland - Awarua Estuary: This estuary near Invercargill is a reliable Grey Teal habitat. Take the Tiwai Road turnoff on the road south to Bluff. Turn left when the bay is reached.

Southland - Lake Manapouri and Lake Te Anau: Grey Teal are often found on both of these lakes. Look for them when driving through this area on route to Cascade Creek and Milford Sound.

General: This is a bird which is relatively easy to find. It is often scary and difficult to approach. Easiest locality is the roadside pools at Miranda just south of the Miranda Naturalists' Trust Centre, when the tide is full.

BROWN TEAL

Brian Chudleigh

Family: Anatidae   **Species:** *Anas aucklandica*
Common name: Brown Teal   **Maori name:** Pateke
Status: Endemic
Size: 480 mm (cf sparrow 145 mm, Grey Teal 430 mm)

Discussion: A very rare endemic, the main population now confined to Great Barrier Island, with several isolated colonies surviving in Northland. Although once a common species found throughout the North Island, South Island, Stewart Island, and on off-shore islands, its range has markedly diminished. Predators, such as mustelids, cats and rats, plus a shrinking wetland habitat, are blamed for its decline. The Brown Teal has been grouped at times with the Australian Chestnut Teal (*Anas castanea*) but the Brown Teal is a bigger bird. It also possesses a cream coloured eye-ring and has less green iridescence on the head and neck. It is closely allied to the Auckland Island Teal, a flightless species, and to the Campbell Island Teal.

Habitat: Remnant populations are generally confined to muddy tidal river estuaries. Previously populations were widespread in swampland and on lakes

135

in most localities. Present river estuary localities usually contain overhanging grasses and mangroves under which the birds can hide during the day.

Range: Great Barrier Island contains most birds. Isolated groups live in areas of Northland, on Tiri Tiri Island and on Little Barrier Island. Occasional reports of sightings come from Fiordland and Stewart Island.

Description - male bird:

Head: Dark brown, with a cream eye-ring around a black eye. **Neck:** Brown, with an indistinct white collar on front of bird. **Upperparts:** Dark brown to brown. **Wings:** Brown, with buff edges to feathers and with a large black speculum with a greenish sheen and white edges. **Breast:** Chestnut. **Underparts:** Buff. **Flank spot:** White. **Bill:** Blue black.

Description - female bird: Generally evenly dull brown all over.

Conspicuous features:

- A small neat looking bird slightly larger than the Grey Teal.
- Cream eye-ring is noticeable.
- The blackish speculum edged with white is noticeable on in-flight birds.
- Lacks the triangle of white to the front of the speculum as on the Grey Teal. This also separates it from the uncommon Chestnut Teal (see photo after Mallard.)
- The white flank-marking on male birds is usually noticeable on both roosting and swimming birds.

Conspicuous characteristics:

- Birds have a habit of loafing in large groups by day.
- Birds become active towards dusk.
- Mainland birds tend to be nocturnal feeders. Great Barrier Island birds feed throughout the day but are more active at dusk.

Call: The male bird has a high-pitched two-syllable "wheeze", and the female a dull rapidly repeated "quack".

Nest: A bowl of grass in dense rushes or grasses. Up to 4 cream eggs are laid.

Best viewing time: Before dusk for mainland birds, but on Great Barrier Island birds can be seen at any time of day.

Chestnut Teal in New Zealand: Many waterfowl breeders have this species within their flocks. Some are free flying and can disperse. Odd reports of "escaped" birds are heard of from time to time.

Artificial breeding programme: Ducks Unlimited, in association with the Department of Conservation, has instituted a breeding programme for Brown Teal and have distributed captive reared birds to localities in the north. To date (2000) results have not been good mainly due to high numbers of predators. Scientific investigation into the habits of this species continue.

Where to find - North Island:

Hauraki Gulf - Great Barrier Island: The beaches around the main town of Tryphena regularly have good sized flocks of birds often swimming off the coastline. Most water holes and small rivers also have this bird as do the sheltered harbours of Port Fitzroy and Whangaparapara. Kaitoke and Medlands Beach also have populations. Day tours to Great Barrier in high-powered catamarans can be arranged from Auckland.

Northland - Helena Bay to Mimiwhangata: To find Helena Bay, which is north of Whangarei, turn of Highway 1 past Hikurangi where the sign says to Russell. At Helena Bay turn right to Teal Bay and after Teal Bay stop at the Owae Stream and search from the road. If unsuccessful here travel on to the Mimiwhangata Farm Park. Once in the park, take the walking track to Trig Point. The lakes near the end of the peninsula and have good populations.

Northland - Whananaki: This area has Brown Teal in two localities. To get to them take the Matapouri turn-off at Hikurangi and drive east. Before Matapouri take Whananaki South Road. At Whananaki South drive south along a river estuary. Look for Brown Teal especially near the last bridge.

Hauraki Gulf - Little Barrier Island: There is a small population here near the manager's house.

North Auckland - Tiri Tiri Island: A small breeding population is surviving on several of the man-made ponds on this island. Here, birds appear in late afternoon but are seldom seen during the day.

NEW ZEALAND SHOVELER

Jim Hague

Family: Anatidae   **Species:** *Anas rhynchotis*
Common name: Shoveler , Spoonbill   **Status:** Endemic
Size: 490 mm (cf sparrow 145 mm, Mallard 580 mm)

Discussion: The Shoveler, in breeding plumage, is New Zealand's most handsome duck. It is also found in Australia and it is from there that New Zealand populations probably stem. Some ornithologists, however, regard the New Zealand species as a distinct sub-species, mainly because some New Zealand birds show whiteness on the breast which the Australian birds lack. This whiteness tends to link the bird with the Northern Shoveler (*Anas clypeata*) of Europe, Asia and North America and not to the Australian Shoveler. It should be noted that Northern Shoveler have turned up in New Zealand from time to time. Ancestry of the Shoveler is linked to the Blue-winged Teal (*Anas discor*) of North America.

Habitat: Shovelers live on ponds and lakes and especially those which have indented rush and raupo covered shorelines. They are also found on slow moving rivers, on estuaries and muddy coastal strips.

Range: Evenly spread through the North and South Islands. Reaches some of the higher altitude lakes especially where seclusion is guaranteed.

Description - male bird in breeding plumage:

Head and neck: Bluish-grey, with black behind bill and a white crescent-shaped stripe in front of the golden eye. **Back:** Brown. **Wings:** Bluish-grey, with dark grey primaries and a green speculum, edged on the leading edge with white. **Breast:** Mottled brown and white. **Abdomen:** Chestnut-brown with a white flank-spot. **Bill:** Grey. **Legs and feet:** Orange.

Description - female bird in breeding plumage:

Upperparts and underparts: Brownish. **Wings:** As for male bird.

Description - eclipse birds:

Upperparts and underparts: Drab brown, although male birds can retain some blue-grey tonings to the head. White flank-spot is absent.

Conspicuous features:

- Look for the white crescent band at base of bill, on male birds.
- The heavy looking "spoon" bill is noticeable.
- The in-breeding plumage male bird is brightly coloured.
- The white flank-spot is noticeable.

Conspicuous characteristics:

- Birds sit lower in the water than Grey Ducks or Mallards.
- Appearance is of a short neck and big head.
- Birds swim in a hunched position.
- When in a group of waterfowl, Shovelers tend to stay together.
- Regularly seen swimming in pairs.
- A fast-flying bird similar in group flight to Grey Teal. In-flight birds show the white wing-markings.
- Birds prefer still water where water insects and larvae can safely breed.
- Seldom seen away from water, unlike the Grey Duck and the Mallard. This is because the heavy pasture seeds and shoots which the Grey Duck and Mallard eat, are not able to be handled by the fine-edged, sieve-like, spoonbills of the Shoveler.

Call: A "cuck cuck cuck", similar to the Grey Teal. Male bird, a clonk sound.

Nest: A bowl of grass lined with down usually in thick vegetation on the ground. Up to 11 bluish eggs are laid.

Where to find - North Island:

Northland - Bay of Islands: Try Lake Owhareiti. (See Australian Little Grebe article.)

North Auckland - Waiwera: Try Strakas Refuge. (See "Places" in back of book.)

Auckland - Mangere Sewage Ponds: Large numbers here.

South Auckland - Miranda: Try the Pukorokoro River-mouth.

Bay of Plenty - Matata Lagoon: Usually a large population can be found here at any time of year. This is a reliable place to see them.

Wellington - Waikanae: Waimeha Lagoon is a small sandhill lagoon on the south end of the Waikanae seaside resort. It always has good numbers of waterfowl including Shoveler and Dabchick. To find it travel down Te Moana Road to Ngapaki Road on the left. Then travel along until you come to the bend in the road. A small signpost indicates the lake on the left. Walk in to a small hide from which to view the birds.

Where to find - South Island:

Marlborough - Lake Elterwater: Usually seen here.

North Canterbury - St Annes Lagoon, Cheviot: This is a reliable place to view them if travelling south.

Southland - Lake Te Anau: Occasionally seen at the southern end.

Southland - Redcliff Wetlands: Usually seen here.

Lake Manapouri: Try the southern end.

SCAUP

Brian Chudleigh

Family: Anatidae   **Species:** *Aythya novaeseelandiae*
Common name: Scaup, Black Teal   **Status:** Endemic
Size: 400 mm (cf sparrow 145 mm, Mallard 580 mm)

Discussion: The Scaup is an endemic species and New Zealand's only true diving duck. It is related to the Lesser Scaup (*Aythya affinis*) of North America and the Tufted Duck (*Aythya fuligula*) of Europe. Its ancestry does not lie with the Australian White-eyed Duck (*Aythya australis*). Although lacking the white flanks and underparts of these two Northern Hemisphere species, and the black tuft on the head of the male Tufted Duck, the Scaup is nevertheless very similar in size, shape, bill configuration and colour. It also shares the yellow eye of male birds, and the overall brownish colouring of female birds. Female scaup

139

also share a white marking at the base of the bill and both sexes share a degree of white on the upperwing secondary feathers.

Habitat: A bird which enjoys deep and clean fresh-water lakes throughout New Zealand including those bordering the coastal sand dunes.

Range: Found through many parts of New Zealand. Common in the Rotorua and Taupo areas. Well spread on the lakes of the South Island.

Description - male bird:

Upperparts and underparts: Glossy black. **Wings:** Black, with a broad white wing-bar on primaries and secondary feathers. **Eye:** Iris is yellow. **Bill:** Blue-black.

Description - female birds:

Head and neck: Dull brown. **Wings and back:** Black with white wingbar as for the male. **Underparts:** Dull brown. **Eye:** Brown. **Bill:** Black, with a white crescent-marking at base of bill.

Conspicuous features:
- The white band on wings is noticeable when birds are in flight.
- Look for yellow iris on male birds.

Conspicuous characteristics:
- Birds in flight fly very quickly just above the water.
- When not swimming together in breeding pairs, birds are usually to be found in large loafing flocks in sheltered water.
- When feeding, birds are continually diving and reappearing at about 15 second intervals.
- When watching pairs with young note how the young birds dive along with their parents.

Call: When sitting loafing in rafts, male birds continually utter a high-pitched rattled whistle.

Nest: A bowl of grass or rushes, lined with down, and close to the water. Up to 8 cream eggs are laid.

Where to find - North Island:

North Auckland - Waiwera: Strakas Refuge is an easy location to see this bird.

Bay of Plenty - Matata Lagoon: There are many Scaup here.

Bay of Plenty - Rotorua lakes: All of these have Scaup.

Bay of Plenty - Rotorua, Lake Okareka: Take the road to the Rotorua airport, Highway 30. At Lynmore turn right up Tarawera Road and follow signposts to the lake. Also look for Dabchick, Little Shag, Little Black Shag, Black Swan, Paradise Shelduck, Mallard, Grey Duck, Shoveler and Scaup.

Bay of Plenty - Lake Rotorua: Scaup regularly loaf in large flocks on this lake behind the Rotorua Gardens. When driving south along Fenton Street take the turning which says to the gardens. (See Dabchick article).

Lake Taupo: Good flocks live around Taupo, especially at the southern end. Also Dabchick, Spotless Crake, Marsh Crake and Fernbird are here.

Where to find - South Island:

Marlborough - Lake Elterwater: Always good numbers here.

North Canterbury - St Annes Lagoon: Good numbers here.

Southland - Lake Te Anau: Scaup are common on the lake-front. New Zealand Falcon can sometimes be seen here predating on them.

Fiordland - Eglinton Valley: Mirror Lakes in the Eglinton Valley south of Cascade Creek always have Scaup and also Grey Duck.

AUSTRALASIAN HARRIER

Brian Chudleigh

Family: Accipitridae   **Species:** *Circus approximans*
Common name: Harrier, Hawk, Kahu   **Status:** Native
Size: 550 mm (cf sparrow 145 mm, New Zealand Falcon 430 mm)

Discussion: Species of birds of prey, in New Zealand, are few they being the uncommon New Zealand Falcon (*Falco novaeseelandiae*) and the very common Harrier (*C. approximans*). Occasional visits of the Nankeen Kestrel (*Falco cenchroides*) are reported from time to time but this species has not been known to breed here. The Harrier is generally regarded as a scavenger rather than a hunter and has benefited from pastoral development. It is also widely spread through the Pacific islands, Australia and New Guinea.

Habitat: A bird of the open countryside rather than forests, occasionally straying over towns and cities.

Range: Found throughout New Zealand and to the off-shore islands.

Description:
    Upperparts: Dark brown. **Underparts:** Reddish-brown streaked with dark brown. **Rump:** White. **Eye:** Yellow, with brown centre. It is very yellow in male birds. **Legs and feet:** Yellow.

Conspicuous features:
- Light colouring of underparts is noticeable.
- Whitish rump is conspicuous on birds in the air.
- Paler colour of older birds is noticeable.

141

Conspicuous characteristics:
- Except at first light when it flies low and level, the Harrier soars and glides and rises on thermals.
- During the mating season Harriers circle and make "scree" type calls.
- It is regularly disturbed on roadsides eating road-killed rabbits or possums.
- Young birds will follow their parents in level flight calling plaintively.
- Occasionally it takes live ducks but not new-born lambs.

Call: The mating "scree" calls are common over the spring months.
Nest: A platform of twigs in among rushes. Up to 5 white eggs are laid.

Differences between the Harrier and the New Zealand Falcon:
- The Harrier is the common raptor of the open New Zealand countryside. The New Zealand Falcon seldom ventures out over farmland in the North Island but does in eastern parts of the South Island high country.
- The Harrier is much larger than the New Zealand Falcon - 550 mm compared with 430 mm.
- The Harrier constantly soars and rises on thermals. The New Zealand Falcon is usually seen flying in a direct manner with a flight pattern similar to a New Zealand Pigeon, although it will rise on thermals.
- The yellow eye colouring separates the Harrier from the New Zealand Falcon which has a brown eye.

Where to find - North and South Islands:
Common throughout all open areas once you have left the edges of the city.

NEW ZEALAND FALCON

Brian Chudleigh

Family: Falconidae　　　　　　　　**Species:** *Falco novaeseelandiae*
Common name: New Zealand Falcon, Bush Falcon, Sparrowhawk
Status: Endemic
Size: 430 mm (cf sparrow 145 mm, Harrier 550mm)

Discussion: The Bush Falcon is an endemic species which is not grouped with any of the five species of Australian falcons. Instead it is grouped with three species known from the southern American states of Texas and New Mexico and from Central America and northern South America (Cade T J 1982). These species are the Orange-breasted Falcon (*F. deiroleucus*), the Bat Falcon (*F. rufigularis*) and the Aplomado Falcon (*F. femoralis*). Its relationship with these three species is to do with similarities of bill shape, tail colouring, sunbathing habits, the excretory habits of nestlings and with their carnivorous eating habits and hunting techniques. The ancestor of the New Zealand Falcon is considered to be an early arrival to New Zealand, it adapting to the New Zealand environment and even progressing towards tameness as did other endemic and ancient species. The rounded wings and the shorter tail of the New Zealand Falcon have evolved to enhance flight manoeuvrability when hunting within dense New Zealand forest (Fleming 1982).

Forms: The New Zealand Falcon is divided into three forms (Fox 1977). These are -

- The Bush Falcon of North Island forests and the forests of the north-west of the South Island, which is a bird of dark plumage having only faint white barring on the wings and breast. This bird is a true forest dweller, living and breeding within the forest. It nests mostly in tall dead trees and especially in the epiphyte called kiekie (*Freycinetia banksii*). Occasional pairs nest on rock ledges (L Hedley, pers. comm.).
- The Eastern Falcon of the South Island which is of paler colouration and is richly barred. This bird lives and feeds over and on open country, nesting on rock ledges inland. Its paleness causes it to blend with the paler eastern South Island environment. It is known to feed more on exotic birds and mammals than on indigenous species and nests on rock ledges.
- The Southern Falcon of Fiordland and Auckland Island which is of colouring intermediate between the Bush Falcon and the Eastern Falcon and has more barring than the Bush Falcon.

Habitat: The Bush Falcon and Southern Falcon are confined to forested areas while the Eastern Falcon is widely spread over pastureland and rough and open high country.

Range: In the North Island widespread south of a line from Kawhia Harbour to the central Bay of Plenty. In the South Island it is widespread throughout but nowhere common. Also on Stewart Island and Auckland Island.

Description - Bush Falcon:

Crown nape and back: Bluish-black. **Wings:** Bluish-black, with grey barring and pure black primary feathers. **Underwings:** Brown, barred with white. **Uppertail:** Black, barred with separate narrow white bars of between 7 to 11 in number (Fox 1988). **Undertail:** Buff with some grey barring. **Throat and breast:** Dark, moustache-like, brown feathers at side of bill and below. Otherwise cream, vertically striped with dark brown. **Flanks:** Cream, horizontally barred with dark brown. **Ceres (above bill):** Yellow. **Eye:** Iris dark brown with a thin yellow eye-ring. **Bill:** Black, with dark markings on sides of chin. **Legs and feet:** Yellow.

Description - Southern Falcon: Similar to the Bush Falcon but paler with more under-barring on male birds.

Description - Eastern Falcon: Paler than the Bush Falcon and the Southern Falcon and more richly barred.

Description - immature birds: Immatures lack the bluish tonings of adult birds and become darker and browner in winter. They lack the bright yellow ceres above the bill of mature birds. Ceres may be blue, grey or brownish.

Conspicuous features:
- Yellow ceres and yellow legs and feet are noticeable.
- The dark brown eye separates it from the Harrier.
- Look for black claws and beak.

Conspicuous characteristics:
- When flying low and straight, with tail out, it can be mistaken for a New Zealand Pigeon or an agitated Long-tailed Cuckoo.
- In fine weather birds will sometimes rise and spiral on thermals.
- Often seen hovering with quick wing beats.
- Falcon have a habit of "greeting" human visitors to a territory by flying out in a slow hovering-type flight, looking, and then returning to a high branch. Such flights are usually accompanied by a rapid "kek kek kek" call. Usually both birds will fly out if they are not nesting.

Call: A rapid high-pitched shrieking "kek kek kek".

Nest: On the ground or a cliff ledge for eastern birds, and high in a tree for northern and southern birds. Up to 3 reddish, brown-blotched, eggs are laid.

Tape-recorders: Birds will respond to taped calls. Play as you enter a known territory and birds will investigate.

Time of day to visit: Birds can be seen at any time of day. Before sundown, though, can be a good time when birds are often more active.

Where to find - North Island:

King Country - Waitomo Caves: This area has several Falcon territories. Most are on private property. Nevertheless a general watch should be kept for this bird if in the vicinity of the famed Waitomo Caves.

King Country - Ruakuri: This territory, near the Waitomo Caves, is not on private land. From Waitomo Caves take Tumutumu Road on left and then first road on right. The territory comprises the bush surrounds of the entrance to the Ruakuri glow-worm cave. Here there is a track into lovely forest from which Pigeon, Tomtit, Whitehead, Tui and Bellbird may also be seen, plus limestone rock outcrops.

King Country - Hauturu Road: From Ruakuri drive west from the Waitomo Caves. Turn up Hauturu Road and travel until you come to heavy bush known as the Houston Memorial Bush indicated by a large roadside stone with an inserted plaque in memory of Robert Houston. Falcons are sometimes seen from the roadside here.

King Country - Pureora: A territory is at the end of Bismarck Road near "The Tower". Another is found near to the small Pureora Museum and toilet block. (See "Places" in back of book.)

Bay of Plenty - Waikaremoana: They are likely to be seen anywhere in this park and near the Hopuruahine Stream. (See Blue Duck article.)

Where to find - South Island:

Westland – Greymouth: Watch for it flying above the forests south of the Paparoa Ranges just north of Greymouth.

Westland - Lake Kaniere: Falcons are regularly seen from Lake Kaniere. This lake is well signposted from Hokitika. It is also a good place to see Great Spotted Kiwi, Crested Grebe, and Marsh Crake in wet verges.

Otago - Makaora: This locality between Haast Pass and Lake Wanaka on Highway 6 is excellent for New Zealand Falcons. Look behind the information centre.

Fiordland - Cascade Creek: Birds can be seen around Lake Gunn. Try the lakeside walk and also try the Cascade Creek walk up the river. Look for a pair after about 10 minutes of steady walking.

Southland - Lake Te Anau: Falcon are known from around the southern lake edge and almost into the town of Te Anau. Their territories extend across from the beech forests on the west edge of the lake.

Southland - Lake Manapouri: Falcons are also known from around the wharf at Pearl Harbour at Lake Manapouri. Search tall trees in this area near to the lake edge.

Southland - Five Rivers to Garston: Birds are regularly seen from Highway 6 especially in the Garston area. This locality is about 35 kms north of Lumsden on the Queenstown Road.

Reference: Fox N C 1988. A taxonomic redescription of the New Zealand Falcon, *Falco novaeseelandiae* Gmelin, 1788. Notornis 35: 270 - 273.

NANKEEN KESTREL

Bev Woolley

Family: Falconidae **Species:** *Falco cenchroides*
Common name: Nankeen Kestrel, Australian Kestrel
Status: Native
Size: 330 mm (cf sparrow 145, New Zealand Falcon 430 mm)

Discussion: The Nankeen Kestrel is a regular visitor to New Zealand from Australia where it inhabits open pastureland and light bush country as well as sometimes moving into urban environments. In New Zealand it appears to prefer similar habitats.

Habitat: Open pastureland.
Range: Isolated reports come from both the North and South Island.

Description - male:
Head and neck: Blue-grey. **Back and upperwings:** Cinnamon-brown with black primaries. **Underparts:** White, with wash of buff on upperbreast. **Tail:** Grey with a black tip. **Ceres (above bill):** Yellow. **Eye:** Brown, with a thin yellow eye-ring. **Bill:** Horn coloured with a black tip. **Legs:** Yellow, with black claws.

Description - female:
Head: Rufous with some black streaking. **Upperparts:** Cinnamon-brown, feathers spotted or streaked black. **Underparts:** Light brown breast to white abdomen. **Tail:** Brown, barred with 10 rows of black and a black tip to tail.

Conspicuous features:
- Small size makes it a distinctive raptor in New Zealand.
- Black feather centre markings are noticeable.
- Has pointed wings and a long tail.

Conspicuous characteristics:
- Hovers in flight above prey before gliding down.
- Tends to fly with fast wing beats and then soars with flat wings.

Call: Shrill, excited chatter.
Nest: It nests in rock cavities, on cliff ledges or in old trees. Up to 5 buff, reddish-blotched eggs are laid. Nesting has not been recorded in New Zealand.

Where to find - recent localities:
Northland - Waipu: In the area around the village of Waipu and along Highway 1 near the town, one bird was recorded in 1996.
Auckland - Taupaki: A bird has been regularly seen in this locality, which is between Waitakere and Kumeu, during the latter part of 2000. Try the area north of the Bethells Road.
North Waikato - Naike: A bird was seen and photographed near the Naike school west of Huntly. Follow the Rotongaro road and carry on until you reach the sign saying Naike. This has been a regular location for this species.
Hawkes Bay - Te Mata: Te Mata peak is well signposted from the south-east of Havelock North town. Drive right to the summit.

General: Birds regularly turn up in both the North and South Island.

CALIFORNIAN QUAIL

Jim Hague

Family: Phasianidae   **Species:** *Lophortyx californicus*
Common name: Californian Quail   **Status:** Introduced
Discussion: This is an imported game bird which has established well. Like the
    Brown Quail, Californian Quail are absent from bare pastoral areas.

Habitat: A bird of rough scrubland, and pastureland which contains sufficient
    wilderness to provide nesting areas. It is a regular roadside species in areas of
    dense roadside verges.
Range: Found in both islands away from forest and away from closely settled
    pastoral land. Absent from Fiordland and some parts of Westland.

Description - male:
    Forehead: Grey to the eye. **Crown:** Black, with a white edge band and a
    black crest feather which leans forward. **Face and chin:** Black, edged with a
    white-curved throat collar. **Neck:** Black and white spotting. **Wings:** Dark grey.
    Breast: Grey. **Underparts:** Buff, feathers edged with black to give a horizontal
    scaly effect. Chestnut hue to middle abdomen. **Bill:** Black. **Legs and feet:**
    Grey.
Description - female:
    Head, breast and upperparts: Duller than the male and tending to brown.
    Crest feather: Shorter than male. **Underparts:** Similar to male.
Conspicuous features:
- Look for the black and white on the head of the male bird.
- Look for top-knot feather which separates it from the Brown Quail.
- Look for the scaly pattern on abdomen.

Conspicuous characteristics:
- Usually to be found in pairs or coveys.
- When disturbed birds run and then fly off with whirr of wings.
- Male birds will call for lengthy periods from a conspicuous perch.

Call: A noisy tri-syllabic "ki kuu kuu".

Nest: A hollow in grasses. Up to 13 cream, brown-blotched eggs are laid. Usually a late breeder with chicks being hatched from mid-December onwards.

Where to find - North and South Islands:

North Island: Common in areas of scrubland and wilderness.

South Island: Common in open countryside with sufficient cover. Absent from Southland, Fiordland and southern parts of Westland.

General: Found in many districts in both islands.

BOBWHITE QUAIL

Brian Chudleigh

Family: Phasianidae   **Species:** *Colinus virginianus*
Common name: Bobwhite Quail   **Status:** Introduced
Size: 230 mm (cf sparrow 145 mm, Californian Quail 250mm)

Discussion: Introduced from North America as a game bird, the Bobwhite Quail has not been successful. Last reports of this bird came from the Ruatahuna district and the Tuai districts near Lake Waikaremoana in 1978.

Habitat: A bird of rough farmland where cover is plentiful.

Range: Unknown but probably still surviving in the Tuai district.

Description - male:
    Crown: Dark brown, edged with black. **Face and chin:** White, with a black stripe under eye to back of head. **Upperparts:** Grey, barred with black. **Underparts:** Grey, lightly barred with black. **Flanks:** Chestnut longitudinal barring. **Bill:** Black. **Legs and feet:** Yellow.

Description - female: Face and chin yellowish-buff with brownish upperparts and underparts lightly barred with black.

Conspicuous features:
- Smaller than the Californian Quail.
- White markings on face and chin are distinctive.

Call: A loud "bobwhite bobwhite bobwhite". Sometimes "bob-bobwhite".

Nest: On ground among grass. Up to 7 white eggs are laid.

Where to find - North Island:

Urewera - Lake Waikaremoana: Try the Ruatahuna district before you reach Lake Waikaremoana.

Tuai district: Look for it when you leave the Urewera National Park, in the first pastureland you come to.

RED-LEGGED PARTRIDGE

Brian Chudleigh

Family: Phasianidae   **Species:** *Alectoris rufa*
Common name: Red-legged Partridge   **Status:** Introduced
Size: 310mm (cf sparrow 145 mm, Californian Quail 250 mm)

Discussion: This species is very similar to the Chukor. It is a recent introduction to New Zealand from England but its establishment is slow.

Habitat: Open pastureland in areas of steeper and poorer pastures.

Range: Releases have been undertaken in several districts from North Auckland to the King Country to Hawkes Bay. Also in Nelson, Marlborough and Canterbury districts. A South Auckland release near Waerenga and the foothills of the Hauraki Plains persists.

Description: As for Chukor but with noticeable black spotting on upperbreast and throat. **Face and chin:** White, the white ringed with a narrow black band. **Neck and throat:** Black necklace-like collar. **Head and nape:** Grey tinged with red. **Upperparts:** Grey. **Underparts:** Grey tinged with brown. **Sides**

149

and flanks: Vertically barred with alternate black, white and chestnut lines. **Bill:** Red. **Legs and feet:** Pink.

Conspicuous features:
- Look for the black, white and chestnut vertical barring on sides and flanks.
- Look for the necklace of black and white spotting.

Call: A loud high-pitched carrying "chuck chuck chuck chukar" call, similar to Chukor.

Nest: A hollow in grasses on ground, among thick cover. Up to 14 olive-brown eggs are laid.

Where to find - North Island:

South Auckland - Mangatarata: Try anywhere along North Road which is the first road to the right at the commencement of Highway 27 near the Hauraki Plains. Try also South Road and Torehape Road in the same district.

South Auckland - Matahura: Leave Highway 27 at Kaihere and take Matahura Road. From Matahura drive north to Stannards Road. Anywhere along these roads this bird might be seen.

South Auckland - Miranda: Mangatarata birds have now spread north and have been sighted at Miranda. Look for them along the Back Miranda Road.

Where to find - South Island:

North Canterbury - Kaikoura: Reports of birds come from the South Bay area on the peninsula, east of the town.

Canterbury - Lake Ellesmere: Some sightings have come from this locality.

Canterbury - Rakaia River: Has been released in rough areas in the upper Rakaia River.

CHUKOR

Family: Phasianidae   **Species:** *Alectoris chukar*
Common name: Chukor   **Status:** Introduced
Size: 310 mm (cf sparrow 145 mm, Californian Quail 250 mm)

Discussion: The Chukor is a native of India. It was introduced into New Zealand in 1926 as a game bird and has since established itself on the dry hills and mountains of Central Otago in the South Island.

Habitat: Lives in rocky areas of low rainfall up to the snow line.
Range: Well spread from Queenstown through Central Otago and north to the Rolleston Range west of Christchurch.

Description:

Head and nape: Grey tinged with red, with a faint white stripe above eye. **Face and chin:** White, the white ringed with a narrow black band. **Upperparts:** Grey. **Underparts:** Grey tinged with brown. **Sides and flanks:** Vertically barred with alternate black, white and chestnut lines. **Bill:** Red. **Legs and feet:** Pink.

Conspicuous features:
- Look for the black, white and chestnut vertical barring on sides and flanks.
- White face with frame of black is distinctive.

Call: Usually a carrying, high-pitched "chuck chuck chuck chukar".

Nest: A hollow in grasses or tussock on the ground. Up to 14 cream, brown-blotched eggs are laid.

Brian Chudleigh

Chukor

Where to find - North Island:

Wairarapa - Herbertville: Chukor were released in Hawkes Bay and there have been regular sightings from the Weber and Herbertville areas, with some increase in numbers being reported. Follow Highway 52 from Eketahuna or the Waitahora Road from Dannevirke. No definite locations are known.

Where to find - South Island:

Central Otago - Crown Range: This road links Wanaka with Arrowtown. It climbs very steeply, zigzagging up the mountain-side through tussock lands. A stop somewhere along this road may find Chukor.

South Canterbury - Lake Alexandrina: Watch for it on the barren looking hills which overlook the lake.

South Canterbury - Lake Tekapo: The Mount John Observatory which is near the eastern end of Lake Alexandrina, has regular sightings of Chukor. The observatory is not accessible to the public although surrounding areas can be accessed from the Lake Alexandrina and Lake McGregor Road.

South Canterbury - Lake Pukaki: The road to Mount Cook is good Chukor country. So too are The Hermitage walking tracks at Mount Cook.

GREY PARTRIDGE

Auckland Fish and Game Council

Family: Phasianidae **Species:** *Perdix perdix*
Common name: Grey Partridge **Status:** Introduced
Size: 300mm (cf sparrow 145 mm, Californian Quail 250 mm)

Discussion: The Grey Partridge was introduced from England in 1962. It was widely liberated. Although an extremely common species in Great Britain and Europe, it has not quickly established itself in New Zealand and its last stronghold in the Winton area of Southland has not recorded sightings for several years. Visitors to this area should watch for it and report sightings.

Habitat: Rough pastureland and roadside verges.
Range: Southland only.

Description - male:
  Head: Face and throat reddish brown, with grey crown. **Upperparts:** Brown, streaked and spotted with buff. **Underparts:** Grey, with wavy lines of grey. **Sides and flanks:** Vertically barred with chestnut and grey lines. **Abdomen:** Grey, with a horseshoe-shaped dark chestnut marking.
Description - female: Similar to male but paler and with indistinct horseshoe-shaped abdomen marking.
Conspicuous features:
  • Look for the dark chestnut abdomen marking.
  • Look for the reddish-brown on face.
Conspicuous characteristics:
  • Has a crouching gait.
  • Never perches above the ground. This separates it from California Quail.
  • A fast flier with whirr of wings followed by a gliding spell.
Call: Loud high-pitched "keev" or "keevit".

Nest: On the ground in wasteland. Up to 12 olive-brown eggs are laid.

Where to find - South Island:
Southland - Heddon Bush: From Winton, north of Invercargill, take Highway 96 to Nightcaps then to Heddon Bush. There have been no recent sightings so the bird may have died out.

BROWN QUAIL

Brian Chudleigh.

Family: Phasianidae　　　　　　**Species:** *Synoicus ypsilophorus*
Common name: Brown Quail, Rat Quail　　**Status:** Introduced
Size: 180 mm (cf sparrow 145mm, Californian Quail 250 mm)

Discussion: The Brown Quail is an Australian introduction. It has had limited success in establishing breeding populations, appearing to be successful only in areas with undisturbed habitat such as in Northland, on the Coromandel Peninsula and in Hawkes Bay. It is considered to be similar in appearance to the now extinct New Zealand Quail (*Coturnix novaezealandiae*). It is also very similar in appearance to the Australian Stubble Quail *(C. pectoralis)*, of which the New Zealand Quail is considered by some authorities to be a race.

Habitat: Inhabits rough country which has plenty of vegetation cover such as manuka, broom, fern and gorse. It also likes areas which have natural roadside verges. It is not plentiful in areas of high fertility pastures.
Range: Found in the North Island from North Auckland to the Coromandel Peninsula, Bay of Plenty, King Country, Poverty Bay, Gisborne and Hawkes Bay.

Description:
　Crown: Dark brown, with a fine black spotting. **Upperparts:** Brown, mottled

with black and chestnut. **Throat:** Buff. **Underparts:** Greyish-buff, with black horizontal barring. **Bill:** Bluish-grey. **Legs and feet:** Yellow.

Conspicuous features:
- Overall brown colouring is distinctive.

Conspicuous characteristics:
- Has a small "rat like" appearance, hence its nick-name "rat quail".
- When disturbed it scuttles away into roadside verges with head down.
- Often seen in family groups over the summer months.
- Flies with a fast whirr of wings.
- Lacks the top-knot feathers of the Californian Quail

Call: Long drawn out, rising "ker-wee ker-wee", whistle.

Nest: A hollow in grass. Up to 12 white, brown-blotched eggs are laid.

Where to find - North Island:

Northland - Far North: The road to Cape Reinga is a good locality.

Northland - Bay of Islands: Regularly seen on roadside verges in this district, especially in the Peria district.

North Auckland - Tiri Tiri Island: Often seen sunning itself on the mown tracks and walkways. Here it is very approachable.

South Auckland - Miranda: Recorded in the hills behind the coastal flats.

Coromandel: Often seen in family parties north of Coromandel town.

Bay of Plenty - Pongakawa Valley: This area, near Lake Rotoiti and Lake Rotoehu has good populations. Try Pongakawa Road near Lake Rotoehu.

King Country - Mapara: Regularly seen here.

PHEASANT

Brian Chudleigh

Family: Phasianidae
Common name: Pheasant
Size: 800 mm (cf sparrow 145 mm)

Species: *Phasianus colchicus*
Status: Introduced

Discussion: Three subspecies of Pheasant were originally introduced to New Zealand for hunting purposes. They were the Black Pheasant (*P. c .colchicus*) from Europe, the White-collared Pheasant (*P. c. mongolicus*) from Mongolia and the Ring-necked Pheasant (*P. c. torquatus*) from China. Today the most common subspecies is the Ring-neck Pheasant. There is also the Melanistic Mutant Pheasant (*P. c. tenebrosus*) breeding true to form in some areas but not recognised as a subspecies by most authorities. It is a well established species which is bolstered by Fish and Game Council releases.

Habitat: Prefers a wooded city or country environment with plenty of cover.
Range: Ranges throughout the North Island away from forests, and in the Canterbury areas of the South Island.

Brian Chudleigh

Female Pheasant with chicks

Description - male bird - *P. c. torquatus*:
   Face: Red. **Head:** Black, with bluish tinge on neck. White neck-collar. Two short ear tufts are on each side of the crown. **Wings:** Grey with light brown. **Back:** Golden-brown with black speckling. **Rump:** Golden-brown. **Tail:** Buff-striped horizontally, with up to sixteen separate black bars. **Underparts:** Golden-buff with some black speckling. **Bill:** Light brown. **Legs:** Grey.
Description - female - *P. c. torquatus*: Overall a dull, buff coloured, bird.
Description - male - *P. c. colchicus*: Less colourful than *torquatus* being darker and lacking the white neck-collar.
Description - female - *P. c. colchicus*: As for *torquatus*.
Description - male - *P. c. mongolus*: Face wattle larger, plumage darker, and neck-collar thinner than *torquatus*. Wings lack grey colouring.
Description - female - *P. c. mongolus*: As for *torquatus*.
Description - male - *P. c. tenebrosus*: Back, breast and underparts, purplish-blue, scalloped with buff and red. Wings olive-black. Tail olive-brown with black horizontal barring.
Description - female - *P. c. tenebrosus*: Purplish-black.

Conspicuous features:
- The short ear-tufts are noticeable.

Conspicuous characteristics:
- Often seen gliding across gullies.
- When disturbed in grass it rises quickly with very fast wing beats.

Call: Loud "kor-r-kok" crow, accompanied whirring of wings before and after calling.

Nest: In dense grasses on the ground. Up to 9 olive-brown eggs are laid.

Where to find - North Island:

Northland: Common in many areas especially in the north.

Northland - Aroha Island: Usually birds here or in the surrounding district.

Auckland: Comes into city parks such as Cornwall Park.

South Auckland - Miranda - Kaiaua: The Melanistic Mutant Pheasant (*P. c. tenebrosus*) is regularly recorded in this area near the town. Further north of Kaiaua and south of Miranda *P. c. torquatus* becomes the common variety.

King Country: Common in many areas.

Where to find - South Island:

Marlborough: Regularly seen from Picton through to Collingwood.

Canterbury: Regularly seen from only Kaikoura south to Oamaru.

PEAFOWL

Brian Chudleigh

Family: Phasianidae **Species:** *Pavo cristatus*
Common name: Peafowl **Status:** Introduced
Size: 1000 mm (cf sparrow 145 mm, Pheasant 800mm)

Discussion: The Peafowl is a garden escape. It was introduced from India and Sri Lanka to adorn established gardens. However, some birds have now set up isolated colonies in the wild.

Habitat: In the wild it is a bird of scrublands and low bush in secluded areas. Also found in exotic pine forests.

Range: Largest colonies are in the Waitangi forest in Northland, along the Wanganui River and on the Mahia Peninsula, Hawkes Bay. Small numbers are found near Kaikoura and the north-western part of the South Island.

Description - male bird:
Crown, neck, breast and inner-wing primaries: Iridescent blue. A tuft of black fan-like feathers, tipped with blue, protrudes from crown. **Face:** White, with a black stripe through eye. **Chin:** Green. **Back:** Green. **Wings:** Tightly barred with buff, black and chestnut. **Underparts:** Iridescent green. **Tail:** This is the most conspicuous part of the male bird, especially in the mating season. When raised it forms a spreading fan of long green-coloured feathers studded with circular whirls of blue and brown.

Description - female:
Crown and neck: Metallic green. A tuft of fan-like feathers, tipped with green, protrudes from the back of head. **Face, chin and throat:** White with brown eye-stripe. **Upperparts:** Brown. **Breast:** Buff coloured. **Underparts:** Whitish.

Conspicuous features:
- The spread tail of the male bird is unmistakable.
- Look for the bright metallic blue on the neck of the male bird.

Conspicuous characteristics:
- At dusk they are very noisy as they gather together in trees for the night.
- Of a gregarious nature, lost birds become agitated, calling madly.

Call: Day call is a loud "may-wee". Evening call is more of a "wail".

Nest: Hollow in grasses and low vegetation. Up to 6 cream eggs are laid.

Where to find - North Island:
Northland - Bay of Islands: A large flock lives in the Waitangi State forest.
North Auckland - Whangaparaoa Peninsula: Try Shakespear Park.
South Auckland - Awhitu: Many on this peninsula
Bay of Plenty - Pongakawa District: Sometimes seen from the roadside.
King Country: Isolated populations in several districts.

Jim Hague
Female Peafowl

BANDED RAIL

Brian Chudleigh

Family: Rallidae   **Species:** *Rallus philippensis*
Common name: Banded Rail, Buff-banded Rail (Australia)
Status: Native
Size: 300 mm (cf sparrow 145 mm)

Discussion: The Banded Rail is a bird of several races which is distributed through South East Asia, Australia, New Zealand, and the Pacific islands east to Tahiti where it is now probably extinct on the main islands. The New Zealand race *assimilis* is found only in swampy areas and tidal estuaries whereas the Pacific and Australian species appear to be widespread through dry land areas, even feeding alongside roads

Habitat: A bird of wet gullies, swamps and lake verges. Coastal populations live in mangrove estuaries and among other types of estuary vegetation which provide sufficient cover. Evidence of its inland presence is sometimes proved by famers' cats catching birds.

Range: Found in the North Island in areas north of Aotea Harbour on the west coast and Ohiwa Harbour in the Bay of Plenty on the east. In the South Island, found in the north-west corner only. Found on Stewart Island.

Description:
    Crown: Chestnut. **Face and throat:** Prominent white stripe above eye. Chestnut stripe through eye with grey chin and throat. **Upperparts:** Olive-brown, marked with black and white. **Breast:** Horizontally striped with black and white with a buff band across the middle. **Underparts:** Horizontally barred with black and white. **Undertail:** Buff with horizontal black bars widely spaced. **Bill:** Brown.

Conspicuous features:
- Look for the white eye-stripe above the eye which extends a short way down the side of the neck.
- The buff-coloured breast band is noticeable.
- Look for the black and white barring on the abdomen.

Conspicuous characteristics:
- Birds feed actively with heads down.
- Bird often chase each other when feeding among mangroves.
- If disturbed birds quickly run for cover with heads down.
- Birds often walk when feeding with a measured gait.

Call: A high pitched "brurururu" sound is often heard from feeding birds. This may be followed by "tick tick tick" calls. At dawn or dusk a harsh "craak" is sometimes heard which sounds like a fence wire being stretched through rusty post staples.

Nest: A cup-shaped bowl in grasses or rushes, well hidden. Up to 5 pinkish, brown-blotched eggs are laid.

Best time of day to view: Birds can be viewed at any time of day. About two hours before or after full tide is a good time for estuary viewing. Birds are definitely more active just on dark when they venture out on to estuary mud from the mangrove or rush verges.

Use of tape-recorders: Birds will respond to tapes.

Telescopes: Because birds are active feeders, rather than fast feeders, they are easy to follow with a telescope.

Where to find - North Island:

Northland - Bay of Islands: Try the causeway verges at the Aroha Island Ecological Centre near Kerikeri. (See "Places" in back of book.)

Northland - Paihia: The Waitangi Estuary near Paihia, has a long verge which is good for Banded Rail. Cross the long bridge which leads towards the Treaty House and walk up the estuary verges.

North Auckland - Wenderholm: Turn down the first road to the right after Waiwera and travel right to the estuary edge where the mangroves start. Search this area. If the tide is full, search along adjacent pastures just in case the birds have come out of the estuary to feed. (See "Places" in back of book.)

South Auckland - Kaiaua: Try the Hauarahi River-mouth by the bridge, just north of the hotel, near where it flows into the Firth of Thames at Kaiaua.

South Auckland - Miranda, Access Bay: Follow the road sign which says "To the Beach", south of the Miranda Naturalists' Trust Centre. Search among the mangroves here. Also search the mangroves on the north side of the gateway into "The Limeworks" area north of the Pukorokoro River. Occasionally birds are seen around the Widgery Lake at the Miranda Naturalists' Trust Centre.

Coromandel - Opoutere: Try the Opoutere Estuary, north of Whangamata, near the first bridge before the cottages start. Look for Fernbirds here too.

Bay of Plenty - Kaituna River-mouth: Look around the lagoon verges.

Bay of Plenty - Matata Lagoons: Try the inland verge of the second lagoon (the east lagoon). After crossing the causeway look back into the verges.

Bay of Plenty - Ohiwa Harbour: From Ohope Beach the road runs around the shoreline of Ohiwa Harbour. Look for shoreline birds from the road.

Where to find - South Island:
Marlborough - Collingwood: The coast around Collingwood has birds.
Marlborough - Waimea Inlet: Verges in this area are worth examining.
Marlborough - Marahau Causeway: This location, just after Kaiteriteri Beach
and before the entrance to the Abel Tasman National Park, is reliable.

Where to find - Stewart Island:
Oban: Walk to Horseshoe Bay north of Oban and search the estuary verges.
Kaipipi Bay: Try Ryans Creek and Kaipipi Bay. To get there walk along the
road to the airstrip behind Oban and turn off into Fern Gully Road. The track
to Paterson Inlet leads off from here.

WEKA

Brian Chudleigh

Family: Rallidae   **Species:** *Gallirallus australis*
Common name: Weka   **Status:** Endemic
Size: 530 mm (cf sparrow 145 mm, Banded Rail 300 mm)

Discussion: The Weka is a large flightless rail, restricted in habitat to a few
forested and isolated areas of New Zealand where it continues to survive in
small numbers. In the North Island, where only a few populations persist,
breeding programmes are being undertaken. Earlier attempts to establish
populations in the Bay of Islands near Russell, at Mangere and Waitakere in
Auckland and in the Karangahake Gorge near Waihi have now failed.

The Weka shares a common ancestor with that of the smaller Banded Rail
(*Rallus philippensis*). This ancestor evolved in predator-free New Zealand, to
become larger in size than the Banded Rail and flightless, in common with
some other New Zealand species such as the Takahe (Fleming 1982). Close
allies of the Weka are the flightless New Caledonian Wood Rail (*Tricholimnas
lafresnayanus*) which is possibly extinct, and the Lord Howe Island Wood
Rail (*Tricholimnas sylvestris*) which survives on Lord Howe Island after a

captive breeding programme from a base of about 30 birds.

Races: The Weka comes in four distinct races based on plumage colour patterns, associated with geographic areas. These races are -
- The North Island race (*greyi*) which is distinguished by its greyish underparts and brown legs.
- The Eastern South Island race (*hectori*) known as the Buff Weka which is distinguished by its sandy-brown colouring and reddish legs.
- The Western South Island race or Black Weka (*australis*) which is distinguished by its dark blackish brown colouration although some birds lack the blackish colouring and appear instead deep chestnut-brown.
- The Stewart Island Weka (*scotti*) which is distinguished by paler colourings all over when compared with the western form. It has grey tonings on the abdomen.

Habitat: The Weka is a bird of forests, scrubland, fringes of estuaries, coastal beaches, roadside verges and rough pastureland.

Range: In the North Island, Weka are confined to isolated areas such as Rakitu (Arid) Island, Kawau Island, the Raukumara Forest Park, Mokoia Island, Tolaga Bay, Gisborne and Kapiti Island. In the South Island the bulk of the population is in the north-west corner, Westland and Fiordland. Also on Stewart Island.

Description:
   Upperparts and underparts: Brown with black markings. (See above under races for variations.)
Conspicuous features:
- Not unlike a slim version of a domestic fowl but with a heavier bill.

Conspicuous characteristics:
- Slinks through the forest with head low to the ground and tail raised.
- An inquisitive bird which will warily approach humans.
- A flightless bird which can raise itself into the air to about one metre.
- Capable of very fast running.
- A bird which defends its territories with fast chases.
- North Island birds are less confiding than South, and Stewart Island birds.

Call: A loud rapidly repeated "cooeet cooeet cooeet", heard day or night.

Nest: A bowl in grasses or low vegetation, on the ground, lined with fine grass. Up to 5 pinkish eggs are laid.

Best viewing times: Can be see throughout the day but birds are usually more active at dusk. At Kawau Island, Pelorus Bridge and Ulva Island, Weka are friendly and come out and investigate the human visitor at any time of day.

Where to find - North Island:

North Auckland - Kawau Island: This is the easiest population to view in the North Island. (See "Places" in back of book.)

Rotorua: An introduced colony of Weka on Mokoia Island in Lake Rotorua provide an opportunity, although the birds here are not very confiding.

Eastland - Toatoa: Take the Motu Road, east of Opotiki and drive into the forests for about 25 kms.

Wellington - Kapiti Island: A good population can be found here.

Where to find - South Island:

Marlborough - Picton to Nelson area: Weka can be found near the road between Picton and Havelock on Queen Charlotte Drive.

Marlborough - Pelorus Bridge: A good locality is at Pelorus Bridge located after Havelock on way to Nelson. It is well signposted.

Westland: Regularly seen on roadside verges in many places in Westland including the Westport and Punakaiki districts.

Westland - Cape Foulwind: Try Wilsons Lead Road, south of Westport and south of the Bullers Gorge Road. This leads west to Cape Foulwind.

Fiordland: Walking tracks throughout Fiordland have Weka. They are seldom seen around Cascade Creek or the Lake Gunn walk although they are probably in the vicinity. Regularly seen at The Divide further up the Eglinton Valley and near the Hollyford Valley.

Where to find - Stewart Island:

Ackers Point: The track to Ackers Point on the arm of Half Moon Bay, usually has Weka, especially near dusk.

Ulva Island: This small island in Paterson Inlet has many Weka.

SPOTLESS CRAKE

Geoff Moon

Family: Rallidae   **Species:** *Porzana tabuensis*
Common name: Spotless Crake   **Status:** Native
Size: 600 mm (cf sparrow 145 mm, Marsh Crake 180 mm)

Discussion: Spotless Crake have a wide distribution through the Philippines, New Guinea, Australia, New Zealand and the Pacific Islands to Tahiti. The genus *Porzana*, which totals 12 species worldwide, is found in many countries throughout the world but not on the continents of North and South America. New Zealand has two species, the Spotless Crake (*Porzana tabuensis*) and the

Marsh Crake (*P. pusilla*). The Spotless Crake is regarded as a fairly recent colonist but because of its secretive habits, it is a relatively little known species.

Habitat: Confined generally to wetland habitat and lake verges. These are usually swamps which contain raupo (*Typha augustifolia*) with an over-storey of manuka (*Leptospermum scoparium*). On the off-shore islands, and on the Poor Knights and Tiri Tiri Island in particular, Spotless Crakes are forest dwellers living away from wetlands. This suggests that mainland birds are living in relic habitats.

Range: Throughout the North Island, and Westland, Marlborough, North Canterbury and Southland in the South Island. The range of Spotless Crakes throughout New Zealand is being added to all the time.

Description:

Head and nape: Black. **Back and wings:** Dull brown. **Underparts:** Dark grey. **Eye:** Red with red eye-ring.

Conspicuous features:
- Look for the red eye.
- The brown of back and wings is noticeable in good light only.

Conspicuous characteristics:
- Birds will fly up from cover if startled by a metallic sound or an engine.
- Birds run quickly when away from cover.

Call: Sounds are varied. The most common is a "mook mook mook mook", often followed by a "brururur" bubbly type call. Also isolated "mook" sounds.

Nest: On the ground in grass or rushes. Up to 4 pinkish-cream eggs are laid.

Response to tape-recorders: Birds will warily investigate recorded sounds at any time of day. They will run across open ground to investigate.

Where to find - North Island:

Northland - Bay of Islands: Try the swampy areas in the Waitangi State Forest. Try the swamp verges at Aroha Island near Kerikeri.

North Auckland - Tiri Tiri Island: Spotless Crakes can usually be heard from the bush tracks. There is a pair beside the pond up from the wharf, and a pair near the seating area on the Wattle Track.

North Auckland - Waiwera: Roadside patches of raupo near Strakas Refuge have birds. Travel along Weranui Road from Waiwera and inspect areas of wetland on the inside road verges for about 2 kms.

South Auckland - Torehape East Road: This locality, on the Hauraki Plains, is accessed from Torehape East Road off Highway 27, approximately 7 kms from the start of the highway. Travel 800 metres east from where the pastureland stops and look for an old gate which leads into the swamp.

North Waikato - Whangamarino: Whangamarino is a large swamp east of the Meremere Power Station off Highway 1. Spotless Crake are known along the causeway. (See Bittern article.)

Waikato - Oparau: From Te Awamutu, south of Hamilton, take Highway 31 to Kawhia. At Oparau turn left and travel for approximately 6 kms when some swampy, raupo type wetlands appear on the left, backed by forest. A causeway runs into a farm property nearby. Fernbirds are also here.

Bay of Plenty - Matata Lagoon: Verges of the lagoons have crake. The best area to try is a gravel road east of the main lagoons which leads down to the mouth of the Tarawera River.

Lake Taupo: Try main road raupo patches about 5 kms south of Taupo. Past Waitahanui drive straight ahead to Lake Rotongaio. The wetlands here have Spotless Crakes.

Lake Taupo - Turangi: Try the wet verges along its southern shores.

Where to find - South Island:

Marlborough - Lake Elterwater: Try the reed verge at south end.

North Canterbury - St Annes Lagoon: This small lake just north of Cheviot has now recorded several breeding pairs in its raupo verges.

Westland: Try any swampy areas in this district.

Westland - Lake Kaniere: Try the swampy verges to this lake.

Southland - Lake Manapouri: Swamp areas in the Blackmount Road area have crake. Marsh Crake are also here.

Southland - Redcliff Wildlife Reserve: From Manapouri town take Weir Road and then turn right into Blackmount Road. Travel along Blackmount Road for about 14 kms.

Southland - Awarua Bay: Try the rough verges of this bay.

Southland - Lake Murihiku: This lake near Invercargill is worth a try. (See Marsh Crake article.)

General: New records show that many localities have both species.

MARSH CRAKE

Brian Chudleigh

Family: Rallidae   **Species:** *Porzana pusilla*
Common name: Marsh Crake, Baillons Crake   **Status:** Native
Size: 180 mm (cf sparrow 145 mm, Spotless Crake 200 mm)

Discussion: Widely spread world-wide, breeding through the southern Mediterranean, Asia, Indonesia, The Philippines, New Guinea, Australia and New Zealand. In New Zealand this species is becoming better known and nests have recently been studied.

Habitat: A bird of swamps and wetlands and the raupo margins of lakes. It shares a similar habitat to that of the Spotless Crake.

Range: Generally considered to be more common in the South Island but as time goes by, more and more North Island localities are being discovered.

Description:
Face, throat and breast: Dark grey. **Crown and upperparts:** Brown. **Wings:** Brown, with black and white mottling on secondary feathers. **Back:** Black, with some white mottling. **Abdomen:** Horizontally streaked with black and white. **Bill, legs and feet:** Greenish.

Conspicuous features:
- A small bird, slightly smaller than the Spotless Crake.
- Look for the undertail barring and white flecking on back and wings.
- Note the paler colouring which differentiates it from the Spotless Crake.

Call: A harsh "krek krek krek" is often heard at night. This is the most common sound made by this bird but a harsh trill might also be heard.

Nest: A platform of grass and twigs in a wet area, often with water under it, attached to a rush bush. Up to 5 olive-brown eggs are laid.

Use of tape-recorders: Marsh Crakes will investigate the recorded songs of Spotless Crakes. When using taped songs, select a place which will cause the birds to come out of the rushes and show themselves.

Best time of day for viewing: Marsh Crakes are known to call more actively at night.

Where to find - North Island:

North Waikato - Whangamarino swamp: A dead bird was found under a bridge on the Meremere causeway in 1989. No sights of live birds have been recorded here. (See Bittern article.)

South Waikato – Lake Ngaroto: This lake is accessed from Te Awamutu. A board walk has been constructed around much of it and Marsh Crakes have been recorded from it.

Lake Taupo: All the swampy roadside verges from Motuoapa to Turangi on Highway 1, and from Turangi to Waihi on Highway 4, are Marsh Crake territory. These localities are at the southern end of the lake. Remember that most areas in this district will also have Fernbird and Spotless Crake.

Bay of Plenty - Tauranga Harbour: Saltmarsh type wet verges to the harbour are suitable Marsh Crake habitat.

Bay of Plenty - Omokoroa: Try the Cooney Reserve at the end of Margaret Place near the Omokoroa camping ground. Search the lagoon verges.

Bay of Plenty - Matata Lagoons: Try the wet areas east of the second lagoon. Take the dirt road by the Tarawera River-mouth and search wet areas on left when heading to the coast.

Bay of Plenty - Ohiwa Harbour: Try the verges of the harbour in accessible areas near the road to Opotiki. (See Banded Rail article.)

Where to find - South Island:

Marlborough - Nelson District: Try the harbour verges of Waimea Inlet near Nelson or the swampy verges along Queen Charlotte Sound.

Marlborough - Kaiteriteri Beach: From Kaiteriteri Beach travel west to Marahau. Look for birds from the Marahau causeway which leads into Abel Tasman National Park. (See Banded Rail article.)

Westland - Lake Kaniere: This lake is due east of the town of Hokitika. Its lake verges are known for Marsh Crake.

Southland - Lake Manapouri: There are some good swampy areas for Marsh Crake on the Blackmount Road.

Southland - Redcliff Wildlife Reserve: Try the swampy areas here. This area is accessed off Blackmount Road.

Southland - Awarua Estuary: The verges of Awarua Bay near Invercargill have Marsh Crake. Take the road to Tiwai Point and the aluminium smelter, which leads south from Woodend. Before the bay is crossed turn east and explore the rough areas well along this road.

Southland - Lake Murihiku: Take Longford Road west of Invercargill City. Turn south into Otatara Road and then west into Coggins Road. Lake Murihiku lies almost at the junction of Hughes and Coggins Road. This is an excellent Marsh Crake habitat.

General: Note that this is a difficult bird to find and one missed by many local birders. A planned strategy, plus a tape-recorder and patience might find it.

Reference: Barlow M; Sutton R R 1975. Nest of a Marsh Crake. Notornis 22

PUKEKO

Brian Chudleigh

Family: Rallidae
Common name: Pukeko, Swamp Hen
Size: 510 mm (cf sparrow 145 mm)

Species: *Porphyrio porphyrio*
Status: Native

Discussion: The Pukeko is a common New Zealand bird and is on the shooting list as a game bird. It is a cosmopolitan species well-spread through parts of southern Europe, Asia, Africa, Australia, New Zealand and many of the Pacific islands. Its ancestry is linked with the Takahe.

Habitat: Generally a bird of wetlands and lake verges but often it can be seen feeding well out into pasture areas and along road verges.

Range: Found throughout North, South and Stewart Islands and on some off-shore islands. A small population is found on the Chatham Islands.

Description:
  Upperparts: Black. **Underparts:** Purple. **Undertail:** White. **Bill and frontal shield:** Red. **Legs and Feet:** Orange-red.

Conspicuous features:
- Look for purple breast and underparts.
- White undertail is noticeable.

Conspicuous characteristics:
- Flies with rapid wing beats and reddish legs trailing.
- If alarmed, runs rapidly through grass or rushes with head down and with white tail patch conspicuous.
- Birds when in territories during the breeding season noisily challenge and fight birds from neighbouring territories.

Call: A variety of harsh screech sounds and a booming "pu-ku pu-ku" are common. Also a rapid "kuweek kuweek".

Nest: A platform of grasses in among rushes. Up to 10 buff, brown-blotched eggs are laid. Birds usually form pairs but polygamous relationships are sometimes established, with all birds sharing incubation and rearing.

Where to find: Common anywhere where there is water.

TAKAKE

Family: Rallidae   **Species:** *Porphyrio mantelli*
Common name: Takahe, Notornis (from *Notornis mantelli*)
Status: Endemic
Size: 630 mm (cf sparrow 145 mm, Pukeko 510 mm)

Discussion: The Takahe was thought to be extinct. It was rediscovered in 1948 by Dr G B Orbell in the Murchison Mountains above the shores of Lake Te Anau on its western side. Following this discovery the area became a sanctuary. Captive reared birds have now been released on Tiri Tiri Island, Kapiti Island, Mana Island (Wellington) and Maud Island (Marlborough Sounds) where they are now breeding successfully.

Ancestry: The Takahe is an ancient New Zealand bird with an ancestry linked to Purple Gallinule stock similar to the common Pukeko. In ancient, predator-free New Zealand this ancestor diverged, becoming flightless, slow moving, large in size and slow breeding. As such it succumbed to predators and the ravages of a changed landscape after settlement by Europeans (Fleming 1982).

Takahe

Habitat: Lives in high tussock-lands where it feeds on tussock shoots, fern roots and alpine grasses. Sub-fossil bone deposits though, link the Takahe to a wide range of habitat from forests to grasslands at lower altitudes.

Range: The Takahe was once widely spread over both the North and South Islands. Today it is naturally confined to the Murchison Mountains.

Description:
> **Head:** Indigo-blue. **Upperparts:** Olive-green. **Wings:** Olive-green. **Underparts:** Indigo-blue. **Undertail:** White. **Bill and frontal shield:** Red. **Legs:** Red.

Conspicuous features:
- Look for its large size, and features similar to a Pukeko.
- Heavy bill is noticeable.

Conspicuous characteristics:
- Birds are slow moving when feeding.
- Its rather cumbersome gait is noticeable.

Where to find - North Island:

North Auckland - Tiri Tiri Island: This island gives a very good chance of seeing this bird. Pairs are now widely spread in territories and are breeding. (See "Places" in back of book.)

Wellington - Kapiti Island: (See "Places" in back of book.)

Where to find - South Island:

Marlborough - Maud Island: To get a permit approach the Department of Conservation at Blenheim. (See "Places" in back of book.)

Murchison Mountains: To get a permit and directions approach the Department of Conservation at Te Anau.

Captive Takahe: Visit the Mount Bruce National Wildlife Centre near Eketahuna or the Te Anau Wildlife Centre. (See "Places" in back of book.)

AUSTRALASIAN COOT

Brian Chudleigh

Family: Rallidae
Common name: Coot
Size: 380 mm (cf sparrow 145 mm, Scaup 400 mm)

Species: *Fulica atra*
Status: Native

Discussion: The Australasian Coot is a recent arrival in New Zealand from Australia with breeding populations establishing themselves in the 1960s in both the North and South Islands. This species is widespread, worldwide, from Europe, Asia, Australia and now to New Zealand where it has built up a sizeable breeding population in many locations.

Habitat: A bird of clean-water lakes where it feeds among the rush and raupo verge, diving for food which is largely of vegetable matter.
Range: In the North Island from North Auckland south, and on the eastern side of the South Island from Kaikoura to Oamaru.

Description:
  Upperparts: Black. **Underparts:** Dull black, sometimes tending to greyish.
  Bill and frontal shield: White. **Legs and feet:** Grey with lobes on toes.

Conspicuous features:
  • White bill and frontal shield is noticeable.
  • Look for lobed toes if birds are out of the water.
Conspicuous characteristics:
  • Flight is low and fast but seldom observed.
  • Has a habit of bobbing its head while it is swimming.
  • Birds regularly dive.
  • Birds bring up food for young and feed them on the water.
  • Birds usually prefer still water and not river currents.
Call: A "krark krark" sound is the usual call.

Nest: A floating platform of rushes and twigs anchored to a rush bush. Up to 8 creamy eggs are laid.

Where to find - North Island:

Auckland - Birkenhead: Try the Chelsea Sugar Refinery lake. Travel down Colonial Road from Mokoia Road until the lake comes into view.

Auckland - Western Springs: Try Western Springs Lake. This is located off Great North Road in the suburb of Grey Lynn. From Karangahape Road at the top of Queen Street follow along into Great North Road and until the sign says Western Springs. There are coots and waterfowl here and sometimes a few Cape Barren Geese which have flown in from the nearby Auckland Zoo.

Hamilton - Lake Rotoroa or Hamilton Lake: From Victoria Street turn west into Collingwood Street and follow to the end. Turn left into Ruakiwi Road and follow along until the lake gates on the right are recognised.

Rotorua: Many of the Rotorua Lakes have coot. Try Lake Okareka which has a large population. (See Scaup article.)

Lake Taupo: Often seen near Motuoapa on Highway 1, approximately 30 kms from Taupo towards Turangi.

Hawkes Bay - Lake Tutira: This lake is situated 30 kms north of Napier on Highway 2. It can be viewed from the road. It has many coots.

Wanganui: Virginia Lake in Wanganui was one of the first lakes colonised by coot and many new colonies have spread from it. Take the New Plymouth road out of Wanganui. Virginia Lake is on the right before you leave the city.

Manawutu - Palmerston North: The Centennial Lake has a large population. Travel along Fitzherbert Avenue towards Massey University and turn left before the Fitzherbert Bridge. Travel along Hardie Street to Jickle Street and then right, and around to the lake.

Where to find - South Island:

North Canterbury - Cheviot: St Annes Lagoon near Cheviot in North Canterbury has a good population. (See "Places" in back of book.)

Canterbury - Lake Ellesmere: Try Timber Yard Road and the domain at Lakeside. From Leeston take the Leeston - Lake Road and turn left into Timber Yard Road and follow to end. (See Mute Swan article.)

South Canterbury - Lake Alexandrina: This lake and Lake McGregor, near Lake Tekapo, have establishing populations. Just south of Tekapo turn right up Lake McGregor Road. After approximately 3 kms turn left into the road which leads into Lake Alexandrina. (See Crested Grebe article.)

Queenstown - Lake Hayes: From Queenstown travel to Frankton and turn left on to the Lake Hayes road. There is a breeding population here. (See Crested Grebe article.)

Southland - Lake Te Anau: Look for birds at its southern end.

SOUTH ISLAND PIED OYSTERCATCHER

Brian Chudleigh

Family: Haematopodidae   **Species:** *Haematopus ostralegus finschi*
Common name: South Island Pied Oystercatcher, S.I.P.O., Redbill
Status: Endemic
Size: 460 mm (cf sparrow 145 mm)

Discussion: The South Island Pied Oystercatcher has increased in numbers since agricultural development started in New Zealand to become its most common wading birds. The Firth of Thames had 29,000 in June 1999. This species (*H. o. finschi*), is closely related to the European Oystercatcher (*H. ostralegus*) with which it shares many similar characteristics such as size, colouration, nesting habits, chick rearing and chick feeding behaviour, and the migration habit to warmer coastal areas in winter.

Habitat - breeding: During the breeding months of August to January birds live in inland areas of Otago and Southland in the South Island. Here they take up nesting territories along riverbeds, on pastureland and among arable crops. A few oystercatchers, probably immature birds, always summer over on the traditional wintering grounds.
Habitat - wintering: From January onwards they move north to coastal estuaries and harbours.
Range: In the North Island, from the Bay of Plenty northwards, especially in the Kaipara and Manukau Harbours and the Firth of Thames in winter. Inland in the South Island over summer months. Also on Stewart Island.

Description:
  Upperparts: Black. **Underparts:** White. **Bill, eyes and legs:** Red.

Differences between South Island Pied Oystercatcher (*H. ostralegus*) and Variable Oystercatcher (*H. unicolor*):

- The South Island Pied Oystercatcher has a clean cut line between the white underparts and the black upperparts - lacking on the Variable.
- The South Island Pied Oystercatcher has two clean cut white shoulder tabs which reach up into the black upperparts - lacking on the Variable.
- The South Island Pied Oystercatcher appears a neater and smaller bird.
- The South Island Pied Oystercatcher has a slimmer bill.

Characteristic differences between South Island Pied Oystercatcher and Variable Oystercatchers:

- The South Island Pied Oystercatcher is an inland nester and does not nest along the coast. The Variable nests along the coast.
- The South Island Pied Oystercatcher has a different starting time for its nesting season, laying its eggs in August, while the Variable starts nesting in mid-October with a second brood in December or early January.
- The South Island Pied Oystercatcher migrates north from the breeding grounds. The Variable tends to form up into small coastal flocks not far from breeding areas. Some remain resident on their breeding territories from one year to the next.

Similar characteristics of each species:

- Both birds have similar, "keeleep keeleep" type calls.
- Both species defend nesting territories with broken wing type displays.
- Both species feed their young until the fledgling stage, being the only wader to actually feed its chicks.
- Both species have similar pale, buffish-brown eggs, marked with black dots and splotches. Clutch size in both species is usually three eggs for the first brood and two eggs for the second or replacement broods.

Call: Noisy "kleep kleep kleep" calls.

Nest: A scrape on the ground. 2 brown, blotched dark-brown eggs are laid.

Where to find - North Island:

Auckland - Manukau Harbour: The Mangere Sewage Ponds are an easy locality to find this bird. (See "Places" in back of book.)

Auckland: Most Auckland beaches have oystercatchers if human interference is not too great. Try Howick Beach or Cockle Bay in east Auckland.

South Auckland - Miranda: Any of the beaches, after leaving Clevedon will have South Island Pied Oystercatcher. The Firth of Thames coast from Matingarahi to Miranda has large numbers at any tide.

Where to find - South Island:

Southland: Very common along the road from Invercargill to Te Anau in spring. Often birds will be seen here with Paradise Shelduck, Spur-winged Plover, Black-fronted Tern and Black-billed Gull all together.

VARIABLE OYSTERCATCHER

Brian Chudleigh

Family: Haematopodidae **Species:** *Haematopus unicolor*
Common name: Variable Oystercatcher, Black Oystercatcher (South Island)
Status: Endemic
Size: 480 mm (cf sparrow 145mm, South Island Pied Oystercatcher 460mm)

Discussion: The Variable Oystercatcher is considered a close relative of the
Australian Sooty Oystercatcher (*H. fuliginosus*) but it differs from the Australian
bird in that it is polymorphic as to colouration, coming in three colour phases
- black all over; with whitish breast markings; or distinctly pied not unlike the
South Island Pied Oystercatcher. Variable Oystercatchers of Southland and
Stewart Island are usually all black.

Habitat: A bird of coastal areas only, which inhabits sandy beaches, mudflats
and rocky promontories.
Range: Found around Northland, the Bay of Plenty and down the east coast to
Wellington and up to Wanganui, but with a gap around the Taranaki coast.
Around the South Island, gaps are found along the coasts of Canterbury and
south Westland.

Description - all black phase:
  Upperparts and underparts: Black. **Bill, legs and eyes:** Red.
Description - pied phase:
  Upperparts: Black. **Underparts:** White of various quantities. **Bill, legs and
  eyes:** Red.
Conspicuous features:
  • Birds appear heavier than South Island Pied Oystercatcher.
  • Look for the red bill, legs and eyes.
Call: A noisy bird with a call similar to South Island Pied Oystercatcher - a
melodic but quite aggressive, "keeleep keeleep".

Nest: A scrape on a sandy beach or rock shelf. Up to 3 brown, blotched dark-brown eggs are laid.

Where to find - North Island:
Northland: Most Northland beaches have breeding birds with territories at approximately 200 metres between nests.
North Auckland - Weiti (Wade) River: Usually birds near the Wade wharf.
South Auckland - Clevedon to Miranda: Always birds on beaches from Kawakawa Bay to Kaiaua, usually with South Island Pied Oystercatchers.
Wellington - Waikanae Estuary: Always birds here of both pied and black markings.

Where to find - South Island:
Otago Peninsula: Common on beaches here and opposite at Aramoana.
South Island: Common away from Canterbury and the lower west coast.

Where to find - Stewart Island:
Ulva Island: Variable Oystercatchers live on most of its small bays.

Identification problems: (See South Island Pied Oystercatcher article.)

CHATHAM ISLAND OYSTERCATCHER
(*H. chathamensis*)

Discussion: Considered a separate, endangered endemic, it is a residential species living on coastal outcrops and sandy beaches, and similar to the pied phase of the Variable Oystercatcher. It has though, a shorter bill and lacks the clean-cut white and black margins of the South Island Pied Oystercatcher.

Brian Chudleigh

174

PIED STILT

Brian Chudleigh

Family: Recurvirostridae   **Species:** *Himantopus himantopus*
Common name: Pied Stilt, Poaka (Maori)   **Status:** Native
Size: 350 mm (cf sparrow 145 mm, South Island Pied Oystercatcher 460 mm)

Discussion: The Pied Stilt is a race of the worldwide genus of Black-winged Stilts which is thought to have invaded New Zealand only since the arrival of the first Europeans. It is now widespread and is known to have interbred with New Zealand's endemic species, the Black Stilt. (See Black Stilt article.)

Similarity to Black-winged Stilts: The Pied Stilt is similar to other black-winged stilts but with the addition of an area of black at the back of the head which extends down the nape to a white collar separating it from the black of the wings.
Habitat: Estuaries, harbours with muddy fringes, wet areas, swamp verges and pastureland. Generally breeds inland although sometimes on coastal fringes. Many birds migrate to northern coastal areas over the winter months.
Range: Found throughout New Zealand where wet habitat is available.

Description:
   Back of neck and wings: Black, separated by a white collar. **Head and underparts:** White. **Bill:** Black. **Legs:** Pinkish.
Description - immature:
   Head: White, with varying amounts of smudgy black. **Wings:** Black, but paler than the adult bird. **Underparts:** White.
Conspicuous features:
- Generally an immaculate bird of black and white.
- Look for the long pinkish legs.

Conspicuous characteristics:
- Birds frequently fly at night indicated by their loud calling.
- Birds harass and scold intruders who come near to the nesting site.

Colour variations: Many New Zealand stilts have variable black colouration. These are hybrid birds, of varying degrees, resultant from a history of inter-breeding with Black Stilts. Immature birds also show some colour variation.

Call: A high-pitched "yep, yep, yep", barking noise.

Nest: Sometimes a colonial nester but often solitary making a cup-shaped nest of grasses on a mound. Up to 4 greenish, blotched with brown eggs are laid

Where to find - North and South Islands:

Auckland: Found on the upper reaches of the Waitemata Harbour, Hobson Bay, Tahuna Torea (see "Places" in back of book), and Howick Beach.

South Auckland - Manukau Harbour: In large numbers during winter in many parts of the harbour. Try Clarks Beach. (See Lesser Knot article.)

South Auckland - Miranda: Large numbers spend the winter here.

BLACK STILT

Brian Chudleigh

Family: Recurvirostridae   **Species:** *Himantopus novaezelandiae*
Common name: Black Stilt, Kaki (Maori)   **Status:** Endemic
Size: 400 mm (cf sparrow 145 mm, Pied Stilt 380 mm)

Discussion: The Black Stilt is an endangered New Zealand species with a population totalling about 34 birds. Its future is being determined by a breeding programme conducted both in captivity and in the wild. So far captive birds have bred successfully.

Historical: Both the Black Stilt and the Pied Stilt escaped notice during Cook's early explorations of New Zealand. Black Stilt were eventually collected in

176

1840 (Fleming 1982) but there were no records of Pied Stilts until the 1870s. This suggests that Black Stilts were the original stilt inhabitant of New Zealand with Pied Stilts coming later, probably from Australia.

Differences in nesting habits of Black and Pied Stilts: The increase in Pied Stilt numbers has paralleled the decline of the Black Stilt, even though Black Stilt and Pied Stilt occupy different nesting niches, with Black Stilt preferring shingle river-beds and Pied Stilt swamp verges, wetlands and coastal areas. Reasons for this decline have not been clearly established. It is currently considered, though, that a reduction in breeding habitat, plus predation by mustelids, rats and cats, on a species adapted to a predator-free environment, with associated slower maturing fledglings, has had something to do with it. Current interbreeding between Black Stilts and Pied Stilts is also suggested as another cause.

Note on melanism: Fleming (1982) noted that the Black Stilt had "followed 'the tendency to melanism' common among New Zealand species (New Zealand shags, oystercatchers, wekas, robins, tits and fantails)". He suggested this had come about because "a species in a predator-free land could relax the need for countershading or disruptive plumage patterns".

Classification: Some authorities have considered the Black Stilt a race of the genus *Himantopus* and have not given it separate species status. However, Pierce (1984), after a lengthy study, discovered that Black Stilts differed from Pied Stilt in the following ways -

- They possessed longer and broader bills. This, he determined, increased their feeding range allowing them to probe under stones for aquatic insects on dry land rather than having to maintain a strictly aquatic, shoreline, feeding station.
- They possessed a shorter tarsus indicating less reliance on water-wading for sustenance.
- They followed a different migration pattern, most Black Stilts wintering in the upper Waitaki River basin, while the hybrids and pieds (plus a few blacks) tended to move north to the harbours of Kawhia and Manukau.
- They returned to their breeding grounds earlier than Pied Stilts.
- They chose different nesting sites, Pied Stilts preferring swamp verges and wetlands, while Black Stilts the shingle embankments in the wide rivers preferably with water surrounding them.
- They preferred to mate with Black Stilts and if Black Stilts were not available they chose a hybrid as second preference.
- Their young had a longer fledgling stage by approximately ten days.
- They had different feeding capabilities in late winter, the Black Stilt being capable of probing beneath stones for aquatic invertebrates, a method which allowed it to overcome cold water temperatures which otherwise would have disallowed feeding. The Pied Stilt did not feed in this manner, a fact which limited the date of its return to the high country from the winter migration.
- They were less defensive on the nesting site lacking the elaborate distraction antics of the Pied Stilt, a factor which supports an ancient evolution in a predator-free environment.

Conclusion: From all this evidence Pierce concluded that the Black Stilt should retain its full species status.

Description - adult bird:
  Upper and underparts: Black. **Legs:** Red. **Bill:** Black.
Description - immature:
  Upperparts: White. **Wings:** Black. **Underparts:** White.
Note: Pierce (1984), observed the progression of young Black Stilts from the nestling stage to third summer and recorded a succession of steps by which the young birds progressed from being black-winged only, to black flanked, to smudgy breasted, to flecked with grey and finally to becoming totally black.
Conspicuous feature:
  • The all black colouring is distinctive.
Call: A yapping, yep yep yep sound, similar to the Pied Stilt.
Nest: A solitary breeder which makes a nest of grass and soft twigs usually on the riverbed. Up to 4 greenish, brown-blotche, eggs are laid.

Where to find - North Island:

South Auckland - Miranda: From time to time Black Stilts are seen here. Also immatures and some hybrids, all of which show varying degrees of white.

South Auckland - Manukau Harbour: Black Stilts are occasional winter visitors to the western shores of Manukau Harbour. Try the mudflats at the end of Gordon Road or Pollok Wharf Road on the Awhitu Peninsula.

King Country - Kawhia Harbour: A flock of between ten and fifteen birds of both pure Black Stilts and hybrids winter in this harbour every year. Chance views may be had from harbour verges near Kawhia town or from harbour glimpses on the Hauturu road which leaves the Kawhia road at Oparau. A boat is really required to see this bird as they roost on a low sand-bank island in the harbour at high tides.

Where to find - South Island:

South Canterbury - Lake Tekapo: Where the Cass River enters Lake Tekapo on its western shores, Black Stilt are sometimes seen. Take the Lake McGregor Road which is just past the Church of the Good Shepherd, almost to the end, and walk into the Cass River Delta. Note that Wrybill nest here.

South Canterbury - Twizel: Drive south from Twizel on Highway 8, for about 5 kms, and search the Ohau River from the main road bridge. If birds cannot be seen from the bridge walk downstream.

South Canterbury - Lake Benmore: Drive south from Twizel on Highway 8 and turn left after the Ohau River bridge at the first road going south. This road leads into Lake Benmore. Drive in past B and C power stations. After C take a left hand track which leads into the lake edge. Sometimes a pair is here.

South Canterbury - Benmore Tarn at Clearburn: This lake is on private land handy to the Omarama to Twizel road, Highway 8, near the junction at Clearburn where the road leads off to Lake Ohau Lodge. Enquire at homestead for permission to walk into the tarn.

South Canterbury - Ahuriri River: This area is west of Lake Benmore and just north of Omarama. Drive south from Twizel on Highway 8 until the road crosses the Ahuriri River about 5 kms north of Omarama. Search here.

South Canterbury - Ahuriri: Travel south from Omarama on Highway 8 and search the Ahuriri River where it meets the road on the right-hand side.

General: To see captive birds visit the Twizel Black Stilt Research Centre, Mount Bruce National Wildlife Centre in the Wairarapa or the Otorohanga Zoological Society Gardens in Otorohanga. (See "Places" in back of book.)

References:

Fleming C A 1982. George Edward Lodge - The Unpublished New Zealand Bird Paintings: 266.

Pierce R J 1984. The Changed Distribution of New Zealand Stilts. Notornis 31: 7-18.

Pierce R J 1984. Plumage, Morphology and Hybridisation of New Zealand Stilts *Himantopus spp*. Notornis 31: 106 - 130.

NEW ZEALAND DOTTEREL

Brian Chudleigh

Family: Charadriidae   **Species:** *Charadrius obscurus*
Common name: New Zealand Dotterel, Red-breasted Dotterel
Status: Endemic
Size: 250 mm (cf sparrow 145 mm, Banded Dotterel 250mm)

Discussion: The New Zealand Dotterel is an endemic species closely related to the Large Sand Dotterel (*C. leschenaulti*) and the Mongolian Dotterel (*C. mongolus*), which have mountain nesting and coastal wintering habits. These two species nest in the highlands of Asia and winter on the sandflats of Africa, through Asia, New Guinea and Australia. The Stewart Island population of the New Zealand Dotterel also nests on the mountains and winters on the coast. North Island birds, though, are coastal nesters.

Dotterel names: In New Zealand most of the plovers are called dotterels. For example, the Greater Sand Plover and the Lesser Sand Plover go by the names of Large Sand Dotterel and Mongolian Dotterel respectively.
Habitat: A bird of sandy coastlines, estuaries and river-mouths.
Range: Widely spread around the North Island coast northwards from Aotea

Harbour on the west coast and the Bay of Plenty on the east coast. A declining population of birds exists on Stewart Island. It is occasionally encountered on the west coast beaches north of Wellington.

Description:
    Head: Brown, with a white forehead and eye-stripe. **Upperparts:** Brown. **Underparts:** White. **Bill:** Black and robust. **Legs:** Grey.

Description - breeding plumage birds:
    Breast: Male birds attain red breasts and abdomens in July. Female birds attain lesser amounts of red colouring.

Conspicuous features:
- A large bird compared with the more common Banded Dotterel.
- The white eye-stripe is noticeable.
- Has a dark eye and bill.
- The red breast is conspicuous when in breeding season.

Conspicuous characteristics:
- It is a bird which is confiding and which can be approached.
- It has the plover habit of running quickly and pausing when feeding.
- Has the appearance of a rounded and hunched bird when standing.
- A strong flier which moves from high-tide roost to high-tide roost when not in breeding territories.
- Blends in well with the high-tide roost and breeding territories.

Call: It often utters a "kreek kreek" call when in flight.

Nest: A scrape in the sand with minimal nest lining. Up to 3 buff-brown, blotched with dark brown eggs are laid. In the North Island, nests are usually found behind the beach in locations which get 360 degree views. Very often, mated pairs occupy territories at the opposite ends of beaches. On Stewart Island birds nest high on the island in prominent positions with good visibility although there are records of sand-dune nests from Mason Bay.

Territorial behaviour: Birds are strongly territorial during the breeding season and keep their neighbours at bay.

Longevity of New Zealand Dotterels: A bird banded on 20.12.50 and known as Wimble, was again sighted in 1987 - at least 37 years old.

Where to find - North Island:

Northland - Bay of Islands, Matauri and Te Ngaire Bays: North of Kerikeri on Highway 10, take the Matauri Bay road to the right. Dotterel live at each end of this bay. Also try nearby Te Ngaire Bay. Usually there is a pair at each end.

North Auckland - Weiti (Wade) River: A small population of New Dotterel can be found on the sand-spit just across from the Weiti (Wade) wharf - that is the first wharf you come to when approaching the boat harbour. (See Reef Heron article.) Should you want a closer view, follow Stillwater Road off East Coast Bays Road. At Stillwater take the walking track at the south end of the beach.

North Auckland – Whangaparaoa: Try the beaches in Shakespear Park.

South Auckland - Kawakawa Bay: If travelling to Miranda via Kawakawa Bay look along the eastern end of the Kawakawa Bay.

South Auckland - Miranda: There is usually a pair of dotterels at "The

Limeworks". (See "Places" in back of book.)

Coromandel - Opoutere: A small spit at the entrance to Wharekawa Harbour has a breeding population of New Zealand Dotterel and Variable Oystercatchers. A ranger supervises visitors in summer. (See Banded Rail article.)

Bay of Plenty - Pukehina Beach: Just past the Maketu turn-off, on Highway 2, turn down Beach Road and follow in to the beach. Try the west end.

Bay of Plenty - Matata: Tarawera River-mouth usually has two pairs.

Where to find - South Island:
Southland - Awarua Bay: Try Awarua Bay.
Southland - Riverton Beach: Sometimes birds here.

Where to find - Stewart Island:
Stewart Island - Ocean Beach: On Stewart Island birds winter along Ocean Beach and on The Neck on the south side of Paterson Inlet. Some though, fly across to the beaches on the south coast of Southland such as at Riverton.

BANDED DOTTEREL

Brian Chudleigh

Family: Charadriidae   **Species:** *Charadrius bicinctus*
Common name: Banded Dotterel, Double-banded Plover (Australia)
Status: Endemic
Size: 200 mm (cf sparrow 145mm, New Zealand Dotterel 250mm)

Discussion: The Banded Dotterel is considered a close relative of the Australian species, the Red-capped Dotterel (*C. alexandrinus*) with which hybridisation has been reported. It is an endemic New Zealand species which breeds along beaches, shellbanks and the wide riverbeds of the South Island. After the breeding season, birds move to the coast in northern areas of the North Island where they congregate in harbours and estuaries such as the Manukau Harbour, and at Miranda in the Firth of Thames. A large number leave New Zealand and migrate to south and eastern Australia, wintering along its coastline but it is not known to breed in Australia. This migration to Australia is similar to that carried out by the Australasian Gannet and the White-fronted Tern. Some birds also turn up in Norfolk Island, Lord Howe Island and Fiji.

Habitat: Both a coastal and inland bird frequenting sandy beaches, shellbanks, braided rivers, well cropped pastureland and sometimes ploughed paddocks. A regular visitor to airport runways.

Range: Generally absent from the Taranaki area in the North Island and from Fiordland in the South Island. Otherwise well spread.

Description - Male in breeding plumage:
Forehead: White patch above bill with black patch above white. **Head:** Brown, with black line from bill to under eye. **Upperparts:** Brown. **Chin:** White. **Under-chin band:** Black, with white under it. **Breast-band:** Rich chestnut. **Underparts:** White.

Description - Female in breeding plumage:
Overall appearance: Similar to male but paler with the lower breast-band being narrower and less distinct.

Description - Immature birds:
Overall appearance: Birds tend to be paler than adult birds and lack the breast-bands. They have a distinct fawny appearance. Shoulder- tabs, brown.

Description - Wintering birds:
Overall appearance: Both sexes are dull, retaining a partial upperbreast band. By July full breeding plumage becomes apparent.

Conspicuous features:
- Much smaller and more petite than the New Zealand Dotterel.
- The double bands are very noticeable in breeding plumage birds.

Conspicuous characteristics:
- Banded Dotterel have the run and pause feeding habit of all plovers.
- Often seen in large flocks standing motionless in ploughed paddocks.

Call: A loud "pit pit" and a trilling "che-ree-a-ree".

Nest: A scrape on the sand. Up to 3 greenish, black-spotted eggs are laid.

Observation problems: It is possible that flocks of Banded Dotterel might also contain vagrant Mongolian Dotterel (*C. mongolus*), Ringed Plover (*C. hiaticula*) and Red-capped Dotterel (*C. alexandrinus*).

Where to find - North Island:
Northland - Bay of Islands, Matauri Bay: Birds nest on this beach but more often seen here in winter. (See New Zealand Dotterel article.)

North Auckland - Weiti (Wade) River: Usually on the sandspit across from the old wharf on the Weiti River. (See New Zealand Dotterel article.)

South Auckland - Kawakawa Bay: Birds are often seen at the eastern end of the beach. (See New Zealand Dotterel article.)

South Auckland - Miranda: Occasional near Pukorokoro River-mouth in wintering flocks at high tide on the grass paddocks.

Bay of Plenty - Matata: Regularly seen at the lagoons.

Manawatu - Manawatu Estuary: Large flocks usually winter here with other waders. (See Royal Spoonbill article.)

Manawatu - Palmerston North: Frequents the Manawatu River living alongside Black-fronted Dotterels. (See Black-fronted Dotterel article.)

Wellington - Waikanae Estuary: Several pairs here. (See Shoveler article.)

Where to find - South Island - Stewart Island:

Canterbury: Regularly seen in many of the wide riverbeds.

Canterbury - Ahuriri River: Search the Ahuriri riverbed from the bridge south of Twizel. (See Black Stilt article.)

South Canterbury - Lake Wainono: This is a coastal lagoon approximately 35 kms south of Timaru. Take Foleys Road from Studholme then turn left into Hannaton Road and right into Poingdestres Road. Stop at the gate and walk out to the shingle bank and turn left along a track inside a stop-bank. Walk for 200 metres to the seaward end of the stopbanks.

Otago - Aramoana: Travel on from Port Chalmers on the north side of Otago Harbour until the beach is reached.

Southland - Cascade Creek: The Eglinton Valley has many breeding pairs in summer. Black-fronted Terns are also here.

Southland - Waituna Lagoon: Travel east from Invercargill and turn right at Kapuka. Travel down Kapuka South Road and then left into Hodgson Road. At Kapuka South turn right down Waituna Lagoon Road until you reach the inner beach. Then travel east along by the shore to the inland arm.

BLACK-FRONTED DOTTEREL

Brian Chudleigh

Family: Charadriidae   **Species:** *Charadrius melanops*
Common name: Black-fronted Dotterel   **Status:** Native
Size: 170 mm (cf sparrow 145 mm, Banded Dotterel 200 mm)

Discussion: The Black-fronted Dotterel is another Australian species which has established itself in New Zealand since the 1950s. It was first discovered breeding in the Hawkes Bay district from where it has now spread.

Habitat: Generally a bird of inland rivers although individuals turn up at coastal estuaries and mudflats from time to time.

Range: In the North Island, found from the Bay of Plenty south to Hawkes Bay, and through the Manawatu Gorge into the riverbeds of the Manawatu, Pohangina and Rangitikei Rivers. In the South Island it is found along the eastern side of the Southern Alps from Marlborough to Southland.

Description:

Crown: Mottled light brown. **Forehead and face:** A black bar passes from the bill through the eye, to back of head. Eyebrow is white. **Upperparts:** Light brown, mottled with darker tonings. **Chin and throat:** White, beneath which is a black V-shaped black band extending to back of neck. **Underparts:** White. **Bill:** Red with black tip. **Legs:** Dull pink.

Conspicuous features:
- Colourful, with contrasting colours of black and white.
- Black forehead and white eyebrow is noticeable.
- Look for deep black V breast-band beneath white throat.

Conspicuous characteristics:
- It is a bird which blends in very easily with the river stones.
- Always found feeding close to water.
- Flight is jerky and dipping.

Call: A fast clicking "tik-tik-tik-tik".

Nest: A scrape on sand or among river pebbles, lined with fine grass. Up to 3 eggs, khaki in colour and marked with brown spots and lines, are laid.

Where to find - North Island:

Bay of Plenty - Matata: Try the eastern lagoon.

Hawkes Bay - Tuki Tuki River: From Napier take the Haumoana Road. Search around the Tuki Tuki bridge and then turn inland soon after. A small side road leads into the river along this road.

Manawatu - Palmerston North: From near the south end of Fitzherbert Ave turn right into Park Road and then left into Ruha Street, then right into Dittmer Drive which runs along-side the Manawatu River.

Where to find - South Island:

Southland - Oreti River: Examine the Oreti River in the area of Branxholme just north of Invercargill.

Southland - Aparima River: Examine the Aparima River from Otautau to Wreys Bush. Follow Wreys Bush Road which touches the river.

LARGE SAND DOTTEREL

Brian Chudleigh

Family: Charadriidae   **Species:** *Charadrius leschenaulti*
Common name: Large Sand Dotterel, Greater Sand Plover
Status: Vagrant
Size: 240 mm (cf sparrow 145 mm, Banded Dotterel 200mm)

Discussion: Breeds in highland areas in a belt from the Caspian Sea through to Mongolia. It winters around the coasts of East Africa, southern Asia, through Malaysia and Indonesia to Australia. A few birds come to New Zealand.

Habitat: A bird of estuaries and harbours.
Range: Likely to be found in the traditional wader haunts of the northern harbours, but can be expected from any estuary.

Description - non breeding plumage:
  Forehead: White extending to above eye. **Upperparts including shoulder tabs:** Grey-brown. **Underparts:** White. **Bill and legs:** Black.
Description - breeding plumage:
  Crown, nape and breast: Reddish-orange. **Forehead:** White, edged with black. **Eye-stripe:** A black marking extends from bill through eye to back of head. **Upperparts:** Brownish. **Chin:** White. **Underparts:** White. **Eye:** Black.
Conspicuous features:
  * As for the Mongolian Dotterel but taller.
  * Look for the dark eye.
Conspicuous characteristics:
  * Has a tendency to stand motionless.
  * Runs and pauses like all plovers when feeding.

Differences between the Large Sand Dotterel and the Mongolian Dotterel:
  * Appears leggy and stands taller than the Mongolian.

- Has a more horizontal posture than the Mongolian.
- White on chin and throat lacks black edge.
- Breast-band in breeding plumage, more orange than the Mongolian.

Where to find - North Island:
North Auckland - Kaipara Harbour: Try Jordans Road. (See Golden Plover article.)
South Auckland - Miranda: Regularly seen in various locations but first try Taramaire and the Stilt Ponds.

Where to find - South Island:
Marlborough - Farewell Spit: (See Mongolian Dotterel article.)
Canterbury - Lake Ellesmere: Try Embankment Road or Kaitorete.
Southland: Try Waituna Lagoon and Awarua Bay.

MONGOLIAN DOTTEREL

Brian Chudleigh

Family: Charadriidae   **Species:** *Charadrius mongolus*
Common name: Mongolian Dotterel, Lesser Sand Plover
Status: Vagrant
Size: 200 mm (cf sparrow 145 mm, Banded Dotterel 200 mm)

Discussion: Two races of the Mongolian Dotterel are recognised. One breeds in central Asia and migrates south to India and East Africa, while the other race breeds in eastern Siberia and migrates down the coastline of the Pacific rim countries to Australia. From Australia, birds consistently straggle to New Zealand. Because of its similarity to the Banded Dotterel when not in breeding plumage, it presents an identification challenge.
Habitat: Found in muddy estuaries and harbours.
Range: Consistently found at such places as Te Hihi on the Manukau Harbour,

Miranda in the Firth of Thames, Ahuriri near Napier, Embankment Road and Kaitorete Spit at Lake Ellesmere, and Farewell Spit at the northern most point of the South Island.

Description - non-breeding plumage:
Forehead: White, extending to a white eyebrow. **Upperparts:** Greyish-brown. **Shoulder tabs:** Greyish-brown. **Underparts:** White. **Eye:** Black, with dark surrounding feathers. **Bill:** Black. **Legs:** Grey.

Description - breeding plumage:
Forehead: White, edged with black. **Face and chin:** White, with a black line through eye to behind eye. **Upperparts:** Greyish-brown. **Chin:** White, faintly edged with black. **Head, breast-band and nape:** Chestnut. **Underparts:** White. **Bill:** Black. **Legs:** Grey.

Conspicuous feature:
- Look for the dark eye in breeding and non-breeding plumage birds.

Conspicuous characteristics:
- When feeding it runs, pauses and then dips its bill forward.
- Associates with Banded Dotterel and Wrybill.

Differences between the Mongolian Dotterel and the Banded Dotterel when not in breeding plumage:
- The Mongolian Dotterel has a brownish crown and head. The Banded Dotterel has tawny tonings.
- The Mongolian Dotterel has dark brownish eye surrounds. The Banded Dotterel is tawny around the eye.
- The Mongolian Dotterel is darkish brown on the upperparts. The Banded Dotterel tends to tawny colouring.

Difference between the Mongolian Dotterel and the Banded Dotterel when in breeding plumage:
- The Banded Dotterel lacks the dark eye.
- The Banded Dotterel has double bands on its breast with a clean white barrier between. The Mongolian has a single wide band.

Where to find - North Island:
North Auckland - Kaipara Harbour: Sometimes seen at Tapora, west of Wellsford. (See "Places" in back of book. See Fairy tern article.)

North Auckland - Kaipara Harbour: Sometimes among waders at Jordans Road.

Auckland - Mangere Sewage Ponds: Records come from here.

South Auckland - Te Hihi: Recorded here but this place is not accessible.

South Auckland - Miranda: Recorded annually here usually among Wrybills.

Hawkes Bay - Ahuriri: Frequently seen here. (See Golden Plover article.)

Where to find - South Island:
Marlborough - Farewell Spit: Sometimes reported from this wading haunt.

Canterbury - Lake Ellesmere: Has been reported from both Embankment Road and the Kaitorete Spit. (See Golden Plover article.)

Southland - Waituna Lagoon: The Banded Dotterel flocks of the Waituna Lagoon and Awarua Bay near Invercargill are worth close examination.

SHORE PLOVER

Brian Chudleigh

Family: Charadriidae **Species:** *Thinornis novaeseelandiae*
Common name: Shore Plover **Status:** Endemic
Size: 200 mm (cf sparrow 145 mm, Banded Dotterel 200 mm)

Discussion: A rare endemic plover considered a close relation of the Black-fronted Dotterel (*Charadrius melanops*) and the Ringed Plover (*C. hiaticula*). The Shore Plover has an ancient New Zealand history illustrated by the fact that it has adapted to the old predator-free New Zealand environment becoming larger than its relatives, slower breeding, with smaller clutch sizes and becoming tame and confiding (Fleming 1982). Population is between 110 and 150 birds.

Habitat: Originally found throughout New Zealand around the coastline on sandy beaches, rocky shelves and in river-mouth estuaries.
Range: Now confined to South East Island in the Chatham Islands group, and to Motuora Island off the North Auckland coast where some transferred birds are now breeding.

Description - male:
  Crown: Greyish-brown above a white head-ring. **Face and neck:** Black from above eye to throat. **Upperparts:** Greyish-brown flecked with black. **Underparts:** White. **Bill:** Red, tipped with black. **Legs:** Orange.
Description - female:
  Overall appearance: Paler than the male bird.
Conspicuous characteristic:
  • Runs with short, fast steps before pausing.
Territorial habits: A sedentary species which stays on its same area of beach or rock shelf throughout the year.

188

Call: A high-pitched "peep peep".
Nest: Usually hidden on the ground under vegetation. Up to 3 buff, brown-blotched eggs are laid.

Where to find - North Island:
North Auckland – Motuora Island: This is best visited by private boat but groups organised by the Department of Conservation in Auckland sometimes charter boats from Sandspit east of Warkworth.

Where to find - coastal New Zealand:
South East Island: It is found only on the one island in the Chatham group. Permission to get on to this island is difficult to obtain mainly because this island is also the main habitat of the endangered Black Robin.

Breeding Centres: Captive birds can now be viewed at the Otorohanga Zoological Society, the National Wildlife Centre near Masterton and at the Te Anau Wildlife Centre. (See "Places" in back of book.)

WRYBILL

Brian Chudleigh

Family: Charadriidae   **Species:** *Anarhynchus frontalis*
Common name: Wrybill   **Status:** Endemic

Discussion: The Wrybill is a unique New Zealand plover, thought to have a closer relationship with the Red-capped Dotterel (*C. alexandrinus*) than to other members of the plover family (Fleming 1982). Its uniqueness is associated with its peculiar bill which has its end segment distinctly curved to the right. It is the only bird in the world with such a bill. A study of this bird (Pierce 1979) concluded that "the bill appears to be pre-adapted for obtaining mayfly and caddisfly from their inactive diurnal positions on the undersurface of submerged stones, where they are not normally visible to Wrybills."

Habitat: Outside of the breeding season, a bird of muddy estuaries and inlets. During the breeding season a bird of the wide riverbeds of the South Island.

Range: Outside of breeding season birds are spread around the North Island coast in Northland, Coromandel, Bay of Plenty, southern Taranaki and Hawkes Bay. Main concentrations are around the Kaipara Harbour, Manukau Harbour, the Firth of Thames and Tauranga Harbour.

Description:

Forehead: White, with white eyebrow to behind eye. **Upperparts:** Grey. **Throat:** A black band crosses the throat when in breeding plumage. **Underparts:** White. **Bill:** Black. **Legs:** Grey-green.

Differences between sexes:

- Male birds can be distinguished from female birds by the presence of a black spot between the white frontal stripe and the grey of crown.
- Male birds have a broader breast-band than females.

Conspicuous features:

- The black breast-band is noticeable but indistinct on wintering birds.
- The bill curved to the right, is clearly visible.

Conspicuous characteristics:

- Birds when feeding have the run and pause habit common to plovers.
- Has a habit of running and suddenly changing direction while feeding.
- Runs in a hunched position, with head pulled back into shoulders.
- A confiding species which can be approached.
- Birds flock during winter at high-tide roosts.

Call: A shrill "weet weet".

Nest: A scrape among the pebbles of the South Island rivers. Up to 2 pale grey, blotched with dark brown eggs are laid.

Breeding grounds: During the breeding season of late July to December, birds are concentrated on the wide riverbeds of the mid-Canterbury area. Nests are placed up to 200 metres apart and are vigorously defended. Birds return to their wintering grounds of the North Island from the end of January onwards. The combined total of wintering birds in the Firth of Thames and the Manukau Harbour is about 5000 birds.

Migrants attracted to high-tide Wrybill roosts: The following species will sometimes roost with Wrybills - Mongolian Dotterel, Large Sand Dotterel, Siberian Tattler, Terek Sandpiper, Turnstone, Sharp-tailed Sandpiper, Curlew Sandpiper and Red-necked Stint.

Where to find - North Island:

North Auckland - Kaipara Harbour: Good numbers can be seen at the end of Jordans Road, north of Kaukapakapa. (See Golden Plover article.)

Auckland - Manukau Harbour: Wrybill can be found at the Mangere Sewage Ponds, not far from Auckland Airport.

South Auckland - Miranda: At high-tide, large flocks assemble at various places along the coast. These places include Pukorokoro, The Hide, the Stilt Ponds, and Taramaire North. At low-tide inspect the mudflat areas north of Taramaire. (See "Places" in back of book.)

South Auckland - Manukau Harbour: Wrybill can be seen occasionally at Clarks Beach on the south coast of the harbour. Drive west from Papakura on the Karaka road and continue to Waiau Pa and Clarks Beach.

Bay of Plenty - Matata: Occasionally seen around the lagoons and at the Tarawera River-mouth.

Where to find - South Island:

Mid-Canterbury: Any of the large rivers, such as the Waitaki, the Rakaia, the Ahuriri or the Cass which flows into Lake Tekapo, will have Wrybill over the breeding season. If looking for Wrybill in these areas expect to find Black Stilt too. Remember that Wrybills will be on scattered breeding territories and not in the huge flocks of the north. (See Black Stilt article.)

Mid-Canterbury - Cass River: South of Tekapo turn right at the Lake Alexandrina - Lake McGregor signpost and travel to the Cass River Bridge. Try down-stream towards the Lake Tekapo river delta.

General: The Wrybill is relatively easy to find. A few birds stay in northern harbours and estuaries over the breeding season and the numbers build up from January onwards.

Flight characteristics: Winter flocks of Wrybill are well known for their aerial displays especially just after the tide has turned. Light patterns on the wings and the sound of wing-rustle are part of it. The collective noun for this behaviour is "A Flung Scarf of Wrybill" (A H Hooper).

Reference: Pierce R J (1979). Foods And Feeding Of The Wrybill (*Anarhynchus frontalis*) On Its Riverbed Breeding Grounds. Notornis 26

PACIFIC GOLDEN PLOVER

Brian Chudleigh

Family: Charadriidae   **Species:** *Pluvialis fulva*
Common name: Golden Plover, Pacific Golden Plover   **Status:** Migrant
Size: 250 mm (cf sparrow 145 mm, Banded Dotterel 250 mm)

Discussion: The Golden Plover breeds in eastern Siberia and Alaska. It migrates south down the countries to the west of the Pacific rim and to Australia. It also spreads out across the Pacific wintering on tropical islands often in association with the Wandering Tattler. Good numbers of birds find New Zealand. It is sometimes confused in New Zealand with the American Golden Plover (*Pluvialis dominica*), which breeds across the Canadian Arctic and generally migrates to South America.

Habitat: Selective as to habitat, preferring muddy estuaries.

Range: Found in traditional wading bird habitats throughout New Zealand, with small flocks occurring in the far north of the North Island, the Manukau Harbour, the Firth of Thames, Lake Ellesmere and at Awarua Bay and the Invercargill Estuary in Southland.

Description - non-breeding:

Head: Brown, with a white stripe above the eye. **Throat:** Buff. **Upperparts:** Brown, with feathers edged with golden-buff. **Breast:** Light brownish. **Abdomen:** White. **Bill:** Black, with white feathers around the base.

Description - breeding plumage:

Crown of head and upperparts: Brown, heavily flecked with golden- yellow and white. **Neck:** A white dividing line, starting at the forehead and travelling behind the eye and down the neck, separates the black underparts from the golden upperparts. This is a very noticeable feature. **Underparts:** Black.

Conspicuous feature:

- The golden tonings are noticeable in non-breeding birds.
- Look for the striking black underparts with white line from head to flanks in breeding plumage birds.

Conspicuous characteristics:

- Golden Plover are usually viewed with head held high.
- They have the usual plover habit of running and pausing while they feed.
- Sometimes they leave the coastline habitat to feed on nearby pastures. This is regularly the case with birds from Manukau Harbour flocks, especially when weather is wet.
- Birds have an "ever alert" stance.
- At high-tide birds will stand motionless for some time.
- Upon landing, birds hold their wings erect for a moment before folding.

Call: Usually a clear two-syllabic "tuill tuill" is heard.

Differences between the Pacific Golden Plover (*P. fulva*) and the American Golden Plover (*P. dominica*):

- When birds are standing, the folded primary feathers of the American Golden Plover extend well beyond the tail. The primary feathers of the Pacific Golden extend minutely past the tail.
- When standing the folded tertial feathers of the American Golden Plover lie well back from the tip of the tail, as compared with the Pacific Golden.
- The Pacific Golden Plover is smaller and slimmer than the American Golden Plover which can be described as "fairly bulky".
- In breeding plumage the Pacific Golden Plover has less shoulder-white than the American Golden Plover.

- In non-breeding plumage the Pacific Golden Plover has an indistinct white eyebrow stripe and a golden head. The American Golden Plover has a much whiter eyebrow stripe and greyish head tonings.
- In non-breeding plumage the Pacific Golden Plover has brown upperparts spotted with bright yellow, while the American Golden Plover has greyish-brown upperparts spotted with pale yellow.

Where to find - North Island:
Northland - Aroha Island, Kerikeri: Usually a small summer flock can be seen on nearby rocky islets about 1 hour before high-tide.
North Auckland - Kaipara Harbour: A very good locality is at the end of Jordans Road, 5 kms north of Kaukapakapa. Take the Helensville road from Auckland. There is no public access to the coast so ask permission to enter.
Great Barrier Island - Whangapoua Beach: Good numbers can be seen with New Zealand Dotterel on the sand estuary east of the Okiwi airstrip.
South Auckland - Miranda: Sometimes present at the "Stilt Ponds".
Bay of Plenty - Kaituna River-mouth: This is a good area to find this species. (See Grey Teal article.)
Hawkes Bay - Ahuriri: This area is on Highway 2 just north of Napier. (See "Places" in back of book.)
Manawutu - Manawatu Estuary: (See Royal Spoonbill article.)

Where to find - South Island:
Canterbury - Lake Ellesmere: The best location to try is Embankment Road at the north end of the lake. From Lincoln travel to Greenpark. Here take Greenpark Road and then left into Davidsons Road. Then right into Embankment Road. Go through the gate at the end to the lake.
Southland - Waituna Lagoon and Awarua Bay: These areas near Invercargill have large numbers. (See Banded Dotterel article.)

Note: This bird is easily viewed along the rocky coastlines of many of the Pacific Islands such as Fiji, New Caledonia, Vanuatu, Rarotonga and Tahiti.

SPUR-WINGED PLOVER

Family: Charadriidae   **Species:** *Vanellus miles*
Common name: Spur-winged Plover, Masked Plover, (Australia)
Status: Native
Size: 380 mm (cf sparrow 145 mm, Variable Oystercatcher 280 mm)

Discussion: The Spur-winged Plover is a recent arrival from Australia which first established breeding populations in Southland in the 1950s. Birds moved north and covered all of the North Island by the late 1980s. In Australia, two races of Spur-winged Plover are recognised. The nominate race (*V. m. miles*) occupies northern Australia, with the race *V. m. novaehollandiae* occupying south-western Australia and south-eastern Australia. The New Zealand population is from the race *novaehollandiae*. This race is distinctive in having a black crown with black markings extending down the neck to the mantle and

to the shoulder. The nominate race has black "scull cap" only.
Habitat: A bird of the coast, estuaries and pastureland.
Range: Found throughout all New Zealand except Fiordland.

Brian Chudleigh
Spur-winged Plover

Description:
  Head: Black crown and neck to mantle and shoulders. **Face:** Yellow facial wattle to behind eye. **Wings:** Brown with black primaries. **Rump:** White. **Tail:** White with a black tip. **Underparts:** White. **Bill:** Yellow. **Legs:** Reddish.
Conspicuous features:
  • Bony wing spur on carpal flexure joint of each wing, is noticeable through a telescope. These appear when birds are showing aggression.
  • Yellow mask is obvious through a telescope.
  • In-flight birds show black wing primary feathers.
  • In-flight birds show a black tail-band with a white rump and white tail-tip.
Conspicuous characteristics:
  • When resting it often stands with head held high and back sloping.
  • Runs and pauses when feeding.
  • Wings look short and rounded when in flight.
  • Has slow wing-beats when in flight but with a faster down-beat.
  • Its high-pitched call gives it away.
Call: A high-pitched agitated "kitter kitter kitter". Calls day and night.
Nest: A scrape on pebbles or pasture with minimal nesting material. Up to 5 khaki, blotched dark-brown eggs are laid. Nests in the autumn in the North Island birds. Main nesting season is from August through until April.

Where to find - North Island:
South Auckland - Miranda: Large numbers in this locality.

Where to find - South Island:
Southland: Common along the roads from Invercargill to Te Anau.

194

TURNSTONE

Brian Chudleigh

Family: Scolopacidae　　　　　　**Species:** *Arenaria interpres*
Common name: Turnstone, Ruddy Turnstone　　**Status:** Migrant
Size: 230 mm (cf sparrow 145 mm, Wrybill 200 mm)

Discussion: The Turnstone is another Arctic nesting migrant which arrives in October. Over the last forty years it has increased to become the third most common migrant. Common in Australia and on the islands of the Pacific.

Habitat: Muddy estuaries and harbours.
Range: Can be expected from all shore-bird bird localities in New Zealand.

Description - breeding:
　Crown: Brown, lightly flecked with white. **Face:** Black and white. **Upperparts:** Neck brown, with a white V on back extending to rump. **Wings:** Brown inner leading edge, black outer leading edge, with white primaries. **Chin:** White. **Breast:** Black. **Abdomen:** Clean white. **Tail:** Black uppertail, then white with broad black tip. **Bill:** Black. **Legs:** Orange.
Description - non-breeding:
　Upperparts and underparts: A dull version of the breeding plumage.
Conspicuous features:
- Black and white colours around head and breast are noticeable.
- Look for white upperwing primary feathers, when bird is in flight.
- Look for uppertail black, white and black tail tip.

Conspicuous characteristics:
- Enjoys washing and preening in fresh water at river-mouths.
- At high-tide roosts, seldom mixes with other species.
- Busily fossicks when feeding, flipping stones.

Where to find - North Island:
South Auckland - Manukau Harbour: Regularly in good numbers at Clarks Beach. (See Bar-tailed Godwit article.)
South Auckland - Miranda: Many birds regularly be found here.
Bay of Plenty - Kaituna Estuary: Regularly seen here.
Bay of Plenty - Matata: An occasional visitor to the eastern lagoon.
Manawatu: Try the Manawatu Estuary. (See Royal Spoonbill article.)
Waikanae Estuary: An occasional visitor. (See Shoveler article.)

Where to find - South Island:
Marlborough - Motueka: Try the sandspit.
Marlborough - Lake Grassmere: Try the Hauwai Road on the south side.
North Canterbury - Kaikoura Peninsula: Look east of the town.
Southland - Awarua Bay: Take Tiwai Smelter Road and turn left at the bay.

CHATHAM ISLAND SNIPE

Brian Chudleigh

Family: Scolopacidae
Common name: Chatham Island Snipe
Size: 200 mm (cf sparrow 145 mm)

Species: *Coenocorypha pusilla*
Status: Endemic

Discussion: This bird is similar in appearance to the European Snipe (*Gallinago gallinago*) and the Woodcock (*Scolopax rusticola*) but close relationships have not been established. It is considered to possess an ancient past and is non-migratory, unlike the Snipes of Europe (Fleming 1982).

Habitat: Confined to scrub and low forests but will venture into the open.
Range: Now confined to the Chatham Islands group especially Mangere Island and South East Island.

Description:
Head: Brown, with a bold light brown central stripe. **Upperparts and throat:** Brownish with black blotching. **Underparts:** Breast brown with dark vertical stripings, and a white abdomen. **Abdomen:** Buff. **Undertail:** White. **Legs:** Fawn.

Conspicuous characteristic:
- Seldom flies but will rise if flushed.

Where to find:
South East Island and Mangere Island: Join a scientific excursion to get here.

NEW ZEALAND SNIPE

Family: Scolopacidae
Species: *Coenocorypha aucklandica,* (sometimes considered a subspecies of the Chatham Island Snipe)
Common name: New Zealand Snipe   **Status:** Endemic
Size: 230 mm (cf sparrow 145 mm, Chatham Island Snipe 200 mm)
Range: Confined to Snares Island, Antipodes, Ewing, and Adams Islands.

Description: Similar to Chatham Island Snipe but larger and darker.

LESSER KNOT

Brian Chudleigh

Family: Scolopacidae   **Species:** *Calidris canutus*
Common name: Lesser Knot, Red Knot   **Status:** Migrant
Size: 250 mm (cf sparrow 145 mm, Wrybill 200 mm)

Discussion: The Lesser Knot is the second most common migrant to arrive in New Zealand over the summer months. It breeds well to the north of the Arctic

Circle in both Siberia and Alaska. Birds spending the summer in New Zealand are generally considered to be of the Siberian race which also summers in Australia. Leg banding has shown that Australian Red Knots also visit New Zealand in the same year. Knots arrive from the end of August with numbers peaking in December.

Habitat: A bird of coastal areas, salty lagoons and harbours.

Range: Found throughout New Zealand. Some harbours, such as the Kaipara, the Manukau and the Firth of Thames, attract very large flocks. Conversely, some harbours which attract godwits, such as Wharekawa and Tairua, on the Coromandel Peninsula, fail to attract knots.

Description - non-breeding plumage:

Upperparts and wings: Greyish-brown with thin white wing-bar. **Underparts:** Greyish-white with some speckling on flanks. **Rump:** Barred with white and grey. **Bill:** Brown. **Legs:** Greyish-brown.

Description - breeding plumage:

Head, neck and breast: Chestnut. **Upperparts:** A mixture of black, dark brown, grey and white. **Abdomen:** Rufous.

Conspicuous features:

- Birds are considerably smaller than the godwits they roost among.
- Birds appear greyish in non-breeding plumage.
- In breeding plumage birds are highly coloured. Hence the name Red Knot. This colouring starts in late summer.
- Have a heavier appearance than the other sandpipers they frequent with.
- Have a squat posture.
- In flight, look for the white wing-bar.

Conspicuous characteristics:

- Have a habit of intermingling with godwits on high-tide roosts. Often they can be found grouped right in the middle of a godwit mob.

Where to find - North Island:

South Auckland - Clarks Beach: This is a very accessible locality. (See Bar-tailed Godwit article.)

South Auckland - Miranda: Large numbers here.

Where to find - South Island:

Marlborough - Farewell Spit: Large numbers here.

Marlborough - Motueka: Good numbers here. (See Whimbrel article.)

Marlborough - Waimea Estuary: Always some birds here. Try Rabbit Island Bridge west of Richmond.

Southland: Try Fortrose Estuary, Waituna Lagoon and Awarua Bay.

General: This is an easy bird to find when it is grouped in large numbers among godwits. However when found singly or when grouped intermittently among Wrybills it is hard to identify. When in doubt look for scattered marking under the folded wings as the first identification pointer.

CURLEW SANDPIPER

Brian Chudleigh

Family: Scolopacidae   **Species:** *Calidris ferruginea*
Common name: Curlew Sandpiper   **Status:** Migrant
Size: 190 mm (cf sparrow 145 mm, Wrybill 200 mm)

Discussion: Breeds in Siberia in Arctic areas and winters in Mediterranean areas, Africa, Asia, South East Asia and in Australia. Some straggle on to New Zealand arriving from October onwards and they leave by early April.

Habitat: Found in muddy estuaries and harbours.
Range: Biggest flocks are found at Miranda and at Lake Ellesmere, although birds can be expected from most shore-bird haunts.

Description - non-breeding plumage:
  Face: Greyish-brown with white eyebrow. **Upperparts:** Grey-brown.
  Wings: Brown, with a thin white line across middle of wings. **Rump:** White.
  Breast: Greyish wash. **Underparts and underwing:** White. **Tail:** White with brown tip. **Bill:** Black, noticeably down-curved at the tip. **Legs:** Black.
Description - breeding plumage - note that female birds are paler:
  Face: White around base of bill and above eye. Otherwise brick red. **Head and neck:** Brick red. **Back and wings:** Red, with flecks of black and silver.
  Breast and underparts: Brick red with black barring. **Rump, undertail and underwing:** White.
Conspicuous features:
  - Smaller than Sharp-tailed Sandpipers and Pectoral Sandpipers.
  - Has a noticeable down-curved tip to the bill.
  - Non-breeding plumage birds have very white underparts unlike other waders usually encountered in New Zealand.
  - The white rump of the bird in flight is noticeable.
  - Birds undergo a colour transformation into breeding plumage in January.

- In-flight birds show the white wing line on upperwings.

Conspicuous characteristics:
- Birds usually feed among Sharp-tailed Sandpipers or Wrybill.
- Birds tend to start feeding immediately the tide has turned.
- Birds are very fast and manoeuvrable fliers when in flocks.

Where to find - North Island:
Auckland - Mangere Sewage Ponds: Regularly found here.
South Auckland - Miranda: Usually found at "The Stilt Ponds".
Other areas: Try Kaituna Estuary, Ahuriri and Manawutu Estuary.

Where to find - South Island:

Marlborough - Farewell Spit: Regularly seen here.
Canterbury - Lake Ellesmere: Try Embankment Road.
Southland: Try Waituna Lagoon, Awarua Bay and Oreti.

SHARP-TAILED SANDPIPER

Brian Chudleigh

Family: Scolopacidae   **Species:** *Calidris acuminata*
Common name: Sharp-tailed Sandpiper   **Status:** Migrant
Size: 220 mm (cf sparrow 145 mm, Wrybill 200 mm)

Discussion: The Sharp-tailed Sandpiper is a regular summer species in some parts of New Zealand. It breeds in Siberia and migrates south to Australia where large numbers occur from October onwards.

Habitat: A bird of muddy estuaries and harbours but one which also likes the verges of salty lagoons and small coastal ponds and lakes.
Range: Can be expected to turn up in all the major shore-bird harbours and estuaries in both the main islands.

200

Description - non-breeding plumage:
   Crown: Traces of rufous colouring over brown. **Face:** Greyish, with a white eyebrow. **Upperparts:** Brown, with buff edges to feathers. **Wings:** Brown, with a faint white line across middle of wing. **Underparts:** Throat brownish, abdomen white. **Tail:** Black outer, white inner, and brown centre feathers. **Bill:** Brown, slightly down-curved at tip. **Legs:** Yellowish-green.
Description - breeding plumage:
   Crown: Rufous. **Head, neck and upperparts:** Rufous tonings over greyish-brown. **Underparts:** Rufous throat and upperbreast, abdomen white, flecked with grey streaks.

Conspicuous feature:
   • Look for the rufous crown.
Conspicuous characteristics:
   • Regularly seen on the edge of roosting Wrybill flocks.
   • Birds tend to remain feeding while other species rest at high tides.

Differences between Sharp-tailed Sandpiper and Pectoral Sandpiper:
   • The Sharp-tailed Sandpiper has a gradual blending of the brown of the breast into the white of the underparts. The Pectoral Sandpiper has a sharp defined line between the two.
   • As they attain breeding plumage, the Sharp-tailed Sandpiper becomes rusty coloured around throat and breast while the Pectoral Sandpiper goes a darker brown on throat and breast, and browner on the upperparts.

Where to find - North Island:
South Auckland - Miranda: Usually to be found at "The Stilt Ponds".
North Island: Kaituna Estuary, Ahuriri, Manawatu Estuary and Waikanae Estuary all have records.

Where to find - South Island:
Canterbury - Lake Ellesmere: Try Embankment Road.
South Canterbury - Lake Wainono: Regularly seen here.
Southland: Try Waituna Lagoon, Awarua Bay.

PECTORAL SANDPIPER

Family: Scolopacidae   **Species:** *Calidris melanotos*
Common name: Pectoral Sandpiper   **Status:** Migrant
Size: 230 mm (cf sparrow 145 mm, Sharp-tailed Sandpiper 220 mm)

Discussion: The Pectoral Sandpiper arrives in New Zealand from October onwards in very small numbers. It is both a Siberian and North American breeding species. The North American birds migrate to winter on the western shores of South America, while the Siberian birds migrate down the western Pacific with a few birds arriving in Australia and New Zealand.

Habitat: Muddy estuaries and harbours.
Range: Can be expected in regular shore-bird haunts.

Brian Chudleigh

Pectoral Sandpiper

Description - non-breeding:
Head, throat and breast: Brown, streaked with dark brown. The brown of the breast ends abruptly in a clean line at the start of white. **Upperparts and wings:** Dark brown with buff edges to feathers, with a thin white line across the middle of the wings. **Abdomen:** Whitish. **Bill:** Brown, with yellow base. **Legs:** Yellow.

Description - breeding:
Upperparts: Feathers become dark brown in breeding plumage with some chestnut and buff feather edges. **Breast:** Brown, heavily streaked with dark brown.

Conspicuous feature:
- Look for the sharp cut-off line between the brown of the breast and the white of the abdomen.

Conspicuous characteristics:
- Usually to be found among flocks of Sharp-tailed Sandpipers.
- Remains feeding at high-tide roosts while other species remain resting.
- Often found on the edges of roosting Wrybill flocks.
- Has a habit of stretching its neck forward while holding wings back.

Where to find - North Island:
South Auckland - Miranda: Regularly one or two birds can be seen here on "The Stilt Ponds" at the high-tide. Look among vegetated verges.
Other areas: Try Kaituna, Maketu, Matata, Ahuriri, and Manawatu Estuary.
Where to find - South Island:
Marlborough - Motueka: Try the sandspit. (See Whimbrel article.)
Marlborough - Nelson: Try the Waimea Estuary. (See Whimbrel article.)
South Canterbury - Lake Wainono: Regularly seen here along with Sharp-tailed Sandpipers. (See Banded Dotterel article.)
Southland: Try Waituna Lagoon and Awarua Bay. (See Banded Dotterel article.)

RED-NECKED STINT

Brian Chudleigh

Family: Scolopacidae **Species:** *Calidris ruficollis*
Common name: Red-necked Stint **Status:** Migrant
Size: 150 mm (cf sparrow 145 mm, Wrybill 200 mm)

Discussion: The Red-necked Stint is the smallest of the wading birds to visit
New Zealand. It breeds in north-east Siberia and in Alaska, and migrates down
the coasts of the countries of the western Pacific rim to Australia. A few straggle
on to New Zealand.

Habitat: A bird of muddy estuaries and harbours.
Range: Found in traditional shore-bird localities with largest flocks usually being
seen at Te Hihi on the Manukau Harbour, Miranda and Lake Ellesmere.

Description - non-breeding plumage:
Forehead and eyebrow: White. **Head and upperparts:** Grey with brownish
tinge. **Neck:** Traces of red on sides of neck. **Wings:** Greyish, with a white line
across the middle of the wings. **Tail:** Whitish outer feathers with black inner.
Underparts: White. **Bill and legs:** Black.
Description - breeding plumage:
**Face, neck, chin and throat: Brick red. New Zealand birds show only
slight reddening prior to departure. Upperparts:** Dark brown with rufous
edges to feathers. **Underparts:** White.
Conspicuous feature:
- The smallest of the Arctic wading birds to come to New Zealand.
- Bill is black, short and straight.
Conspicuous characteristics:
- Prefers to feed on areas of mud with a thin film of water over them.
- Feeds busily, with sewing-machine action, with little runs here and there

- Usually found towards the edges of Wrybill flocks.
- Often feeds in the company of other sandpipers and Wrybills.
- In flight, birds fly low and direct in a compact group.

Where to find - North Island:
North Auckland - Kaipara Harbour: Try Jordans Road.
South Auckland - Manukau Harbour: At Te Hihi on the south Manukau Harbour a flock of between 10 and 20 birds is regularly seen over the summer. There is no public access to this roosting area.
South Auckland - Miranda: Regularly seen at the "Stilt Ponds" where up to 5 birds have been encountered. This is the easiest location to find this bird.
Other areas: Try Ahuriri, Manawatu Estuary and Waikanae Estuary.

Where to find - South Island:
Canterbury - Lake Ellesmere: Try Embankment Road. Larger numbers may be seen in Kaitorete Spit area but this area is fairly inaccessible to the public.
Southland: Try Waituna Lagoon and Awarua Bay.
Other areas: Expect to find one or two birds in most shore-bird localities such as the Waimea Estuary. (See Whimbrel article.)

EASTERN CURLEW

Brian Chudleigh

Family: Scolopacidae   **Species:** *Numenius madagascariensis*
Common name: Eastern Curlew, Long-billed Curlew
Status: Migrant
Size: 630 mm (cf sparrow 145 mm, Bar-tailed Godwit 390 mm)

Discussion: This large Arctic nesting bird breeds in north-east Siberia and spends the northern winter in countries of the western Pacific rim with large numbers arriving in Australia. Small numbers straggle on to New Zealand where they become noticeable due to their size and their down-curved bills.

Habitat: Found in estuaries and harbours.

Range: Can be expected in any harbour or estuary. Birds favour the harbours of Northland, Auckland and Farewell Spit. Records come from places such as Maketu Estuary, Manawatu Estuary, Awarua Bay and Waituna Lagoon.

Description:

    Upperparts: Dark brown mottled with buff. **Underparts:** Buff, longitudinally striped with dark brown. **Eyebrow:** Whitish. **Bill:** Dark brown, noticeably curved and darker on the tip. **Legs:** Bluish-grey.

Conspicuous features:

- Look for the long down-curved bill.
- The large size is noticeable.

Conspicuous characteristic:

- Birds generally remain apart from other birds on high-tide roosts, usually staying on the edges of the flock, and so they are readily spotted.

Call: The song of the curlew, a long "kroo-lee kroo-lee", is especially noticeable when the bird takes off.

Where to find - North Island:

South Auckland - Kaiaua: Up to 11 birds have been known to winter at Kaiaua, just south of the beach houses. These tend to congregate with South Island Pied Oystercatchers on the beach at the high tide.

South Auckland - Miranda: Regularly on the shellbank near "The Hide" at Access Bay or at the Pukorokoro River-mouth. Also, frequently seen further north at the Taramaire River-mouth.

Bay of Plenty - Maketu: Sometimes at the Kaituna River-mouth.

Manawatu Estuary: Sometimes at the Manawatu Estuary in association with other waders and the Royal Spoonbill. (See Royal Spoonbill article.)

Where to find - South Island:

Southland - Waituna Lagoon: Try Waituna Lagoon and Awarua Harbour in Southland. (See "Places" in back of book.)

WHIMBREL

Family: Scolopacidae   **Species:** *Numenius phaeopus*
Common name: Whimbrel   **Status:** Migrant
Size: 430 mm (cf sparrow 145 mm, Bar-tailed Godwit 390 mm)

Discussion: The Whimbrel is a bird which nests across northern North America, Europe and Asia. It migrates south in the northern winter and the Asiatic race (*N. p. variegatus*) winters around the western Pacific rim and in particular in northern Australia. The American race (*N. p. hudsonicus*) winters on central Pacific islands. Both arrive in New Zealand in estuaries and harbours from time to time.

Habitat: Found in estuaries and harbours.

Range: Expected in small numbers from the northern harbours to Southland.

Brian Chudleigh

Whimbrel

Description:
Head: Brown, with a white centre-stripe on crown and with white eyebrows.
Upperparts: Brown, streaked with buff. **Underparts:** Light brown, streaked longitudinally with buff. **Rump:** Whitish (Asiatic), warm brown (Hudsonian).
Tail: Grey and black barred. **Bill:** Dark brown and curved downwards. **Legs:** Bluish-grey.

Conspicuous features:
- The white head striping is noticeable.
- The Whimbrel looks like a small curlew.
- Look for down-curved bill.

Conspicuous characteristics:
- When resting at high tide, Whimbrels keep to the edge of the godwit flocks and often remain alert with heads up and curved bills noticeable.

Call: A rippling trill of seven "ti ti ti ti ti ti ti" notes, identifies this bird on the summer (wintering) mudflats or sandflats. Birds will call throughout the night.

Where to find - North Island:
South Auckland - Miranda: Access Bay near "The Hide" is one of the best and easiest places to look for it.
Bay of Plenty - Kaituna River-mouth: Sometimes found here.
Bay of Plenty - Matata: Try for it at the lagoons.
Manawatu Estuary: Try for it here.

Where to find - South Island:
Marlborough - Farewell Spit: (See "Places" in back of book.)
Marlborough - Nelson: Try for it at Nelson near Tic Toc Road and Rabbit Island Bridge areas, west of Richmond. These are high-tide roosts.
Marlborough - Motueka Sandspit: Turn north from High Street at a sign which says "golf course" and travel down to the estuary.
Southland: Try for it at Waituna Lagoon and Awarua Bay.
General: Look for Whimbrels in any godwit flock in any harbour.

BAR-TAILED GODWIT

Brian Chudleigh

Family: Scolopacidae   **Species:** *Limosa lapponica*
Common name: Bar-tailed Godwit, Kuaka (Maori)   **Status:** Migrant
Size: 390 mm (cf sparrow 145 mm, Black-tailed Godwit 390 mm)

Discussion: The Bar-tailed Godwit is New Zealand's most common migrant
wader. This species breeds in both Siberia and the western Arctic regions of
North America. It migrates to Australia and New Zealand. It arrives in large
numbers from September onwards, reaching a peak in December.

Habitat: A bird of large muddy harbours and estuaries. It is less numerous on
sandy harbours but often present.
Range: Found throughout New Zealand and to Stewart Island.

Description - non-breeding plumage:
   Upperparts: Greyish, streaked with brown. **Underparts:** Whitish. **Rump
and tail:** Barred white and brown. **Bill:** Brownish pink with a black tip and
curved upwards. **Legs:** Greyish.
Description - breeding plumage - male birds:
   Head: Brick red with whitish stripe above the eye. **Upperparts:** Dark brown
with buff edges to feathers. **Neck and underparts:** Chestnut. **Underwing:**
Whitish. **Tail:** Brown, barred with white. **Bill:** Brownish-pink.
Description - breeding plumage - female birds:
   Upperparts: Greyish, streaked with brown. **Breast:** Buffy tinge of various
amounts. **Underparts:** Whitish, with fine barring on edges of abdomen.
Conspicuous features:
- A large greyish-brown wading bird. Note that female birds are slightly
larger than male birds.
- Bill is long and up-curved. Female birds have a longer bill than males.

Conspicuous characteristics:
- Birds fly in loose and straggly skeins.
- Birds congregate in large numbers on high-tide roosts.
- Birds feed busily once the tide recedes.
- Birds dig bills deeply into the mud, so often seen with muddy faces.
- Male birds develop rufous tonings towards the end of summer.
- Auckland birds are often seen changing harbours in straggly skeins.

Call: A soft "kit kit kit" or a "kew kew" call, is heard from flying birds. Just prior to departure, birds become very excited and noisy when on roosts.

Arrival dates: From mid-September.

Departure dates: Birds congregate in northern harbours from late-January onwards in places like Manukau Harbour and the Firth of Thames, and start leaving from mid-March.

Overwintering birds: At any time of year including winter, godwits in small numbers, often in breeding plumage, can be seen in many harbours.

Where to find - North Island:

North Auckland: All harbours are worth investigating for godwits.

Auckland - Tahuna Torea: This is an excellent viewing place for this bird. (See "Places" in back of book.)

Auckland - Howick: Beaches in the Howick area regularly attract godwits.

South Auckland - Manukau Harbour: Try the Mangere Sewage Ponds. Other roads lead to the Manukau harbour in the vicinity of Auckland Airport.

South Auckland - Manukau Harbour: Sometimes godwits can be seen in the estuary at Bottletop Bay at mid-tide. From the motorway off-ramp at Papakura drive west in the direction of Karaka. Turn down Bottletop Road 1.5 kms from the off-ramp and travel to end.

South Auckland - Clarks Beach: Birds regularly feed along the mudflats at Clarks Beach at half-tide, usually with knots. Clarks Beach is approximately 22 kms west off the Papakura off-ramp. Roads lead to the beach.

South Auckland - Kawakawa Bay: This bay, just past Clevedon, is an excellent place to see birds from the car. It is good at any tide.

South Auckland - Miranda: This is an excellent place to see this bird. It can be seen here at any tide if the viewer takes a telescope. Search the more northern parts of the Firth around the township of Kaiaua if the tide is low. At high-tide large numbers congregate in the Miranda area on the shellbanks.

Coromandel Harbours: Try Colville, Coromandel near Coromandel town, Tairua, Wharekawa near Opoutere, and Whangamata. To view at Tairua stop when harbour comes into view approximately 3 kms before the town.

Bay of Plenty: Try Tauranga, Maketu and Ohiwa Harbours. At Ohiwa Harbour birds can often be seen from the road approximately 3 kms on from Ohope Beach towards Opotiki.

Where to find - South Island:

Marlborough - Nelson: Try the Waimea Estuary. (See Whimbrel article.)

Marlborough - Motueka: Try the Motueka Estuary. (See Whimbrel article.)

Canterbury: Try Embankment Road at Lake Ellesmere.

Otago: Try Hoopers Inlet. (See Grey Teal article.)

Southland: Try Waituna Lagoon, Awarua Bay and Oreti.

BLACK-TAILED GODWIT
INCLUDING COMMENTS ABOUT THE HUDSONIAN GODWIT
L.haemastica

Brian Chudleigh

Family: Scolopacidae   **Species:** *Limosa limosa*
Common name: Black-tailed Godwit.   **Status:** Migrant
Size: 390 mm (cf sparrow 145 mm, Bar-tailed Godwit 390 mm)

Discussion: The Black-tailed Godwit straggles to New Zealand in small numbers. Birds which come to New Zealand breed in Siberia and migrate southward around the western Pacific rim to Australia where they occur in large numbers. New Zealand also records a few Hudsonian Godwit (*L.haemastica*), a similar looking bird, but one which breeds in central Canada and migrates to South America with a few reaching the western Pacific islands and New Zealand.

Habitat: Found in estuaries and harbours.
Range: Regular sightings come from the Manukau Harbour, the Firth of Thames and Southland.

Description - non-breeding plumage:
  Upperparts: Smooth grey. **Upperwings:** Grey, with black edges to the secondary feathers, under which is a white band which passes through the black primaries. **Underwing:** White, edged with black. **Underparts:** Whitish. **Rump:** White, the white extending down the tail to a broad black tip. **Bill:** Greyish with a black tip.
Description - breeding plumage:
  Head, neck and breast: Chestnut. **Eyebrow:** Whitish. **Upperparts:** Brownish, with individual feathers having buff edges. **Abdomen:** White, with some side barring with brown. **Legs:** Lead grey.

Conspicuous features:
- Similar in size to a Bar-tailed Godwit.
- Smoother grey than a Bar-tailed Godwit.
- In flight, the white upperwing marking is noticeable.
- The white tail and black tail-tip band is noticeable.
- Has an almost straight bill, not up-curved like the Bar-tailed Godwit.

Conspicuous characteristics:
- In flight, legs trail behind the bird in a conspicuous manner, they being longer than those of the Bar-tailed Godwit.
- Is scary and quickly takes to the air when disturbed.

Call: When put to flight a loud "wicka wicka wicka" call is made.

Differences between the Black-tailed Godwit and the Hudsonian Godwit:
- The Black-tailed Godwit has a straight bill. The Hudsonian Godwit has a slightly up-curved bill.
- Underwing of the Black-tailed Godwit is white, edged with black.
- Underwing of the Hudsonian Godwit is dark brown on the "armpits", tips of primaries and secondaries, but has a whitish band in the centre of the underwing.
- The Black-tailed Godwit has lead-grey coloured legs. The Hudsonian Godwit has bluish-grey legs.
- The Black-tailed Godwit has less abdominal chestnut colouring in the breeding season with the chestnut not extending to undertail feathering.

Quick observation points when watching godwits:
- Look for white on wings of flying birds (Black-tailed or Hudsonian).
- Look for dark "armpits" on flying birds or on raised wing birds (Hudsonian).
- Look for straight bill (Black-tailed) or slightly curved (Hudsonian).

Where to find - North Island:
North Auckland - Kaipara Harbour: Try Jordans Road at Kaukapakapa. (See Golden Plover article.)
South Auckland - Miranda: Each year small flocks of up to five birds arrive here during late October. "The Stilt Ponds" and the Taramaire and Pukorokoro River-mouths have been regular visiting spots over recent years.

Where to find - South Island:
South Canterbury - Lake Wainono: Regularly seen here.
Southland - Waituna Lagoon: This area has records of Black-tailed Godwit.

WANDERING TATTLER

Family: Scolopacidae   **Species:** *Tringa incana*
Common name: Wandering Tattler   **Status:** Migrant
Size: 270 mm (cf sparrow 145 mm, Bar-tailed Godwit 390 mm)

Discussion: This species regularly arrives in New Zealand. It breeds in coastal Alaska and migrates south across the tropical islands of the Pacific where it is regularly seen.

Brian Chudleigh

Wandering Tattler

Description: (See Siberian Tattler article.)

Differences between the Siberian Tattler and the Wandering Tattler:
- Wandering Tattler is bigger than the Siberian Tattler.
- In the hand, the length of the nasal groove can be seen to be longer in the Wandering Tattler, about double the length of that of the Siberian Tattler.
- In breeding plumage the Wandering Tattler has undertail barring and barring on the abdomen and lower breast. The Siberian Tattler has indistinct barring undertail and lighter barring on breast and abdomen. Birds seen in New Zealand usually show only traces of barring.
- The Wandering Tattler has a very narrow eye-stripe behind the eye and less white in front of the eye than the bolder stripe of the Siberian Tattler.
- The Wandering Tattler has longer wings, making its tail appear shorter.
- The Wandering Tattler is an overall darker bird.
- The Wandering Tattler has a distinctive call. It is musical trill of "tew tew tew tew tew tew teeew" notes which differ greatly from the less musical Siberian Tattler whose call is a two syllable "two-eet two-eet", the second note being of higher pitch than the first.

Call: Call is a musical "tew tew tew tew tew tew teeew".

Where to find:
South Auckland - Miranda: Wandering Tattler have been recorded here in association with South Island Pied Oystercatchers roosting birds.
Other localities: See localities from Siberian Tattler.

PacificIslands: This bird is best seen in the Pacific Islands, such as Tahiti, Rarotonga, Vanuatu and Fiji. Here it is a conspicuous bird which sits on shoreline rocks about the lagoons. It regularly calls as it flies from one roost to another. Often it can be seen feeding side by side with Golden Plover.

SIBERIAN TATTLER

Brian Chudleigh.

Family: Scolopacidae   **Species:** *Tringa brevipes*
Common name: Siberian Tattler, Grey-tailed Tattler   **Status:** Migrant
Size: 250 mm (cf sparrow 145 mm, Wandering Tattler 270 mm)

Discussion: A migrant which arrives in New Zealand every summer in very small numbers. It breeds in eastern Siberia and migrates down the western Pacific rim to winter in countries such as The Philippines, Malaysia, Indonesia, Papua New Guinea and Australia. Odd birds eventually find New Zealand.

Habitat: Found on muddy estuaries and sandspits.
Range: Can be expected from places where shorebirds gather. These include Manakau Harbour, the Firth of Thames at Miranda, Tauranga Harbour, Manawatu Estuary, Waikanae Estuary, Lake Ellesmere, Papanui Inlet, Hoopers Inlet, Fortrose Estuary, Waituna Lagoon and Awarua Bay.

Description - non-breeding:
  Head: Grey, with white eyebrow, and a dark stripe beneath eye. **Upperparts:** Smooth grey. **Chin:** White. **Underparts:** Grey breast with white abdomen. **Sides and flanks:** Some light horizontal barring. **Tail:** Grey, with some white indistinct cross-barring. **Bill:** Black, heavy in structure. **Legs:** Yellow.
Description - breeding:
  Upperparts: Smooth grey. **Underparts:** Heavily barred dark grey with white undertail.
Conspicuous features:
- The long and heavy bill is noticeable.
- Has a squat posture which is heavier than most shorebirds.
- Look for the yellow legs.

Conspicuous characteristics:

- At the high-tide, it usually roosts close to the mud-line.
- When alerted, bobs head and dips tail.
- Is easily alerted and put to flight.
- Usually a solitary species.

Call: A "two-eet two-eet", the second note being a higher pitch than the first.

Where to find - North Island:
North Auckland - Kaipara Harbour: Try Jordans Road.
South Auckland - Miranda: This is a most likely place. At Access Bay or Pukorokoro River-mouth, search the seaward sides of the shellbanks and examine any birds which are alone.
Bay of Plenty - Matata: Try here. (See "Places" in back of book.)
Manawatu - Foxton Estuary: Try here. (See Royal Spoonbill article.)
Wellington - Waikanae Estuary: Try here. (See Shoveler article.)

Where to find - South Island:
Southland - Waituna Lagoon and Awarua Bay: Records come from here.

MARSH SANDPIPER

Brian Chudleigh

Family: Scolopacidae **Species:** *Tringa stagnatilis*
Common name: Marsh Sandpiper **Status:** Migrant
Size: 220 mm (cf sparrow 145 mm, Wrybill 200 mm)

Discussion: A species which breeds in Central Asia migrating to Africa, southern Asia and Australia. Since 1959, when it was first recorded in New Zealand, numbers have grown to a record 8 birds being seen together in one flock at Miranda in 1998. Closely related to the Greenshank.

Habitat: A bird of harbours and estuaries usually preferring still-water areas.
Range: Birds turn up from time to time in all the main wading-bird area

Description - non-breeding:
  Upperparts: Pale grey, with a dark edge to folded wings. **Underparts:** White.
  Eyebrow: White. **Bill:** Black, slim and pointed. **Legs:** Dark grey.
Description - breeding:
  Upperparts: Grey, flecked with brown. **Throat and breast:** Grey, lightly
  flecked with brown. **Bill:** Black. **Legs:** Yellow.

Conspicuous features:
  * Has an elegant stilt-like appearance but much smaller than a stilt.
  * Has a long slender bill.
Conspicuous characteristics:
  * In flight shows a distinctive white V marking on the back which separates
    it from the Lesser Yellowlegs (*Tringa flavipes*).
  * At high-tide it keeps feeding in shallow water while other species roost.
  * A fast flier.
  * When in flight it usually calls.
Call: Widely spaced "twee twee" notes.

**Difference between Marsh Sandpiper and Lesser Yellowlegs when in
breeding plumage:**
  * Marsh Sandpiper has a white V marking on the back, seen when in flight.

Where to find - North Island:
South Auckland - Miranda: "The Stilt Ponds" are a good place to look.
South Auckland - Manukau: One bird was seen Clarks Beach in 1998.
Manawatu - Foxton Estuary: Try here. (See Royal Spoonbill article.)

Where to find - South Island:
Canterbury - Lake Ellesmere: Try the Embankment Road area.
Southland - Waituna Lagoon: (See Banded Dotterel article.)

TEREK SANDPIPER

Family: Scolopacidae   **Species:** *Xenus cinereus*
Common name: Terek Sandpiper   **Status:** Migrant
Size: 230 mm (cf sparrow 145 mm, Wrybill 200 mm)

Discussion: The Terek Sandpiper is a regular migrant which arrives in New
  Zealand over the summer months along with other Northern Hemisphere
  migrants. It breeds in northern Europe and migrates to areas which include
  East Africa, India and the countries of the western Pacific rim including
  Australia. A few straggle on to New Zealand.

Habitat: A bird of muddy estuaries and harbours.
Range: Recorded in places such as the Manukau Harbour, Miranda, Kaituna
  Estuary, Ahuriri, Manawatu Estuary, Waituna Lagoon and Awarua Bay.

Brian Chudleigh

Terek Sandpiper

Description - non-breeding:
   Upperparts: Brownish-grey. **Eyebrow:** White. **Breast:** Grey, with darker shoulder-tabs. **Abdomen:** White. **Bill:** Brown, with a yellow base. It is longish and up-curved. **Legs:** Yellow.

Conspicuous features:
   - Look for the long up-curved bill.
   - Look for the yellow legs.
   - The bird has a squat posture standing on short legs.

Conspicuous characteristics:
   - When the bird lands it tends to bob both its head and its tail.
   - Feeds with agile running movements, sometimes very fast. Will wade through shallow water when feeding.
   - Tends to associate with flocks of Wrybill roosting on the flock edge.
   - At high-tide it usually roosts along the waterline.
   - When with Wrybills it looks a more solid bird.
   - Sometimes it winters over, staying in close contact with Wrybill flocks.

Call: A trilling "turloop too".

Where to find - North Island:
South Auckland - Miranda: Look for it at Pukorokoro River-mouth, "The Stilt Ponds" or at Taramaire.
Manukau Harbour - Te Hihi: Turns up at high-tide roosts.
Hawkes Bay - Ahuriri: Regularly found here.
Manawutu: Try the Manawatu Estuary near Foxton.
Where to find - South Island:
Southland - Waituna Lagoon and Awarua Bay: Often found here. (See Banded Dotterel article.)

BROWN SKUA

Charles A Fleming

Family: Stercorariidae   **Species:** *Catharacta skua lonnbergi*
Common Name: Brown Skua or Southern Skua   **Status:** Native
Size: 630 mm (cf sparrow 145 mm, Black-backed Gull 600 mm)

Discussion: Skuas can be described as predatory gulls, with the Brown Skua
being well known as both a predator and a scavenger content to raid nesting
colonies of penguins, shearwaters, gulls and terns. Although it is bigger than
the South Pole Skua (*C. maccormicki*) it has a wide size range and so can be
confused with it, and with the immature Black-back Gull.

Habitat: A coastal species during the breeding season which ranges into deeper
waters over the winter months.
Range: The New Zealand subspecies (*C. s. lonnbergi*) ranges around the south
of the South Island, Stewart Island, Snares Island and to the islands further
south. It sometimes is seen around Cook Strait when not breeding.

Description:
 Upperparts and underparts: Dark brown. **Wings:** Dark brown with white
 wing-flashes on both sides of the wing primary feathers.
Conspicuous feature:
 • Look for the white wing-flashes.
Call: "Charr-charr-charr" at nesting site only.
Nest: Breeds either in loose colonies or as a solitary breeder, making a scrape of
 a nest lined with grasses, twigs and dried seaweed placed on a promontory. Up
 to 2 light brown, blotched with dark brown eggs are laid.

Differences between the Brown Skua and the immature Black-backed Gull:
 • The Skua is heavier looking.
 • The Skua has wider wings.

- The Skua has very conspicuous white on the wings.
- The Skua has a thicker neck.
- The Skua has a much heavier bill with a hook on the end.

Differences between the Brown Skua and the South Pole Skua:
- Brown Skua appears of heavier build.
- Brown Skua is of a warmer brown colouring.
- The South Pole Skua is of a generally darker brown except around the face and neck where it has creamy tonings.

Where to find: South Island.
Cook Strait: Watch for it from the Cook Strait ferry on the off chance.

Where to find - Stewart Island:
Ackers Point: Brown Skuas can been seen from Ackers Point on the south side of Half Moon Bay. A track leads to the light-house on the point. Look for Skuas from here along with other seabirds.
Paterson Inlet: Islands at the entrance of Paterson Inlet provide suitable nesting localities.

ARCTIC SKUA

Family: Stercorariidae   **Species:** *Stercorarius parasiticus*
Common name: Arctic Skua, Arctic Jaeger   **Status:** Migrant
Size: 430 mm (cf sparrow 145 mm, Pomarine Skua 480 mm)

Discussion: Arctic Skuas are summer migrants to New Zealand and are easily identified by their habit of chasing White-fronted Terns to rob them of their recently caught prey.

Morphs: The Arctic Skua comes in both a dark and light morph. They are known for a great variation of colour so the descriptions below are approximate only.

Description - non-breeding - dark morph:
   Upperparts and underparts: Brown, with crown darker. **Wings:** Brown, usually with conspicuous white-flashes at the base of the primary wing feathers on the underwings and with traces of white on the upperwings. The wing-flashes are sometimes missing.
Description - non-breeding - light morph:
   Crown, neck and upperparts: Dark brown. **Chin and throat:** White. **Breast:** Brown band. **Underparts:** White. **Tail:** Brown, with a protruding central tail feather.
Conspicuous features:
- Looked for the prominent tail feather but not on non-breeding plumage birds.
- White underwing flashes are noticeable.
Conspicuous characteristics:
- Flies steadily and level when searching for feeding terns.
- Sits on the water like a gull.
- Extremely manoeuvrable when in flight chasing terns.

Arctic Skua

- Has the habit of approaching fishing boats and sitting on the water nearby.
- Will roost on beaches in the vicinity of other birds such as Caspian Terns.

Breeding localities of the Arctic Skua: Birds breed north of the 58th parallel in loose colonies on off-shore islands, open tundra and on open sandspits.

Migration: Birds head southwards in July to the 46th parallel. They return north in March. Some immatures are known to stay on.

Where to find - North Island:
Northland: Found in any coastal water where White-fronted Terns feed.
North Auckland - Tiri Tiri Island: Often seen in these waters.
South Auckland - Miranda: Seen here from land near nesting terns.

Where to find - South Island:
Cook and Foveaux Strait: Can be seen in these waters from the ferries.

Arctic Skua chasing White-fronted Terns

POMARINE SKUA

Bob Gill

Family: Stercocariidae   **Species:** *Stercocarius pomarinus*
Common name: Pomarine Skua, Pomarine Jaeger   **Status:** Migrant
Size: 480 mm (cf sparrow 145 mm, Arctic Skua 430 mm)

Discussion: The Pomarine Skua is considered to be less common than the Arctic
Skua. Where they occur together at sea they are impossible to separate.

Similarities of Pomarine Skuas with Arctic Skuas:
- Both species come in two morphs.
- Both species have similar colouration.

Differences between Pomarine Skuas and Arctic Skuas:
- The Pomarine Skua is a larger and heavier bird.
- The Pomarine Skua nests further north on the Arctic tundra only.
- The tail of the Pomarine Skua is more elongated with central protruding
  feathers rounded. The central tail feathers of the Arctic Skua are pointed.
- The light morph of the Pomarine Skua has whiter wing-flashes.

BLACK-BACKED GULL

Family: Laridae   **Species:** *Larus dominicanus*
Status: Native
Common name: Black-backed Gull, Dominican Gull (after the black and white
colours of the Dominican friars). Colloquially known as Mollyhawk.
Size: 600 mm (cf sparrow 145 mm, Pomarine Skua 480 mm)

Black-backed Gull

Discussion: The Black-backed Gull is a non-equatorial species found around New Zealand, the south-eastern shores of Australia, South America and southern Africa. It is also a non-migratory species unlike the Lesser Black-backed Gull (*Larus fuscus*) of the Northern Hemisphere. In Australia, it overlaps with the Pacific Gull (*Larus pacificus*) which is not found in New Zealand. Currently very common but not recorded from Cook's first voyage.

Habitat: Found around the coast and over pastureland.
Range: Found throughout New Zealand and its off-shore islands.

Description:
  Head, neck and underparts: Pure white. **Wings and back:** Black, with primaries edged with white. **Bill, legs and feet:** Yellow.
Description - immature birds until year three:
  Upper and underparts: Dull brown streaked with dark brown. **Bill and legs:** Brown.
Conspicuous features:
  • The overall brown of juveniles is obvious.
  • The Black-backed Gull is the only big bird on most beaches.
Call: A clear yodel of some volume.
Nest: Nests in loose colonies on open pastureland, or around the coast. Nest is a mound of grass and sticks. Up to 4 greenish, brown-blotched eggs are laid.

Where to find - North Island and South Island:
South Auckland - Miranda: Nests at the mangrove verge among rough pasture. This colony tends to move its location from time to time.
Bay of Plenty - Mount Tarawera: A nesting colony is located near the summit of Mount Tarawera, near Rotorua.
General: A very common species. Black-backed Gulls are known for their scavenging habits around city rubbish dumps. They also peck at cast sheep.

Brian Chudleigh

Immature Black-backed Gull

RED-BILLED GULL

Brian Chudleigh

Red-billed Gull with immature

Family: Laridae   **Species:** *Larus novaehollandiae*
Common name: Red-billed Gull, Silver Gull (Australia)   **Status:** Endemic
Size: 370 mm (cf sparrow 145 mm, Black-billed Gull 370 mm)

Discussion: Red-billed Gulls are a common species around the shoreline of
New Zealand. Races are also recognised in Australia and South Africa with
differences being based mainly on bill size, bill structure and the white patches
(mirrors) in the black of the wing tips. They are also found in New Caledonia,
especially on the south-east coast. Red-billed Gulls, which at times overlap

with Black-billed Gulls in some New Zealand coastal wintering areas, are not grouped with Black-billed Gulls. Instead, they share a relationship with the North American Laughing Gull (*Larus atricilla*) and the Black-headed Gull of Europe, (*Larus ridibundus*).

Habitat: A shoreline species that sometimes ventures inland.
Range: Found around the coast of New Zealand and its off-shore islands but inland at Lake Taupo and Lake Rotorua.

Description:
   Head, neck and underparts: White. **Wings:** Grey, black tipped on upper and undersides with white markings. **Bill and legs:** Red. **Eye:** Iris white, with a red ring around it.
Description - immature birds:
   Wings: Soft grey, with brownish speckles. **Bill, legs and feet:** Black or brownish-black. **Iris and eye-ring:** Brown.
Conspicuous feature:
   • Look for the bright red bill and legs of adult Red-billed Gulls.
Conspicuous characteristics:
   • Immature birds utter persistent, food-begging, "cheeting" cries.
Call: Familiar "kek kek kek" associated with strident screams and "kwaar kwaar kwaar" sounds.
Nest: A colonial nester making a mound of sticks and seaweed on a sandbank or rock ledge. Up to 2 light brown, dark brown-blotched eggs are laid. Sometimes they nest alongside Black-billed Gulls and White-fronted Terns.

Differences between mature Red-billed Gulls and Black-billed Gulls:
   • The Red-billed has a red bill. Black-billed has black bill.
   • The Red-billed has a shorter and heavier bill than the Black-billed.
   • The Red-billed has red legs. The Black-billed has reddish-black legs.
   • The Red-billed has distinctive black wing-tips with a triangle of black on the end of wings and a white marking among the black.
   • The Red-billed has a heavier head with the eye appearing to be less well balanced within it than the Black-billed.
   • The Black-billed has only an edge of black on the wing-tips showing much more white on the wings when in flight.
   • The Black-billed has a softer appearance than the Red-billed.
   • Some Black-billed Gulls have black tail dots on the end of the upper tail.
Differences between immature Red-billed Gulls and Black-billed Gulls:
   • The Red-billed Gull has a black bill in the fledgling stage and blackish legs.
   • The Black-billed Gull has a reddish bill with a dark tip and dark reddish legs in the fledgling stage.
Ecological differences between Red-billed Gulls and Black-billed Gulls:
   • The Red-billed Gull takes a wide range of sea foods. It is also a recognised scavenger well known for its rubbish tip feeding habits.
   • The Black-billed Gull is a specialised feeder taking estuarine fish and crustacean matter as well as worms and insects common on pastureland. It has a regular habit of following the plough in parts of the South Island.

Habitat and nesting differences between Red-billed Gulls and Black-billed Gulls:

- The Red-billed Gull is mainly a coastal bird.
- The Black-billed Gull is predominantly an inland bird.
- The Red-billed Gull is a coastal nesting species.
- The Black-billed Gull nests inland on the wide riverbeds of the South Island. In the North Island it is recorded nesting on sand and shell-spits.

Where to find:

Nesting colonies: Common around the coast on rock stacks and cliff edges. Places such as Aroha Island, Tiri Tiri Island, Motuihe Island and Rangitoto Island all have colonies detached from the main island.

BLACK-BILLED GULL

Brian Chudleigh.

Family: Laridae   **Species:** *Larus bulleri*
Common name: Black-billed Gull   **Status:** Endemic
Size: 370 mm (cf sparrow 145 mm, Red-billed Gull 370 mm)

Discussion: The Black-billed Gull is an endemic species, common in the southern half of the South Island where its feeds over pastureland and breeds in the wide riverbeds. Here it is often seen feeding with Black-fronted Terns when its tern-like flight sometimes causes confusion. Over recent years it has spread to the North Island breeding at Te Hihi on the Manukau Harbour and Miranda, while regularly being seen at Tauranga Harbour, Lake Rotorua, and the Manawatu and Waikanae Estuaries. Its closest relative is thought to be the Slender-billed Gull (*Larus genei*), a species which ranges through southern Europe and North Africa to Pakistan.

Habitat: Pastureland and riverbeds with a coastwards and northwards movement in winter.

Range: Well-spread through inland South Island pastureland areas. In the North Island it is scattered around coastal estuaries northwards to Miranda and Manukau Harbour.

Description:

Head, neck and underparts: Pure white. **Wings:** Soft grey. **Primaries:** Soft grey, edged with black and a trace of white. **Bill and legs:** Black.

Note: See Red-billed Gull article for differences between species, immature birds and habitats.

Conspicuous features:

- Look for the black bill and black feet which separate mature Black-billed Gulls from Red-billed Gulls.
- Black-billed Gulls have far less black on primary feathers, showing more white on wings when in flight.

Call: As for Red-billed Gull.

Nest: A colonial nester which makes a nest of twigs and seaweed on sand or river pebbles. Up to 2 pale greenish, brown-blotched eggs are laid.

Where to find - North Island:

South Auckland - Wattle Downs Ponds: Regularly seen here. Birds are from Manukau Harbour breeding colony. (See Dabchick article.)

South Auckland - Manukau Harbour: Clarks Beach often has odd birds among the Red-billed Gulls. (See Bar-tailed Godwit article.)

South Auckland - Miranda: Usually seen at "The Hide", especially over summer months. Birds breed on the shellspit from time to time.

Bay of Plenty - Rotorua: A breeding colony is easy to locate at Rotorua behind the Polynesian Pools. Visit by driving through the Centennial Gardens and then turn right and in behind the old Bath House complex.

Where to find - South Island:

Southland - Fiordland: Try the Eglinton Valley near Cascade Creek where birds nest alongside Black-fronted Terns.

Southland: Try the wide areas of the Oreti River just north of Mossburn on Highway 94 for nesting colonies. Generally common throughout inland areas.

WHITE-WINGED BLACK TERN

Family: Sternidae   **Species:** *Chlidonias leucopterus*
Common name: White-winged Black Tern   **Status:** Migrant
Size: 230 mm (cf sparrow 145 mm, White-fronted Tern 400 mm)

Discussion: A small species of marsh tern which breeds in eastern Europe and Siberia and migrates south to east Africa, south-eastern Asia, Indonesia and Australasia. A few end up in New Zealand where they have bred.

Habitat: Generally a coastal species which feeds over muddy pools and takes mainly aquatic insects. Moves inland to lakes and wet areas near the coast.

Brian Chudleigh

White-Winged Black Tern

Range: Records come from both islands of New Zealand.

Description - breeding plumage:
    Head, neck, back and underparts: Black. **Wings:** White, with pale grey primaries black tipped. **Underwing:** Coverts black, with primaries grey and black tipped. **Tail:** White above and below. **Bill and legs:** Red.

Description - non-breeding (as in photo above):
    Head: White forehead with indistinct partial black cap. **Upperparts:** White. **Wings:** White, with grey leading edges and primaries. **Rump and underparts:** White. **Bill and legs:** Black with reddish tinge.

Conspicuous features:
- Smaller than the Little and Fairy Terns.
- Indistinct black cap, in non-breeding birds, separates it from Little Terns.

Conspicuous characteristics:
- Feeds while hovering just above the water.
- Very buoyant when in flight almost dancing in the air.
- Will alight and settle among other terns or on sticks or posts.

Call: "keet keet keet".

Where to find - North Island:
Northland - Karikari: Try Lake Waiporohita. (See Little Grebe article.)
Auckland - Mangere Sewage Ponds: Odd records from here.
South Auckland - Manukau Harbour: Te Hihi often has a bird.
Hawkes Bay - Ahuriri Estuary: This area has recorded a flock of 15 birds.
Manawatu - Manawatu Estuary: Try the estuary-mouth.
Wellington - Waikanae Estuary: Odd records from here.

Where to find - South Island:
Canterbury - Lake Ellesmere: Records come from Embankment Road.
Canterbury - Sedgmere: Try Cooper Lagoon just south of Lake Ellesmere and

almost on the coast, accessed east of Leeston, off McEvedys Road.

Canterbury - Lake Wainono: Records come from here. This is accessed east of Studholme on Poingdestres Road. (See Banded Dotterel article.)

Canterbury - Tekapo: The Cass River-mouth sometimes produces a record.

Southland: Try the Invercargill Estuary or Awarua Bay.

BLACK-FRONTED TERN

Brian Chudleigh

Family: Sternidae   **Species:** *Sterna albostriata*
Common name: Black-fronted Tern   **Status:** Endemic
Size: 290 mm (cf sparrow 145 mm, White-fronted Tern 400 mm)

Discussion: The Black-fronted Tern is an endemic species which breeds along the South Island riverbeds. It belongs to the marsh tern group and is closely related to the Whiskered Tern (*Chlidonias hybrida*), a tern which has widespread distribution through Africa, Asia and Australia. It is the only inland tern of the South Island. The occasional visit of a White-winged Black Tern (*C. leucopterus*) is not likely to confuse as sightings of this bird are rare.

Habitat: A bird of inland waterways and especially the wide braided rivers of Mid-Canterbury. It also feeds over farmland, especially recently ploughed earth, arable crops and recently flooded irrigated land.

Range: It is found east of the Southern Alps in the South Island and particularly in Canterbury. In winter some birds move to the coast spreading south to Stewart Island or north into the North Island and up the east coast as far as Tauranga Harbour.

Description:
    Crown: Velvet-black. **Under-eye:** White. **Upperparts:** Soft bluish-grey.
    Cheeks, throat and underparts: Soft bluish-grey. **Rump:** White, with a grey

forked tail. **Bill and legs:** Orange.

Description - immature birds:
Crown: White behind bill then mottled with black. **Wings:** Grey. **Bill:** Dusky brown with a reddish base.

Conspicuous features:
- Look for the orange bill and legs.
- Look for the black crown coming right to the bill.
- Look for blue grey underparts.

Conspicuous characteristics:
- Birds flit and dart when in flight.
- Upon spotting prey, birds hover with fast wing beats.
- Birds blend with the riverbed stones when on the ground.

Call: A high-pitched "kit kit kit". It is more brittle than the call of the White-fronted Tern. Birds can "bark" angrily at intruders near their nests.

Nest: A scrape among the pebbles of the riverbeds in loose colonies. Up to 2 greyish, brown-blotched eggs are laid.

Differences between Black-fronted Terns and White-fronted Terns:
- The Black-fronted Tern has an orange bill and feet. The White-fronted Tern has a black bill and black legs.
- The Black-fronted Tern has bluish grey delicate underparts. The White-fronted Tern has clean white underparts.
- The Black-fronted Tern has a white forehead above the bill. The Black-fronted Tern has black coming right to the bill.
- The Black-fronted Tern is generally an inland bird except during winter months. The White-fronted Tern is coastal.

Where to find - North Island:

Bay of Plenty - Tauranga Harbour: Regularly recorded from the sandbanks in the harbour at the northern end. Follow the Athenree road from Highway 2 and then the Bowentown road, and travel to the end of the spit. Examine the harbour in this vicinity. This is a winter location.

Bay of Plenty - Kaituna River-mouth: This is a winter location only.

Bay of Plenty - Matata Lagoon: Occasionally sighted here and at the Tarawera River-mouth. This is a winter location.

King Country - Kawhia Harbour: Regularly seen here in winter near the town. Boats would be needed to see them on the sandbars.

Manawatu - Manawutu Estuary: This is a winter locality.

Manawatu - Rangitikei River-mouth: To get here, take Parewanui Road north of the river and travel west to the end. This is a winter locality.

Wellington - Waikanae Estuary: Regularly seen here. This is a winter locality. (See Shoveler article.)

Where to find - South Island:

Marlborough: Try the Wairau River north of Blenheim, either where the road to Nelson crosses it on SH 6 or where the road to Picton crosses it on SH 1.

Canterbury: In the breeding season, trips up most rivers in the South Island will produce this tern. In cropping areas, inspections of ploughed land will often reveal terns feeding with Black-billed Gulls. Anywhere along the

Rangitata River, south of Ashburton, should have this bird.

Southland: Good locations are the wide riverbeds of the Oreti and Aparima Rivers. Inspect these rivers when driving to Te Anau and the Eglinton Valley. It pays to stop the car and walk along the river stones.

Fiordland - Te Anau: Birds can often be seen flying along the shoreline of Lake Te Anau.

Fiordland - Eglinton Valley: Birds nest right along the Eglinton River, their nests being placed well out on the riverbed and often hidden among flowering Russell lupin (*Lupinus polyphyllus*).

CASPIAN TERN

Brian Chudleigh

Family: Sternidae   **Species:** *Sterna caspia*
Common name: Caspian Tern   **Status:** Native
Size: 510 mm (cf sparrow 145 mm, White-fronted Tern 400 mm)

Discussion: The Caspian Tern is a common coastal bird which breeds around the New Zealand coastline on secluded sandspits and coastal beaches. It is more common in northern waters. This tern is a cosmopolitan species with a range worldwide which extends through Britain, southern Europe, Asia, Australia, New Zealand and to the United States of America. It is absent in South America, northern North America, Asia and Europe. It is the largest of the world's terns and closely related to the Crested Tern (*Sterna bergii*).

Habitat: Sandy stretches of coast.
Range: Found right around the New Zealand coastline and sometimes inland to lakes such as Lake Taupo, the Rotorua lakes and Hamilton Lake.
Description - breeding:
  Crown: Black to below the eye. **Upperparts:** Grey. **Underparts:** White. **Bill:** Bright red. **Feet and legs:** Black.

Description - non-breeding:
Crown: White, flecked with black through eye and round back of head.
Conspicuous features:
- Larger than the White-fronted Tern with which it frequently associates.
- The black cap, extending from the bill base on forehead, separates it from the smaller White-fronted Tern.
- Body looks long and legs short.

Conspicuous characteristics:
- Has a squat posture when standing.
- Usually birds feed alone flying slowly above water with heads down. The heavy bill is obvious in this position. When a fish is spotted, birds hover momentarily and then dive forcefully, in a similar fashion to gannets.
- Birds rest on sandbanks and high-tide roosts, often among shore-birds such as oystercatchers. When resting they spread through them.

Call: A guttural "kaar-kaa kaar-kaa kaar" noise, different from the higher-pitched "kee-eet" call of the White-fronted Tern. Immature birds make a "petulant" whistle.

Nest: A colonial nester which makes a scrape in the sand. Up to 2 greyish, brown-blotched eggs are laid.

Where to find - North Island:
Northland waters: Common in these waters.
South Auckland - Miranda: Always good numbers here.

Where to find - South Island:
Kaikoura: Try the road east of the town.

General: Common in most coastal areas so no special localities are needed to find it. Common around most of the South Island.

WHITE-FRONTED TERN

Family: Sternidae   **Species:** *Sterna striata*
Common name: White-fronted Tern, Kahawai Bird   **Status:** Endemic
Size: 400 mm (cf sparrow 145 mm, Little Tern 250 mm)

Discussion: The White-fronted Tern is a well known New Zealand endemic tern which is common right around the coast where it nests in colonies on rock ledges, off-shore islands and rock stacks.

Migration: Juvenile White-fronted Terns migrate across the Tasman and winter around the south-east Australian coast and the northern coast of Tasmania where they are now known to have bred.

Tern migrants: Some identification confusion has arisen with the irregular identification of the Arctic Tern (*Sterna paradisaea*) and the northern hemisphere Common Tern (*Sterna hirundo*), in the Tauranga Harbour. Also the Antarctic Tern (*Sterna vittata*), which breeds to the south of Stewart Island, is sometimes seen in northern waters.

White-fronted Tern

Habitat: A bird of coastal waters preferring indented and rocky coastlines which are suitable for nesting. Will fish well up rivers.

Range: Especially common around northern coasts in the North Island and the northern coast of the South Island but generally well spread right around New Zealand and to the off-shore islands.

Description - breeding:
Forehead: White above bill. This distinguishes it from the Black-fronted Tern of the South Island and the Antarctic Tern. **Crown:** Black. **Upperparts:** Soft grey, sometimes with a pink breast-tinge. **Underparts:** White. **Bill:** Black. **Legs:** Dull red.

Description - non-breeding:
Crown: Receded black cap at back of a white head.

Description - immatures:
Crown: Receded black caps at back of white head. **Upperparts:** Dark grey wing markings on light grey.

Conspicuous features:
- Look for the white forehead.
- Look for the forked "swallow-like" tail.

Call: A high-pitched "kee-eet kee-eet" or a soft "zeet zeet". It has other more rasping notes used at times of communal feeding.

Nest: A colonial nester making a scrape in the sand or shell or using a rock crevice. Up to 2 green, lightly-spotted brown eggs are laid.

Where to find:
Auckland - Muriwai: Birds nest on the cliffs near to the gannet colony.

South Auckland - Miranda: Birds nest near "The Hide".

General: A common coastal bird found on many beaches throughout New Zealand. Often referred to as Kahawai Birds by fishermen because of their habit of flocking in and around feeding kahawai fish.

230

ANTARCTIC TERN

Charles A Fleming

Family: Sternidae   **Species:** *Sterna vittata*
Common name: Antarctic Tern   **Status:** Endemic
Size: 360 mm (cf sparrow 145 mm, White-fronted Tern 400 mm)

Discussion: A bird which is slightly smaller than the White-fronted Tern, differentiated by its heavier bill which is red coloured rather than black and its red legs. It is also an overall heavier looking build.

Habitat: A bird of coastal islands and rock stacks where it nests usually in small colonies. Sometimes isolated nests might be found.
Range: Known from the waters around the south of Stewart Island and Snares Islands, Auckland Island, Campbell Island and Antipodes Island.

Description:
   Crown: Black. **Upperparts and underparts:** Soft grey. **Rump, undertail and uppertail:** White. **Bill and legs:** Bright red.
Conspicuous features:
- Look for red bill and legs.
- Look for black cap which extends to base of bill.
- When in flight, tail has a gently curved fork.

Conspicuous characteristics:
- Birds flock together into feeding groups during the months of February to November when away from the breeding colonies.
- Generally a slow flier above the sea when looking for prey.
- Its dives for prey are not as forceful as those of the White-fronted Tern or the Caspian Tern.

Where to find: Stewart Island.

Paterson Inlet: Sometimes on the rock stacks and islands off Paterson Inlet.

Port Pegasus: If on a boat trip further south from Half Moon Bay this tern will be frequently seen.

FAIRY TERN

Brian Chudleigh

Family: Sternidae   **Species:** *Sterna nereis*

Common name: Fairy Tern (Not to be confused with the White Tern (*Gygis alba*), a tropical species, which sometimes goes by the name of Fairy Tern.)

Status: Native

Size: 250 mm (cf sparrow 145 mm, Little Tern 250 mm)

Discussion: The New Zealand Fairy Tern, (*S. n. davisae*) is considered a sub-species of the Australian Fairy Tern and is separated mainly by an enlarged area of black feathering in front of the eye. It is one of New Zealand's most endangered species totalling about 30 birds. It nests in very small numbers along two stretches of the Northland east coast and on one small stretch of the Northland west coast. This bird is easily confused with the migrant Little Tern which ranges from Africa through Asia to Australia and in places over-laps with the Fairy Tern.

Habitat: A coastal species which in New Zealand appears to prefer long sandy beaches in spring and summer but winters in harbours and estuaries.

Range: On the Kaipara Harbour it sometimes can be found in a pre-breeding flock. Otherwise found in Northland near the Kaipara Heads or on the east coast from Pakiri in the south to Whangarei Heads in the north. Records of isolated birds also come from Miranda and the Tauranga Harbour.

Description - breeding plumage:
    Forehead: White with a rounded recess to above the eye. **Crown and nape:**

232

Black, which encircles the eye. **Back and wings:** Light grey, but primary feathers darker. **Neck and underparts:** White. **Tail:** White and forked. **Bill:** Yellow-orange. **Legs:** Orange.

Description - non-breeding:

Crown: White of forehead extends to mid-crown.

Conspicuous features:

- Look for yellow bill right to the tip.
- Look for the black eye surround.
- Look for the white rounded recess above the eye.
- Look for the forked tail.

Call: Both Fairy and Little Terns make high-pitched "cheet" or "peep" calls.

Nest and chicks: The Fairy Tern is a solitary nester which lays two eggs in the sand relying on camouflage to protect the chicks from aerial and other predators. Chicks on hatching cryptically blend with the colour of the sand. By day 21 birds have taken on grey plumage feathers barred with dark grey and have assumed a rusty coloured head, colouring which tends to help them blend in with the dead shells and especially those of golden oysters.

Differences between breeding Fairy Tern and Little Tern:

- Fairy has a yellow bill. Little has a yellow bill which is black-tipped.
- Fairy has a black cap which extends around the eye in a soft S curve. This black does not extend right to the bill. Little has a neat black cap which extends around the eye in a sharp V which then extends to the bill.
- Fairy is paler grey on wings and back and lacks the dark grey primary wing feathers of the Little Tern.
- Fairy has a rounded forehead. Little a swept back forehead.

Differences between non-breeding Fairy Terns and Little Terns:

- The Fairy Tern has more black on the crown.
- The Little Tern has a swept back crown with black towards the nape.

Differences between immature Fairy Terns and Little Terns:

- Immature birds are inseparable. Birds of both species have black bills and indistinct white crowns mottled with black feather scalation.
- Fairy Terns always have a higher crown.

Field characteristics which can help separate the two species:

- Fairy Terns are more communal and feed in company, while Little Terns are more solitary when feeding.
- Fairy Terns dive boldly, more akin to the Caspian Tern, while the dives of Little Terns are gentle splashes.
- Fairy Terns' flight is usually level and direct, not unlike the Caspian Tern, while Little Terns tend to hover with fast wing beats, with heads down, not unlike Marsh Terns.
- Little Terns intermingle on high tide roosts with other birds such as Lesser Knots, while Fairy Terns tend to roost alone.

Where to find - North Island:

Northland - Mangawhai: Birds nest on the sand "island" near the entrance to the heads. Areas are fenced from intruders. As the island is now joined to the spit enter the sand dunes via Pacific Road to the south of the Mangawhai shopping centre and walk northwards.

Northland - Waipu: At the Uretiti Reserve off Highway 1, about 4 kms north of the Waipu turn-off, drive down to a carpark and walk to the beach. Walk in a southerly direction towards the Waipu Spit.

Northland - Waipu: From Waipu town drive to the river-mouth and turn into Johnsons Point Road. Drive to the end and park. Cross the river in a southerly direction (at low tide only). Nesting birds are fenced off.

North Auckland - Tapora: Tapora is west of Wellsford on the Kaipara Harbour. Roads are gravel and dusty for much of the way. From Tapora take Okahukura Road. At Te Ngaio Point Road travel a further 2 kms and look for a track on the left with locked gate and shed on left. Walk in for 1.5 kms and cross the sand or shallow water to Big Sand Island. The crossing point on either side of the island is likely place for Fairy Terns.

North Auckland - Kaipara Harbour: Drive from Helensville to the end of South Head into the Trig Road rest area. Walk to the lagoon. Go at low-tide and wade across the lagoon. This area is known as Papakanui Spit.

EASTERN LITTLE TERN

Brian Chudleigh

Family: Sternidae   **Species:** *Sterna albifrons*
Common name: Little Tern or Eastern Little Tern   **Status:** Migrant
Size: 250 mm (cf sparrow 145 mm, Fairy Tern 250 mm)

Discussion: Little Terns are a wide ranging species known from Europe, North and South America, Africa and Asia. A few straggle to New Zealand probably from Australia, where they breed from Tasmania to northern Queensland.

Habitat: Harbours and estuaries.
Range: The Manukau Harbour and the Firth of Thames host most of the summer

population. Up to 25 birds turn up at summer counts and up to five at winter counts. Frequently recorded also from the Bay of Plenty and Farewell Spit in small numbers.

Description - breeding plumage:
  Forehead: White, extending to a white line above the eye. **Crown:** A black line extends from base of bill through the eye to the black head cap. **Back:** Grey. **Wings:** Grey with dark edges to primaries. **Underparts:** White. **Tail:** White and forked. **Bill:** Yellow-orange with a black tip. **Legs:** Yellow.

Description - non-breeding:
  Crown: Receded black cap at back of head. **Bill:** Pale yellow with dark tip.

Note: See Fairy Tern article for differences between Little Tern and Fairy Tern. Birds in breeding plumage are more easily separated from Fairy Terns.

Conspicuous features:
- Look for yellow-orange bill with black tip.
- Look for the partial black cap and the black line through eye to bill.
- Look for the white line above the eye.

Conspicuous characteristics:
- Sits with roosting shorebirds at high tide usually near the tide line.
- Hovers in an agitated manner before diving.
- Very dainty when in flight.

Call: Urgent "peet peet" sounds.

Where to find - North Island:

North Auckland - Kaipara Harbour: Try Jordans Road north of Kaukapakapa. Permission is required to go through private land here.

South Auckland - Manukau Harbour: The best area is at Te Hihi but this has no public access.

South Auckland - Miranda: Visit "The Hide" at high-tide, Taramaire River-mouth or further north. Little Terns may be found roosting among waders or resting on fence posts which are isolated in the mud.

Bay of Plenty - Matata Lagoon: Look for them flying over the lagoons.

GREY TERNLET

Family: Sternidae   **Species:** *Procelsterna cerulea*
Common name: Grey Ternlet   **Status:** Native
Size: 280 mm (cf sparrow 145 mm, White-fronted Tern 400 mm)

Discussion: A bird of the tropics and sub-tropics which breeds on the Kermedec Islands, on West Island in the Three Kings group and Volkner Rocks off White Island.

Habitat and range: Coastal and islands in Northland and the Bay of Plenty.

Description:
  Crown: Whitish with dark eye. **Upperparts:** Delicate blue-grey with dark primaries on wings. **Wings:** Blue-grey with a thin white trailing edge. **Underparts:** Light grey

Grey Ternlet

Where to find:
Bay of Islands: Often seen in deeper water.
Bay of Plenty: Often seen on route to White Island from Tauranga.

NEW ZEALAND PIGEON

Family: Columbidae　　　　　**Species:** *Hemiphaga novaeseelandiae*
Common name: New Zealand Pigeon, Kereru, Kukupa (Northland)
Status: Endemic
Size: 510 mm (cf sparrow 145 mm, Rock Pigeon 330 mm)

Discussion: New Zealand has only one endemic pigeon. It has missed out on any major spread of the order Columbiformes from Australia and further afield. Australia has some 22 species, while New Caledonia and Vanuatu both have five and Fiji has ten. The ancestor of the New Zealand Pigeon is considered an early arrival later adapting and spreading to Norfolk Island and the Chatham Islands.

Habitat: A bird of both secondary forest and old forest, in particular of those which contain fruiting varieties such as puriri, kohekohe, taraire, tawa and miro. It will also enter suburban gardens to feed on flowering or fruiting trees.
Range: Found throughout the forested areas of New Zealand and on the off-shore islands. It is a very common bird on Stewart Island.

Description:
　Upperparts: Greenish, with feathers showing a metallic purplish iridescence, especially around the neck. **Underparts:** White, this white appearing like a white "apron" on abdomen.

New Zealand Pigeon

Conspicuous features:
- The white abdomen "apron" on a roosting pigeon, is conspicuous.

Conspicuous characteristics:
- Pigeon flight "swish" noises are audible as it flies from branch to branch.
- Open-country flight is level and steady.
- Courtship display habit of soaring out from high up in trees, gaining altitude and then suddenly stalling and swooping earthward is often seen.

Call: Usually silent but often soft "kuu kuu kuu" sounds are heard in the breeding season.

Nest: A loose structure of sticks at about four metres above ground. 1 white egg only is laid.

Where to find - North Island:
Northland - Bay of Islands: Kerikeri often has birds in old trees.
Northland - Waimate North: Old puriri stands here have birds.
North Auckland - Waiwera: Try Wenderholm Park off Highway 1 north of Waiwera. (See "Places" in back of book.)
North Auckland - Whangaparaoa: Follow Wade River Road at Whangaparaoa down to the Weiti River. Search roadside forests by the wharf.
North Auckland - Tiri Tiri Island: Several pairs live on the island. Expect one from the boardwalk on the northern end.
King Country - Pureora: Common at the forest park. (See "Places" in back of book.)

Where to find - South Island:
Dunedin: Common in Dunedin in gardens, and the botanical gardens.
Fiordland: Cascade Creek and the Hollyford Valley have good numbers.

Where to find - Stewart Island:
Half Moon Bay: Large numbers of pigeon can be seen around Oban.
General: Expect them in forested localities away from the Far North.

ROCK PIGEON

Brian Chudleigh

Family: Columbidae   **Species:** *Columba livia*
Common name: Homing Pigeon   **Status:** Introduced
Size: 330 mm (cf sparrow 145 mm)

Discussion: Introduced by pigeon fanciers, this bird is common in most New Zealand cities where it breeds high up on building ledges or under bridges. It has also established populations on cliff faces in places like Napier, Rangitikei and inland Canterbury.

Habitat: Cities, parks, pastureland and mudflats.
Range: Throughout both the main islands usually close to cities.

Description:
Head and upperparts: Variations of dark grey and blue-grey with some purple iridescence on neck. **Wings:** Usually blue-grey with two black bars on primaries. **Rump:** White.

Where to find:
North and South Islands: Common in many cities and towns.

BARBARY DOVE

Family: Columbidae   **Species:** *Streptopelia roseogrisea*
Common name: Barbary Dove   **Status:** Introduced
Size: 280 mm (cf sparrow 145 mm, Homing Pigeon 330 mm)

Discussion: Introduced by pigeon fanciers, this bird originates from Asia. It is closely related to the Ring-necked Doves of Africa (*S. decipens* and *S. capicola*)

238

Brian Chudleigh

Barbary Dove

and to the Collared Dove of Europe and Asia, (*S. decaocta*). Feral populations in New Zealand remain tenuous.

Habitat: A bird of old gardens and parkland where tall trees are plentiful.
Range: Isolated populations occur in Kerikeri, Whangarei, Mangere, Clevedon, Whakatane and Havelock North.

Description:
   Upperparts and underparts: Creamy buff, with brown wing edges. **Neck:** Black collar across the back of the neck. **Tail:** Fawn, with white tips to outer tail feathers.
Conspicuous feature:
   • Look for the brown neck collar which separates it from the Spotted Dove.
Call: Call is a soft "kru ku". Don't mix with the Morepork. It is also different from the tri-syllabic call of the Spotted Dove.
Nest: A twiggy, flimsy structure built at about four metres from the ground. 2 white eggs are laid.

Where to find - North Island:
Northland - Kerikeri: Birds are seen around the town especially in the area near the "Stone Store".
Auckland: The suburb of Mangere has a growing population some of which associate with Spotted Doves on Puketutu Island across the causeway from the Mangere Sewage Ponds.
South Auckland - Clevedon: A small colony is establishing just east of Clevedon in the direction of Kawakawa Bay.
Rotorua: Try Rainbow Springs north of Rotorua town on Highway 5.
Hawkes Bay - Napier: A small population exists in the Napier gardens.
Hawkes Bay - Havelock North: A small population here is sustaining itself in the Holiday Park area.

SPOTTED DOVE

Brian Chudleigh

Family: Columbidae **Species:** *Streptopelia chinensis*
Common name: Spotted Dove, Lace-necked Dove, Malay Spotted Dove
Status: Introduced
Size: 300 mm (cf sparrow 145 mm, Homing Pigeon 330 mm)

Discussion: This dove is an escaped cage bird. Its origins lie in Asia and it is considered a bird of the tropics. In New Zealand its spread has been limited mainly to Auckland and nearby districts although bird sightings have come from other places such as Te Puke in the Bay of Plenty. In Australia its spread has been wider and even into Tasmania. It is also common in some of the Pacific islands such as Fiji, New Caledonia and Samoa.

Habitat: A bird of old gardens, parks, and forest verges.
Range: Common in many suburbs of Auckland and now slowly spreading both north to Albany and south to Clevedon and Pukekohe.
Description:
  Head: Grey. **Neck:** Delicate white spots, sprinkled over a wide black half-collar, on back of neck. **Upperparts:** Grey-brown. **Underparts:** Grey with a pinkish flush. **Tail:** Brown, with outer feathers white, noticeable when in flight.
Conspicuous features:
  - The undertail black and white is noticeable when in flight.
  - Look for the spotted neck-collar.
Conspicuous characteristics:
  - A fast flying dove which shows a long tail when in flight.
  - Feeds especially on gravel driveways and on mown lawns.
  - Calls from roof tops or chimneys.
  - Commonly seen at dusk carrying out display flights, swooping steeply upwards and then stalling, dropping downwards before swooping up once

again. These displays are part of its courtship ritual.

Call: A tri-syllabic, "ku kuu kuk", distinguishes it from the Barbary Dove which is bi-syllabic. Both species can be mistaken for the evening calls of the Morepork which is also heard in some Auckland suburbs.

Nest: A twiggy structure at about four metres. 2 white eggs are laid.

Where to find - North Island:

Auckland - Epsom: Look for it in the One Tree Hill, Mount Eden and Epsom areas of Auckland. Try Cornwall Park in Epsom.

Auckland - Remuera: Usually found in wooded areas from Mount Hobson to Hobson Bay.

Auckland - Westmere: A large population lives about the Auckland Zoo and Western Springs.

Auckland - Mangere: A sizeable population is to be found at Puketutu Island across the causeway from the Mangere Sewage Ponds. Here, Barbary Doves may also be seen.

Auckland - Howick: A sizeable colony exists on Point View Drive about 3 kms along from the Whitford Road junction.

South Auckland - Clevedon: Small populations have spread east to Whitford, Clevedon and Kaiaua.

Bay of Plenty: Records come from Katikati to Te Puke with an increasing population in the Te Puke area.

SULPHUR-CRESTED COCKATOO

Family: Cacatuidae   **Species:** *Cacatua galerita*
Common name: Sulphur-crested Cockatoo   **Status:** Introduced
Size: 500 mm (cf sparrow 145 mm, Kaka 450 mm)

Discussion: The Sulphur-crested Cockatoo population in New Zealand is considered to have derived from cage-bird escapes although it may have been added to over the years by windblown stragglers from Australia from where it originates. In Australia it is extremely common being found in eastern and northern states. It is also found in Papua New Guinea and eastern Indonesia. In New Zealand this bird has never built up large populations but numbers are growing in some localities.

Habitat: Found in native forest remnants, exotic plantations and especially in eucalypt trees.

Range: The main North Island populations are found in small groups in areas to the west from Awakino in the south to Muriwai Beach in the north. Other populations exist near Miranda, Hunterville and Waikanae. The South Island range is limited to populations near Christchurch and south of Dunedin.

Description:
  Crest and behind eye: Yellow. **Upperparts and underparts:** White.
  Bill and feet: Greyish-black. **Eye:** Brown with a blue eye-ring.
Conspicuous feature:
- A large white parrot with a sulphur coloured crest.

Brian Chudleigh
Sulphur-Crested Cockatoo

Conspicuous characteristics
- In the breeding season regularly seen in pairs, but out of the breeding season it is to be found in large and mobile flocks which are often noisy.

Call: Harsh and raucous screeches.

Nest: A hole high up in a tree, usually with 2 white eggs.

Feeding habits: It feeds and roosts in tall trees by day, and congregates in them over-night. From time to time it will feed on the ground with some sentry birds posted around in taller vegetation.

Where to find - North Island:

South Auckland - Onewhero: Take the Onewhero signs from Tuakau and then try Nolan Road, Brien Road, Matakitaki Road and Baker Road.

South Auckland - Miranda: It is often seen near the gravel pit area at Whakatiwai Bay and in the Mangatangi Road area.

Waikato - Waingaro near Ngaruawahia: Birds are often seen in this area.

Waikato - Horhsam Downs to Te Kowhai near Hamilton: Birds come to areas of tall gum trees in these districts.

Manawautu - Hunterville: Populations are known from east of Hunterville at the headwaters of the Rangitikei River, and west of Hunterville towards the headwaters of the Turakina River near Turakina Valley Road.

Wellington - Waikanae: Look for birds near the cemetery in Ngarara Road.

Where to find - South Island:

Christchurch: Try Greendale just south of Christchurch.

Southland - Owaka: Establishing near Owaka.

GALAH

Brian Chudleigh

Family: Cacatuidae   **Species:** *Cacatua roseicapilla*
Common name: Galah   **Status:** Introduced
Size: 360 mm (cf sparrow 145 mm, Kaka 450 mm)

Discussion: A recent Australian cage-bird escape which is establishing itself in the South Auckland areas of Clevedon, Kawakawa Bay, Mangatangi, Mangatawhiri and Waitakaruru. Also on Ponui Island off Kawakawa Bay.

Habitat: Pastureland, maize stubble, hedgerows and eucalypt trees.
Range: South Auckland from the Waitemata Harbour through to the lower Waikato areas and east to the Firth of Thames.

Description:
  Crown: White. **Upperwings:** Grey. **Neck, abdomen and underwing coverts:** Pink. **Underwing:** Grey with dark primary feathers. **Rump:** White. **Undertail:** Grey. **Bill:** Off-white.
Conspicuous features:
- Pink abdomen extending to underwing coverts and neck, gives birds away when in flight.
- White crown is conspicuous on ground feeding birds.

Conspicuous characteristics:
- Often in fast moving flocks outside of breeding season.
- Noisy when in flocks.
- Feeds among maize stubble.

Call: A high pitched "chi chi chi".
Nest: It usually nests in a hole in an old tree. Up to 5 white eggs are laid.

Where to find - North Island:

Auckland - Ponui Island and Pakihi Island: These islands lie off the coast near Kawakawa Bay, east of Clevedon.

South Auckland - Clevedon: Birds are regularly seen in this district and towards Kawakawa Bay. Inspect eucalyptus trees.

South Auckland - Miranda: Birds have been seen moving through this district and to Waitakaruru and Mangatangi.

South Auckland - Pokeno: Birds are regularly seen along Highway 2 in the Mangatawhiri district. Try Lyons Road just before the Mangatawhiri shop and petrol station. Look in the paddocks with maize stubble.

South Auckland - Mangatawhiri: Try Bell Road just past the Mangatawhiri shops.

General: The total number of birds in New Zealand is now over 100 birds (2000). Birds seem to be very mobile and outside of the breeding season cover a lot of territory. Nesting birds have not yet been found. Main breeding territories are as yet unknown.

KAKAPO

Don Merton

Family: Cacatuidae **Species:** *Strigops habroptilus*
Common name: Kakapo **Status:** Endemic
Size: 630 mm (cf sparrow 145 mm, Kaka 450 mm)

Discussion: The Kakapo is an ancient New Zealand species probably related to the Australian Night Parrot (*Pezoporus occidentalis*) and the Ground Parrot (*Pezoporus wallicus*). In predator-free New Zealand it has become large, slow breeding and flightless (Fleming 1982). It is a nocturnal species which feeds and carries out its courtship behaviour at night. Now totalling about 64 birds it is confined to Little Barrier Island, Codfish Island off Stewart Island and Maud Island in the Marlborough Sounds. Intensive efforts to raise the population are underway and four chicks have now been reared (2000).

Description:
  Upper and underparts: Greenish-yellow. **Tail:** Brownish.

Call: A "booming" noise, made when male birds are on lek "booming bowls".

General: Only Department of Conservation staff and helpers have any opportunity of seeing this bird in the wild. For further information enquire at Department of Conservation offices or visit - www.kakaporecovery.org.nz.

KAKA

Charles A Fleming

Family: Nestoridae   **Species:** *Nestor meridionalis*
Common name: Kaka   **Status:** Endemic
Size: 450 mm (cf sparrow 145 mm, Kea 460 mm)

Discussion: A bird of relatively ancient origin with stocky build, brush-tipped tongue, short tail and ceres bristles. This suggests an evolution separated from other parrots. Its adaptation to a temperate climate reinforces this. Its closest relatives are the Australian lorikeets, all of which have brush-tipped tongues and nectar-eating habits (Fleming 1982). The South Island Kaka (*N. m. meridionalis*), is larger than the North Island bird (*N. m. septentrionalis*) with more grey colouring on the cap.

Habitat: A bird of old forests, which seeks remnant forests, gardens, orchards and even suburban gardens outside of the breeding season.

Range: In the North Island, birds are concentrated in the centre of the island and on the off-shore islands. It is well-spread in South and Stewart Island.

Description:
  Head: Cap greyish on the North Island Kaka and grey on the South Island Kaka. Behind the eye is orange. **Upperparts:** Brown, with tonings of green and red. **Breast:** Brown, with tonings of green and red. **Abdomen:** Brown,

with crimson tonings. **Underwing:** Red.

Conspicuous features:
- A large overall brown looking parrot.
- The rather large head of the in-flight bird is noticeable.

Conspicuous characteristics:
- Harsh calls of in-flight birds give it away.
- Flying birds always appear to be poorly proportioned with large head.
- Rounded wings are noticeable.
- The sound of breaking sticks can indicate a feeding Kaka.

Call: Usually harsh guttural calls but also sweet musical notes.

Nest: Usually a hole in an old tree high up. Up to 5 white eggs are laid.

Where to find - North Island:

Great Barrier Island - Tryphena: Good populations here.

King Country - Pureora Forest: This is an easy place to find them. Look for them in the Bismarck Road area. (See "Places" in back of book.)

Urewera - Lake Waikaremoana: Try the Lake Waikareiti Track, signposted from the area of Lake Waikaremoana Park information centre.

Taupo - Lake Rotopounamu Track: Take Highway 47 from Tokaanu. Lake Rotopounamu is over the saddle and signposted. (See Rifleman article.)

Where to find - South Island

West Coast - Lake Brunner: Generally Kaka can be expected from any West Coast forests. (See Great Spotted Kiwi article.)

Fiordland - Cascade Creek: It is a common species here, sometimes seen with Kea.

Where to find - Stewart Island:

Oban: Common around the town.

KEA

Family: Nestoridae   **Species:** *Nestor notabilis*

Common name: Kea   **Status:** Endemic

Size: 460 mm (cf sparrow 145 mm, Kaka 450 mm)

Discussion: Kea are a close relative of the Kaka. They are renowned for being the only alpine parrot in the world. The species stems from an ancestor closer to the forest Kaka than the alpine Kea (Fleming 1982). In the past they have gone through phases of persecution by high-country farmers being blamed for killing sheep. Today, though, they are protected and numbers have increased.

Habitat: They are restricted to subalpine and alpine environments.

Range: Found only in the South Island. They are well-spread across the Southern Alps and into much of Westland and throughout Fiordland.

Description:

Upperparts and underparts: Olive-green. **Underwing:** Scarlet. **Rump:** Dull red. **Tail:** Has a touch of blue on longer feathers. Otherwise green.

Brian Chudleigh

Kea

Conspicuous features:
- A large green parrot.
- Look for sharp-hooked bill.
- Some yellow flecking is noticeable on body feathers.
- The red underwing is easily seen when birds are frolicking.

Conspicuous characteristics:
- A bird which is very confident on the ground and which is constantly clambering around and over rocks in search for food.
- Vocally noisy when in flight. This gives away its presence.

Kea behaviour: Kea behave in their alpine environment in a similar comical way as do Kaka in the forest. They are, though, far more interested in human activities than Kaka. For example, cars parked in alpine areas are quickly investigated. Kea are known to slide down windscreens, pull on wind-screen wipers, hook on to half-open windows and peck tyre rims and valve stems. The public are warned to guard their cars in Kea localities.

Call: The Kea screech is commonly heard in all alpine regions. It sounds like its name "kee-aaa kee-aaa kee-aa". Usually the screech comes from above because birds tend to perch high up. It is also uttered when birds are in flight.

Nest: In holes in the ground or under fallen logs. Up to 4 white eggs are laid.

Where to find - South Island:

Marlborough - Lake Rotoiti: Tracks lead from this lake into the alpine environment. They are worth a try. (See Brown Creeper article.)

West Coast - Franz Josef Glacier: Try the carparks at either Franz Josef or Fox Glacier.

Canterbury - Arthurs Pass: Take Highway 73 from Christchurch. After Arthurs Pass village try the alpine screes.

Fiordland - Eglinton Valley: Try Cascade Creek, The Divide, Hollyford Valley, the Homer Tunnel entrance and the road up to the Homer Tunnel.

CRIMSON ROSELLA

Brian Chudleigh

Family: Platycercidae   **Species:** *Platycerus elegans*
Common name: Crimson Rosella   **Status:** Introduced
Size: 350 mm (cf sparrow 145 mm, Eastern Rosella 320 mm)

Discussion: The Crimson Rosella is an introduced species and a close relative of the Eastern Rosella. Occasional birds are seen from time to time.

Habitat: Similar to that of the Eastern Rosellas frequenting both native and exotic trees.

Range: Main population is in the Wellington city area and in particular the Botanical Gardens and Karori. Scattered reports of birds have come from Waiwera (1995) and South Manukau Harbour and Whangaparaoa (1998).

Description - mature birds:
  Head and underparts: Red. **Face and throat:** Blue. **Wings:** Black and red with blue primaries. **Tail:** Light blue outer feathers, and dark blue inner feathers.
Description - immature birds:
  Head: Crimson. **Face and throat:** Blue. **Upperparts and underparts:** Green. **Wings:** Green, black-blotched with blue primaries. **Tail:** Crimson with blue outer feathers.
Conspicuous features:
  • General appearance of a mature bird is of an all-over red bird.
  • A striking bird to see.
Conspicuous characteristics:
  • Will associate with Eastern Rosellas.
  • Direct, fast-flying flight, with out-stretched tail.
Call: A loud "kwink kwink kwink", similar but of deeper notes than the Eastern Rosella. It also has a musical song not unlike the Eastern Rosella.
Nest: Cavities in trees about five metres up. Up to 6 white eggs are laid.

Where to find - North Island:
North Auckland - Wenderholm: A sighting in 1997 was made in the park.
North Auckland - Whangaparaoa: A sighting from this area was made in 1997 at the east end of Manly beach where the bird was viewed eating ripe plums in January. If on the Whangaparaoa Peninsula watch out for this bird.
South Auckland - Clarks Beach: One bird seen here in 1998.
Wellington: The Botanical Gardens and Brooklyn Park occasionally have these birds and juveniles have been recorded here. This is probably the best area to try.
Wellington - Karori: The reservoir area is worth trying.
Wellington - Kelburn: Try its wooded areas.

General: New reports suggest that this species could be extending its range.

EASTERN ROSELLA

Brian Chudleigh

Family: Platycercidae   **Species:** *Platycercus eximius*
Common name: Eastern Rosella   **Status:** Introduced
Size: 320 mm (cf sparrow 145 mm)

Discussion: This colourful species is a cage-bird escape which is now widely spread. It is a native of Australia where it is to be found in Tasmania, Victoria, New South Wales and south Queensland.

Habitat: In New Zealand a bird of both exotic and indigenous forests and of scattered vegetation.
Range: Now wide-spread through the northern North Island from Taupo northwards and continuing a southern spread. Also to be found around Wellington with a northward spread occurring. A small population lives around Dunedin in the South Island.

Description:
  Head, neck and breast: Bright red. **Lower cheeks and throat:** White. **Wings:** A mixture of yellow and black with blue primaries. **Underparts:** Yellow. **Tail:** Blue and green.
Conspicuous feature:
  • The most gaily coloured of New Zealand's birds.
Conspicuous characteristics:
  • Usually seen flying in pairs.
  • A difficult bird to see once it has landed in a tree, as it tends to move into the middle of the tree.
  • Birds often call from high up.
Call: The usual call is a metallic "kwink" heard from high up in the forest. They also have an attractive musical song.
Nest: Is found in cavities in trees. Up to 6 white eggs are laid.

Where to find- North Island:
North Auckland - Waiwera: Common at Wenderholm Park.
North Auckland - Whangaparaoa: Common at the Weiti (Wade) River.
South Auckland - Kawakawa Bay to Orere Point: Common here.
Waikato - Te Kowhai: In this area they frequent the clumps of kahikatea forest and occasionally share them with Sulphur-crested Cockatoos.
Bay of Plenty - Matata to Rotorua: Regularly seen through these forests.
King Country - Otorohanga: Common in most lightly wooded areas.
Wellington - Waikanae: Look in areas of bush around the town.

Where to find - South Island:
Dunedin: The Botanical Gardens, town belt and the Portobello areas all have occasional birds.

ANTIPODES ISLAND PARAKEET

The Antipodes Island Parakeet (*Cyanoramphus unicolor*): This lives side-by-side with Reischeks Parakeet *(C. novaezelandiae hochstetteri)*. It is considered to have evolved from a very early arrival of a Red-crowned ancestor. This bird is all green in colour, larger than Reischeks being 360 mm in length, and is ground feeding. It clambers around on the ground using its beak and its wings as added support, and has been likened to a small Kakapo. Although it can fly, it seldom does.
Captive birds: This bird can now be seen at Mount Bruce National Wildlife Centre, and at Te Anau Wildlife Reserve where it is breeding well in captivity.

RED-CROWNED PARAKEET

Family: Platycercidae   **Species:** *Cyanoramphus novaezelandiae*
Common name: Red-crowned Parakeet, Kakariki   **Status:** Endemic
Size: 280 mm (cf sparrow 145 mm, Yellow-crowned Parakeet 250 mm)

Brian Chudleigh
Red-crowned Parakeet

Discussion: New Zealand Parakeets, which include the Red-crowned Parakeet, the Yellow-crowned Parakeet and the Antipodes Island Parakeet, are thought to share a common ancestry with the Australian rosellas. This common ancestor is thought to have differentiated in New Zealand and then spread to New Caledonia, Lord Howe Island, Norfolk Island and Tahiti in the north, and to the Chatham Islands, Macquarie Islands, Auckland Islands and Antipodes Islands in the south (Fleming 1982).

Habitat: On the main islands of New Zealand it is a bird of tall, old forests. On off-shore islands it is a bird of the rocky cliff faces, low scrub areas, secondary forests, as well as older and taller forests.

Range: Seldom found on either the North or the South Islands but abundant on many of the off-shore islands. Birds are occasionally seen in the forests of the central North Island. It is also occasionally seen in North Auckland and Northland the birds probably arriving there from off-shore islands such as Tiri Tiri. Stewart Island has good populations everywhere.

Description:
　Forehead: A red cap extends from bill to above the eye. **Upperparts:** Green. **Wings:** Green with violet-blue primaries. **Underparts:** Yellowish-green.
Conspicuous features:
- A small parakeet but bigger than a budgerigar.
- When in flight the bird appears to have a long tail for its size.

Conspicuous characteristics:
- Its chattering call is very noticeable.
- The fast flight is conspicuous.
- Birds enjoy the security of the canopy and are usually found right in by the trunk of a tree or on the heavier inside branches. They seldom sit on outer branches. They appear more visible at dawn.

- When feeding on low coastal vegetation they are bold and easy to see.

Call: A rapid series of "chit chit chit chit" notes, is made when in flight. The sound has thin rattle-like, over-tones. It is constantly made when flying from one flax bush to the next.

Nest: Usually in holes in trees about five metres up, but also low to the ground in flax bushes, rock crevices and undergrowth. Up to 7 white eggs are laid.

Where to find - North Island:
North Auckland - Tiri Tiri Island: This is a guaranteed locality.
North Auckland - Whangaparaoa: Sometimes seen in Shakespear Park which is a short flight from Tiri Tiri Island.
Bay of Plenty: Recently found on Motuhora (Whale) Island.

Where to find - Stewart Island:
Oban and Ulva island: Widespread in these localities.

New Caledonia: Common in Blue River Reserve and at Yate along the roadsides. These areas are about a one hour drive north and inland from Noumea and are generally very good bird-watching places to visit.

REISCHEKS PARAKEET

Charles A Fleming

Family: Platycercidae   **Species:** *Cyanoramphus novaezelandiae hochstetteri*
Common name: Reischeks Parakeet   **Status:** Endemic
Size: 320 mm (cf sparrow 145 mm, Red-crowned Parakeet 280 mm)

Discussion: Reischeks Parakeet is a Red-crowned Parakeet subspecies and is found on the Antipodes Islands south of New Zealand. Its yellowish colour caused it to be regarded as a separate species at one time.

YELLOW-CROWNED PARAKEET

Brian Chudleigh

Family: Platycercidae   **Species:** *Cyanoramphus auriceps*
Common name: Yellow-crowned Parakeet, Kakariki (Maori)
Status: Endemic
Size: 250 mm (cf sparrow 145 mm, Red-crowned Parakeet 280 mm)

Discussion: This species, has stabilised in the old forests of the North Island and is more often encountered than its close relative the Red-crowned Parakeet. It occupies a niche higher in the trees than the Red-crowned and does not feed on or near the ground.

Habitat: A bird of mature forests. On off-shore islands it penetrates lower secondary type forests.

Range: Found in northern Northland and the central North Island. Well-spread through the forests of the South Island and particularly common in the tall beech trees of Fiordland and in the Catlins and Chaslands forests of Southland. Common on Stewart Island and its off-shore islands.

Description:
    Forehead: Yellow to above the eye. **Upperparts:** Green. **Wings:** Green, with violet-blue on the primaries. **Underparts:** Yellowish-green.

Conspicuous features:
- Smaller than the Red-crowned Parakeet.
- Look for yellow crown on head.

Conspicuous characteristics:
- Rattled song in the tree-tops indicates a parakeet.
- Birds usually land on the heavy upper branches of the forest.
- Long tail and fast flying habit are conspicuous.

Call: Similar to the Red-crowned Parakeet. Call is a constant chatter of "chit chit chit" notes, but when alarmed, such as when a Long-tailed Cuckoo strays into its territory, notes become rattled and agitated.

Nest: These are in holes in old trees up to six metres. Up to 7 white eggs are laid.

Best viewing time: Throughout the day but especially active at day break.

Where to find - North Island:

Northland - Puketi Forest in the Bay of Islands: Small populations are found here. (See Kokako article.)

North Auckland - Tiri Tiri Island: Note that Yellow-crowned Parakeets are not on this island but they are on Little Barrier Island, the Hen and Chicken Islands and the Poor Knights Islands.

King Country - Pureora Forest: Can be seen from the area about the campground and in the Bismarck Road area, usually high up in podocarps. (See "Places" in back of book.)

Urewera - Whirinaki Forest near Minginui: To get to Whirinaki follow Highway 5 from Rotorua and then left into Highway 38. Minginui is signposted after Murupara. Follow down to the village. Walking tracks lead into this forest from the village. Alternatively enter Whirinaki by a side road which leads into the forest from Highway 38 about 5 kms before the Minginui signpost.

Lake Waikaremoana and the Waikareiti Track: This is a reliable locality.

Taupo - Lake Rotopounamu near Tokaanu: This place, at the southern end of Lake Taupo, is good for parakeets and all bush birds. (See Kaka article.) Expect to see birds from the top of the Te Ponanga Saddle on Highway 47, prior to arriving at the lake signpost when travelling from Tokaanu.

Where to find - South Island:

Fiordland - Cascade Creek: This is an excellent locality. Especially good is the Mirror Lake roadside "board walk" area and the Cascade Creek and Lake Gunn walk. While in this locality look for bush birds. Note that the Mirror Lakes are particularly attractive when viewed with the mountain reflections on them in early morning. (See "Places" in back of book.)

West Coast - Lake Brunner near Greymouth: Try this area near the campground. (See Great Spotted Kiwi article.) Try any West Coast forest.

Where to find - Stewart Island:

Oban: The taller forests around the town have Yellow-crowned Parakeet frequently overlapping with Red-crowned.

Ulva Island: The walks here should reveal both species of parakeet.

ORANGE-FRONTED PARAKEET

Family: Platycercidae   **Species:** *Cyanoramphus malherbi*
Common name: Orange-fronted Parakeet

Discussion: This parakeet has recently (2000) been confirmed as a separate species after extensive DNA testing and habitat observation (Department of Conservation in prep.). Originally it was grouped with the Yellow-crowned

Parakeet (*Cyanoramphus auriceps*), following cross-breeding experiments carried out in captivity. These showed that the original two species were colour morphs of the same species (Taylor R H 1998. Notornis 45: 49 – 63). It is now though proven to be closer to the Red-crowned Parakeet with two known localities in the Hawdon Valley near Arthurs Pass and the Hurunui Valley near Lake Sumner, North Canterbury.

General: Kakariki are easy to breed in captivity and some captive birds have been released into the wild. These released birds though have proved to be vulnerable to predation.

SHINING CUCKOO

Brian Chudleigh

Family: Cuculidae **Species:** *Chrysococcyx lucidus*
Common name: Shining Cuckoo **Status:** Endemic
Size: 160 mm (cf sparrow 145 mm)

Discussion: The Shining Cuckoo is noted for its habit of laying its eggs in the nests of other birds, so causing the other species to rear its young. It is also a migratory species which winters to the north-west of New Zealand in the Solomon Islands, the Bismarck Archipelago north-east of Papua New Guinea, Papua New Guinea and eastern Indonesia. It breeds in Australia, New Caledonia, Vanuatu and New Zealand. It is not unlike the Didric Cuckoo (*Chrysococcyx caprius*), of Africa, as to size, colour, call and its habit of "domed nest" parasitism, the Shining Cuckoo parasitising the Grey Warbler's domed nest, the Didric Cuckoo, the domed nests of weaver birds.

Habitat: A bird of scrublands, secondary forests and old forest. Also vegetated suburban gardens where Grey Warblers live.
Range: Found throughout the North, South and Stewart Islands wherever there is sufficient bush and vegetation.

Description:

Upperparts: Shining green. **Underparts:** White, finely barred with metallic green.

Conspicuous features:

- Barring on the breast is visible on perching birds.
- A flash of green often gives the bird away when it is in flight.

Conspicuous characteristic:

- Mating birds tend to congregate in tall trees and in particular eucalypt species, where they carry out noisy behaviour. This often includes fighting between males and courtship feeding with moths between pairs.
- The song gives the bird away.

Call: An easily recognised "tu-wee tu-wee tu-wee tu-wee tee-wuu", whistle. Upon arrival in New Zealand in the spring, birds are very noisy. Cuckoo song is seldom heard after the end of January. There is evidence to suggest that Shining Cuckoos, when in New Zealand, are in fact a territorial species, actually living throughout the breeding season within a defined area of territories of several pairs of Grey Warblers. Cuckoo song might therefore be a proclamation of territory as well as a way of attracting a mate.

Nesting: The Grey Warbler's nest is the preferred host but Silvereyes and Fantails are also on record as having reared cuckoo chicks. One olive-green egg is laid in the Grey Warbler's nest. How the egg is placed in the nest is unknown but it is possible that the cuckoo might push its way in, after which the Grey Warblers then repair the damage.

Date of arrival: It arrives in northern New Zealand from the first week in September.

Date of departure: Probably early February but some birds are still here at the end of March. These may be young birds of a late brood.

Where to find: Expect them anywhere where there is vegetation. They are widespread throughout forested areas. Listen for them, especially when near manuka or kanuka forests which are favourite haunts of the Grey Warbler.

LONG-TAILED CUCKOO

Family: Cuculidae   **Species:** *Eudynamis taitensis*
Common name: Long-tailed Cuckoo   **Status:** Endemic
Size: 400 mm (cf sparrow 145 mm, Shining Cuckoo 160 mm)

Discussion: A migratory cuckoo which winters in the Pacific Islands both to the north-east and north-west of New Zealand, from New Guinea in the east to Rarotonga, Tahiti and the Marquesas Islands in the east. It returns to New Zealand to breed where it parasitises in particular, the nests of Whiteheads, Yellowheads and Brown Creepers.

Habitat: Confined to tall forests especially in areas where Whiteheads live in the North Island and Yellowheads and Brown Creepers in the South Island. Birds can be found outside of these areas during times of migration.

Range: North, South, Stewart Island and off-shore islands, particularly Little

Geoff Moon

Long-Tailed Cuckoo

Barrier, Great Barrier and Kapiti Islands, with concentrations in central North Island native and exotic forests, and forested areas of the South Island.

Description:

Upperparts: Rich brown, barred with black. **Underparts:** Creamy-white, boldly streaked with brown and black longitudinal markings. **Tail:** Prominent horizontal barring on undertail and uppertail.

Conspicuous features:

- One of the bigger birds of the New Zealand forest.
- The long tail is noticeable especially when in flight.

Conspicuous characteristics:

- The screeching song uttered from a high perch is most characteristic.
- Birds are known to spiral when in flight, often screeching at the same time.
- Could be mistaken for a New Zealand Falcon when in flight.
- Whiteheads, Yellowheads and parakeets will often mob cuckoos if they enter their territories.

Call: A long, harsh, drawn out "tuuueet", not unlike the introduced Greenfinch but on an ascending scale rather than a descending one, is the usual call. Also a musical song of ringing warbled, short notes.

Nesting: Lays a creamy-white egg usually in the nest of the Whitehead, Yellowhead or Brown Creeper. Sometimes it also lays in nests of Silvereyes and Fantails.

Arrival and departure dates: Arrives in New Zealand in early October. Departs in early March. Birds are seldom heard after the end of January.

Where to find - North Island:

King Country - Pureora: This is an accessible locality. Listen for them near the camp-ground and at Bismarck Road. (See "Places" in back of book.)

Urewera - Waikaremoana: Common throughout these forests.

Central Plateau - Whakamaru: Found in pine forests here.

Where to find - South Island and Stewart Island:
Marlborough - Pelorus Bridge: Try the walking tracks here.
Westland: Found in all tall forests.
Fiordland - Eglinton: Expect it at Cascade Creek and the Hollyford Valley.
Oban: Look for it around the township and also on Ulva Island.

MOREPORK

Brian Chudleigh

Family: Strigidae   **Species:** *Ninox novaeseelandiae*
Common name: Morepork, Ruru (Maori)   **Status:** Native
Size: 290 mm (cf sparrow 145 mm, Little Owl 230 mm)

Discussion: The Morepork is a nocturnal owl and a race of the Australian
   Boobook Owl. Also on Lord Howe Island and originally an inhabitant of
   Norfolk Island but this population has died out. In New Zealand it has handled
   development well, even establishing breeding territories in urban areas.

Habitat: A bird of old forests, modified forests, exotic forests and even well-
   vegetated suburban gardens. Most of the big cities have breeding populations
   in their wooded suburbs but it is not found in Christchurch.
Range: North Island, South Island and Stewart Island but it is absent from pastoral
   areas of limited vegetation.

Description:
   Head: Brown, sometimes with a white ring around the crown and with whitish
   eyebrows. **Upperparts and underparts:** Mostly brown. Feathers are lightly
   flecked with white, tan or creamy colouring, especially around eyes and breast.
   Eyes: Yellow set in a dark face. **Legs:** Brownish-yellow, with brown feathers
   and brown toes.

Conspicuous features and characteristics:
- Look for the staring eyes placed on the front of the face.
- Nocturnal in feeding and calling habits. This is different from the diurnal Little Owl (*Athene noctua*), the introduced European species, which is widespread over much of the South Island, east of the Southern Alps.
- The Morepork is silent in flight. The viewer senses its arrival.
- Will sit on power wires near a street light and catch attracted insects.
- Tends to favour the same daylight roosting branch from day to day.

Call: This is a monotonous "more-pork more-pork more-pork" (probably male bird only). This song probably proclaims the bird's territory. Also a series of "more more more", and a "cree cree cree" screech when hunting. Don't confuse in Auckland with the tri-syllabic, "kik ku koo" of the Spotted Dove.

Nest: Usually a heap of sticks or debris in an old trunk or fork of tree. On off-shore islands there is often the remains of the native rat, *(Rattus exulans)* and insects such as the Weta (*Hemideina thoracica*) and the Huhu Beetle (*Prionoplus reticularis*) scattered below. Up to 3 white eggs are laid.

How to locate: Spotlighting calling birds just on dark will locate them. By day, search for roosting birds in calling territories. Usually birds will sit tight.

Where to find - North Island:
Northland - Kerikeri: Aroha Island is an excellent locality.
Northland - Waitangi: Many in the Waitangi pine forests.
Northland - Paihia: The Haruru Falls walking track, just past the Haruru Falls, is good for Moreporks. Kiwis are also to be found here.
Auckland - Cornwall Park: Regularly heard here.

Where to find - South Island - Stewart Island:
Fiordland - Cascade Creek: Common in this area.
Oban: Common about the town.

General: The Morepork can be found in most vegetated areas.

LITTLE OWL

Family: Strigidae   **Species:** *Athene noctua*
Common name: Little Owl, German Owl   **Status:** Introduced
Size: 230 mm (cf sparrow 145 mm, Morepork 290 mm)

Discussion: A European introduction which is widespread and well known for its diurnal habits of hunting in full view in late afternoon. In New Zealand it has become common in the South Island and noted for its diurnal appearances when disturbed in old barns and hedgerows.

Habitat: Frequents open farmland and arable land which has sufficient scattered vegetation or hedging to provide cover. Prefers hedging varieties such as pine (*Pinus radiata*) or macrocarpa (*Cupressus macrocarpa*).

Range: South Island only with largest populations in Southland but fairly widely spread from Southland north to the Marlborough Sounds.

Jim Hague

Little Owl

Description:
Head: Grey brown, finely streaked with cream above eyes and on cheeks.
Upperparts: Grey-brown, speckled with white. **Underparts:** Grey-brown,
flecked with white vertical markings. **Eyes:** Yellow.
Conspicuous features:
- Smaller in size than the native Morepork.
- Yellow eyes are obvious.
Conspicuous characteristics:
- When disturbed it will fly out from cover and will often sit on a wire or a
  branch in full view.
- Has an undulating flight pattern.

Where to find - South Island:
Christchurch: Found around the city and in Hagley Park.
Southland: Best locations are in areas where roadside hedges are dense and
  trimmed. These give good shelter. Sometimes, when walking along these
  hedges, birds can be flushed. Also expect them to fly out from open barns.
Southland - Winton: Good numbers can be found in this area. If travelling to
  Fiordland stop in likely hedged areas.

KOOKABURRA

Family: Alcedinidae   **Species:** *Dacelo novaeguineae*
Common name: Kookaburra   **Status:** Introduced
Size: 450 mm (cf sparrow 145 mm, Kingfisher 240 mm)

Discussion: The Kookaburra was introduced from Australia in the 1860s. It
  failed to establish itself throughout the country but a small colony has persisted
  in the Waiwera district just north of the Whangaparaoa Peninsula. The absence
  of snakes in its diet in New Zealand could be a reason for its inability to

Charles A Fleming

Kookaburra

increase its numbers. In Australia this bird is widespread in the eastern states, and south of Perth in the west. Also it is found in northern Tasmania. Note that the Blue-winged Kookaburra *(Dacelo leachii)* was not introduced to New Zealand.

Habitat: Lives in areas of scattered vegetation and light forest.
Range: Mainly found in the Waiwera district of North Auckland and surrounding areas, and on Kawau Island.

Description:
   Head and underparts: Whitish with darker on crown. **Wings:** Dark brown with some blue-grey flecking. **Tail:** Brown, with darker brown barring. **Bill:** Large, with black above and yellow below.
Conspicuous features:
   - Larger than the Kingfisher in size.
   - Similar to the Kingfisher in shape and habit.
Conspicuous characteristics:
   - Commonly sits on power wires or the exposed branches of tall trees.
   - Regularly feeds on the ground.
Call: Call is a raucous laugh - "kuk kuk kuk and a he and a ho and a haw haw haw". Heard mainly in the early morning and at sunset, these being the best viewing times, but also through the day.
Nest: A hole or cavity in an old tree. Up to 3 white eggs are laid.

Where to find - North Island:
Northland - Whangarei: The Glenbervie district, north-east of Whangarei, has regular sightings. Search old trees and power wires.
North Auckland - Kawau Island: Look for it here if visiting to see Weka.
North Auckland - Puhoi district: This area north of Waiwera has regular sightings. Examine power wires in early morning for it.

North Auckland - Waiwera: Look for it in the Wenderholm Park.
North Auckland - Wainui and Waitoki: These districts are west of Silverdale. Birds have been recorded breeding here.

KINGFISHER

Brian Chudleigh

Family: Alcedinidae   **Species:** *Halcyon sancta*
Common name: Kingfisher, or Sacred Kingfisher, a name derived from Polynesian reverence which all kingfishers were traditionally given.
Status: Native
Size: 240 mm (cf sparrow 145 mm)

Discussion: The New Zealand Kingfisher has a sub-species in Australia, Lord Howe Island, Norfolk Island and New Caledonia. The New Zealand bird, though, is of larger size and more brilliant in its plumage, especially at breeding time. The Australian species appears to be more restricted as to habitat than the New Zealand bird probably due to competition from several other species of Australian kingfishers. A common species throughout New Zealand although less obvious in Southland.

Habitat: A bird of forests, rivers, creeks and the coastline. Commonly seen sitting on rural power wires. Often encountered well inside old forests. Although a forest kingfisher for much of the year, it drifts coastwards in the winter months. It also drifts northwards.

Range: Throughout New Zealand and its off-shore islands but not on the Chatham Islands.

Description:
  Cap: Blue-green. **Face:** A buff line extends above eye from bill to just beyond eye. Around the eye is black. Behind eye is blue. **Neck:** A white collar extends from chin to nape. **Upperparts:** Greenish-brown, with deep blue wing

262

primaries. **Underparts:** Orange-tan. **Tail:** Deep blue. **Bill:** Black.

Conspicuous features:
- The blue of the wings and tail is very noticeable, especially in flight.
- Look for the heavy black bill.

Conspicuous characteristics:
- Has a habit of sitting on power wires, fence wires, or high up on the branches of dead trees.
- Sits on foreshore rocks.
- Commonly sits in trees above rivers or lakes.
- Will suddenly leave its perch to take an insect or worm from the ground or from water.

Call: A continuous and often monotonous "ki-ki-ki-ki". At times, when in full song, a syllable is added. Near the nest it has a guttural screech.

Nest: A hole in a clay bank or old tree. Up to 5 white eggs are laid.

Where to find - North Island:
North Auckland - Waiwera: Good numbers at Wenderholm.
Urban and coastal areas: Common, especially in areas where rock pools or mud rivulets are found.

Where to find - South Island:
Southland: Not very common here but occasionally it is seen in areas near the coast such as in the Fortrose and Tokanui districts.

RIFLEMAN

Rod Morris

Family: Xenicidae
Common name: Rifleman
Size: 80 mm (cf sparrow 145 mm, Grey Warbler 100 mm)

Species: *Acanthisitta chloris*
Status: Endemic

Discussion: The family of Xenicidae is considered New Zealand's most ancient bird family apart from the Kiwi (Apterygidae). Relationship of this family to other world bird families is unclear but it may be closest to the Kingfisher (Fleming 1982). This family is a good example of adaptive radiation, the original ancestor separating into the Rifleman (*A. chloris*), a middle and upper forest dweller, the Bush Wren (*X. longipes*), a bird of the forest floor and understorey, the Rock Wren (*X. gilviventris*), a bird of alpine "rock garden" areas, and the Stephen Island Wren (*X. lyalli*). The Stephen Island Wren and the Bush Wren are both extinct.

Habitat: A bird of old forests which has not adapted to exotic pine forests. In the South Island it comes into bush remnants and forest verges.

Range: Found throughout New Zealand, including Stewart Island, although seldom encountered from the upper North Island, and North and South Canterbury.

Description - male:
Head: Bright yellow-green, with white eye-stripe. **Upperparts:** Bright yellow-green. **Wings:** Green, with a noticeable yellow bar. **Underparts:** Whitish. **Tail:** Brown, and white-tipped.

Description - female:
Head: Brown, slightly "zebra-striped" with white. **Eyebrow:** White. **Upperparts:** Brown, slightly "zebra-striped" with white. **Wings:** Brown, with faint yellow bars on the secondary feathers and faint white markings on the inner edges of primary feathers. **Underparts:** Whitish. **Tail:** Brown, and white-tipped.

Conspicuous features:
- The smallest bush bird.
- Smaller than the conspicuous Grey Warbler.
- Appears tailless in comparison to the Grey Warbler.
- White eyebrow is conspicuous on both male and female birds.
- White tip to tail and pale yellow wing-bars are noticeable.

Conspicuous characteristics:
- Has a habit of working up tree trunks hopping from one side to the other.
- Sometimes it "wing-flicks" as it feeds.

Call: A high-pitched "zit zit zit zit", which is difficult to hear.

Nest: A hole or cavity in an old tree. Up to 4 white eggs are laid.

How to locate: Can be called up with Audubon callers and by making squeaking sounds. Can be found any time of day.

Where to find - North Island:

King Country - Pureora Forest: This is a very easy locality. A track leads into the forest almost opposite to the information centre and this is a good place to start. (See "Places" in back of book.)

Rotorua - Mamaku: The Mamaku Ranges are north of Rotorua. Try Galaxy Road where it crosses Highway 5, north of the Oturoa Road turnoff. Search in the native forest verges before the pine forests start.

Taupo - Opepe Reserve: This reserve is on Highway 5 about 14 kms from Taupo on the left. It is the first area of bush along this road after Taupo, on the left and has a good walking track. Expect Rifleman where the older trees are encountered within the forest.

Taupo - Lake Rotopounamu: At Turangi follow Highway 41 to Tokaanu and then turn left into Highway 47. Travel over Te Ponanga Saddle. The lake is signposted on the left. The track around this lake is a good locality.

Urewera - Lake Waikaremoana: Try the Lake Waikareiti track near the Lake Waikaremoana Park headquarters. (See Kaka article.)

Where to find - South Island:

Marlborough - Pelorus Bridge: Pelorus Bridge is on Highway 6 north of Blenheim and towards Nelson after Havelock. It is signposted. Good walking tracks lead into the forests**.**

Marlborough - Lake Rotoiti: Follow Highway 63 from Blenheim for about 90 kms. After St Arnaud turn left up Mount Roberts Ski-Field Road. Good walking tracks léad into beech forests.

Canterbury - Akaroa: Try Hinewai Reserve. (See Brown Creeper article.)

Canterbury - Alford and Peel Forests: These forests, inland from Ashburton, are well signposted and have very good walking tracks.

West Coast - Haast Pass: Any forests in this area are worth a visit.

Fiordland - Cascade Creek: This is a good locality. Take the Lake Gunn walkway. (See "Places" in back of book.)

Fiordland - Eglinton and Hollyford: All these forests have Rifleman.

Dunedin: Ross Creek Reservoir Reserve off Cannington Road and Burma Road north of the city, have wooded areas where Rifleman can be found. Try below the golf course on Cannington Road.

Southland - Omaui Bush: This bush is located near the Invercargill to Bluff road. Turn right at Greenhills and follow in until forests are found. It also has Brown Creeper.

Where to find - Stewart Island:

Oban: Rifleman are in the tall inaccessible forests beyond Oban.

Ulva Island: They are not on this island.

ROCK WREN

Family: Xenicidae   **Species:** *Xenicus gilviventris*
Common name: Rock Wren   **Status:** Endemic
Size: 100 mm (cf sparrow 145 mm, Rifleman 80 mm)

Discussion: The Rock Wren is a rare species and difficult to find. It is an alpine bird and an example of a divergence from a common wren ancestor in a similar manner as the Kea, an alpine parrot, diverged from the ancestral stock of the Kaka. Similar adaptations are known in the tree genus *Nothofagus* (beech) and in the insect genus *Maoricicada* (cicadas) (Fleming 1982).

Habitat: Alpine areas above the tree line, in "rock gardens" of scattered low vegetation along either side of the Southern Alps.

Rock Wren

Range: South Island only. It is found right along the Southern Alps but populations are higher in the Fiordland area.

Description - male:
   Head: Olive-brown. **Eyebrow:** White, edged with black. **Upperparts:** Olive-brown. **Underparts:** Grey-brown. **Flanks:** Yellow.
Description - Female:
   Upperparts and underparts: Similar to the male bird but duller.
Conspicuous features:
   - Larger than the Rifleman.
   - White eyebrow is distinct.
   - Yellow on flanks under folded primaries is conspicuous.
   - Look for large toes, with prominent hind-toe.
Conspicuous characteristics:
   - When birds are standing they continually bob their bodies.
   - Birds will suddenly appear.
   - Birds hop quickly from rock to rock with some use of wings.
   - At times they undertake longer flights and have the appearance when in flight of that of a young sparrow trying its wings.
   - Feeds on moths and insects among the rocks.
Call: A high-pitched three syllable "zit" sound, the first note being rather .piercing. The call is not often heard but is distinctive. Do not muddle with the louder Pipit's "scree" call which is often heard in Rock Wren territory.
Nest: A hole in a bank or rock crevice on the ground. Up to 3 creamy eggs are laid.
How to locate: Because Rock Wrens live in areas of rocks and low vegetation it is easy for the viewer to find a vantage point from which a wide area can be scanned with binoculars. Pipits and Chaffinches are usually the only other birds in the area. If vegetation is taller, say to two metres, Grey Warblers may also be around.

Best viewing times: Can be found throughout the day. During rain or snow, birds shelter and are impossible to find.

Where to find - South Island:

Canterbury - Arthurs Pass National Park: There are several roads into the Craigeburn National Park area, off Highway 73, west of Christchurch, before you get to Arthur's Pass, which lead up to ski fields, and to Rock Wren territory. All are worth investigation. (See "Places" in back of book.)

Canterbury - Arthurs Pass National Park: From the village, travel to the top of the Pass, a distance of 5 kms. After the top of the Pass look for a pull-in area on the left (west) with an information board and map for Lake Misery. Follow the walking track for 30 minutes to a bridge over a stream and then walk for another 20 minutes to rock screes. Also climb rocks screes around the top Arthurs Pass. Kea will also be in these areas.

Canterbury - Mount Cook: Mount Cook is accessed from Highway 80 north of Twizel. The road to it runs alongside Lake Pukaki. Take the walking tracks which lead from The Hermitage carpark.

West Coast - Franz Josef and Fox Glacier: These places have Rock Wren within easy walking distances from the carpark.

Fiordland - Gertrude Valley: A road leads up to Gertrude Valley about 1 km before the Homer Tunnel on the Hollyford side. Drive in past the Alpine Sports Huts and walk into the valley. This area is useful if weather or avalanches preclude using the Homer Tunnel site.

Fiordland - Homer Tunnel: This is an accessible locality on the road to Milford Sound. The Homer Tunnel is a half hour drive from Cascade Creek. The tunnel links the Hollyford Valley with Milford Sound and its portal is in the alpine zone. The portal surrounds are excellent Rock Wren territory. Explore up to 500 metres away from the tunnel entrance. You may also see Kea here. There is some risk in parking here because of rock avalanches and Kea damage to vehicles.

Fiordland - Milford Sound side of tunnel: Rock Wrens also live on the screes on the Milford side. Drive through the tunnel and park on any available wide area of road. Note that two cars can pass in the tunnel and a coach and a car can safely pass in the tunnel.

Fiordland - Glenorchy: Glenorchy is up the western end of Lake Wakatipu about 45 kms from Queenstown. North of Glenorchy, walking tracks lead from the road in various directions - for example to the Dart River, Mount Earnslaw and the Routeburn. Any of these tracks might have Rock Wren. In particular try the start of the Routeburn Track. Soon after crossing the river Rock Wrens may be encountered in rock garden areas when weather is good. This area is one of the easier places to find this bird. Look here also for Weka, Kea and a good range of bush birds.

General: This is not an easy bird to find. The main requirement is to be patient and a wait of about 30 minutes is usually needed at all sites before birds show up. It also requires good weather and is easier to find in summer.

SKYLARK

Brian Chudleigh

Family: Alaudidae   **Species:** *Alauda arvensis*
Common name: Skylark   **Status:** Introduced
Size: 180 mm (cf sparrow 145 mm)

Discussion: The Skylark, for nostalgic reasons, was introduced from Britain by the early European settlers. Since then it has spread widely and is now a common bird in areas of pastureland and open grassland up to the snow line in many areas. Those who have looked for this bird in its native England usually conclude that it is easier to find in New Zealand. In England, it appears restricted to wilderness areas and coastal cliff faces.

Habitat: Open pastureland and wilderness grassland areas.
Range: Throughout New Zealand away from forests and alpine areas but not subalpine areas. Found on some of the off-shore islands.

Description:
     Head: Brown, streaked with light brown. A crest is sometimes noticeable.
     Upperparts: Brown, streaked with light brown. **Underparts:** Buff. **Tail:** Dark brown, the outer feathers being white.
Conspicuous features:
- Look for crest on head.
- White tail feathers are noticeable when bird is in flight.

Conspicuous characteristics:
- The Skylark sings purposefully from the sky.
- Crouches on gravel country roads, flying off just as traffic approaches.
- Frequently sits on fence posts.
- Flies up in front of intruders when in long grass.
- Raises its crest when carrying out courtship and mating procedures.

Call: Song, delivered by the male bird, is a liquid trill uttered when flying above nesting territories. Sometimes, though, it is delivered from atop a fence post or even when sitting on the ground. Birds can remain singing in the air for some time. Seven minute song spans are commonly heard in spring months with the longest timed song being 20 minutes (pers. obs.). Song period is concentrated in the months of July to February. Over the autumn months song is heard much less but is not totally absent. Birds disturbed on the ground utter a "chirrup" call.

Nest: A neat grass-lined cup on ground or in clump of grass. Up to 4, greyish-brown, speckled eggs are laid.

Differences between Skylarks and Pipits: See Pipit article.

Where to find - North Island:
South Auckland - Miranda: Very good populations here.

General: Skylarks are common everywhere and even in towns. Larger numbers, though, are seen and heard in areas of rough grassland.

WELCOME SWALLOW

Brian Chudleigh

Family: Hirundinidae   **Species:** *Hirundo tahitica*
Common name: Welcome Swallow, Pacific Swallow   **Status:** Native
Size: 150 mm (cf sparrow 145 mm)

Discussion: The Welcome Swallow arrived in New Zealand from Australia in the 1950s when it established a small breeding colony in the far north of Northland. From then onwards a southward spread occurred until it became established over the whole country. Early populations had preferences for nesting under bridges and in culvert pipes, but currently their nests can be found on the sides of buildings, under eaves as well as along cliffs and banks.

It is considered a race of the Pacific Swallow with some subtle differences, the Pacific Swallow having a higher forehead and being more solitary. In Australia the Welcome Swallow is well-spread except in the dry parts of Western Australia and the Northern Territory.

Habitat: Found over waterways, open pastureland and wilderness areas but seldom over forested areas. Regularly seen over estuaries and mudflats.

Range: Throughout New Zealand but seldom seen in drier South Island areas and Fiordland.

Description:
Crown: Blue-black. **Forehead, throat and breast:** Rusty-brown.
Upperparts: Metallic blue-black. **Underparts:** Greyish-white.

Conspicuous features:
- Rusty-brown of the chin and throat is noticeable.
- Look for the forked tail.

Conspicuous characteristics:
- When feeding over water birds continually dip into the water surface.
- In winter it can be seen feeding over dams and ponds in large flocks.
- Often seen sitting along power wires in large numbers, usually towards the end of the breeding season.

Call: A short "peep peep" is heard when birds are feeding. Sometimes a rapid twittering is uttered from a perch.

Nests: These are found under bridges, under eaves, commonly in milking sheds, as well as along cliffs and banks of rivers. They are cup-shaped and carefully sculptured with mud pellets made of clay mixed with saliva. They are lined with straw, feathers and wool. Up to 4 pink, brown-flecked eggs are laid.

Where to find:
North and South Islands: Can be found almost anywhere away from old forests although uncommon in Fiordland. It is often more common where there is water, or where water is handy.

NEW ZEALAND PIPIT

Family: Motacillidae   **Species:** *Anthus novaeseelandiae*
Common name: Pipit, Richards Pipit   **Status:** Endemic
Size: 190 mm (cf sparrow 145 mm, Skylark 180 mm)

Discussion: The Pipit is widely spread throughout the world with the European, Asian and Australian races being known by the name of Richards Pipit. In some countries it is migratory and tends to move east and south during the winter, turning up in western Europe, the United Kingdom and Africa. The Pipit was collected on Cooks voyage of 1783, and painted by George Forster, the ship's naturalist. This painting was used to describe the "New Zealand's Lark" and this name was Latinised by Gmelin in 1789, *Alauda novaeseelandiae* (Fleming 1982). Hence, the cosmopolitan Pipit carries the species name of *novaeseelandiae*.

New Zealand Pipit

Habitat: A bird of the open countryside but preferring wilderness, unkempt areas, to improved pastureland. Prefers areas where scrubby roadside verges exist and roads are gravelled. Also is commonly found on beaches.

Range: Found throughout New Zealand but seldom in the improved farming districts. Absent from forested areas.

Description:

Head: Brown, streaked with light brown and with a white eyebrow. **Upperparts:** Brown, streaked with light brown. **Chin:** White. **Breast:** White, streaked with light brown. **Underparts:** Whitish. **Tail:** Dark brown with white outer feathers.

Conspicuous features:

- The whitish eyebrow is noticeable, especially on birds in breeding plumage.
- White outer tail feathers are noticeable.

Conspicuous characteristics:

- Has a tendency to bob the tail especially upon alighting.
- Has a tendency to signal its arrival by a loud high-pitched "scree" note.
- Has a tendency to rise up in front of approaching traffic on dusty country roads and then fly in undulating swoops alongside or in front of cars. Birds seen doing this should be watched carefully as they often will land on a roadside fence post and reward the driver with an excellent view.

Call: This is either a high-pitched "tueet tueet" or "scree scree" sound.

Nest: A grass cup among tall grasses or in the base of a rush bush. Up to 4 creamy eggs blotched with brown are laid.

Differences between the Pipit and the Skylark:

- The Pipit lacks the Skylark's crest and rather square head.
- The Pipit is of upright stance standing higher than the Skylark, which instead is inclined to sit back on its haunches with a sloping back posture.
- The Pipit has a habit of landing nearby and being a friendly and confiding

bird. At such times it will bob its tail vigorously.
- Skylarks are vigorous aerial singers. Pipits sing from a perch although they will utter their "scree" note when on the wing.

Where to find - North Island:
Northland - Cape Reinga: Large populations around the light-house at the far north of New Zealand.
Northland - Awanui: Dusty roads to the north of Awanui frequently have Pipits. While on these dusty roads keep a look out for the introduced Australian Brown Quail which is in good numbers in Northland.
Northland - Matauri Bay to Whangaroa: These roads are generally good. Turn off Highway 1 about 12 kms north of Waipapa and head out to the coast. Also New Zealand Dotterel on beaches in this area.
Northland - Bay of Islands: Try the Rawhiti Road, south-east of Russell.
North Auckland - Waiwera: Try the roads beyond Strakas Refuge.
South Auckland - Miranda: Occasionally birds are seen on the foreshore.
Rotorua: The dusty roads of the Central Plateau areas of the North Island, in districts such as Rotoiti, Pongakawa and Manawahe, have good populations. Try Manawahe Road off Highway 30, which runs into Lake Rotoehu. Then try Hamiltons Road.
Urewera - Waikaremoana: It is well-spread along Highway 38 through the Murupara to Waikaremoana district even in forested areas.
Tongariro - Desert Road: Often seen on the Desert Road, Highway 1, after Turangi. Drive off the Desert Road down one of its tracks and wait. Sometimes Banded Dotterel are also here.

Where to find - South Island:
Marlborough - Picton: Try Queen Charlotte Drive from Picton to Havelock. Birds are regularly seen along the roadside here.
Marlborough - Seddon: Roadside birds can be seen on side roads from Highway 1, south of Blenheim.
Westland: Many of the West Coast highways have Pipits.
Fiordland - Te Anau: It is well-spread through the Manapouri, Te Anau area. Usually seen on Highway 94, just north of Te Anau town. Watch out for it when on the way to Cascade Creek and Milford Sound.
Fiordland - Homer Tunnel: Common around the Homer Tunnel area of Highway 94, even above the bushline. Rock Wrens are also here.

HEDGE SPARROW

Family: Prunellidae   **Species:** *Prunella modularis*
Common name: Hedge Sparrow, Dunnock   **Status:** Introduced
Size: 140 mm (cf sparrow 145 mm)

Discussion: The Hedge Sparrow was introduced from England in the second half of the 19th century. Its spread was generally slow but by 1940 it had colonised most parts of New Zealand. It is now a common species in most districts but absent from some.

Brian Chudleigh

Hedge Sparrow

Habitat: Hedge Sparrows inhabit low vegetation and second growth. Also found in pine forests, well established suburban gardens, but only on the verges of native forested areas.

Range: Found throughout New Zealand

Description:

Head and upperparts: Grey, streaked with brown. **Face, throat and collar and underparts:** Soft grey. **Wings:** Brown, streaked with dark brown.

Conspicuous features:

- Has fine bill as opposed to a House Sparrow's blunt bill.
- Appears similar to a female House Sparrow but finer and smaller.

Conspicuous characteristics:

- Its habit of singing in a regular and conspicuous place, often from a roadside verge, alerts the viewer.
- Regularly feeds low down in shrubs and often on the ground.
- It will venture out on to lawns sometimes in the company of House Sparrows.
- A neat looking bird, although of sombre colouring.

Call: Its song, uttered by the male bird, is a fragile warble of "sweedle sweedle swee swee" notes. It is the first of the introduced songsters to commence singing in the autumn and birds are in full song by mid-April in the north. Because of the general silence of other songsters at this time, the Hedge Sparrow's song can be learnt. The song period extends to the end of January.

Nest: A cup of twigs lined with moss, wool or feathers, usually deep among foliage but near the ground. Up to 4 blue eggs are laid.

Where to find - North Island:

North Auckland - Waiwera: Try Wenderholm Park.

North Auckland – Whangaparaoa: Often seen in Shakespear Park.

South Auckland - Kaiaua: Try the Waharau Park just north of Miranda.
Auckland: Seldom heard in Auckland gardens or parks.
Waikato: Common in rough roadside verges.
Bay of Plenty - Matata: Good numbers in the low vegetation to the seaward side of the lagoons. (See "Places" in back of book.)
Wellington: Common throughout the suburbs.

Where to find - South Island:
Canterbury - Lake Tekapo: Large numbers throughout this area.
Fiordland - Lake Te Anau and Lake Manapouri: Good numbers can be found in lake verges and the scrubby wilderness areas in these districts.
Dunedin: Common in the Dunedin Botanic Garden.
Southland - Invercargill: Common in the town park.

Where to find - Stewart Island: Common around the town of Oban where birds seem very tame. Sings near the hotel and along the roads near Stewart Island School.

BLACKBIRD

Brian Chudleigh

Family: Muscicapidae
Common name: Blackbird
Species: *Turdus merula*
Status: Introduced
Size: 250 mm (cf sparrow 145 mm, Song Thrush 230 mm)

Discussion: Blackbirds are another introduced species brought to New Zealand by the early settlers. They are now spread over all of New Zealand. North American birders always note their similarity to the American Robin (*Turdus migratorius*).

Habitat: The Blackbird has adapted to a wide range of habitat from the suburban garden to the pastoral countryside, to native and exotic forests.

Range: Found throughout New Zealand and on off-shore islands.

Description - male bird:
   Upperparts and underparts: Black. **Bill:** Bright yellow in the breeding season. **Eye-ring:** Yellow.

Description - female bird:
   Upperparts: Dark brown. **Chin:** Grey. **Breast and underparts:** Light brown speckled with dark brown. **Bill:** Orange in breeding season. Otherwise brown.

Description - immatures:
   Upper and underparts: Dark brown with some breast speckling.

Conspicuous features:
- All black colour is noticeable.
- The yellow eye-ring on the male bird is noticeable.
- Look for the yellow bill.

Conspicuous characteristics:
- When on the ground it hops rather than walks.
- Birds pause when feeding, often with head turned and ear to ground.
- When disturbed, birds will fly off making an alarm call.
- Have a habit of sunbathing, lying under full sun with wings spread.
- Birds moult heavily over late summer, more so than the Song Thrush.

Call: Song period is from August through to January but the "tok tok tok tok" alarm call can be heard at any time of year. The song of the male Blackbird is melodious and fluid with notes being uttered in phrases with distinct pauses between each. It does not repeat notes as does the Song Thrush but instead runs a variety of notes together. Blackbirds sing strongly at dawn and dusk.

Nest: A bulky cup of grass, twigs and leaves bound with some mud and lined with fine grasses. Up to 4 greenish, brown-speckled, eggs are laid.

Where to find: Common in most places below the snowline.

Brian Chudleigh

A female Blackbird - compare with Song Thrush

SONG THRUSH

Brian Chudleigh

Family: Muscicapidae   **Species:** *Turdus philomelos*
Common name: Song Thrush   **Status:** Introduced
Size: 230 mm (cf sparrow 145 mm, Blackbird 250 mm)

Discussion: The Song Thrush, along with other European birds, was introduced to New Zealand by the early settlers. It has since become widespread and said to be more common here now than in Britain.

Habitat: Lives in any vegetated area from the suburban garden to hedged rural areas, exotic plantations and to the edges of native forest. Does not penetrate as deeply into native forest as does the Blackbird.
Range: Found throughout New Zealand and the off-shore islands.

Description:
    Upperparts: Olive-brown. **Underparts:** White, speckled with brown. **Bill:** Brown, with a speck of yellow at the gape.
Conspicuous feature:
- Look for the breast streaking.

Conspicuous characteristics:
- Feeds mainly on the ground where it takes worms, snails and insects.
- Hops when feeding rather than walks.
- Often heard breaking snails on hard surfaces.
- Note that the female Blackbird, which is of brownish colouring, is sometimes mistaken for the Song Thrush.

Call: Male birds start singing in the north at the end of April and continue through until January. Their song is often confused with that of the Blackbird. However, whereas the Blackbird sings in short phrases of a variety of notes, the Song Thrush repeats the same note forming brackets, which it runs into the next

276

bracket without a pause.

Nest: A large bulky cup is made of grasses, twigs and moss, bound with some mud and lined with mud. It is usually two to three metres above the ground. Up to 4 greenish, black-spotted eggs are laid.

Where to find: Common in most places away from native forests.

FERNBIRD

Brian Chudleigh

Family: Sylviidae   **Species:** *Bowdleria punctata*
Common name: Fernbird, Matata (Maori)   **Status:** Endemic
Size: 180 mm (cf sparrow 145 mm)

Discussion: The Fernbird is considered a derivative of the Australian genus of grass birds, *Megalurus*. It shares some similarities such as a wetland habitat, similar colouration and its manner of song delivery (Fleming 1982). The Fernbird's habit of climbing high among the vegetation and peering out, and its habit of flying above the vegetation for short distances with tail held down, are also obvious similarities. It differs in the structure of its tail feathers, which are scrawny and possess disconnected barbs not unlike a kiwi feather.

Name: Buller W L 1873, has the Fernbird's habitat as the vast areas of fern-covered hills of much of New Zealand. The Fernbird was in those days a bird of the fern-lands and so hence its name. It is possible, though, that the birds "fern-like" tail also had something to do with its name.

Subspecies: These are recognised for the North Island species, the South Island species and for those on Codfish Island, Stewart Island, Chatham Island and Snares Island.

Habitat: Found in wet swampy areas and semi-wet tidal verges on the main islands. Also in low fern and rush, away from wet areas, such as on Great Barrier Island.

Range: In the North Island found from Tongariro north and on Great Barrier Island. In the South Island found from north-east Marlborough down the west coast to Otago and Southland. It is also found on Stewart Island.

Description:
    Upperparts: Brown, streaked with dark brown. **Eyebrow:** White.
    Underparts: White, streaked with brown from throat to abdomen.
Conspicuous features:
- The spiky fern-like tail is conspicuous.
- The vertical brown streaking on the breast is noticeable.

Conspicuous characteristics:
- Birds often do short low flights above the vegetation.
- Tail is often held in a downwards position when in flight.
- Birds often just arrive and seem to peer from the vegetation at head height.
- Feeding birds have a habit of fossicking quickly through the vegetation, appearing and disappearing at speed.

Call: Usually a rather feeble "tick tick tick" or "uu-tik uu-tik" or a melodic "too-tok too-tok", with the last note on a descending scale. Pairs are known to duet with one bird singing the first note, the second bird finishing the second note.

Nest: A cup of woven grasses among rush stems or raupo. Up to 4 pale pink, brown-blotched eggs are laid.

Response to callers: Fernbirds are attracted by tape-recorded songs, Audubon callers, whistle calls and polystyrene rubbed on wet bottles.

Best time of year for viewing: Spring and summer months are best. In cold weather birds seem to lie low and are hard to find.

Observation difficulties in the field: In many Fernbird swamps Redpoll, Skylark and Pipit are also present. These birds can cause confusion due to similar colouration. Their behaviour is less secretive than that of the Fernbird.

Where to find - North Island:

Northland - Kerikeri - Aroha Island: Found at the beginning of the causeway. Spotless Crakes are also here. (See "Places" in back of book.)

Northland - Bay of Islands: All the swamp areas around Paihia and Waitangi have good populations.

Northland - Paihia: An obvious wet area between Paihia and Haruru is very good for Fernbirds and Spotless Crakes. When travelling from Paihia the swamp is on the right.

Great Barrier Island: Expect them on the Mount Hobson walkway after about 30 minutes walking.

South Auckland - Whangamarino wetland: Good populations exist in this swamp under the coal cableway. When travelling south from Auckland, turn left down Island Block Road just north of the Meremere Power Station. Travel along under the Cable Way and then walk in from the gate to No 73 pylon, where a boardwalk extends into the swamp. Fernbird can be seen from the boardwalk. Use a caller.

South Auckland - Miranda: Records come from the coastal verges in the area near the Miranda Hot Springs. Walk in by the pump station and over the stopbank, and then head south for about ten minutes.

South Auckland - Hauraki Plains: A good locality is on Torehape East Road which is located off Highway 27. This is south of Miranda. On Torehape East Road drive down through the farmlands until the swamp is encountered. Look for an old fallen down gate about 800 metres from the farmland verge on the south side. Walk in for a few minutes and use a caller.

Bay of Plenty - Matata Lagoon: Can be found in any of the lagoon verges. Also try the Tarawera River verges just east of the lagoons. Also here are waterfowl plus Banded Rail, Spotless Crake and Marsh Crake.

Taupo District: The southern areas of Lake Taupo, near Turangi and Tokaanu are excellent Fernbird habitat. Almost all of the roads leading to the Tongariro River fishing pools have Fernbirds along their swampy verges, as do the Turangi lake verges.

Taupo - Waiotaka Reserve: The easiest locality in the Turangi area is the Waiotaka Reserve on Highway 1, about 1 km west of the Waimarino River and 7 kms from Turangi. Drive down Frethey Drive and search the verges.

Taupo - Waihi Village: Follow Waihi Road off Highway 41. Search the swamp verges. Also in this area are Dabchicks, Little Shags, Little Black Shags, Scaup, Black Swans, Spotless Crakes and Marsh Crakes.

Tongariro - The Chateau: Usually found in the vicinity of The Chateau near the Department of Conservation camping ground.

Where to find - South Island:

Westland - Lake Brunner: The swampy areas near the lake are worth searching.

Southland - Fiordland: Fernbirds are not recorded within the National Park. A handy location when in the general Fiordland area is Horseshoe Bend on the Waiau River, 8 kms from Te Anau on the Manapouri Road. A track here leads in to wet areas.

Southland - Manapouri: Swamp areas near Blackmount Road have Fernbirds. This road leads off the Manapouri to Lumsden Road in a southerly direction. Most Fernbird areas are on private land.

Southland - The Redcliff Wetland Reserve: Along Blackmount Road, about 20 kms from Manapouri, are the Redcliff Wetlands. This area is well worth a visit.

Otago - Lake Waihola: Berwick Swamp, south of Dunedin on Highway 1, is worth a try. Turn inland at the sign that says Berwick. Look for a small picnic area which overlooks Lake Holm. This area is surrounded by wetlands.

Otago - Sinclair Wetlands: While in the area of Berwick Swamp, visit the Sinclair Wetlands, a good area for waterfowl. This area is signposted.

Southland - Awarua Bay: This area, which is south-east of Invercargill, is a good place for Fernbirds around its swampy verges. It is also good for shorebirds.

Southland - Bushy Point on the New River Estuary: This area, considered to be one of the easiest locations to find Fernbirds in the South Island, is almost in Invercargill and is located at Otatara. Find Stead Street and then turn left into Marama Avenue South, right into Bryson Road and left into Grant Road. Drive to the end of Grant Road and enquire at the house of Ian and Jenny Gamble for permission to enter their boardwalk which takes you right into the swamp without getting your feet wet. There is no charge to enter even though this is a private walk on private land. This area of swampland and its nearby forest are noted for a range of native birds including New Zealand Pigeon. White-faced Herons nest here and Harriers are prevalent with some nesting, while from March to August the area is a colonial roosting site for this species. Marsh Crake are also recorded here.

Southland - Lake Murihiku: This lake is located west of the Invercargill airport. Take Coggins Road and then north into Hughs Road. The lake is on the right.

Southland - Tautuku: This area is between Papatowai and Progress Valley on Highway 92. Fernbirds live in the coastal salt marshes of the area.

WHITEHEAD

Brian Chudleigh

Family: Pachycephalidae   **Species:** *Mohoua albicilla*
Common name: Whitehead, Bush Canary   **Status:** Endemic
Size: 150 mm (cf sparrow 145 mm)

Discussion: Unlike its close relative the Yellowhead, the Whitehead has increased in numbers over the last fifty years. This spread has continued along the Coromandel Peninsula in a northerly direction. It has also spread through many of the man-made pine forests (*Pinus spp.*) of the central North Island where it thrives on the large moth-food resource to be found there.

Habitat: Found in a range of forests including podocarp, beech, secondary forest and exotic pine forests.

Range: North Island only and on Little Barrier Island, Tiri Tiri Island and Kapiti Island. Absent from forests north of Mount Pirongia to the west, and Table Mountain, behind the town of Thames, to the east. Widely spread through the forests of the central North Island south to Wellington.

Description:
   Head and underparts: White, with male birds being whiter than female birds.

Wings, back and uppertail: Pale brown. **Bill, legs and feet:** Black. **Eye:** Black.

Conspicuous features:
- Look for the white head and underparts.
- The black eye is obvious.

Conspicuous characteristics:
- In most forests it feeds high in the canopy but regularly comes down into the middle-storey forest.
- Has a habit of working up tree trunks usually in a hurry.
- Often sings in short melodic bursts as it feeds.
- Makes short, almost hopping-like flights, from tree-top to tree-top.
- In winter it forms noisy flocks which move through forests in a mass.

Call: This bird has two songs. One is a canary-like chatter made up of "swee swee swee chir chir chir" notes. Some of these notes could be confused with the introductory notes of a Chaffinch song. Its other song is melodic and carrying, and is not unlike some notes of the Bellbird and the Robin.

Nest: Cup-shaped made of twigs bound with cobwebs and lined with feathers, wool or tree-fern hair, usually built towards the end of branches, about four metres above the ground. Up to 4 white, brown-speckled eggs are laid. Nests are parasitised by the Long-tailed Cuckoo, this bird laying 1 creamy-white egg in the Whiteheads nest.

Best time of day for viewing: Easily located at any time of day. It is noisy just after sunrise, although it has no excessive dawn-chorus period.

Best time of year for viewing: Can be viewed in any month but probably easiest to find in spring when birds are in territories. Birds respond to taped songs and Audubon callers.

Problems with observations in the field: Usually Chaffinches will be sharing the same habitat as Whiteheads. Chaffinches, though, frequently fly up from the ground. Whiteheads are not ground feeders. Further, Chaffinch song is consistent. Whitehead song is more variable. When a bird is glimpsed in flight and white is seen on tail and wings, it can be assumed to be a Chaffinch.

Where to find - North Island:

Tiri Tiri Island: This is a very good locality and accessible. Whiteheads are now well spread here.

Waikato - Mount Te Aroha: Note that birds are moving north along the Kaimai Range. Try the walking track to the summit of Mount Te Aroha which leads up from near the thermal pools.

Waikato - Kaimai Range: Try the Kaimai hill on Highway 29 to Tauranga where sign says "To Kauri". (See New Zealand Robin article.)

King Country - Pureora: Look for Whiteheads when in these forests.

King Country - Waitomo: Try the Ruakuri Caves walkway. From Waitomo Caves drive west and turn left up Tumutumu Road. Take the first road to the right down to a carpark and the walkway. Good numbers here.

Bay of Plenty - Mount Otanewainuku: Whiteheads are common here just a few metres up the track from the carpark. (See Brown Kiwi article.)

Rotorua - Mamaku: Galaxy Road, a forestry road north of Oturoa Road, has Whiteheads in both the pine and native forest road verge. The pine tree populations are particularly good. (See Rifleman article.)

Rotorua - Blue Lake: The forests here and the background pine forests are all worth visiting. Take the Tarawera Lake road near the Lynmore shopping centre on the east side of Rotorua Lake. Walk in from the Blue Lake lakeside area.

Rotorua - Central Plateau forests: Pine forests of the central North Island are the easiest locations to find this bird.

Rotorua - Atiamuri: The forests opposite the Atiamuri Hydro Station, alongside Highway 1, always have Whiteheads, Robins and Tomtits. Stop in the rest area and walk a short distance into the pines. Logging roads run into these forests and provide easy access. These forests are privately owned but people are not forbidden as long as they do not drop cigarette butts or litter.

Birds of the pine forests include:

Pigeon	Eastern Rosella	Shining Cuckoo
Long-tailed Cuckoo	Morepork	Kingfisher
Whitehead	Robin	Tomtit
Grey Warbler Fantail	Blackbird	Thrush
Silvereye	Bellbird	Tui
Chaffinch	Greenfinch	

Taupo - Opepe Reserve: This small reserve on the Taupo to Napier road is always good for Whiteheads. Rifleman and many other bush birds can also be seen here.

Taupo - Lake Rotopounamu: Whiteheads are here. (See Rifleman article.)

YELLOWHEAD

Don Hadden

Family: Pachycephalidae   **Species:** *Mohoua ochrocephala*
Common name: Yellowhead, Mohua (Maori)   **Status:** Endemic
Size: 150 mm (cf sparrow 145 mm)

Discussion: A bird which has speciated from the common ancestor of both the Brown Creeper and the Whitehead and which has been variously grouped over the years with finches (Fringillidae), warblers (Muscicapidae) and tits (Paridae). Now they are placed in the family of Whistlers (Pachycephalidae). It is a rare species, its range having been continually depleted as forests have become altered or felled.

Habitat: A bird of old forests with a special liking for beech forests, but also lowland podocarp.

Range: It is found in the South Island only, mainly confined to Fiordland National Park and further north in the Mount Aspiring National Park. Other populations survive in the Catlins and Blue Mountains in Southland, the Hawdon River Valley in the Arthurs Pass National Park, north-west of Christchurch, and at Mount Stoke near the Marlborough Sounds.

Description:
   Head and underparts: Yellow. **Upperparts:** Olive-brown. **Bill and feet:** Black. **Eye:** Black.
Conspicuous features:
   - The yellow head and the black eye and bill are very noticeable.
   - Bright yellow underparts readily distinguish this bird.

Conspicuous characteristics:
   - Has a habit of feeding in the middle to high canopy.
   - Movements are urgent and often noisy with birds making buzzing notes.
   - If birds are disturbed by a Long-tailed Cuckoo they become very agitated. Often they will be joined by Brown Creepers, Robins and Yellow-crowned Parakeets in an attempt to repel it.
   - When feeding, Yellowheads often hang upside down.

Call: The song is sweet and gentle and less canary-like than the Whitehead. It is louder than the Brown Creeper. Because it shares a habitat with the Brown Creeper their songs, although different, can sometimes be confused.

Nest: It nests in holes of old trees, usually above four metres, making a structure within the hole of twigs bound with cobwebs. Up to 4 pink, lightly speckled with brown eggs, are laid. The hole-nesting habit of Yellowheads could be the main reason for their decline. Not only are holes easy for predators like rats and stoat to access, but they have also become in short supply with the clearing of forests. Nests of Yellowheads are parasitised by Long-tailed Cuckoos which may be another cause for the bird's decline. Because birds nest in holes, any likely hole should be watched during the nesting season for an arriving or departing bird.

Best viewing times: Late spring and summer are the best months. Birds can be found at any time of day but are silent during wet weather.

How to attract: Yellowheads respond to tape-recorded Yellowhead song. They will also come and investigate Audubon caller sounds as well as the sound of polystyrene rubbed against a wet bottle. However, birds can readily be found without the use of callers. Out of the breeding season they can be found in flocks and usually not too high up in the canopy.

Where to find - South Island:

Marlborough - Mount Stokes: From Picton take Queen Charlotte Sound Drive. At Linkwater, turn into Kenepuru Road and follow up past Portage to Kenepuru Saddle. A track leads into the forest from near Graham's Lookout.

Canterbury - Arthurs Pass: Follow Highway 73 from Christchurch. At Cass just past Lake Grasmere, turn right where sign says Lake Sarah. Cross the river and walk into heavy beech forests.

Otago - Haast Pass: There are 3 places to try -

- **Makarora:** Try the forests near the information centre.
- **Davis Flat:** Follow north from Makarora for 14 kms and stop at Davis Flat campsite/picnic area. A walking track leads along the Haast River and over a foot bridge. Look for Yellowheads here.
- **Gates of Haast:** An old bridal trail leads west along the Burke River at the north end of the Mount Aspiring National Park. Here look for bush birds and Yellowheads.

Fiordland - Eglinton Valley to Milford Sound: Once inside the park look for the Transit New Zealand depot. Take the small road beside it into the forest. Alternatively try the forests behind Knobbs Flat or at Cascade Creek. At Cascade Creek walk the Lake Gunn track. Birds can be found right beside Cascade Creek a short distance from Highway 94. This is an excellent birding place. For a full list of likely species for this area see "Places" in back of book.

Fiordland - Milford Sound: Try the forests before the Homer Tunnel and those around Milford Sound above the wharf road.

Southland - Owaka Valley: From Owaka take Owaka Valley Road towards Clinton and the Catlins State Forest Park. Turn left into Chloris Pass Road and drive to top of hill where good numbers of Brown Creeper live in roadside scrub. Next, at the bottom of the hill turn left into Wisp Camp Ground near the top of the Catlins River walking track. Good numbers of Yellowheads can be found here and on the riverflat areas. Also Yellow-crowned Parakeet, Red-crowned Parakeet, Shining Cuckoo and Long-tailed Cuckoo are here.

Southland - Chasland Forest: This forest is also part of the Catlins State Forest Park. It is about 15 kms south of Owaka. Turn into Puketiro Road and stop at the Puketiro Camp Ground. Cross the river and walk into the forests.

Southland - Blue Mountains: This forest is north of Gore on Highway 90. Near Crookston at Black Gully, turn east into Black Gully Road and drive into the carpark.

Reference: Read A F and O'Donnell C F J 1988. Notornis 34: P 307 - 315. Abundance of Yellowheads in the Hawdon River Valley, Arthur's Pass, in 1983 and 1984.

BROWN CREEPER

Geoff Moon

Family: Pachycephalidae   **Species:** *Mohoua novaeseelandiae*
Common name: Brown Creeper   **Status:** Endemic
Size: 130 mm (cf sparrow 145 mm)

Discussion: The Brown Creeper is closely related to the Whitehead and the Yellowhead and grouped with the Whistlers in the family Pachycephalidae.

Habitat: Found in any type of forest and even small remnants, from mid-storey to canopy. Occasionally in scrubland and roadside verges.

Range: Found over much of the South Island but not the Canterbury Plains. Also on Stewart Island and its outlying islands including Codfish Island. Absent from the North Island.

Description:
   Crown: Bluish-grey colouring to below eye. **Face and neck:** Ash-grey with white eyebrow behind eye. **Upperparts:** Cinnamon-brown. **Underparts:** Buff.
Conspicuous features:
   • A distinct line, well below the eye, separates the bluish-grey eye surround from the buff underparts. The eye is almost impossible to see except when viewing in good light and at close range.
Conspicuous characteristics:
   • Outside of the breeding season birds congregate in large noisy flocks and move through the canopy in this manner.
   • Moves secretively through low vegetation.
Call: A rapid "ddee did dee dee", of fragile quality. It is not unlike the Yellowhead's song. This can confuse where these two species overlap.
Nest: A cup-shaped nest of bark, twigs and mosses, bound with cobwebs and lined with feathers, wool or grass is made. Up to 4 white, speckled reddish-brown eggs are laid.

How to attract: Brown Creepers are easily attracted with taped song recordings, Audubon callers or even polystyrene rubbed on a wet bottle.

Where to find - South Island:
Marlborough - Pelorus: Look in forests at Pelorus Bridge on Highway 6, between Havelock and Nelson. (See Weka article.)
Marlborough - Lake Rotoiti: Try the tracks around the lake and the Mount Roberts track. This lake is off Highway 63 at St Arnaud.
Canterbury - Banks Peninsula: The Hinewai Reserve is a good location for Brown Creeper. It is a ten minute drive from Akaroa. Follow the Goughs Bay signpost. Tracks lead into the reserve just before the Long Bay and Goughs Bay road junctions. Also to be seen here are Rifleman and Tomtit.
Fiordland - Cascade Creek: Common around Lake Gunn and up Cascade Creek. Most of the roadside beech forests of the area have Brown Creeper such as those around Mirror Lakes, and those behind Knobbs Flat.
Southland - Catlins State Forest Park: (See Yellowhead article.)
Southland - Invercargill: Try the Greenhills Bush area and the Omaui Bush. To get to these areas turn right at the Omaui signpost on the road to Bluff.

Where to find - Stewart Island:
Ackers Point walkway: Try for them here.
Ulva Island: The Boulder Beach track is good for Brown Creepers.

GREY WARBLER

Brian Chudleigh

Family: Acanthizidae   **Species:** *Gerygone igata*
Common name: Grey Warbler, Riroriro (Maori)   **Status:** Endemic
Size: 100 mm (cf sparrow 145 mm)

Discussion: Closely related to the Australian *Gerygone* genus and to the New Caledonian, Yellow-sided Warbler, (*Gerygone flavolateralis*). The Grey Warbler is one of New Zealand's most common species. Its sweet but plaintive song can be heard anywhere there is sufficient vegetation for the bird to hide in. A choice habitat for this bird is scrubland containing manuka (*Leptospermum scoparium*).

Habitat: Found from low secondary vegetation to tall forests.
Range: Found throughout New Zealand and on off-shore islands where vegetation exists.

Description:
Upperparts: Grey-brown. **Face, throat and breast:** Pale grey. **Underparts:** Whitish. **Tail:** Grey with white tips, the white being absent on the central tail feathers. The long tail separates the bird from the smaller Rifleman.
Conspicuous features:
- The long tail with white end markings is noticeable.
- Smaller than a House Sparrow but larger than the Rifleman.

Conspicuous characteristics:
- Has a habit of feeding on the wing and fluttering its wings quickly as if trying to fan the leaves to dislodge insects.
- Moves quickly through the branches usually in the middle canopy.
- Regularly warbles as it feeds.
- Often to be seen flying high above the canopy chasing other warblers in territorial "battle".

Call: Song is a sweet and fragile warble. Dialects vary from district to district although the bird is always identifiable. Birds quiver right to tip of tail when in full song. Male birds can be heard singing at any time of year but they are particularly vocal throughout the spring and summer breeding season.
Nest: Nests are of domed construction, pear-shaped, with a small hole on the side for an entrance. They are made of twigs, lichen, bark and moss, and lined with feathers. Up to 4 white, brown-speckled eggs are laid.
Cuckoo parasitism: The Grey Warbler is the major foster parent of young Shining Cuckoos. Therefore they nest early so that one brood of warblers is on the wing before the arrival of the cuckoo in September or October. In northern New Zealand the first brood is usually fully-fledged by early August. The Shining Cuckoo lays one olive-green egg in the warbler's nest. This egg is larger than the Grey Warblers but the host birds accept it. Although it is not known how the cuckoo's egg is placed through the small entrance hole of the closed nest of the warbler, it is likely the cuckoo breaks in when the warbler is away. The warbler then returns to tidy up the damage.

Where to find:
This bird is found wherever there is vegetation. It is often in suburban gardens and parks. It is a bird which can be found without even leaving the city environs. It is present in all the areas where the rarer forest birds might be sought. It may confuse the viewer searching for Rifleman.

CHATHAM ISLAND WARBLER

Brian Chudleigh

Family: Acanthizidae   **Species:** *Gerygone albofrontata*
Common name: Chatham Island Warbler   **Status:** Endemic
Size: 120 mm (cf sparrow 145 mm, Grey Warbler 100 mm)

Discussion: A close relative of the Grey Warbler but larger and browner in colour, and with a larger bill.

Habitat: Similar to the Grey Warbler.
Range: Chatham Island, Pitt Island, Mangere Island and South East Island.

Description:
     Forehead and eyebrow: White. **Upperparts:** Olive-brown. **Underparts:** White, with flanks tinged with yellow. **Tail:** Brown, with obscure white spots on outer feathers.
Call: Fragile warble of three weak notes and a pause, before another three notes and a pause. Delivered by the male bird.
Nest: Heavy domed nest bulkier than the Grey Warbler. 3 white eggs are laid.

Where to find: Chatham Island group.

FANTAIL

Family: Monarchidae   **Species:** *Rhipidura fuliginosa*
Common name: Fantail   **Status:** Endemic
Size: 160 mm (cf sparrow 145 mm, Grey Warbler 100 mm)

Discussion: The New Zealand Fantail is a race of the Australian species the Grey Fantail (*Rhipidura fuliginosa*). It is also closely related to the fantails of

Vanuatu, New Caledonia, Fiji and those of the islands eastwards to Samoa. Whereas New Zealand only has one species, most of the islands in the Pacific have two species - the Grey Fantail (*R. fuliginosa*) and the Speckled Fantail (*R. rufifrons*), each Fantail occupying separate niches within the bush. There are subtle differences between the Grey Fantail and the New Zealand race, the New Zealand bird showing less white on the eyebrow and lacking the white "tear-drop" behind the eye. It is also a more confiding bird than the island or Australian variety, living in suburban situations where vegetation is sufficient to provide feeding and nesting habitat. It will sometimes enter houses.

Phases: This bird comes in both a pied phase, similar to the Grey Fantail, and a black phase. The black phase is more common among South Island birds, especially in areas of the Marlborough Sounds, south of Christchurch and north of Dunedin. In the North Island, black birds are only rarely encountered.
Habitat: Found anywhere where there is vegetation. This might be a suburban garden, scrubland, wetland or native or exotic pine forest.
Range: Throughout New Zealand and the off-shore islands. Absent from alpine areas and areas of vast grassland.

Jim Hague

Pied Fantail with the black form inset

Description - pied phase:
Head: Brownish-black with a white eyebrow. **Upperparts:** Brown. **Chin:** White, below which is a black bar. **Underparts:** Tan colouring but yellowish when in full breeding plumage. **Tail:** The two central feathers, black. The outer feathers are white.
Description - black form:
Upperparts and underparts: Black. Usually a faint white tear-drop can be seen behind eye.
Conspicuous feature:
- Look for the white, showy, fan-like tail, noticeable from within dark foliage.

289

Conspicuous characteristics:
- During winter birds flock over grass and hawk insects close to the ground.
- Will enter houses and sit on lamp-shades, while all the time shifting position with sideways movement of its tail.

Call: A high-pitched "cheet cheet" communication call. When in nesting territories male birds have a vocal and constant repetitive chattering call.

Nest: A neat, wineglass-shaped cup, made of grass, bark, moss and cobwebs, about three metres from the ground. Up to 4 white, brown-speckled eggs are laid. Nesting birds usually give away the presence of a nest by suddenly stopping singing as an intruder approaches. Commonly nests around creeks and rivers.

How to locate: Responds to all squeaking lure sounds.

Where to find: Fantails can usually be found in any vegetated area.

TOMTIT

Jim Hague

Male Tomtit - North Island (left), Female Tomtit (right)

Family: Eopsaltriidae   **Species:** *Petroica macrocephela*
Common name: Tomtit   **Status:** Endemic
Size: 130 mm (cf sparrow 145 mm, Grey Warbler 100 mm)

Discussion: A New Zealand endemic species which is closely related to the Australian genus of *Petrocia* but larger in size. The Tomtit is divided into four subspecies, the Pied Tit of North Island forests, the Yellow-breasted Tit of South Island forests, the Chatham Island Tit of the Chatham Islands and Snares Island Tit found on Snares Island to the south of Stewart Island. The Tomtit appears to be increasing its numbers in many areas and is usually easy to find. It is a confiding bird which is not quickly frightened.

Habitat: A bird of old forests, secondary forest and exotic pine forests. Absent from scrublands.

Yellow-breasted Tomtit (South Island)

Range: Can be found in most forested areas throughout New Zealand including Stewart Island, but absent from large areas of farmland in the Waikato and Canterbury. Also on off-shore islands, but not on Tiri Tiri Island.

Description - male bird:
Head, throat and upperparts: Black. **Frontal dot above bill:** White. **Wings:** Black with a conspicuous white wingbar. **Underparts:** Pure white on the North Island bird and white, washed with yellow, on the South Island and Chatham Island birds. **Tail:** Black with white edges.

Description - female bird:
Upperparts: Brownish. **Frontal dot above bill:** Less conspicuous than on male bird and sometimes absent. **Wingbar:** White, but less obvious than on male birds. **Chin and breast:** Grey-brown. **Underparts:** Greyish.

Conspicuous features:
- Bigger and heavier than the Grey Warbler.
- Has prominent eye, considerably larger and bolder than the Grey Warbler.
- Its black and white under pattern is distinctive.

Conspicuous characteristics:
- The confiding nature of this bird is engaging. Birds seem to just arrive and they have the habit of peering down with head on one side.
- Although usually to be found inside the forest, Tomtits will venture out for short spells from forest verges into cleared areas.
- Birds often are seen clinging on to the side of trunks with head down.
- Birds often seek out people, look, and then fly off.

Call: Song, delivered by the male bird, is a fragile "sweedle sweedle sweedle swee". Male birds in nesting territories can be very vocal.

Nest: A bulky structure of twigs, fern, moss and cobwebs, lined with feathers and tree-fern hairs, on a branch fork or a cavity in a bank. Up to 5 cream, yellow-speckled eggs are laid.

How to locate: Tomtits respond well to taped calls, Audubon callers and "pishing" sounds.

Where to find - North Island:

Northland - Bay of Islands: Try Puketi Forest. From Waipapa take Pungaere Road and travel to junction. Go right for the boardwalk and left for the park tracks.

Northland - Warkworth: At the Dome north of Warkworth, stop at the Dome tearooms at the summit of the Dome. Take the nearby walking track into forest for about 500 metres.

South Auckland - Waharau: North of Miranda find the Waharau Park. Take a walking track into the hills.

King Country - Pureora: Look for Tomtits on the track near the Pureora Park headquarters or try Bismarck Road. Enquire at the forest park headquarters.

Rotorua - Mamaku: Try Galaxy Road, north of Oturoa Road off Highway 5. Look in the pine forests beyond the native forest fringe.

Rotorua - Hongis Track: This forest area between Lake Rotoiti and Lake Rotoma on Highway 30 always has birds and is very accessible. The road runs right through it.

Rotorua - Whakarewarewa: Tracks lead into this forest of exotic pines and redwoods about 10 kms south of Rotorua on Highway 5. Eventually you come to Lake Rotokakahi (Green Lake) which is good for waterfowl.

Central Plateau - Atiamuri: Try the forests around Atiamuri Hydro Station on Highway 1. Robins and Whiteheads are also here.

Taupo - Opepe Forest: This place, 14 kms from Taupo on Highway 5, is a very easy location to see Tomtits. Take the short forest trail.

Taupo - Lake Rotoponaumu: (See Rifleman article.)

Where to find - South Island:

Marlborough - Pelorus Bridge: Take the walking tracks here.

Canterbury - Alford Forest: These forests east of Ashburton are signposted and have good walking tracks.

West Coast: All the roadside forests here are good for Tomtits.

Fiordland - Cascade Creek: This area, the Hollyford Valley, and Milford Sound, are excellent localities. (See Yellowhead article.)

Where to find - Stewart Island:

Oban: Can be seen in the forests around Oban.

Ulva Island: This small island in Paterson Inlet has good numbers.

SNARES ISLAND TOMTIT

Family: Eopsaltriidae   **Species:** *Petroica macrocephala dannefaerdi*
Common name: Snares Island Tomtit   **Status:** Endemic
Size: 130 mm (cf sparrow 145 mm)

Discussion: Snares Islands are a small group lying to the south of Stewart Island on about the 48th parallel south. This Tomtit shares similar habits to the birds

Charles A Fleming

Snares Island Tomtit

of the North and South Islands and the Chatham Islands.

Habitat: A bird of secondary and tall forests.
Range: Snares Island only.

Description:
  Upper and underparts: Black.
Call: The song, delivered by the male bird is as for mainland species - "sweedle sweedle sweedle swee".
Nest: As for North and South Island Tomtits.

General: To see this bird a permit from the Department of Conservation, Invercargill would be required.

NEW ZEALAND ROBIN

Family: Eopsaltriidae   **Species:** *Petroica australis*
Common name: New Zealand Robin   **Status:** Endemic
Size: 180 mm (cf sparrow 145 mm, Tomtit 130 mm)

Discussion: The New Zealand Robin, along with the Tomtit, is closely related to the Australian robins of the genus *Petroica* and stems from an early *Petrocia* ancestor which, in predator-free New Zealand, became larger, ground feeding and confiding, unlike the Australian genus which is a smaller, more active dweller of the middle forest strata (Fleming 1982). It obtained its vernacular name from early British settlers who, on first contact with it, saw similarities to that of the European Robin Red-breast (*Erithacus rubecula*). Although slightly bigger than Robin Red-breast, the New Zealand Robin is of similar character. It has the large head, the bold dark eye and the noiseless flight.

David Stonex-Snapshotz /Jim Hague
New Zealand Robin (female left, male right)

Robin Red-breast, though, is placed in the family of thrushes (Muscicapidae) whereas the New Zealand Robin is placed with the Australasian robins in the family Eopsaltriidae.

Subspecies: New Zealand Robins are divided into North and South Island forms. The Chatham Island Robin, which is all black in colour, is considered a separate species.

Habitat: A bird of large, dark, old forests and seldom found in small remnants. It has, though, adapted to the large exotic pine forests of the central North Island and these forests have stopped its decline.

Range: In the North Island confined to central areas and to Little Barrier Island, Tiri Tiri Island and Kapiti Island. Also Mokoia Island in Lake Rotorua. In the South Island known from the forests of the north-west, areas in Westland, Fiordland, Kaikoura, Dunedin and Southland. Known from central Stewart Island but absent from the surrounds of the town of Oban, the Paterson Inlet area and Ulva Island in Paterson Inlet.

Description - North Island Robin:
  Upperparts: Almost black. **Frontal dot above bill:** White, especially in breeding plumage. **Lower breast and abdomen:** Greyish-white.
Description - South Island Robin:
  Upperparts: Almost black. **Frontal dot above bill:** White, especially in breeding plumage. **Lower breast and abdomen:** Yellowish-white.
Description - female birds: Distinctly drabber than male birds.
Conspicuous features:
  • Larger than the Tomtit but smaller than the introduced Blackbird.
  • Look for the bold eye.
  • Look for the breast and abdomen markings.
  • The frontal dot is noticeable.

Conspicuous characteristics:
- Has a confiding nature and will approach humans.
- Has a habit of just appearing nearby.
- Scratches through leaf litter on the forest floor like a Blackbird.

Call: The song, delivered by the male bird, is a ringing "tueet tueet tueet tueet tooo" on a descending scale. Birds are very vocal in mid-morning, especially if the day is warm and will continue to sing for periods of up to one hour. They also have a distinctive alarm call, often issued when standing on the ground, not unlike the alarm call of the introduced Blackbird. Birds sing throughout the year although not as strongly as in springtime when territories are firmly defined.

Nest: A bulky cup of twigs, fern and moss, bound with cobwebs and lined with feathers, wool or tree-fern hairs. Up to 4 cream, brown-speckled eggs are laid.

How to locate: Birds rapidly respond to taped calls and to Audubon callers.

Where to find- North Island:

North Auckland - Tiri Tiri Island: This is a very easy place to see them. Go first to the northern boardwalk.

Waikato - Kaimai Ranges: About 3 kms up from where Highway 29 climbs the Kaimai Range on the western slopes, watch for a parking area on the right. A short walk from here through paddocks takes you to the bush. Robins can be found just inside the bush along with good Tomtit and Whitehead populations. Past the Rapurapu River the track goes on to a large kauri tree after numerous river crossings.

King Country - Pureora Forest: Take the level walking track into tall podocarps near the information centre.

Rotorua - Mamaku Ranges: Try Galaxy Road north of Oturoa Road on Highway 1 and walk into the pine forests.

Rotorua - Atiamuri: The pine forests in this district, beside Highway 1, and especially those opposite the Atiamuri Hydro Station, are good localities.

Urewera - Waikaremoana: Try the track which leads into Lake Waikareiti.

Taupo - Lake Rotoponaumu: This is another Robin locality.

Where to find - South Island:

Marlborough - Mount Stokes: Try the track as for Yellowheads.

Marlborough - Pelorus Bridge: Try the walking tracks here.

Marlborough - Lake Rotoiti: Try the Mount Roberts Track. Take Mount Roberts Ski Field Road, off Highway 63. Tracks lead into beech forests.

West Coast - Okarito: Try the forests which lead to Okarito Beach.

West Coast - Haast Pass: Try the bridal track as for Yellowheads.

Fiordland - Eglinton Valley - Cascade Creek: Birds can be found right along this valley. Try first at the Mirror Lakes and then at Lake Gunn.

Dunedin: The bush in the environs of Dunedin contains Robins. Try the Douglas Fir plantations on the Three Mile Hill Road. (See Rifleman article.)

BLACK ROBIN

Brian Chudleigh

Family: Eopsaltriidae **Species:** *Petroica traversi*
Common name: Black Robin or Chatham Island Robin **Status:** Endemic
Size: 150 mm (cf sparrow 145 mm, New Zealand Robin 180 mm)

Discussion: Found only on South East Island and Mangere Island in the Chatham
Island group. Its survival is due to a major breeding campaign between 1979
and 1988 by the then Wildlife Service of the Department of Internal Affairs.
This set about reversing the declining numbers of the Black Robin from a
remaining stock of one female bird and four male birds which had persisted on
Little Mangere Island. From Little Mangere Island, birds were transferred to
nearby Mangere Island and later South East Island where eggs from the
remaining female bird, known as "Old Blue", were transferred to the nests of
foster parents (warblers and tits). Current population is over 200 birds.

Description:
Upper and underparts: All black.
How to view: Contact the Department of Conservation in Wellington.

SILVEREYE

Family: Zosteropidae **Species:** *Zosterops lateralis*
Common name: Silvereye, White-eye, Grey-backed Silvereye (Australia)
Status: Native
Size: 120 mm (cf sparrow 145 mm, Grey Warbler 100 mm)

Discussion: The Silvereye is a self-introduced bird which colonised New Zealand
in the 1850s, probably from Australia. It is also found around the Pacific on
many islands such as Norfolk Island, Lord Howe, Vanuatu, New Caledonia,

Silvereye

Fiji and Tahiti. It is very common in New Zealand where it is popular as a bird which comes to bird tables and feeders. Has a brushed-tongue for the taking of nectar from flowers.

Habitat: Found anywhere where there is suitable vegetative cover from suburban gardens, to hedgerows, to exotic plantation and native forests.

Range: Throughout New Zealand and the off-shore islands.

Description:
Head, nape and rump: Green. **Back:** Grey. **Wings:** Green, primaries edged with brown. **Chin:** Yellowish. **Underneck and breast:** Pale grey. **Flanks:** Pinkish-brown. **Abdomen:** Whitish. **Eye-ring:** White. **Tail:** Above green, edged with brown, with white undertail.

Conspicuous features:
- It appears as a small green bird.
- The white eye-ring is very noticeable.
- Look for the grey back.

Conspicuous characteristics:
- Gathers into large winter feeding flocks which work through areas of vegetation in a noisy manner and are easily detected.
- Often seen feeding alongside the Grey Warbler in canopy trees. The white tips to the Grey Warbler's tail separates it from a distance.

Call: Several Silvereye songs have been detected. The alarm note is a noisy "tchirrup", while the territorial song, delivered by the male bird, is rapid and warbled, not unlike a thin rendition of a Blackbird's song. In autumn, birds often sing softly from within trees and shrubs.

Nest: A rather flimsy cup woven from fine grasses, mosses and twigs, hung between two branches, and very often placed at the extremity of branches, up to three metres from the ground. Usually 3 pale blue eggs are laid.

Breeding habits: Because Silvereyes very often place their nests on the end of flimsy branches, it is likely that they are beyond the reach of rats (*Rattus rattus*) in most instances. It breeds from September through to March.

Where to find:
Suburban gardens, parks, rural patches of vegetation, orchards, forests and roadside verges all have this bird.

STITCHBIRD

Simon Fordham/Jim Hague

Female Stitchbird (inset)

Family: Meliphagidae   **Species:** *Notiomystis cincta*
Common name: Stitchbird, Hihi   **Status:** Endemic
Size: 180 mm (cf sparrow 145 mm, Bellbird 200 mm)

Discussion: The Stitchbird is thought to be linked to the Australian honeyeaters showing some resemblance to the White-cheeked Honeyeater (*Phylidonyris nigra*) but from which it has markedly deviated (Fleming 1982). It is a rare endemic which has a main population on Little Barrier Island north-east of Auckland. Small numbers have been transferred to the predator-free islands of Tiri Tiri in the Hauraki Gulf, Mokoia Island in Lake Rotorua and Kapiti Island near Wellington, from Little Barrier Island. The Stitchbird is one of two world honeyeaters to nest in cavities, the other being the Hawaiian Honeyeater (*Moho braccatus*).

Habitat: A bird of both secondary and mature native forest. At times when favourite plants are in full flower it can be drawn from forest margins to feed. Flax flowers draw birds out into the open on Little Barrier Island.
Range: Little Barrier Island, Tiri Tiri Island, Mokoia Island and Kapiti Island.

Description - male:
  Head: Velvet-black with white erectile tufts behind eyes. **Upperbreast and back:** Black. **Wings:** Feathers are black with light brown edges and a conspicuous white wingbar at base of primaries. **Lowerbreast:** A band of yellow crosses the lowerbreast and the folded wings. **Rump and underparts:** Pale brown.

Description - female:
  Upper and underparts: Olive-brown, similar to the female Bellbird.
  Wings: Brown with a white wingbar.

Conspicuous features:
  - White wingbar separates the female Stitchbird from the female Bellbird.
  - Both male and female birds have whiskers at the gape.
  - Ear tufts on the male bird are noticeable.

Conspicuous characteristics:
  - Birds are usually in pairs. In the nesting season they are strongly territorial.
  - Out of the nesting season on Little Barrier Island, individual birds can often be found following large flocks of Whitehead through the forest.
  - Stitchbirds have a habit of alighting on a branch with the tail held high or even over their backs or with heads facing down and tails kinked.

Call: A resonant "tik tik tik tik" and loud "t-zit". Females make "pek pek pek", alarm notes similar to the Bellbird.

Nest: In holes or cavities high up, made of twigs, with a cup lined with feathers or tree-fern hairs. Up to 4 white eggs are laid.

Where to find:
Little Barrier Island: This is the stronghold of this species.
North Auckland - Tiri Tiri Island: Regularly seen here.
Rotorua - Mokoia Island: Tourist launches leave from the Lake Rotorua lakeside twice a day. (See "Places" in back of book.)
Kapiti Island: Birds are breeding here.

BELLBIRD

Family: Meliphagidae   **Species:** *Anthornis melanura*
Common name: Bellbird   **Status:** Endemic
Size: 200 mm (cf sparrow 145 mm, Tui 300 mm)

Discussion: The Bellbird is a honeyeater which shares many of the characteristics of Australian honeyeaters. Its busy feeding habits, fast, low and noisy flight and its loud and persistent dawn chorus all illustrate similarities. Although a bird of large populations upon the arrival of James Cook to New Zealand in 1769, its populations declined seriously with the arrival of the colonists to a point where many thought extinction was likely. It has since recolonised many areas.

Habitat: A bird of both old forests, secondary forests, scrublands and in some areas even in suburban gardens.
Range: Well-spread throughout the forested areas of the South Island and forested

Simon Fordham/Jim Hague

Female Bellbird (inset)

areas of the North Island north to the Waikato and the top of the Coromandel Peninsula. Establishing on the Whangaparaoa Peninsula. Also on off-shore islands but not Great Barrier Island.

Description - male:
   Head: Olive-green with purple iridescence on foréhead and crown. **Upperparts:** Olive-green. **Wings:** Dark bluish-black with yellow at bend of folded wing. **Tail:** Bluish-black and slightly forked. **Underparts:** Pale green. **Eye:** Red. **Bill:** Black.

Description - female bird:
   Upperparts: Tending to olive-brown. **Cheek:** Whitish stripe under eye from gape. **Wings and tail:** Brownish-black, tail slightly forked. **Underparts:** Pale green. **Bill:** Black.

Conspicuous features:
 • Green of the male bird is noticeable.
 • Look for the purple head tonings on the male bird.
 • The curved honeyeater bill is conspicuous.
 • Female bird is duller than the male.
 • Look for the slightly forked tail.

Conspicuous characteristics:
 • The Bellbird is renowned for its early morning chorus.
 • It has a habit of taking nectar from flowers in an acrobatic manner.
 • Flight is fast with noisy wing rustle. In the forest it flies low and is manoeuvrable. In the open its flight becomes direct with some undulation.

Call: Bell-like, liquid, clear and melodic which starts well before sunrise. The dawn chorus is memorable. Both sexes sing, male birds being of stronger and more persistent voice. Also has a "pek pek pek" alarm call.

Nest: A loosely built structure of twigs and fern leaves, lined with fine grasses, usually in a fork of a tree, at about four metres from the ground. Up to 4 white, brown-blotched eggs are laid.

How to locate: A tape of Bellbird or Tui song will draw birds.

Where to find - North Island:

North Auckland - Whangaparaoa: From Highway 1 take Whangaparaoa Road and follow to Shakespear Park at the end of the Whangaparaoa Peninsula. At the park take the sign to Te Haruhi Bay. Look for Bellbirds in the trees above the beach and parking area.

North Auckland - Tiri Tiri Island: Large numbers are found here.

Auckland - Motuihe Island: This small island in the Auckland Harbour has a good population but requires a boat to get there.

South Auckland - Waharau Regional Park: This park, which is north of Kaiaua on the Firth of Thames, has an increasing population of Bellbirds. Follow the walking track from the parking area.

Thames - Kauaeranga Valley: This road leads into the valley from the south end of Thames. It always has good numbers of Bellbirds once in the forest.

Thames - Ruamahunga Bay: Follow the motel sign and drive to end.

Coromandel Range: Follow Highway 25a, the road from Kopu to Hikuai. At the summit try the Kaitarakihi track which leads north.

King Country - Pureora: Try the walk by the Information Centre.

Taupo - Opepe: Large numbers here. (See Rifleman article.)

Taupo: Often seen in the parks in the town.

Taupo - Turangi: The forests around the southern end of Lake Taupo are easy places to find this bird. Try Frethey Road, east of Turangi.

Where to find - South Island:

West Coast: Common nearly everywhere where there are trees.

Fiordland - Te Anau: Can be seen in lakeside trees.

Fiordland - Cascade Creek: This is an excellent location.

Where to find - Stewart Island:

Oban: Common everywhere.

TUI

Family: Meliphagidae   **Species:** *Prosthemadera novaeseelandiae*
Common name: Tui, Parson Bird (old settlers' name   **Status:** Endemic
Size: 300 mm (cf sparrow 145 mm, Blackbird 250 mm)

Discussion: A common endemic brush-tongued honeyeater quite unlike any of the Australian honeyeaters from which descendants are usually sought. This suggests an ancient New Zealand history.

Habitat: A bird of forests, secondary forests and vegetated suburban areas in many towns and cities. Tui can be found from sea level to sub-alpine forests.

Range: Well-spread throughout the North Island but generally absent in districts of intense farming activity such as the Waikato. In the South Island it is found throughout most forested areas but is absent from Canterbury grassland areas and is seldom seen in the beech forests of Fiordland. Common on Stewart Island.

Brian Chudleigh

Tui

Description:

    Upperparts and underparts: Black, with green-purple iridescence. **Wings:** Black, with white wingbars, conspicuous when in flight. **Neck and nape:** Black, with a lacy white collar. **Throat:** Black, with two white throat tufts. **Bill:** Black.

Conspicuous features:

- A bird of glossy plumage with considerable iridescence in good sunlight.
- Look for the conspicuous white feather, throat tufts.
- Slightly larger than the common Blackbird.
- White wingbars are noticeable in flight.

Conspicuous characteristics:

- Flight is jerky and erratic. Usually after about six wing beats, the bird pauses in flight before resuming. Sometimes birds will rise vertically to great heights, with very rapid wing beats, before plunging down again.
- A noisy flier and especially fast and manoeuvrable when chasing unwanted birds from nesting territories.
- Regularly feeds on flax (*Phormium tenax*), five-finger (*Pseudopanax spp.*), kowhai, (*Sophora spp.*) and the coastal pohutukawa tree (*Metrosideros excelsa*).

Call: The song, delivered by both sexes, is of bell-like notes, similar to the Bellbird, but less pure, incorporating many guttural notes and gurgles. Some notes are beyond human hearing. Dialects have developed in some areas. When in full song, birds will sing from vantage points. It is one of the first birds to start singing in the morning usually uttering its first notes at least an hour before sunrise. In summer birds will sing from day-break to dusk. Birds sing throughout the year.

Nest: A platform of sticks, lined with fine grasses, in a fork of a tree or on an outer branch at about four metres above ground. Up to 4 white, brown-blotched eggs are laid.

Where to find - North Island:
Northland - Aroha Island: Common here.
North Auckland - Wenderholm: Always common here.
Auckland: The Tui is a resident in many parts of the city.
Auckland - Cornwall Park: Always birds here.
Waikato - Hamilton: Not heard in the city. Closest birds are found in the Te Kowhai area north-west of Hamilton in remnants near the Hakarimata Range.
King Country - Pureora: Common here. (See "Places" in back of book.)
Taupo - Opepe: Good populations are found here often feeding on the nectar from fuchsia flowers. (See Rifleman article.)
Central North Island: Found in all areas of forest and secondary forest, and even in the large pine forests (*Pinus spp.*) which have a native under-storey.

Where to find - South Island:
Marlborough - Pelorus Bridge: Very common in forested areas.
West Coast: Common in all forests.
Canterbury: Try Alford and Mount Peel forests west of Ashburton.
Southland: Common in forested areas away from Fiordland and especially the eastern Southland forests of Catlins and Chaslands.

Where to find - Stewart Island:
Oban: It is a very common species which is easily seen in the town of Oban.

SEASONAL FEEDING PREFERENCES OF TUI

Spring: Feeds on the nectar of flowers and in particular, of the kowhai tree. These are yellow, bell-shaped and rich in nectar.
Summer: Feeds on nectar from coastal pohutukawa and inland rata flowers.
Autumn: Feeds on fruiting podocarp trees and takes large numbers of cicada species especially (*Amphispalta cingulata*) and (*A. zelandica*).
Winter: Feeding largely on the flowers of exotic eucalypts. Will travel large distances to find winter food.

YELLOWHAMMER

Family: Emberizidae   **Species:** *Emberiza citrinella*
Common name: Yellowhammer   **Status:** Introduced
Size: 160 mm (cf sparrow 145 mm, Chaffinch 150 mm)

Discussion: Introduced from England, the Yellowhammer has spread widely and is probably now more abundant in New Zealand than in Great Britain. Although widespread, it is a bird which seldom comes into suburban areas.

Habitat: A bird of open country and areas of second growth.
Range: Found throughout New Zealand and on many off-shore islands.

Jim Hague

Yellowhammer (male left, female right)

Description - male bird:
   Head and throat: Yellow, with some widely spaced brown markings. **Wings:** Brown, streaked with dark brown. **Breast:** Yellow, washed with brown and streaked with dark brown. **Underparts:** Yellow. **Rump:** Rufous. **Tail:** Brown, with black outer feathers edged with white.

Description - female birds:
   Upperparts and underparts: Similar to male birds but paler and with more brown streaking.

Conspicuous features:
   • Yellow plumage is noticeable.
   • Tail is slightly forked.
   • White outer tail feathers are noticeable when in flight.

Conspicuous characteristics:
   • Flocks in large numbers in winter on to pastureland where they feed on grass seeds and in particular *Poa* species.
   • Can be found looking for discarded grass seed in areas where farmers have recently fed out hay.

Call: The song, "chitty chitty chitty chitty swee", made by the male bird, is commonly translated as "little bit of bread and no cheese". It is usually delivered from a post or a low shrub which is conspicuous. New Zealand birds seem to omit the "cheese" note, except when in full song in mid-December. Singing period starts in September and ends in February.

Nest: A cup of grass, lined with wool, feathers or moss and usually close to the ground in low growing vegetation or tall grass. Up to 4 white, scribbled over with brown, eggs are laid. It is a late nester starting in October.

Where to find - North Island and South Island:
Common in all areas of pastureland and wilderness. Not in forests. Birds form large flocks in winter.

CIRL BUNTING

Brian Chudleigh

Family: Emberizidae **Species:** *Emberiza cirlus*
Common name: Cirl Bunting **Status:** Introduced
Size: 160 mm (cf sparrow 145 mm, Yellowhammer 160 mm)

Discussion: The Cirl Bunting is the least known of the introduced passerines mainly because it has not spread widely, its main populations being confined to the north of the South Island. In recent years records have come from other localities indicating an on-going distribution spread.

Habitat: A bird of open pastureland and low vegetation.
Range: North Island records come from Whangarei, Rotorua, Gisborne, Hawkes Bay and Wellington areas. Most South Island records come from eastern areas from Nelson, south to South Otago and occasionally Westland.

Description - male:
   Crown and nape: Dark grey, striped with black and yellow. **Face:** Yellow, with bold black stripe through eye. **Chin and throat:** Black, with yellow band below. **Neck and upperbreast:** Pale brown. **Wings:** Brown, edged with dark brown. **Underparts:** Pale yellow, lightly streaked with brown. **Rump:** Olive-brown. **Tail:** Olive-brown, with black outer feathers, edged white.
Description - female:
   Upperparts and underparts: Dull yellow, streaked heavily with dark brown on the crown and light brown elsewhere. **Rump:** Olive-brown.
Conspicuous features:
   • Yellowhammer size.
   • At first sight similar to a Yellowhammer.
   • Overall a dark Yellowhammer.
Conspicuous characteristics:
   • Feeds on the ground, especially among fed out hay, with Yellow-hammers.

- Hops while feeding on ground.
- Often crouches close to ground like a Yellowhammer.
- Twitters in flight when in family parties.

Differences between female Cirl Buntings and female Yellowhammers:
- Cirl Buntings have olive-brown rumps.
- Yellowhammers have rufous rumps.
- Cirl Buntings are darker with less yellow.

Differences between male Cirl Buntings and male Yellowhammers:
- Cirl Buntings have a greyish crown.
- Yellowhammers have yellow crowns.
- Cirl Buntings have a yellow face separated by a bold black eye-stripe.
- Cirl Buntings have a black chin.

Call: Song, made by the male bird, is a thin, metallic high-pitched rattle, "tirree tiree tirree tiree" delivered from a conspicuous perch. It is not unlike the Yellowhammer's song. Song period is from October to March, this bird still singing when all the other introduced songsters have stopped. Birds also call when in flight and have a variety of "zit" type communication calls.

Nest: Is a cup of dried grass and moss in thick vegetation at about two metres above the ground. It places its nest higher up than does the Yellowhammer. Up to 4 bluish green, streaked with black eggs are laid.

Where to find - North Island:

Northland - Whareora: From Whangarei take the Whareora Road, east of the town. Turn into Mount Tiger Road. Search towards the top of Mount Tiger Road. Look for birds here in late spring when they are in full song.

Other localities: No reliable localities are known. Odd birds turn up in North Auckland (Muriwai), Rotorua (Okere Falls), Gisborne (Kaiti Hill), Hawkes Bay (Mangakuri Beach and Clive).

Where to find - South Island:

Marlborough - Nelson: Most of the pastureland around Nelson has this bird. It is especially easy to find during winter when farmers are feeding out hay. Try Polestead Road in Stoke, Monaco near Stoke, Nelson Haven coastal fringes north of the city, and generally any rural land in the district.

Marlborough - Motueka: Try Beach Road and the sandspit area.

Marlborough - Abel Tasman Park: Try the pasture areas prior to the park.

Marlborough - Blenheim: Try rural areas south of the town.

Marlborough - Seddon: Drive south from Blenheim to Seddon. Before Seddon at Dashwood take the Awatere Valley Road and search the area.

Marlborough - Lake Grassmere: Try the areas around Lake Grassmere and Lake Elterwater, south of Seddon.

Canterbury - Oamaru: Try the Oamaru Racecourse. This is about 4 kms north of the town on Highway 1, located between Redcastle Road and Russell Road on the left. It is a consistently good locality.

Otago - Taiaroa Heads: Regularly recorded near the heads.

Otago - Berwick: Try Berwick swamp and the Lake Waihola districts, south of Dunedin. Try along Berwick Road from Highway 1.

CHAFFINCH

Jim Hague

Chaffinch (female left, male right)

Family: Fringillidae
Common name: Chaffinch
Size: 150 mm (cf sparrow 145 mm)

Species: *Fringilla coelebs*
Status: Introduced

Discussion: The Chaffinch was introduced into New Zealand during the late 19th century and has now spread widely to become one of New Zealand's most common birds. It is equally at home in almost every environment other than alpine regions above the snowline.

Habitat: Lives everywhere from suburban gardens, to parkland, to farmland, to scrublands and forests. Large populations exist in the exotic pine forests.
Range: Found throughout New Zealand and on the off-shore islands.

Description - male bird:
    Forehead: Black. **Crown and nape:** Bluish-grey. **Face, throat and breast:** Pinkish-brown. **Back:** Reddish-brown. **Wings:** Blackish, with two conspicuous white wingbars on each wing, one of which is on the shoulder. **Rump:** Olive. **Underparts:** Pinkish-brown, tapering to white under the tail. **Tail:** Brown, with outer feathers black with white edges.
Description - female bird:
    Upperparts: Brownish-grey. **Wings:** As for male bird. **Rump:** Green. **Underparts:** Greyish-brown. **Tail:** As for male bird.
Conspicuous features:
 • Look for the bluish-grey on the crown.
 • Look for the pinkish-brown around face, throat and upperbreast.
Conspicuous characteristics:
 • Feeds on the ground but flies up for cover when disturbed.

- Shows a lot of white on wings and tail when in flight.
- In flight, when in forests, it is faster and more direct than native birds.
- Has a habit of hawking insects like a flycatcher, especially over water.
- Continually sings during the breeding season.
- During winter and early spring joins mixed flocks of other finches.

Call: Its song, delivered by the male bird, is a happy "cherry cherry cherry cheery swee swee" repeated many times throughout the day. Throughout the year both sexes utter a metallic "pink pink" note. Song period is July to January.

Nest: A neatly constructed cup of dry grass and moss, camouflaged with silver lichen, at about three metres from the ground, firmly placed on a branch or in a fork of a tree. Up to 4 bluish, purple-blotched eggs are laid.

Where to find: Common everywhere. In parks, birds become tame enough to beg for crumbs from the picnicing public.

GREENFINCH

Brian Chudleigh

Greenfinch

Family: Fringillidae   **Species:** *Carduelis chloris*
Common name: Greenfinch   **Status:** Introduced
Size: 150 mm (cf sparrow 145 mm, Chaffinch 150 mm)

Discussion: An introduced European finch which has readily adapted to New Zealand and which is common in both urban and rural environments.

Habitat: Found everywhere from suburban gardens to rural pastureland and especially in areas which are hedged. It is does not penetrate heavy forest.
Range: Found throughout New Zealand and on some off-shore islands.

Description male:
   Face: Grey, a black marking going from the upper bill to behind the eye.

Eyebrows: Bright yellow. **Upperparts:** Olive-green. **Wings:** Primaries are black on outer feathers, grey on inner feathers, with a bright yellow bar in middle of wing. **Underwing:** Grey and yellow. **Breast:** Yellowish-green above, with yellow patch on belly. **Underparts:** Olive-green. **Rump:** Yellowish. **Tail:** Greyish inner feathers, yellowish outer feathers, with a dark tip. **Undertail:** Yellow on outer feathers and grey on the inner feathers. **Eye:** Brown.

Description - female:
Upper and underparts: Similar to the male bird but much duller.

Conspicuous features:
- Look for the dark eye.
- Look for the green head and back.
- The yellow leading edge of wing of the standing bird is noticeable.

Conspicuous characteristics:
- Sings from high in conifers.
- Flocks in winter and spring with other finches.
- During the breeding season singing males will fly from perch to perch assuming a bat-like flight with wings beaten in a staccato fashion.
- Tail is slightly forked and slightly splayed in flight.

Call: Song, delivered by the male bird, is a drawn out "tuusweeet". Also a melodious "chichichichi - tuu tuu tu" warble. Songs are uttered from high perches especially from conifer trees. Note that its song is often mistaken for that of the Long-tailed Cuckoo. The Greenfinch, though, has notes arranged on a descending scale while the cuckoo has notes arranged on an ascending scale. Song period starts in September and continues into February.

Nest: A bulky cup-like structure of twigs, leaves and moss, lined with fine dry grass, wool or feathers, placed near the top of a bush, in a fork or on a branch. Up to 5 pale blue, brown-blotched eggs are laid.

Where to find: Common in most areas away from tall forest. Likely on the edge of forests only. They prefer conifer trees.

GOLDFINCH

Family: Fringillidae   **Species:** *Carduelis carduelis*
Common name: Goldfinch   **Status:** Introduced
Size: 130 mm (cf sparrow 145 mm, Chaffinch 150 mm)

Discussion: The Goldfinch is another very common introduced European species which is well known due to its habit of feeding in large gaily coloured flocks right in suburban gardens and even among flowers right next to houses.

Habitat: Found in many localities from gardens and parks to pastureland and open country. Also found in exotic forests but not into tall indigenous forest.
Range: Found throughout New Zealand and on some off-shore islands.

Brian Chudleigh

Goldfinch

Description:
Crown: Black from centre crown to back of head. **Face:** Red to under chin, with broad patch of white behind the eye and on the throat. **Back:** Brown. **Wings:** Primaries and secondaries black with a gold bar between and some white on ends of feathers. **Breast:** White, with a brown wash. **Underparts:** White. **Rump:** White. **Tail:** Black, spotted white near the tip.

Conspicuous features:
- Sexes are alike.
- Look for the red and white of face.
- Look for the gold bar on wings.

Conspicuous characteristics:
- Forms into large flocks after the breeding season.
- Regularly feeds on the ground on sow thistle seed (*Sonchus oleraceous*) and grass seed (*Poa annua*), but also high up in trees such as alder trees (*Alnus glutinosa*).
- Flies with undulating flight showing slightly forked tail.
- Utters a fragile twitter while in flight. Don't mix with Redpoll flight-song which is loud and clear by comparison.

Call: Song, delivered by the male bird, is a rather thin but persistent jingling twitter, usually uttered from power wires or a high perch. Song period is from October to February.

Nest: A neatly made cup of fine twigs and grasses camouflaged with silver lichen and lined with feathers or wool, placed on a branch or in a fork of a tree, high up. Up to 5 blue, brown-spotted eggs are laid.

Where to find:

South Auckland - Miranda: Large winter flocks of up to 500 birds regularly assemble here on the coastal flats with Greenfinches.

General: Common in all suburban areas and in all open country.

REDPOLL

Brian Chudleigh

Family: Fringillidae   **Species:** *Carduelis flammea*
Common name: Redpoll   **Status:** Introduced
Size: 120 mm (cf sparrow 145 mm, Chaffinch 150 mm)

Discussion: An inconspicuous and less well known European introduction which has a widespread but uneven distribution in New Zealand.

Habitat: A bird of open country and wasteland. Avoids areas of high fertility pastures. Found in both native and exotic forests and even to above the snowline in some areas.

Range: Found throughout New Zealand but with sparse populations in some areas, such as in the intensive dairying areas of South Auckland and the Waikato. It is very common in the South Island.

Description - male bird:
   Head: Dark behind bill then a reddish crown to the back of the head. **Neck, nape and back:** Brownish. **Wings:** Dark brown on primaries with distinctive whitish wingbar. **Chin:** Black. **Breast:** Brownish, with a reddish flush in the breeding season. **Underparts:** Greyish, with some scattered dark brown striping.

Description - female:
   Crown: Reddish. **Upperparts:** Greyish-brown, with noticeable dark brown striping, but less coloured than on the male bird. **Underparts:** Whitish, with light brown striping but lacking the reddish flush of breeding plumaged males.

Conspicuous features:
   • The smallest of the introduced finches.
   • Whitish wingbar is noticeable.
   • Look for red on forehead.
   • Look for the black chin on male birds.

311

- Streaking on the back of head and mantle is noticeable.

Conspicuous characteristics:
- Noisy flight-song is conspicuous.
- Feeds on the ground often among other finches.
- Will feed close to buildings and houses in some localities.
- Enjoys feeding over stubble paddocks.

Call: Song, which is delivered by the male bird, is a loud, direct, rippling trill, more often heard in flight than from a perch.

Nest: A neat cup of dried grass and fine twigs, lined with wool and feathers, placed in a fork of a tree, or on a branch in a low shrub. Up to 4 blue, brown-spotted and streaked eggs are laid.

Where to find:
Expect it in any locality but it is more common in the South Island and Stewart Island than in many North Island localities. Very common in inland Canterbury, Central Otago and on the Otago Peninsula.

HOUSE SPARROW

Jim Hague

House Sparrow (female left, male right)

Family: Ploceidae   **Species:** *Passer domesticus*
Common name: Sparrow   **Status:** Introduced
Size: 145 mm (cf Chaffinch 150 mm)

Discussion: The House Sparrow was introduced to New Zealand for insect control in crops and has multiplied rapidly. Today it inhabits areas close to people, where it forms symbiotic relationships as far as food scraps are concerned, but largest populations are now in rural areas.

Habitat: It is found in towns and suburbs and in rough open countryside.
Range: Found throughout New Zealand and on some of the outlying islands.

Description - male:

Crown: Grey. **Face:** Light grey with a black band from forehead, through the eye to back of neck. **Upperparts:** Brown, streaked black on back. **Wings:** Primaries grey, secondaries brownish, with a white wingbar. **Chin:** Black, increasing to a black bib in the breeding season. **Underparts:** Greyish-white. **Rump:** Grey. **Tail:** Dark grey.

Description - female:

Upperparts: Brown, with buffy patches to sides of face and neck. **Wings:** As for male bird but lighter. **Underparts:** Grey.

Conspicuous features:

- Look for the black bib on male birds.
- Look for the whitish wingbar.
- Don't confuse the female House Sparrow with the Redpoll
- House Sparrows have greyer wings than Redpolls.

Conspicuous characteristics:

- Tends to flock in large numbers on pastureland and roadside verges. Can be confused with other finches in these places.
- Returns to evening roosts outside of the breeding season.
- A late nester from early October, when it can be seen carrying streamers of straw into the tree tops or under house eaves.

Call: A noisy "chirrup" and chattering sound is the usual song. At dawn and dusk House Sparrow evening roosts become very noisy. The dawn chorus starts after the Blackbird and Song Thrush have finished singing.

Nest: An untidy bundle of straw formed into a dome with a side entrance. The cup is lined with feathers or wool. It nests high up in conifers and exotic evergreens but also in buildings and under roofs. Breeding tends to be solitary but occasionally noisy nesting colonies of three or four pairs are found. Up to 5 whitish, brown-blotched and streaked eggs are laid.

Where to find:

Common in every town and around the open countryside.

STARLING

Family: Sturnidae

Common name: Starling

Size: 210 mm (cf sparrow 145 mm)

Species: *Sturnus vulgaris*

Status: Introduced

Discussion: The Starling was introduced from Europe for pest control reasons and has become very plentiful throughout the country with some farmers providing nesting boxes for them to breed in.

Habitat: A bird of towns, cities and open pastureland.

Range: Found throughout New Zealand away from forests and alpine areas.

Description:

Note: Three plumage changes should be noted for this bird. This helps prevent confusion.

Starling (immature left, mature right)

Description - immature bird:
> **Upperparts:** Greyish-brown, with darker wing striping. **Underparts:** Greyish. **Eye:** Black, with a dark brown area in front of it and behind. **Bill:** Brown.

Description - winter bird:
> **Upperparts:** Black, with buff coloured head and with white overall spotting to the neck. **Wings:** Black, feathers edged with light brown. **Underparts:** Blackish with very conspicuous white spotting. Note that the female is more spotted than the male bird. **Bill:** Brown.

Description - breeding bird:
> **Upperparts and underparts:** Glossy black with a purple sheen. Some faint remnant whitish spotting on flanks. **Wings:** Black, with a greenish sheen and feathers edged with brown. **Bill:** Yellow.

Conspicuous features:
- Look for the yellow bill in the breeding season.
- Look for the white speckling on birds not in full breeding plumage.
- Look for the dark eye on juvenile birds.

Conspicuous characteristics:
- Outside of the breeding season Starlings flock by night in large communal roosts, gathering in groups before dusk, before flying off.
- Birds feed on paddocks in large groups outside of the breeding season.If disturbed these flocks look spectacular as they take to the air.
- Birds fly constantly backwards and forwards to nests in breeding season.

Call: The Starling is a recognised mimic of such birds as the Californian Quail, Shining Cuckoo, and the alarm calls of the Blackbird. Its own song is a warble of a variety of thin notes uttered from a high perch. Wings are clapped when the bird is singing.

Nest: A bundle of straw and sticks in holes or under the eaves of buildings. Egg laying starts in the first week in October. Up to 6 pale blue eggs are laid.

Where to find: Common everywhere.

INDIAN MYNA

Brian Chudleigh

Family: Sturnidae   **Species:** *Acridotheres tristis*
Common name: Myna   **Status:** Introduced
Size: 240 mm (cf sparrow 145 mm, Starling 210 mm)

Discussion: This introduced species is a common bird in the more northern parts of the North Island of New Zealand. Here, its loud call provides a tropical atmosphere especially during the autumn months when most of the European songsters have stopped singing.

Habitat: A bird of towns, roadside verges and pastureland, seldom venturing into forests, although occasionally seen along forest verges.

Range: North Island of New Zealand only. Largest populations are to the north of Lake Taupo but scattered numbers are found south to Wellington.

Desription:
    Head and neck: Glossy black, with a bare yellow patch behind eye. **Upperparts:** Cinnamon-brown. **Wings:** Brown, with black primaries and a prominent white patch. **Underparts:** Light brown. **Underwing:** White. **Tail:** Black with white tip and white undertail. **Bill, legs and feet:** Yellow. **Eye-ring:** Yellow.

Conspicuous features:
* White patches are very visible on wings when birds fly.
* White on tail is visible.
* Yellow bill is very visible.

Conspicuous characteristics:
* Mynas have a habit of feeding on tarmac roads in late afternoon, where they eat traffic-killed insects and side-step cars.
* Usually seen flying in pairs or in groups of up to ten.

Call: Song, delivered by both sexes, is a loud bell-like assemblage of notes which is more conspicuous in the autumn months.

Nest: A bundle of grass and sticks in a hole, in a bank, or in an old building. Up to 5 greenish-blue eggs are laid.

Where to find:

North Island only: Very common in any roadside situation in the north of the North Island.

General: Mynas tended to explode into northern localities in the 1940s and 50s. They have since settled back to levels which the environment can sustain. Farmers claim they, along with Starlings, are beneficial to pastures taking good numbers of pasture pests.

Note: The Jungle Myna (*Acridotheres fuscus*), which is found in Fiji and particularly in Suva parks, is not found in New Zealand. Although similar to the Indian Myna, the Jungle Myna lacks the yellow eye surround and has a small crest on the forehead above bill. It is a smaller and neater bird than the Indian Myna.

KOKAKO

Geoff Moon

Family: Callaeidae   **Species:** *Callaeas cinerea*

Common name: Kokako, North Island bird - Blue-wattled Crow, South Island bird - Orange-wattled Crow.

Status: Endemic

Size: 380 mm (cf sparrow 145 mm, Saddleback 250 mm)

Discussion: The Kokako is considered to have diverged further from the original wattle-bird ancestor than the Saddleback and the Huia, with a difference being the Kokako's predominant diet of vegetation and fruits, associated with old forests, rather than a diet of fruits, insects, insect larvae, spiders and even nectar as adopted by the Saddleback and Huia. It is an ancient New Zealand bird which commenced an evolutionary path of adaptation associated with a predator-free New Zealand environment. This partial evolution has caused it to sacrifice some flight mobility in return for energy consuming, walking ability. With an increase in leg length at the expense of wing size, it has become a fast and agile walker among the branches (Fleming 1982). Those who have seen the Australian Apostlebird (*Struthidea cinerea*) will see a likeness in it to the Kokako although no relationship between the two species has been established.

Conservation status: The Kokako has suffered significantly since the arrival of European people to New Zealand. Not only have farmers destroyed vast Kokako habitat but European settlement brought with it possums, rats and mustelids to the original predator-free environment. All of these have taken their toll. Consequently, this is now a rare species found only in isolated pockets of bush. Predator control is helping it to survive in some isolated localities such as Mapara. (See "Places" in back of book.) Birds liberated on predator-free Little Barrier and Kapiti Islands are showing a general increase in numbers. In the South Island the orange-wattled Kokako is thought to be extinct.

Habitat: The Kokako is a bird of podocarp and tawa-type forests. The isolated populations of this bird seem to prefer forested areas of easy contour.

Range: Found in the forests of the Bay of Islands, the Hunua Ranges just south of Auckland, Coromandel Ranges and those of the central North Island. The South Island Kokako, if not extinct, may still survive in areas of Marlborough, Fiordland (Mitre Peak) and on Stewart Island.

Description:

Forehead and face: Covered with a black mask to behind the eye. **Wattles:** Found just below gape, are blue on the North Island bird and orange on the South Island bird. **Upperparts:** Grey. **Wings:** Grey, with a touch of black on edges of primaries. **Underparts:** Grey. **Bill and feet:** Glossy black.

Conspicuous features:
- Look for the heavy, almost parrot-like, black bill.
- The black mask and blue wattles are conspicuous.
- The long black legs are conspicuous.
- Wings are of rounded appearance and short in comparison to size of bird.
- The tail appears long when the bird is in flight.

Conspicuous characteristics:
- In flight the bird has rapid wing beats.
- Has a habit of running along branches.
- Will often arrive without notice.

Call: The song, delivered by both birds, often in duet, is known as the "organ music" of the forest. It is a rich melody of notes, interspersed with periods of pure silence, some notes being distinctly like that of the Tui and Bellbird. When singing, birds claps their wings in time with the notes. Birds also have a variety of "took took took" notes, issued in sparse phrases and sometimes barely audible. Birds commence song with first-light and continue singing for up to two hours after day-break.

Nest: A platform of twigs and leaves, the cup lined with tree-fern hairs or fine grasses at about four metres. Up to 4 grey, brown-blotched, eggs are laid.

How to locate: Birds will respond to tapes. However, they are sensitive to dialectal differences. Therefore, it is best to arrive at a locality at daybreak and then attempt to locate birds as they start calling. Refrain from using tapes during the breeding season as they are thought to upset the pair-bonding process.

Where to find - North Island:

Northland - Bay of Islands: Puketi Forest near Kerikeri has a declining population of Kokako amounting to about 15 birds (1999). Enquire about their status at the Department of Conservation in Landing Road, Kerikeri, or try the Bramleys Ridge area. Plan to be in the area at daybreak.

Northland - Trounson Park: This forest, located on Trounson Park Road off Highway 12, north of Dargaville, is now a "mainland island" forest and controlled for predators. It has a Kokako population and is also good for Brown Kiwi. (See "Places" in the back of book.)

Northland - Little Barrier Island: Good numbers have now bred here.

North Auckland - Tiri Tiri Island: Birds are now breeding on this island after release, making this a very good locality to see this bird. It is not essential to be there at daybreak. Try the "Wattle track".

Bay of Plenty - Lake Rotoma: Sightings are rare here. To give it a try turn off the Whakatane Road, Highway 30, just past Lake Rotoehu. Then at the Rotoehu Hot Springs turn right. Follow up this road for about 2 kms. Here, there is a remote chance of hearing or seeing a bird.

Bay of Plenty - Pongakawa Valley: From Highway 30, at Lake Rotoehu, follow Pongakawa Road beside Lake Rotoehu. Follow up the hill and turn left at Hamilton Road and then right into Rotoehu Road. About 2 kms along Rotoehu Road a small forestry road leads in to the left. Try here.

King Country - Mapara: This forest is located on Mapara South Road. (See "Places" in back of book.)

King Country - Pureora: There are several pairs of birds here surviving because of predator control near nest sites. Enquire at the Department of Conservation headquarters about where to find birds.

King Country - Rangitoto: (See "Places" in back of book.)

Wellington - Kapiti Island: Birds are breeding here. A permit from the Department of Conservation in Wellington would be needed to visit.

SADDLEBACK

Family: Callaeidae   **Species:** *Philesturnus carunculatus*
Common name: Saddleback, Tieke (Maori)   **Status:** Endemic
Size: 250 mm (cf sparrow 145 mm, Blackbird 250 mm)

Discussion: The Saddleback is a member of the family of New Zealand Wattlebirds which include the Kokako and the extinct Huia. The relationship of this bird family to other world bird families is still unclear (Fleming 1982). Saddebacks are a rare New Zealand species, originally widely spread in both islands but recently confined only to Hen Island off the Northland coast and several small islands off the south-west coast of Stewart Island. Since 1964 they have been transferred to ten islands off the North Island and 12 islands off the South Island, these having first been cleared of introduced predators. Saddlebacks have also been successfully bred in captivity and so their future

Brian Chudleigh

Saddleback

now looks relatively secure as long as their haunts remain predator-free.

Subspecies: The North Island and South Island species of Saddleback represent two distinct subspecies. The North Island Saddleback (*P. c. rufusater*) is characterised by having a faint yellow band across the top of its chestnut coloured saddle. The South Island Saddleback (*P. c. carunculatus*) lacks this and is distinctive in that its immature birds lacks the chestnut coloured saddle in the juvenile phase. The absence of the saddle on the juvenile South Island bird initially had this bird classified as a separate species known as the "Jack Bird".

Habitat: A bird of both old and secondary type forest.

Range: Found on Hen Island and ten islands off the North Island, and on Mokoia Island in Lake Rotorua. Found on 12 islands off the South Island and Stewart Island, including Motuara Island and Pickersgill Island in Queen Charlotte Sound, Marlborough.

Description:

    Upperparts and underparts: Glossy black all over. **Wing coverts and back:** Chestnut, with a thin buff line above on the North Island subspecies, which is absent on the South Island bird. **Wing primaries:** Black. **Rump:** Chestnut. **Tail:** Black, with undertail chestnut. **Bill:** Black, with orange-red wattles at the gape and below.

Conspicuous features:

- The chestnut saddle is visible on mature birds of both subspecies and on the North Island juvenile only.
- Orange-red wattles below gape are visible, especially on breeding birds.
- Buff line above saddle is noticeable on the North Island bird.

Conspicuous characteristics:

- Birds are often seen on or near ground.
- Birds are territorial and will even challenge human intruders with song.
- Birds are often seen running up branches.

- Generally they are very active and noisy among the vegetation.

Call: Song, delivered by both birds, sometimes in duet, is a loud staccato "whuu huhuhu hook", in one chattering phrase, or variations of this. Notes are usually rhythmic and uttered in a see-sawing fashion. Separate localities often have their own dialects. Birds sing from day-break till dusk all the year.

Nest: Nest is in tree and rock cavities and holes, usually close to the ground, the nest being made of twigs, grasses and leaves and lined with tree-fern hairs. Up to 4 white, brown-blotched eggs are laid.

Where to find - North Island:

North Auckland - Tiri Tiri Island: This is easiest place to see the Saddleback. (See "Places" in back of book.)

Bay of Plenty - Mokoia Island: This island in the centre of Lake Rotorua, is a very easy location. (See "Places" in back of book.)

Where to find - South Island:

Marlborough - Motuara Island: Take the Dolphin Watch excursion from the wharf at Picton. (See "Places" in back of book.)

HUIA

Charles A Fleming

Family: Callaeidae   **Species:** *Heteralocha acutirostris*

Common name: Huia   **Status:** Endemic

Size: 450 mm (cf sparrow 145 mm, Saddleback 250 mm)

Discussion: This now extinct bird is included here in the hope that some birder in some remote corner of the North Island may come across an unknown pair. It has, though, not been seen since 1907. The Huia was distinctive by way of its dimorphism, not as to plumage colouration as in most birds, but as to sexual differences in bill shape. The male Huia had a short heavy bill very like the Saddleback while the female bird had a slender curved bill. Current thinking suggests that the two different shaped bills evolved to expand the Huia's feeding niches and therefore survival chances.

General: It is worth visiting a museum to see a mounted specimen. Try the Auckland Museum.

Reference: Jamieson I G 1996. The bill and foraging behaviour of the Huia (*Heteralocha acutirostris*): were they unique? Notornis 43: 14 - 18.

AUSTRALIAN MAGPIE

Family: Cracticidae   **Species:** *Gymnorhina tibicen*
Common name: Magpie   **Status:** Introduced
Size: 410 mm (cf sparrow 145 mm, Rook 450 mm)

Discussion: The Magpie is an introduction from Australia which has colonised widely over both islands and is now a common bird. Two races of Magpie are found in New Zealand. They are the more common White-backed Magpie (*G. t. hypoleuca*) and the Black-backed Magpie (*G. t. tibicen*).

Habitat: A bird of the suburbs, parks and open countryside. Especially plentiful in areas of steep hill country. Seldom in forests.

Range: Throughout much of New Zealand but absent from Westland.

Description:
    Head and underparts: Black. **Nape and mantle:** White. **Back:** Black-backed Magpie (black), White-backed Magpie (white). **Wings:** Black, with conspicuous white patch on secondary feathers. **Uppertail and undertail:** White, black tipped. **Bill:** White, with a black tip.

Description - female birds and juveniles:
    Upperparts: The white areas of the male birds are grey coloured. **Underparts:** On juvenile birds brownish-grey. **Bill:** On juveniles, brownish.

Conspicuous features:
- The bold black and white colouring is noticeable.
- Look for the heavy white bill.

Conspicuous characteristics:
- Birds feed on the ground in small parties of up to about 14 birds.
- Aggressive if intruders (including humans) approach a nest.

Call: A chuckle of bell notes.

Nest: A platform of twigs and grasses, the cup lined with fine grass or wool. Up to 4 green, olive-blotched eggs are laid

Where to find:
Common roadside rural bird. Not in old forests or alpine areas.

General: Magpies are disliked by many who believe they plunder the nests of passerine birds. Observations of the plundering of Skylarks and Tui nests have been recorded. Conversely, though, they have been recorded doing environmental good in eating agricultural pests such as black field crickets, porina caterpillar and grass-grubs.

Brian Chudleigh

White-backed Magpie

Brian Chudleigh

Black-backed Magpie

ROOK

Family: Corvidae   **Species:** *Corvus frugilegus*
Common name: Rook   **Status:** Introduced
Size: 450 mm (cf sparrow 145 mm, Australian Magpie 410 mm)

Discussion: Rooks were introduced from England in the 1860s. They established colonies in both the Hawkes Bay and mid-Canterbury districts. Because they were blamed for damage to arable crops, many thousands were poisoned and numbers restricted. Main damage done by these birds seems to be to maize seedlings and walnut crops.

Habitat: Rooks are birds of open country not venturing into towns and cities as

do Australian Magpies.

Range: Hawkes Bay province to southern Hawkes Bay and Woodville. Scattered colonies are found in the Manawatu, Matamata, Hauraki Plains and Miranda areas. In the South Island mainly in mid-Canterbury and on Banks Peninsula.

Description:

Face: The area of rough skin on the face beneath the eye is greyish. **Upper and underparts:** Glossy black. **Wings:** Black and "fingered" at tips. **Legs:** Greyish-brown with shaggy black-feathered thighs. **Bill:** Greyish with dark tip. **Tail:** Black and rounded at tip.

Conspicuous features:

- An overall black bird.
- Look for the greyish face and bill.

Conspicuous characteristics

- Birds feed on the ground usually in groups, but occasionally alone.
- Feeding birds often play, chasing each other into the air and tussling.
- At dusk birds seek communal roosts.

Call: A "caw caw" is the usual call. Birds are extremely noisy when they leave their communal rookeries at daybreak.

Nest: Birds are communal nesters. Nests are made of grass and twigs and placed high up in conifers. Up to 4 bluish, brown-blotched eggs are laid.

Where to find - North Island:

South Auckland - Miranda: Always some birds in this vicinity.

Hawkes Bay: Rooks are often seen on the road from Wairoa to Napier and generally throughout Hawkes Bay.

Where to find - South Island:

Canterbury - Banks Peninsula: Birds are regularly seen here.

Canterbury - Ashburton and Geraldine area: Regularly seen in this area.

Otago - Middlemarch: This area, west of Dunedin and on Highway 87, once had a colony. Small numbers are still recorded here.

BIRD PLACES

OF

NEW ZEALAND

THE NORTH TO SOUTH GUIDE TO BIRD-WATCHING PLACES IN NEW ZEALAND

INTRODUCTION

The object of this section is to give people a variety of places which have a variety of birds. Many places have birds but not all places have special birds. This section is written to help people find places which have both a variety of birds and special birds.

THE PLACES

These have been selected for several reasons. They include ones which –

- have consistently come up with a special bird or birds.
- provide a variety of habitats.
- are accessible to the public.
- are handy to main travel routes.
- are generally attractive localities to visit.

HABITATS

Because of the variety of landscape in New Zealand, a wide range of bird habitats can be found with a consequential wide range of bird species inhabiting them. Habitats include -

Gardens and city parks: In these areas birds are mainly of introduced varieties such as finches, blackbirds, thrushes, starlings and sparrows. However many gardens also have native species such as Morepork, Grey Warbler, Tui, Silvereye and Kingfisher. Occasionally special birds come into gardens and parks such as the New Zealand Pigeon and Bellbird.

Pastures: These are mostly inhabited by introduced varieties such as Skylarks, Blackbirds, Thrushes, finches, Starlings, Magpies and Rooks. The main native species is the Harrier. The Pukeko is common on pasture verges and Mallards are anywhere where there is water. Spur-winged Plovers, Pied Stilts and oystercatchers also frequent these areas in some localities.

Forests, including pine forests: In these areas, native species are dominant. These include such birds as Kiwi, New Zealand Pigeon, Tui, Bellbird, Tomtit, Robin and Whitehead. Sightings of Kiwi, Kaka, Kakariki, Long-tailed Cuckoo and New Zealand Falcon are special species which bird-watchers look for.

Swamps: In these areas Pukeko are the main species. Sightings of Banded Rail, Fernbird, Spotless Crake, Marsh Crake and Bittern are special birds here and are what bird-watchers hope to see.

Lakes: These areas usually contain the introduced Mallard and Black Swan. However sightings of native species such as Grey Duck, Shoveler, Grey Teal, Scaup and Dabchick are what bird-watchers look for.

Estuaries and mudflats: These areas support a wide range of birds from shags, common gulls, godwits in summer, and oystercatchers. Special birds which can occasionally be found here include rare migrants such as Red-necked Stint, Sharp-tailed Sandpiper and Curlew Sandpiper. Because of their variety of bird species, these areas provide a challenge for bird-watchers.

Oceans: The oceans around New Zealand, together with their scattering of off-shore islands, make New Zealand a locality rich in seabirds. Birds feed on the oceans and nest on the islands. Common shoreline species here are gulls, gannets and shags but in the deeper waters these soon give way to albatrosses, petrels, shearwaters and prions. These are the special birds for which bird-watchers look.

TARGET BIRDS

All birds are interesting. Some birds, usually the hard to find varieties, are even more interesting, with their discovery providing a special challenge. Generally these are called special birds.

Bird-watchers term them target species as they are generally the reason for their visit to an area. Target species are therefore listed in this book in each locality so as to give the bird-watcher or visitor to the area a definite task and challenge. In some particularly good birding spots, complete bird-lists are included. The hope is that birders will tick off the species as they find them.

BIRD-WATCHING

Where to look for birds has always been a problem for the beginner to bird-watching. Many people, because they have never known where to look, have lacked the motivation necessary to go out and find birds. This in turn has prevented them from learning about them. Consequently they have been denied a rewarding and enriching experience of knowing birds and being able to put names to them.

This section takes people who are interested in seeing more than the common garden varieties, to some interesting and rich birding spots. It gives them an opportunity of adding new species to their lists. It also provides them with the challenge of finding and identifying the target species at each spot. Such identification requires further knowledge about birds and this data can be found in the previous pages of this book.

The exciting part of bird-watching is actually finding the promised bird at the promised spot. However even recognised birding spots do not always come up with what is promised but when they do it is a satisfying experience.

BIRD-WATCHING REQUIREMENTS

Before embarking on a bird-watching adventure the following items will be needed –

Field guides: This "BIRDS OF NEW ZEALAND – LOCALITY GUIDE" aims to provide a total bird-watchers' package in the one volume. However it is recommended that the "Field Guide to the Birds of New Zealand" (Viking), by Barrie Heather and Hugh Robertson, is also included with bird-watching requirements. It provides descriptions of all birds recorded in New Zealand plus notes about their breeding and habitat details. This can also be purchased in a slim volume which contains bird plates only, if required.

Binoculars and telescopes: Both of these are essential requirements for satisfying bird-watching. However if birding only in the bush is contemplated, 8 x 40 binoculars are sufficient. These have a wide field of vision which allow plenty of light to enter and also allow sharp focus of birds which are often only of a short distance from the viewer. If birding over lakes or estuaries, telescopes are essential for accurate observation. 25 magnification is usually sufficient.

Notebooks: It pays to carry a notebook with you when bird-watching. Make notes as you go along. Sightings, which include the date and the place and obvious bird characteristics and features, help with the learning process and allow bird-watchers to consolidate at a later time. Small spring-bound notebooks with a pencil attached are the best.

It pays to make three entries of the bird seen. Note it on a general page, on a particular species page (for example on a page for Tui) and a locality page (for example on a page for Rotorua).

PREPARATION FOR AN EXCURSION TO A BIRDING SPOT

There are two ways to embark on a bird-watching adventure. These are -
- Select a locality and go and visit it and see what can be found.
- Select a bird species and go to a locality which has this bird and try and find it there.

For beginners the best way is to select a locality and go and see what can be found. As the bird list grows, localities can then be selected with a particular species in mind.

LOCALITIES IN "BIRDING PLACES"

"Birding Places" does not try to cover all of New Zealand. All it does is highlight selected localities which are attractive, accessible to the public and which give the bird-watcher the greatest chance of getting to know most New Zealand bird species. Its aim is to give a selection of bird-watching places.

THE FIRST LOCALITY TO VISIT

Beginners should look in their gardens first and see what is feeding on the lawn. Usually most lawns have House Sparrows, Starlings, Blackbirds and Song Thrushes. In most months they also have Goldfinches, Greenfinches and Silvereyes. All of these can present identification problems. For example who can separate-
- the brownish female Blackbird from the Song Thrush, especially during the moulting season.
- the juvenile greyish Starlings from their black coloured parents.
- the brownish female House Sparrow from the Redpoll or Hedge Sparrow.

So there is plenty to do right alongside the house. When things are sorted there, it is then time to branch out and try a locality elsewhere.

BIRDING PLACES

FROM CAPE REINGA TO STEWART ISLAND
(From north to south, and north again to Farewell Spit)

The following places listed below are not guaranteed but they give the bird-watcher a good opportunity of seeing a wide range of birds. They do not include all of New Zealand. Rather they provide places in proximity to main tourist routes. They start at Cape Reinga in the Far North and travel through the country to Paterson Inlet, Stewart Island and up the West Coast to Farewell Spit. They are all accessible to the public unless stated in the text.

FAR NORTH

THE FAR NORTH AND CAPE REINGA

Locality description: This remote northern most part of New Zealand is wilderness and farmland. Roads are good and traffic is light. There is accommodation at several places north of Awanui. Cape Reinga at the end of the road provides expansive views out to sea of the surrounding landscape and west to Cape Maria van Diemen.

How to get there: Tours leave from several Bay of Islands locations and from Awanui. These usually travel up the Ninety Mile Beach and back on Highway 1. The direction of travel depends on tides. Independent travellers leave Awanui, north of Kaitaia, and drive north on Highway 1 to the end. Places to visit and things to observe on the way include -

- Rangaunu Bay accessed from Camp Road north of Waiharara. Here at low tide many birds may be seen feeding on the exposed sandflats.
- Houhora Heads accessed from Heads Road further north, which also has wading birds on the flats at low tide.
- Parengarenga Harbour accessed from the Paua Peninsula, north again, which leads into the harbour flats where wading birds and Royal Spoonbills are often seen.
- Te Paki wetland on the west side of Highway 1, which has waterfowl and Spotless Crakes.
- Cape Reinga Road (Highway 1) past Te Paki which has large numbers of Pipits alongside it, which fly up and give good views.
- Cape Reinga at the end of the road, where seabirds might be seen, and in particular Black-winged Petrels. Look to the west towards Cape Maria van Diemen and to Motuopao Island where they nest.

Target birds: Royal Spoonbills and wading birds in Houhora and Parengarenga Harbours, Pipits, which are very common from Houhora northwards, and Black-winged Petrels which are sometimes seen from the Cape Reinga light-house.

KARIKARI - LAKE WAIPOROHITA

General: This is an attractive area of water in a very accessible situation where viewing can be done from the car. The greater area is wetland and farmland with a lonely wilderness feel about it.

How to get there: From Awanui north of Kaitaia, follow Highway 10 eastwards. After 13 kms turn left (north) up Inland Road and travel for 14 kms to the T junction with Rangiputa Road. Lake Waiporohita is on the corner of Inland Road and Rangiputa Road.

Target birds: Dabchick, Australian Little Grebe, White-winged Black Tern.

LAKE ROTOKAWAU

General: This small lake lies to the west of Highway 1 about 5 kms north of Awanui. It is one of several sand dune lakes in the area and has a large population of Australian Little Grebe. It is a small lake which can be viewed from the road through pine trees. Permission to enter the land must be sought should you want a closer look.

How to get there: From Awanui north of Kaitaia, travel north on Highway 1 for 5 kms. Turn left (west) into Lake Rotokawau Road and look for Lake Rotokawau on the left (south) after 1 km.

Target birds: Dabchick, Australian Little Grebe, shags and waterfowl.

MATAURI BAY AND TE NGAIRE BAYS

How to get there: From Kerikeri travel north on Highway 10 and take the Matauri Bay road to the right (east). Travel to Matauri Bay which is signposted and after Matauri Bay travel on to Te Ngaire Bay.

Target birds: Variable Oystercatcher and New Zealand Dotterel nest on these beaches.

PUKETI FOREST

General: Puketi Forest contains many large kauri trees (*Agathis australis*). Its interest to birders is its small population of Kokako (*Callaeas cinerea*). This population is now down to about 15 birds (2000). To see them try the Bramleys Ridge track at day-break.

How to get there: From Kerikeri drive north up Highway 10 to Waipapa and then turn left (west) into Pungaere Road. Follow along to Waiare Road. Turn left, and then right into the forest headquarters. An information board gives track details and a map. A walking track into the forest also leads in from Puketi Road. To find this track travel south down Waiare Road and into Puketi East Road. Look for the Forest Road sign on the right.

For further details: For details about the Kokako population and where to find them enquire at the Department of Conservation office, Landing Road, Kerikeri, or write: P O Box 128, Kerikeri, or phone: +64 09 407 8474.

Target birds: Tomtit and Kokako.

Birds likely to be seen include -

Brown Kiwi (night)	Blackbird
New Zealand Pigeon	Fantail
Eastern Rosella	Tomtit
Shining Cuckoo (summer)	Grey Warbler
Long-tailed Cuckoo (summer)	Tui
Morepork	Silvereye
Kingfisher	Chaffinch
Song Thrush	Kokako

MANGINGANGINGA BOARDWALK

How to get there: Follow the directions for Puketi Forest but at the junction with Pungaere Road and Waiare Road turn right (north) and travel along for about 1 km, north. The boardwalk is signposted on the left. It takes you among old kauri trees. Here bird life is scarce but you may find the kauri snail (*Paryphanta busbyi*).
Target bird: Tomtit.

AROHA ISLAND ECOLOGICAL CENTRE

General: This small island in the Kerikeri Inlet is linked to the mainland by a causeway. It has been developed by its owners the Queen Elizabeth II National Trust as an ecological centre. It has a small feral population of Brown Kiwi as does the adjoining Rangitane Scenic Reserve.
How to get there: From Kerikeri, follow down Kerikeri Road to the Stone Store. Follow north along Landing Road to the first round-about where signposts take you out to Aroha Island. Alternatively leave Highway 10 at Kapiro Road about 3 kms north of the Kerikeri road junction. Turn down Kapiro Road and then left (north) along Redcliffs Road. Then right down Rangitane Road and right into Kurapari Road. 150 metres along Kurapari Road turn left at the Aroha Island sign and follow down to the Centre.
Accommodation: There is accommodation on the island. This includes a cottage, home-hosting accommodation, and camp-sites. This is a relaxing place to stay offering a harbour coastline, bush walks, and a mangrove forest which can be explored by canoes.
Target birds: Brown Kiwi, Reef Heron, Golden Plover, Banded Rail, Spotless Crake, Morepork, Shining Cuckoo, Fernbird, Fantail and Tui.
For further details: Contact: Aroha Island Ecological Centre, P O Box 541, Kerikeri. Phone: +64 9 407 5243. Fax: +64 9 407 5246.
Email: kiwi@aroha.net.nz
Web: www.aroha.net.nz

WAITANGI FOREST

General: The Waitangi Forest, not far from the coastal town of Paihia in the Bay of Islands, is administered by Rayonier NZ Ltd. It is known for its populations of Brown Kiwi. This forest is mainly of exotic pines (*Pinus radiata*) but there are other plantation species plus areas of understorey native trees and ferns. In 1988, a domestic dog ran wild in it for some months and predated on

Brown Kiwi. Numbers were reduced but it is still worth a visit.

How to get there from Paihia: Follow the road to Haruru. Turn left up Haruru Road past the floodlit waterfall to Mount Bledisloe. Entry to this forest is through a gate near Mount Bledisloe on the left-hand (north) side of Mount Bledisloe. On your return to Paihia drive back down Haruru Road and turn left at the first junction. This road takes you back to Paihia via the boundary of the forest and the golf course. Along this road stop from time to time and listen for Brown Kiwi in the forest.

How to get there from Kerikeri: Follow Cobham Drive into Inlet Road. After the pine trees appear on the right (south) look for a gate which leads into the forest. This gate is signposted and advises the public that they may enter on foot or bicycle but not in a vehicle.

Night excursions into the forest: When in the forest listen for Brown Kiwi calls. Other noises in the night might be Moreporks calling "more-pork, more-pork", shearwaters and petrels returning to island colonies to the east, and maybe possums.

Day excursions into the forest: During the day enter the forest north of Paihia and past the Waitangi Treaty House at Wairoa Bay. Walk parallel to the coast until wet areas are located. Search any of these for Fernbird and Spotless Crakes. Look also for Brown Kiwi probe holes, holes in the pine needles with circular whirls of needles at the entrance. These areas could be noted for an evening visit as they indicate the bird's presence. Also, watch out for kiwi burrows where birds may be sleeping by day. Active ones often have dung at the entrances.

Birds likely to be seen include -

Brown Kiwi (night)	White-faced Heron
Bittern	Fernbird
Brown Quail	Grey Warbler
Californian Quail	Song Thrush
Peafowl	Blackbird
Pheasant	Hedge Sparrow
Banded Rail	Pipit
Spotless Crake	Tui
Pukeko	Silvereye
New Zealand Pigeon	Greenfinch
Eastern Rosella	Goldfinch
Shining Cuckoo (summer)	Chaffinch
Morepork	Yellowhammmer
Kingfisher	Sparrow Starling
Skylark	Myna
Welcome Swallow	Magpie
Fantail	

Note: Reef Herons might be seen in the Waitangi estuary.
For further details: Contact: Rayonier NZ Ltd. Phone: +64 9 438 9174.

LAKE OWHAREITI

How to get there: At Pakaraka south of Kerikeri, at the junction of Highway 1 and Highway 10, travel north and turn left (west) into Ludbrook Road. Travel along until Lake Owhareiti comes into view as a gate is reached. View the lake arm from here.

Target birds: Dabchick, Australian Little Grebe, shags and waterfowl.

LAKE OMAPERE

How to get there: From Pakaraka, south of Kerikeri, travel north on Highway 1 through Ohaeawai until Lake Omapere comes into view on the left. View from Highway 1 or turn left down Te Pua Road. The lake can be viewed from various places on Te Pua Road and later on Lake Road, which eventually ends up at Okaihau after circling the lake. A telescope is needed to view this lake.

Target birds: Dabchick, Australian Little Grebe and waterfowl.

NORTHLAND

HELENA BAY - MIMIWHANGATA

General: At Teal Bay follow past the houses and stop at the Owae Stream, the first stream after the houses. This stream has a population of Brown Teal and these can often be seen from the road. If unsuccessful here, travel on to the Mimiwhangata Farm Park. Once in the park, follow the walking track to Trig Point. The lakes are near to the end of the small peninsula and have good populations. While here, look for seabirds from the coast.

How to get there: From Whangarei travel north on Highway 1 for 23 kms. Turn right (east) at Russell Road and follow through to Helena Bay. Turn right (south) at Helena Bay and travel along to Teal Bay.

Target bird: Brown Teal and seabirds.

TROUNSON PARK

General: This is a unique kauri forest which recently has become a "mainland island" after having undergone extensive predator control. The result is a very good population of Brown Kiwi, and Kokako were released there in 1996. There are now good numbers of forest bird species such as Tui, Fantails, Tomtits and Grey Warbler.

How to get there: From Dargaville travel north on Highway 12 for approximately 32 kms. After Kaihu turn into Trounson Park Road on the right (east). The forest park is well signposted and there is a camp ground on site.

Night time excursions: A commercial operator takes excursions into the forest at nights to see kiwi. These follow wide board walks and the chances of seeing birds on one of these is very good.

Target birds: Kiwi, Tomtit, Kokako

For further details: Contact Waipoua Forest Visitor Centre, Private Bag, Dargaville. Phone: +64 9 439 0605.

For night time forest walks: Phone: +64 9 439 0621.

KAIIWI LAKES

General: These two sandhill lakes lie north of Dargaville. They are well signposted. A small side road leads into them running between Lake Kaiiwi and Lake Taharoa. Examine Lake Kaiiwi (the southern lake) first for both Dabchick and Australian Little Grebe. The larger lake, Lake Taharoa, is used extensively for recreation and so birdlife tends to be sparse.

How to get there: Follow Highway 12 from Dargaville and then after 25 kms turn left into Omamari Road and right into Kaiiwi Road.

Target birds: Dabchick, Australian Little Grebe, shags and waterfowl.

WHANGAREI – BEACH ROAD, ONERAHI

How to get there: From Whangarei follow the airport and Onerahi signs. After the airport, follow on along Church Street and down Hill Street to Beach Road. From Beach Road, look for waders and Royal Spoonbills. Most birds are seen by looking west towards Port Whangarei.

Target bird: Royal Spoonbill.

WHANGAREI - MOUNT TIGER

How to get there: Travel north from Whangarei towards Kamo. Before Kamo turn right (east) at the Glenbervie sign. Next turn right at Whareora Road and continue along past Abbey Caves Road until Mount Tiger Road is arrived at on the right. Up this road on broken farmland can be found the Cirl Bunting.

Target bird: Cirl Bunting.

WAIPU - URETITI RESERVE

How to get there: About 4 kms north of the Waipu town turn-off on Highway 1, look for Uretiti Reserve on the right (east). Here drive down to a carpark and walk to the beach. Walk in a southerly direction towards the Waipu Spit.

Target birds: Caspian Tern, Fairy Tern and White-fronted Tern.

WAIPU COVE

How to get there: From the Waipu town turnoff on Highway 1, follow in past the town to Waipu Cove. Find Johnsons Point Road and drive to the end and park here. Walk across the estuary in a southerly direction if the tide is low. It is too deep to cross at high-tide. Once on the sandspit, walk in a northerly direction. Do not enter fenced off areas where Variable Oystercatchers, New Zealand Dotterel and Fairy Terns nest.

Target bird: Fairy Tern.

MANGAWHAI HEADS

How to get there: From Waipu Cove drive south to Mangawhai Heads. After the shopping centre follow Mangawhai Road. Look for Black Swamp Road and then take Bull Road on left (north). Park at the end of Bull Road, without blocking private entrances, and walk to the coastline and across the estuary. Follow the coastline north through the sand-dunes to the fenced Fairy Tern nesting areas. This walk should be undertaken at low tide only. Alternatively travel on along

Black Swamp Road, then left into Pacific Road. Park at end and walk north along the beach to the sandspit.

Target birds: Fairy Tern, White-fronted Tern and Caspian Tern.

THE DOME FOREST - WARKWORTH

How to get there: The Dome is approximately six kms north of Warkworth on Highway 1. At the summit, stop near the restaurant. Follow the walking track from behind the restaurant and walk into the forest. Bush birds, including Tomtits, can be found after a 500 metre walk up at least three lots of steps.

Target bird: The Tomtit.

TAPORA - BIG SAND ISLAND

General: Tapora lies to the west of Wellsford on the Kaipara Harbour.

How to get there: Follow the Port Albert sign at Wellsford and then Wharehine and the Tapora signs. Roads are sealed to Wharehine and then gravel, but are of a good standard. From Tapora take Okahukura Road which heads south. After Te Ngaio Point Road junction, travel a further 2 kms along Okahukura Road and look for a track on the left with locked gate (sometime unlocked) and a shed on left of gate. Park here and walk in for 1.5 kms to the Department of Conservation reserve. Cross the sand, or shallow water if tide is in, to Big Sand Island. Don't be put off if the tide is full, for at high tide it is not more than waist deep, and it is firm under foot. There are no channels. At the island look for Fairy Terns at the arrival point. The track into Big Sand Island is privately owned but a legal easement allows public access. Should you wish to drive in, contact the owners, as below.

For further details and for permission to enter by vehicle: Contact, Gary and Wendy Inger. Phone: +64 9 423 8972. Write: P O Box 113, Wellsford.

Birds likely to be seen here include -

South Island Pied Oystercatcher	Turnstone
Variable Oystercatcher	Lesser Knot
Spur-winged Plover	Sharp-tailed Sandpiper
Golden Plover	Pectoral Sandpiper
Grey Plover	Curlew Sandpiper
New Zealand Dotterel	Red-necked Stint
Banded Dotterel	Pied Stilt
Mongolian Dotterel	Arctic Skua
Large Sand Dotterel	Black-backed Gull
Wrybill	Red-billed Gull
Eastern Curlew	Black-billed Gull
Whimbrel	Caspian Tern
Asiatic Black-tailed Godwit	Fairy Tern
Bar-tailed Godwit	Little Tern
Siberian Tattler	White-fronted Tern
Terek Sandpiper	

NORTH AUCKLAND

GOAT ISLAND MARINE RESERVE:

How to get there: Turn east at Warkworth and follow the road to Leigh. 3 kms east of Leigh is the Goat Island Marine Reserve which is signposted. From the Goat Island Marine Reserve carpark follow a marked walking track behind the Marine Reserve buildings. These lead to a cliff-top vantage point above the sea. Here seabirds come into telescope range.

Target birds: Bullers, Flesh-footed, and Fluttering Shearwaters.

KAIPARA HARBOUR - JORDANS ROAD

How to get there: From Helensville take the Kaukapakapa sign on Highway 16, and travel north. Jordans Road is 5 kms north of Kaukapakapa on the left. Drive to the end and ask permission at the farm house to enter.

Target birds: Golden Plover plus most birds listed for Tapora.

KAIPARA HARBOUR - SOUTH HEAD

How to get there: When travelling north from Auckland on Highway 16, turn left at the Parakai - South Head sign and follow north up the south head of the Kaipara harbour. Travel for approximately 25 kms to near the end of South Head Road, turn left into the Trig Road and follow to the carpark and rest area. Walk to the lagoon. Go at low-tide and wade across the lagoon. This area is known as Papakanui Spit.

Target birds: Fairy Tern and Caspian Tern nest here.

KAWAU ISLAND

General: Kawau Island is well known for its Weka which are easily seen as birds regularly feed along the beaches and near the wharf at Mansion Bay where the boats tie up. There is also a resident Brown Kiwi population on the island but this is less easy to find and requires night time searching near Bon Accord Harbour. Kookaburra and Eastern Rosellas are also here, the Kookaburra being placed here by a Governor of New Zealand, Sir George Grey. Wallabies, monkeys and zebra were also released but only the wallabies remain. On a windy day seabirds can be seen on the trip to Kawau Island. The most likely ones are Bullers Shearwater, Flesh-footed Shearwater, Fluttering Shearwater, Diving Petrel and Fairy Prion. To see further seabirds, a journey out beyond Kawau Island would be necessary.

How to get there: Kawau Island lies off the Northland coast, east of Warkworth. It can be visited on a daily basis by boat from the small east coast settlement of Sandspit. To get to Sandspit turn of Highway 1 at the north approach to Warkworth. Follow the Sandspit signposts.

Target birds: Kookaburra, Weka.

For further details: Contact: Fullers Kawau Ferries Ltd, Phone: +64 9 425 7307.

LITTLE BARRIER ISLAND

General: Because all of Little Barrier Island's birds, apart from the Kakapo, can now be found at other places, bird-watchers are not encouraged to go to this island. It is easier, for example, to see the Brown Kiwi on Aroha Island, the Little Spotted Kiwi, Takahe, Stitchbird, Saddleback and Kokako on Tiri Tiri Island and a further range of bush birds at Pureora.

A few facts about Little Barrier Island, or Hauturu, are though, still of interest. The island is situated off the east coast of Northland, 25 kms east from the coastal township of Leigh. It is 3080 hectares (7544 acres) in size and is heavily forested. It is of steep terrain rising to 722 metres (2370 feet) on Mount Hauturu. About 15 hectares at Te Titoki Point is flat and this has been cleared and is used as a small farmlet by a resident ranger. A few sheep are grazed here. The ranger's house is also here looking across the paddocks to the sea.

For further details: Contact the Department of Conservation, Private Bag 68-908 Newton, Auckland. Phone: +64 9 307 9279.

THE HAURAKI GULF - FROM SANDSPIT

General: The waters of the Hauraki Gulf, especially those between the town of Sandspit and Little Barrier Island, are a good place for a pelagic excursion.

How to get there: The easiest and cheapest way to get into these waters is on a commercial launch from Auckland. Fullers Ferry run regular excursions to Great Barrier Island and birds can be seen from these. Launch excursions can also be organised from Sandspit. The Sandspit excursions get you into the best waters for seabirds very quickly. (See Kawau Island Island article for location of Sandspit.) Beyond Kawau Island the first seabirds will be seen. Two important species for these waters are Black Petrel and Cooks Petrel both of which nest on Little Barrier Island. A chance sighting of Pycrofts Petrel is also likely.

Birds likely to be seen here include –

Blue Penguin	Little Shearwater
Giant Petrel (winter)	White-faced Storm Petrel
Cape Pigeon (winter)	Diving Petrel
Grey-faced Petrel	Gannet
Cooks Petrel	Black Shag
Pycrofts Petrel	Pied Shag
Fairy Prion	Little Shag
Black Petrel	Red-billed Gull
Bullers Shearwater	Black-backed Gull
Flesh-footed Shearwater	Caspian Tern
Sooty Shearwater	White-fronted Tern.
Fluttering Shearwater	

For further details: Contact: Fullers Ferry and Cruise Centre. Phone: +64 9 367 9102 or contact, Kawau Kat Cruises, Sandspit Road, Warkworth. Phone: +64 9 425 8006 or Fax: +64 9 425 7650.

MOTUORA ISLAND

General: Motuora Island lies off the end of the Mahurangi Heads north of Waiwera on the east coast of North Auckland. It can be seen from Wenderholm Regional Park. For some years it was farmed with sheep and cattle but more recently it is being revegetated back into secondary forest in a similar manner as Tiri Tiri Island. There are plans to eventually release endangered forest birds there, as has happened on Tiri Tiri. The first release of these has been the rare Shore Plover from Rangitira Island (South East Island) in the Chatham Islands group. After various releases, with some birds abandoning the island for the mainland, breeding success resulted in 1999.

How to get there: The public can visit this island by boat from Sandspit. (See Kawau Island above.) There is also a camping ground there but campers must take all provisions.

For further details: Contact: Auckland Regional Council, Park Line. Phone: +64 9 303 1530. Fax +64 9 366 2127.

Target bird: Shore Plover

WENDERHOLM REGIONAL PARK

General: The estuary on the edge of the park is a good place to find Banded Rail. Do not turn into the park gate but instead travel straight ahead to the end of the road where it meets the estuary. Birds can usually be seen among the mangroves. High tide viewing is not recommended as birds hide away out of view. A half tide is the best. In the park itself are New Zealand Pigeon, Kookaburra, Eastern Rosella, Robin and Tui. The Kookaburras are often heard in the pohutukawa trees near the beach. The Robins were released into the park in 1998 after the forested area was cleared of predators. They have since bred successfully and it is hoped that the population will maintain itself. To see the Robins follow the signposted walking tracks from the carpark area.

How to get there: Wenderholm Regional Park is located just north of Waiwera and about one hour's drive north of Auckland. From Highway 1, about 1 km north of Waiwera, turn right and down into the park.

Excursion note: Wenderholm is very close to the waterfowl habitat of Strakas Refuge (see below).

STRAKAS REFUGE

General: Look for Black Swans and Mallards in the middle of the lake and Grey Ducks, Shoveler, Grey Teal and Scaup around the verges. Dabchicks are often seen near the reed verge of the eastern end. Little Shags sit on obstacles in the lake. In the small swampy areas containing raupo (*Typha orientalis*) on the inland side of the road, Spotless Crake have been seen.

How to get there: Strakas Refuge is a waterfowl habitat found 1.8 kms along Weranui Road, west of the township of Waiwera. To get to it turn right off Highway 1 when travelling north at the sign which says Waiwera. This is 6 kms north of the township of Orewa. Turn right at the first junction into Weranui Road. On the right is the Waiwera River. The Waiwera Sewage Ponds are seen on the right and Strakas Refuge is about .5 km further along on the left. It is opposite some estuary mangroves and difficult to see from the road. Do not drive into the nearby farm-house as the refuge can be viewed from the road

without need to enter private land.
Birds likely to be seen here at the refuge or in its vicinity include –

Dabchick
Black Shag
Little Black Shag
Little Shag
White-faced Heron
Cattle Egret
Bittern

Black Swan
Canada Goose
Paradise Shelduck
Mallard
Grey Duck
Grey Teal

Shoveler
Scaup
Banded Rail
Spotless Crake
Pukeko
Fernbird

WAIWERA SPIT

How to get there: Turn right off Highway 1 when travelling north, at the sign which says Waiwera and travel into Waiwera village. Then walk north along the beach to the sandspit where the Waiwera River enters the sea.
Target birds: Reef Heron, Variable Oystercatcher and New Zealand Dotterel.

MURIWAI BEACH GANNET COLONY

General: The Muriwai gannet colony is a mainland breeding colony situated within easy access of Auckland. The walk from the carpark to the colony is over well formed tracks and is of easy grade for most of it. Viewers can get very close to the birds, although binoculars are important as they allow viewing of the off-shore Oaia Island. White-fronted Terns and Red-billed Gulls nest on nearby cliffs and the occasional Spotted Shag might be seen on the cliff ledges.
How to get there: Follow the north-western highway, Highway 16, from Auckland. Travel through Kumeu and Huapai and just past Waimauku turn left (west). The gannet colony is signposted to Muriwai Beach.
Target bird: Australasian Gannet.

TE HENGA (BETHELLS) BEACH

How to get there: Should you have all day in this area follow Oaia Road, slightly to the south of Muriwai, and then Constable Road. From the end of Constable Road take the walking track to Te Henga (Bethells) Beach and look for Spotted Shags on Erangi Point. This point is a noticeable headland jutting into the beach just north of the Bethells Beach carpark. Birds can often be seen high on the cliff faces.
Target bird: Spotted Shag.

MURIWAI BEACH TO STRAKAS

How to get there: After a visit to see the gannets at Muriwai, travel on to Wenderholm and to Strakas Refuge. From the Muriwai - Waimauku turnoff, travel north along Highway 16 through Helensville and turn right at the Waitoki turnoff just before Kaukapakapa. At Waitoki follow the Waitoki Road which leads to Wainui. At Wainui turn left on to Monowai Road then right along Weranui Road. Strakas Refuge is on the south side of the road almost opposite where the mangroves start along the estuary.
Target bird: Dabchick.

MURIWAI BEACH TO JORDANS ROAD

How to get there: Another place to visit after seeing the gannets could be the Jordans Road wader roost north of Kaukapakapa on the Kaipara Harbour. (See Kaipara - Jordans Road. Note permission to enter is required.)

Target Bird: Golden Plover.

LAKE KERETA

How to get there: From Auckland follow Highway 16 as for the Muriwai gannet colony. Before Helensville turn left at the Helensville - Parakai junction and travel north up South Head Road. At Wilson Road, just past Shelley Beach Road, turn left and travel down to Lake Kereta. There are Dabchicks on this lake. Bitterns and Fernbirds have been recorded nearby. Australian Little Grebe could be looked for on Kereta South Lake which is just south of the larger lake.

After Lake Kereta, travel onto Papakanui Spit and look for Fairy Tern. (See Page 336.)

Target birds: Dabchick, Australian Little Grebe, Bittern and Fernbird.

TIRI TIRI MATANGI ISLAND

General: This island, commonly known as Tiri, lies off the end of the Whangaparaoa Peninsula north of Auckland. It is open to the public. Here can be seen Little Spotted Kiwi, Takahe, Brown Teal, Stitchbird, Kokako and Saddleback among others. A visit makes a pleasant one day excursion from Auckland.

How to get there: Fullers' ferries go to the island on a regular basis departing from Auckland or from Gulf Harbour, Whangaparaoa. To get to Gulf Harbour turn off Highway 1 after Silverdale, 37 kms north of Auckland and travel along the peninsula for approximately 11 kms until you see the sign Gulf Harbour on the right, past Tindalls Bay. At the Gulf Harbour Marina the ferry leaves from the seaward end of the marina.

Details about the island: From Gulf Harbour the trip to Tiri Tiri Island takes 25 minutes over a short channel of water from which sometimes can be seen Blue Penguins, Bullers Shearwaters, Flesh-footed Shearwaters, Fluttering Shearwaters and Diving Petrels, plus shags, gannets, gulls and terns.

At the island the rangers meet the boat and give instructions about where to walk. Take your lunch as you cannot purchase food on the island but you will be offered a cup of tea. There is a small shop which sells mementoes and books, proceeds from which go to help the island's finances.

Tiri Tiri Island is an area of 226 hectares rising to 75 metres at the highest point where a lighthouse is situated. Originally it was farmland except for some gully remnant bush. Since 1975 an ambitious revegetation plan carried out mainly by volunteers, has been undertaken, and now 65% of the island is low bush with some taller trees in the remnant areas.

Tiri Tiri Island's greatest appeal is its richness of birds. Birds are everywhere enjoying a predator-free environment, giving a feel of what the original New Zealand was really like. A small pond near the wharf has a pair of Brown Teal and again Spotless Crakes are usually heard near to it. Up the road from this the "Wattle Track" between the wharf and the light-house is also rich in birds. Spotless Crakes are usually heard and Brown Quail are regularly seen here, and at night

Little Spotted Kiwi.

The island has an extensive system of board-walks on the northern end. The walk north along the coast to the boardwalk gives good views of Red-crowned Parakeets, Bellbirds, Tui and Saddlebacks and maybe a Takahe. Once on the board-walk Robins, Whiteheads and Stitchbirds might be seen and Spotless Crakes heard.

The following 69 species have all been recorded on the island -

Little Spotted Kiwi	Takahe	Fantail
Blue Penguin	Variable Oystercatcher	Whitehead
Grey-faced Petrel	Spur-winged Plover	Grey Warbler
Bullers Shearwater	Red-billed Gull	Robin
Flesh-footed Shearwater	Black-backed Gull	Tomtit
Fluttering Shearwater	Caspian Tern	Song Thrush
Diving Petrel	White-fronted Tern	Blackbird
Australasian Gannet	Arctic Skua	Hedge Sparrow
Black Shag	New Zealand Pigeon	Stitchbird
Pied Shag	Barbery Dove	Bellbird
Little Shag	Spotted Dove	Tui
Reef Heron	Kaka	Silvereye
White-faced Heron	Galah	Greenfinch
Black Swan	Eastern Rosella	Goldfinch
Paradise Shelduck	Red-crowned Parakeet	Redpoll
Mallard	Long-tailed Cuckoo	Chaffinch
Grey Duck	Shining Cuckoo	Yellowhammer
Brown Teal	Morepork,	Sparrow
Harrier	Spine-tailed Swift	Starling
Brown Quail	Kingfisher	Saddleback
Spotless Crake	Skylark	Kokako
Weka	Pipit	Myna
Pukeko	Welcome Swallow	Magpie

For further details: Phone: Tiri Tiri Island, +64 9 479 4490 or Fullers Ferry and Cruise Centre, +64 9 367 9102.

WEITI (WADE) RIVER

How to get there: From Whangaparaoa Road, at Pacific Harbour Shopping Centre, turn right at the traffic lights and follow along Wade River Road until the wharf is reached. A small population of New Zealand Dotterel and other waders can be found on the sandspit just across the river from the wharf. Reef Herons are also here.

How to get there - alternative route: Should you want a closer view of the sandspit return to Silverdale. Travel south from here on Highway 1 to the traffic lights and turn left into East Coast Bays Road and then right into Stillwater Road. At Stillwater take the walking track at the south end of the beach.

Target birds: Pied Shag, Reef Heron, Banded Dotterel, New Zealand Dotterel, Bar-tailed Godwit, Turnstone.

WHANGAPARAOA - SHAKESPEAR PARK

General: This park lies at the end of the Whangaparaoa peninsula. It is open to the public during daylight hours and has areas of bush, farmland and wetlands as well as two swimming beaches.

How to get there: From Highway 1 north of Silverdale, turn right (east) and follow along the Whangaparaoa Peninsula to the end. At the gate to the park on the left is a small pond. Park here and do the bush track to a waterfall. Look for Red-crowned Parakeet, Tui and Bellbird. Then proceed through the park to Te Haruhi Bay where forested areas come close to the carpark. Here look for Bellbirds. A range of both introduced and native birds can also be found and sometimes Banded and New Zealand Dotterels on the beach.

Target birds: Red-crowned Parakeet, Tui, Bellbird.

AUCKLAND

LAKE CHELSEA - CHELSEA SUGAR REFINERY - AUCKLAND

General: This lake is on the north shore of the Waitemata Harbour and has a good population of waterfowl.

How to get there: After crossing the Auckland Harbour Bridge when travelling north, turn off Highway 1 on to Onewa Road at the first off-ramp. Follow Onewa Road to the first round-about and continue straight ahead into Mokoia Road. Travel along and then turn left down Colonial Road. Follow until the lake comes into view.

Target birds: Waterfowl and Australasian Coot.

WESTERN SPRINGS LAKE- AUCKLAND

General: This lake is located off Great North Road in the suburb of Grey Lynn. It can be seen from the road. There are good waterfowl populations here and also sometimes a few Cape Barren Geese which have flown in from the nearby Auckland Zoo.

How to get there: From Karangahape Road at the top of Queen Street, follow along into Great North Road and until the sign says Western Springs.

Target birds: Black Shag, Little Shag, White-faced Heron, Black Swan and Australasian Coot.

THE AUCKLAND MUSEUM

General: The Auckland War Memorial Museum has a very fine bird hall and it is a good place to visit to consolidate bird knowledge. It is situated on a prominent hill in Parnell.

How to get there: Access to it is off Parnell Road or Grafton Road. Some tour companies run excursions there on a twice daily basis.

For further details: Contact Auckland Museum. Phone: +64 9 377 3932.

ORAKEI BASIN - HOBSON BAY

General: This basin, which is part of the Hobson Bay area of the Auckland Harbour on the outskirts of Remuera, is a tidal area with water levels controlled by a floodgate. It is usually full of water so a good place to see Little Black Shags and Little Shags. Hobson Bay also has a walkway leading from Shore Road not far from its junction with Orakei Road and Upland Road. It leads around the mudflats where Pied Stilts, White-faced Herons and Pied Oystercatchers can be seen.

How to get there: From Auckland drive east along Tamaki Drive. After Hobson Bay on the right (south) turn right up Ngapipi Road. At the first traffic lights turn right into Orakei Road and cross over the bridge. After the bridge look for a small road on the left which leads down to the Orakei Basin Reserve.

Target birds: Little Shag, Little Black Shag, White-faced Heron, Pied Stilt.

TAHUNA TOREA NATURE RESERVE

General: This nature reserve is located in Auckland on the edge of the Tamaki Estuary, an arm of the Auckland Harbour. It is to the east of central Auckland in the suburb of Glendowie. Walking tracks lead around the reserve. A full tide is best when the wading birds come in close to the shore on to high tide roosts.

How to get there: Follow Tamaki Drive from the city and turn right into St Heliers Bay Road at the St Heliers village. Follow St Heliers Bay Road and then turn left down West Tamaki Road and travel to the end.

Target Birds: South Island Pied Oystercatcher, Variable Oystercatcher, Banded Dotterel, Bar-tailed Godwit, Knot and Turnstone.

MANGERE SEWAGE PONDS

General: These ponds are located on the Manukau Harbour between Puketututu Island and Mangere near the Auckland International Airport. Recent developments here confine birdwatchers to signposted viewing areas.

How to get there: From Auckland follow the airport signs. Leave Highway 20 at the Walmsley Road off-ramp and turn right and cross the motorway. Then turn left into McKenzie Road. Follow along McKenzie Road. and turn right into Ascot Road and then right again into Greenwood Road. Then turn left into Island Road and follow to end. Also drive across the causeway to Puketutu Island. Spotted Doves and Barbary Doves are sometimes seen on Puketutu Island.

Rarities: Chestnut-breasted Shelduck, Bairds Sandpiper, White-rumped Sandpiper, Broad-billed Sandpiper, Grey Phalarope and Red-necked Phalarope have all been recorded here.

Birds likely to be seen include -

Black Shag	Royal Spoonbill
Little Shag	Cattle Egret
White-faced Heron	Black Swan

Paradise Shelduck
Mallard
Grey Duck
Grey Teal
Shoveler
Pukeko
Australasian Coot
South Island Pied Oystercatcher
Variable Oystercatcher
Spur-winged Plover
Golden Plover
Banded Dotterel
New Zealand Dotterel

Wrybill
Bar-tailed Godwit
Turnstone
Lesser Knot
Curlew Sandpiper
Red-necked Stint
Pied Stilt
Red-billed Gull
Black-backed Gull
Caspian Tern
White-fronted Tern
Spotted Dove

WATTLE FARM RESERVE - MANUREWA

General: This reserve has two lakes which at one time were the sewage ponds for the district. The northern lake always has the most waterfowl on it. There is plenty of parking here. This is a handy place to see Dabchick near Auckland.

How to get there: Follow Highway 1 south of Auckland to the Takanini off-ramp. At the off-ramp turn right (north) and follow along the Great South Road to Mahia Road on the left. Travel down Mahia Road, turn left into Coxhead Road and then into Wattle Farm Road.

Target Birds: Dabchick, Royal Spoonbill, Grey Teal and Black-billed Gull.

POINT VIEW RESERVE - HOWICK

General: This small reserve is to the south-east of Auckland and behind Howick. Walking tracks (wet in winter) lead in from Caldwells Road near the corner and from these a small range of bush birds can be seen.

How to get there: From Howick follow Cook Street at the east end of the town to Whitford Road. Follow Whitford Road and turn right at a round-about which says Point View Road. Travel to the top until Caldwells Road is encountered on a bend. The reserve is on the corner of Caldwells Road and Point View Road.

Target birds: New Zealand Pigeon, Spotted Dove, Tomtit.

CLIFTON BEACH – WHITFORD

General: This beach is located in the Whitford district just past the town of Howick. It is a good wading bird haunt especially in the autumn.

How to get there: From Howick follow Cook Street at the east end of the town. Then follow Whitford Road until you get out into the countryside. After Whitford turn down Clifton Road on the left (north), and then left again into Potts Road and follow to the end.

Target birds: New Zealand Dotterel, Bar-tailed Godwits and Lesser Knots. An American Whimbrel has also been seen here.

SOUTH AUCKLAND

TE HIHI - MANUKAU HARBOUR

General: This the best high-tide wader roost on the Manukau Harbour and maybe in all New Zealand, and always has good numbers of rare birds. It is, though, inaccessible to the public being surrounded by privately owned farmland but it is mentioned here because sometimes local birders can obtain permission to enter and visit the area in groups.

Location: Te Hihi is located 12 kms west from the Papakura off-ramp on Highway 1 on the seaward side of Te Hihi School.

Birds likely to be seen here include –

Pacific Golden Plover
Banded Dotterel
New Zealand Dotterel
Mongolian Dotterel
Large Sand Dotterel
Wrybill
Whimbrel
Black-tailed Godwit
Bar-tailed Godwit
Siberian Tattler
Great Knot
Lesser Knot
Marsh Sandpiper
Terek Sandpiper
Turnstone
Sharp-tailed Sandpiper
Curlew Sandpiper
Red-necked Stint
Pied Stilt
Black-billed Gull
White-winged Black Tern
Little Tern.

Target birds: Mongolian Dotterel, Large Sand Dotterel and White-winged Black Tern.

CLARKS BEACH - MANUKAU HARBOUR

General: By boat, from the boat ramp at Waiau Beach or Clarks Beach, a visit can be made to a very large Pied Shag colony. Head south along the coast to Waitete Point and then turn left up the Taihiki River for 1 km and look north.

From side roads at Clarks Beach, South Island Pied Oystercatcher, Variable Oystercatcher, Bar-tailed Godwit and Lesser Knot can all be seen at any tide.

How to get there: From Highway 1 south of Auckland leave the motorway at the Papakura off-ramp and drive west through Karaka, Te Hihi, Kingseat, Waiau Pa and at the end of the road is Clarks Beach which can be accessed by side roads.

Target birds: Pied Shag, Bar-tailed Godwit, Lesser Knot.

AWHITU PENINSULA – GORDON ROAD

General: A small high tide roost is located at the bottom of Gordon Road which is about 7 kms up the Awhitu Peninsula from Waiuku. Royal Spoonbill, Black Stilt, Bar-tailed Godwit and Lesser Knots have all been recorded here.

How to get there: After Waiuku follow up the Awhitu Peninsula. Gordon Road is the sixth road running east after Sandspit Road which is on the outskirts of Waiuku. Drive to the end and the roost is found to the right.

After visiting here proceed up the peninsula to the Awhitu Regional Park on Brook Road and look for Fernbirds in the swampy areas.

Target bird: Black Stilt, Marsh Sandpiper.

KAWAKAWA BAY

General: Kawakawa Bay is located east of Clevedon and to the east end of the Waitemata Harbour. Look for shorebirds at the west end of the beach arrived at after descending the hill into the bay. Here New Zealand Dotterel and Banded Dotterel are regularly seen plus Pied Oystercatchers, Variable Oystercatchers, Bar-tailed Godwits and Pied Stilts.

How to get there: From the southern motorway, Highway 1, leave at Takanini and travel south along the Great South Road until the Clevedon sign shows up on the left. Follow to Clevedon and then follow the Kawakawa Bay sign.

Target birds: New Zealand Dotterel and Banded Dotterel.

MIRANDA - ON THE FIRTH OF THAMES

General: Miranda is a coastal mudflat area located at the base of the Firth of Thames on its western shores. The Firth of Thames is an area of 8500 hectares of mudflat at the low tide, this mud providing a vast feeding ground for wading birds.

In the winter the area hosts up to 28,000 South Island Pied Oystercatchers, a bird which breeds in the riverbeds and open country of the southern half of the South Island. It also hosts in winter Wrybills which breed in the mid-Canterbury riverbeds and migrate north to northern harbours, including Miranda. Over 3000 or two thirds of the world's population, winter here.

In the summer Miranda hosts Bar-tailed Godwits and Lesser Knots from Siberian and Alaskan breeding grounds and included with these are sprinklings of many other Arctic breeding birds.

How to get there - via the scenic route: The scenic route to Miranda is via the Pacific Highway. Follow the southern motorway, Highway 1, south from Auckland and turn off near Manurewa at the Pacific Highway sign. If you miss this sign turn off at the Takanini off-ramp. At Takanini proceed south along the Great South Road and turn left at the Clevedon sign. Follow to Clevedon, Kawakawa Bay and Kaiaua. Miranda is 6 kms further south from Kaiaua.

How to get there – via the quick route: From Auckland follow Highway 1, the southern motorway, from Auckland. This motorway leads over the Bombay Hills. At the southern side of the Bombay Hills turn left on to Highway 2 which says to Thames. Beyond Mangatawhiri, where there is a shop designed like a castle, travel on for a further 3 kms and follow left to Mangatangi and Miranda. This leads down to the coast. At the Miranda junction turn left (north) and travel along the coast road for 2 kms until the Miranda Naturalists' Trust, shorebird centre is seen on the left.

Accessible viewing locations starting from the north are:

Kaiaua: At the river-mouth at Kaiaua just north of the hotel, look for Banded Rail from the bridge. Just south of the town is a high-tide roost where Eastern Curlews are often seen.

Rangipo or Taramaire North: About 3 kms south of Kaiaua where the sea comes close to the road, walk into a shell beach where Wrybills often roost.

Taramaire River-mouth: Further south, at the first river-mouth north of the Miranda Shorebird Centre, drive over Department of Conservation land to the coast. Birds congregate around the river-mouth.

"The Hide": Look for "The Hide", a bland looking plywood building on the sea-edge, opposite "The Stilt Ponds". Here at full tide, a narrow channel of sea separates the birds from the viewers giving the birds security, which means they sit quietly within close view.

"The Stilt Ponds": These ponds and the surrounding land on the road edge just north of Pukorokoro River are owned by the Lane family. They often have large numbers of birds including Grey Teal, sandpipers and Wrybills, as well as many stilts.

"The Limeworks": This site is near the Pukorokoro river-mouth. It was once the site of a lime-works. Birders may enter and walk to the coast. Look for New Zealand Dotterel here.

Birds likely to be seen her include -

Little Egret	Bar-tailed Godwit
White Heron	Siberian Tattler
Cattle Egret	Terek Sandpiper
Reef Heron	Turnstone
Bittern	Lesser Knot
Royal Spoonbill	Sharp-tailed Sandpiper
Grey Teal	Pectoral Sandpiper
Shoveler	Curlew Sandpiper
Banded Rail	Marsh Sandpiper
South Island Pied Oystercatcher	Red-necked Stint
Variable Oystercatcher	Pied Stilt
Golden Plover	Black Stilt
Banded Dotterel	Hybrid Stilt
New Zealand Dotterel	Arctic Skua
Mongolian Dotterel	Black-billed Gull
Large Sand Dotterel	Caspian Tern
Black-fronted Dotterel	Fairy Tern
Wrybill	Little Tern
Eastern Curlew	Pipit
Whimbrel	Fernbird
Asiatic Black-tailed Godwit	Rook

Note: Extreme rarities have been excluded from this list.

THE MIRANDA NATURALISTS' TRUST

General: The importance of Miranda as a birding place is highlighted by the fact that bird-watchers have got together to form a group called the Miranda Naturalists' Trust. This Trust purchased land at Miranda in 1989 and has built there a visitor information centre plus accommodation for up to 25 people. The accommodation, which includes bunkrooms plus two self-contained flats, is available for use by both members and non-members. Visitors should take sleeping bags and food but some bedding is available for hire.

For further details: Phone/fax: +64 9 232 2781. Email: shorebird@xtra.co.nz, or write to R D 1, Pokeno.

THAMES - COROMANDEL

THAMES - THE HIDE

General: Look for waterfowl and wading birds here.

How to get there: From the town of Thames drive north along the Queen Street by-pass and turn left after the Goldfields round-about into Brown Street. Follow along until a mown grass verge on the left (west) comes into view. The small hide among the mangroves is accessed from here.

Target birds: Pied Oystercatchers, Bar-tailed Godwits and Pied Stilts.

THAMES COAST - WAIOMU BEACH

General: At the north end of Waiomu Beach, New Zealand Dotterel can usually be found. Further along the coast large numbers of Spotted Shags can be seen on off-shore rocks.

How to get there: Follow the road north of Thames along the Coromandel Peninsula. At the 2 kms mark look for dead pine trees on the right which provide a nesting place for a Pied Shag colony. From the 5 kms mark start looking for Spotted Shags on the rocks and also again at about the 17 kms mark after Waiomu Beach.

Target birds: Pied Shags, Spotted Shags, New Zealand Dotterel.

COROMANDEL - COLVILLE:

How to get there: Drive north from Coromandel town for about 15 kms. The road soon follows the coast and from these places Bullers Shearwaters are regularly seen and Spotted Shags.

Target birds: Bullers Shearwaters and Spotted Shags.

COLVILLE HARBOUR

General: Colville Harbour is 80 kms up the Coromandel Peninsula from Thames.

How to get there: Drive north from Coromandel and once at Colville drive north for about 1 km until the harbour comes into view. From the roadside rest area the harbour is easily scanned for wading birds.

Target birds: Pied Oystercatchers, New Zealand Dotterel and Banded Dotterel.

TAIRUA HARBOUR

General: This harbour on the east coast of Coromandel Peninsula has good numbers of waders.

How to get there: From Thames drive south on Highway 26 and then follow left (east) on to Highway 25 which goes to Tairua and Pauanui. Follow the Tairua signs and stop and view the harbour at suitable places once it comes into view on the right (south).

Target birds: Banded Dotterels, Bar-tailed Godwits and Lesser Knots.

OPOUTERE

General: When driving into Opoutere stop over the bridge which is just before the start of the first houses. Look up the river verges from here, especially on dusk, for Banded Rail. Fernbirds can also be found here and on the harbour fringes generally. The main ocean beach at Opoutere is accessed over a foot bridge just past the backpackers' lodge. Here New Zealand Dotterel nest out on the sandspit along with Variable Oystercatchers.

How to get there: From Highway 25 at the Hikuai junction, instead of going north to Tairua turn right (south) towards Whangamata. After about 8 kms the sign to Opoutere is seen on the left. This leads into the Wharekawa Harbour and the Opoutere beach settlement.

Target birds: Banded Rail, Pied Oystercatcher, New Zealand Dotterel, Fernbird.

HAURAKI PLAINS

TOREHAPE EAST ROAD

General: Torehape East Road is on the western verges of the Hauraki Plains, south of the Miranda Shorebird Centre. Much of it is a vast swamp which has Fernbirds.

How to get there: Leave Highway 2, when travelling south, at Highway 27 which is the road to Matamata. Follow Highway 27 for about 8 kms and before the Kaihere hills turn left (east) down Torehape East Road. Follow to the Torehape swamp which is a manuka-scrub Fernbird locality. Travel on for a further 800 metres until an old gate is seen on the right and enter here.

Target bird: Fernbird.

LAKE PATETONGA

General: Lake Patetonga is a small lake on the western edge of the Hauraki Plains. It is a good place to see Bitterns and place and waterfowl. It regularly has one or two Glossy Ibis and occasionally a Chestnut-breasted Shelduck. Many Grey Teal live on this lake. Note that after the shooting season (May) birds can become scarce and those that remain are scary.

How to get there: From the start of Highway 27 travel south for about 17 kms to Patetonga. At Patetonga which is a shop and a garage, turn left (east) down Tramline Road to the end and park beside the Piako River. Then walk for about 800 metres northwards along the river until the lake comes into view.

Birds likely to be seen here include -

Black Shag	Glossy Ibis	Grey Duck
Little Shag	Black Swan	Shoveler
Little Black Shag	Canada Goose	Grey Teal
White-faced Heron	Chestnut-breasted Shelduck	Scaup
Cattle Egret	Paradise Shelduck	Spotless Crake
Bittern	Mallard	Pukeko
		Coot

MOUNT TE AROHA

General: Robins, Tomtits and Whiteheads could all live in the forests here so it is a place to try for them. They are found a few kilometres further south. Follow the walking track to the summit. This leads up from near the Te Aroha thermal pools.

How to get there: Follow Highway 27 south from Patetonga and turn left (east) at the Tatuanui junction. Te Aroha is about 15 kms from here.

Target birds: Robin, Tomtits and Whiteheads.

WAIKATO

MEREMERE AND WHANGAMARINO

General: Whangamarino is a large wetland in the north Waikato and is known for its Bitterns, Spotless Crakes, Marsh Crakes and Fernbirds.

How to get there: Follow Highway 1 south of Auckland to the motorway's end at Mercer. At the old Meremere Power Station on Highway 1, about 5 kms south of Mercer, turn left (east) at the signpost which says Island Block. This road leads into dense wetlands known as Whangamarino. Search anywhere along this road for Bitterns. At a closed gate walk along the gravelled road until you reach Pylon 73. A small board-walk (sometimes hard to see) extends into the swamp here and Bitterns, Spotless Crakes and Fernbirds have been seen from it.

Target birds: Bittern, Spotless Crake, Marsh Crake and Fernbird.

FINLAYSON ROAD, MARAMARUA

General: Extensive ponds and wet areas can be found along Finlayson Road, east of the Whangamarino wetlands. These are frequently inhabited by waterfowl and Bitterns.

How to get there: Leave Highway 1 at the sign which says Island Block, as for the Whangamarino wetlands. Follow this east until Falls Road is reached. Here turn left (north) and follow along until Finlayson Road on the right is reached. Look for the wetlands on the right and further along on the left. The most likely place for Bitterns is the first wetland on the right.

Target birds: Bittern and a wide range of waterfowl including Black Swan, Canada Goose, Paradise Shelduck, Mallard, Grey Duck, Grey Teal and Shoveler.

LAKE WAIKERE

General: This lake lies to the east of Highway 1 at Rangiriri. Vantage points along Lake Road give good views of the lake and its waterfowl. At the southern end of the road waterfowl are in greater numbers. In spring months the many kowhai trees along this road are always full of Tui.

How to get there: From Highway 1 turn left (east) at the Te Kauwhata signpost. Travel through the town of Te Kauwhata and on until the first road on the right (south) is encountered. Turn down Lake Waikere Road and travel along until the lake comes into view.

Target birds: Little Black Shag, Black Swan and waterfowl.

RANGIRIRI - CHURCHILL EAST ROAD

General: This area south of Mercer on Highway 1 has been a place to see Cattle Egrets for many years. Occasional Glossy Ibis also visit from time to time and live with the Cattle Egrets.

How to get there: From Mercer, on Highway 1, drive south for a further 10 kms. At Rangiriri turn right (west) at the sign for the bridge which crosses the Waikato River. Before crossing the river turn right into Churchill East Road and follow along examining the dairy herds for Cattle Egrets. Birds are more likely to be found after about 3 kms. This flock arrives in New Zealand from Australia in the middle of May.

Target birds: Cattle Egret, Glossy Ibis.

RANGIRIRI - LUMSDEN ROAD

How to get there: Back on Highway 1, turn south and examine the dairy herds along the banks of the Waikato River. Then turn left into Tahuna Road and then hard left (north) into Lumsden Road. At the end of Lumsden Road among the cattle on the right, Cattle Egrets and maybe a Glossy Ibis are sometime seen.

Target birds: Cattle Egret, Glossy Ibis.

RANGIRIRI - LAKE WHANGAPE

General: Lake Whangape lies on the west side of the Waikato River near Rangiriri. Good views of the lake can be made from roadside vantage points. The large numbers of Black Swans here provide a waterfowl spectacle although birds are quite some distance from the road and a telescope is required for good viewing. Dabchicks have also been recorded here.

How to get there: From Highway 1 near Rangiriri, turn west at the Waikato River bridge sign and cross over the river. Over the river follow south for a short distance and then turn right towards Glen Murray. Travel along until the lake comes into sight on your left (south).

Target birds: Black Swan and waterfowl.

HUNTLY - LAKE HAKANOA

General: Just north and east of the Huntly town centre, and across the railway line, lies Lake Hakanoa. This lake has more Grey Ducks on it than Mallard. Also to be seen here are Black Shag, Little Shag and Little Black Shag, along with good numbers of Black Swan and sometimes Shoveler and Grey Teal.

How to get there: Travel south on Highway 1 to Huntly. At Bell Crossing Street, turn left (east) and cross the railway line. Turn right into Hakanoa Street and then left down Park Avenue and follow on to the lake. It is signposted. It can also be viewed from several Huntly side-roads. These give views into its distant corners.

Target bird: Grey Duck, Grey Teal and Shoveler.

HUNTLY - LAKE WAAHI

General: This lake, not far from the western banks of the Waikato River, can be viewed from the boat launching ramp. The lake verges have Bitterns. In deeper water towards the middle of the lake can be seen Black Swans and Canada Geese.

How to get there: From the Huntly town centre drive south on Highway 1 and cross the Waikato River at the second traffic lights. Follow west through two intersections until the Lake Waahi sign is encountered at Weavers Crossing Road. Drive along this road until the Lake Reserve sign is found.

Target bird: Australasian Bittern, Canada Goose.

TAUPIRI WETLAND

General: Often Bittern and sometimes White Herons are seen on the far side of this swamp which is a few minutes drive from Highway 1 at Taupiri on the Gordonton road, just past the 100km sign. South of the wetland near a small cemetery, Spotless Crakes have been seen. Suspected calls of Marsh Crakes have also been recorded. Note that a record of a Plumed Egret comes from this swamp in 1990.

How to get there: From Highway 1 at Taupiri, 8 kms south of Huntly, turn left (east) into Gordonton Road. Travel for about 1.5 km to just past the last house and some roadside plantings and look for the wetland on the left (east) side of road.

Target birds: White Heron, Australasian Bittern, Spotless Crake and Plumed Egret.

HAMILTON - LAKE ROTOROA

General: This lake always has good numbers of Coot, plus Black Swan, Canada Geese and many Mallards. Black Shags and Little Shags roost in the trees on the western shore and occasionally Pied Shags have bred here and a Caspian Tern has been seen.

How to get there: From Victoria Street in Hamilton, turn west into Collingwood Street and follow to the end. Turn left into Ruakiwi Road and follow along until the lake gates on the right are recognised. A road runs right around the lake allowing viewing along the rush verges on the western side.

Target bird: Australasian Coot.

TE AWAMUTU - LAKE NGAROTO

General: This lake is used for yachting and rowing. It nevertheless retains a waterfowl population with its main feature being its rush verge from which both Spotless Crakes and Marsh Crakes have been observed as well as Bitterns and Fernbirds. A boardwalk skirts the lake verge giving good access to these birds. This leads off from near the yacht club.

How to get there: The easiest approach to Lake Ngaroto is from Te Awamutu. Follow Paterangi Road from the centre of the town and then right into Bank Rd. The lake is signposted from the junction. Other roads lead to the yacht club from Highway 3 south of Ohaupo which are of similar distance.

Target birds: Bittern, Spotless Crake, Marsh Crake, Fernbird.

KAIMAI RANGE FROM HIGHWAY 29

General: A short walk through paddocks leads to the Kaimai Forest. Here Robins can be found just inside the forest edge along with Tomtits and Whiteheads. A further walk leads to the Rapurapu River. Past the river the track goes on to a large kauri tree after numerous river crossings.

How to get there: From Hamilton follow Highway 1 south. Just past Karapiro turn left (east) into Highway 29 and follow through and to the Kaimai hill. About 3 kms up the Kaimai hill look for a rough parking area on the right. A track leads from here.

Target Birds: New Zealand Robin, Tomtit and Whitehead.

KING COUNTRY - CENTRAL PLATEAU

OTOROHANGA ZOOLOGICAL SOCIETY

General: The Otorohanga Zoological Society runs a kiwi house at Otorohanga, a country town 60 kms south of Hamilton. It has had considerable success with the breeding of kiwi and other birds. As well as the kiwi house there are also large waterfowl ponds, a giant aviary, tuatara cages and a deer park. There is a Blue Duck enclosure with special waterfall facilities and a Kokako enclosure. Free-flying flocks of waterfowl such as Mallard, Grey Teal and Paradise Shelduck, come and go from the lakes, so it is a good place to study waterfowl.

How to get there: From Hamilton follow Highway 3. This is signposted from the south end of the main street called Victoria Street. Otorohanga is a 45 minute drive from Hamilton and the Otorohanga Zoo is signposted from the north end of the main street of the town.

For further details: Phone: +64 7 873 7391. The park is open from 10 a.m. to 4.30 p.m. every day of the week.

WAIMAHORA - RANGITOTO STATION

General: Rangitoto Station is a protected area of native forest owned by the Forest Restoration Trust. It is located 35 kms east from Otorohanga and it has good populations of bush birds which include the rare kokako. Visitors can hire a cottage on the station for overnight stays. Enquiries should be made to the Trust prior to visiting.

How to get there: From Otorohanga follow the Otewa sign from the south end of the town. From Otewa follow Waipa River Road to the Toa Bridge. After the bridge follow Waimahora Road. Past the junction with Owawenga Road the road surface deteriorates and sometimes in winter four wheel drive is required.

Target birds: New Zealand Falcon, Kaka, Kokako.

For further details: Write: New Zealand Native Forests Restoration Trust, P O Box 80-007, Green Bay, Auckland 7, New Zealand.

OPARAU

How to get there: From Otorohanga follow Highway 31 to Kawhia. Just before Oparau at about the 40 km mark, turn left towards Hauturu and travel for approximately 6 kms when some very swampy, raupo-type wetlands appear on the left (south). These wetlands are backed by forest. A causeway runs into a farm property nearby. This is an excellent roadside place to find Spotless Crake and Fernbird.

Target birds: Spotless Crake, Fernbird, Bellbird.

WAITOMO - RUAKURI CAVES

General: A walkway here which is signposted crosses a river and then climbs into the bush. It runs around rocky limestone outcrops. Birdlife here includes New Zealand Falcon, New Zealand Pigeon, Tomtit, Whitehead, Tui and Bellbird. The Ruakuri Glow Worm Caves nearby are worth a visit if they are open.

How to get there: From Otorohanga drive south on Highway 3 and turn right (west) at the sign which says Waitomo Caves. From Waitomo Caves drive west for 1 km and turn left up Tumutumu Road. Take the first road to the right and then right again and drive down to a carpark.

Target birds: New Zealand Falcon, New Zealand Pigeon, Tomtit, Whitehead, Tui, Bellbird.

MAPARA WILDLIFE RESERVE

General: Mapara Wildlife Reserve is a managed area of forest remnant in which predator control is sustained on a year round basis. The reason for this constant control is that this area contains a large population of Kokako and other bush birds. Results from this control work are now conclusive. In 1996 18 pairs of birds out of a total of 24 pairs fledged 55 chicks, an unprecedented success story and this type of increase has continued but declined in 1998 when control measures were eased.

How to get there: To get to Mapara follow Highway 3 from Otorohanga and travel south to Te Kuiti. From Te Kuiti take the New Plymouth road (also Highway 3) and travel a further 12 kms to the Eight Mile Junction. Turn left (south) on to Highway 4 where the signpost says Taumarunui. Travel along this road past Pukerimu Road and Mapara North Roads for approximately 14 kms. Turn left at the junction which says Aratora, Pukerimu and Kopaki. Then turn right into Mapara South Road and travel along until you come to a Department of Conservation notice board. A track leads into the bush from here and a Kokako locality is about 20 minutes walk in from it.

Target birds: New Zealand Falcon, New Zealand Pigeon, Shining Cuckoo, Long-tailed Cuckoo, Whitehead, Tomtit, Bellbird, Tui and Kokako.

For further details: Phone: +64 7 878 7862, for the manager of the Mapara Scenic Reserve.

PUREORA FOREST

General: This forest, which contains many old podocarp trees, is found south of Te Kuiti and north of Lake Taupo, almost in the middle of the North Island. As a place to see a wide range of bush birds there is no better one. There are two main places to visit. One is "The Tower" on Bismarck Road to the east of the entrance road, and the other is the "Totara Walk", walking track near to the information centre almost opposite the main carpark.

How to get there: From Highway 3 in Te Kuiti follow Highway 30 from the south end of the main street of the town. Travel to Benneydale. Approximately 23 kms past Benneydale look for the signpost to Pureora on the right (south) which leads into the park headquarters. Enquire at the headquarters about the whereabouts of Kokako.

How to get to "The Tower": After leaving Highway 3 at the Pureora signpost, travel into the park and turn left (east) at the first road which is signposted Plains

Road. (Note some signposts might be missing.) Then turn right into Pikiariki Road and travel along to Bismarck Road, the first road on the left. Drive down and then up to a carpark. Walk from here to "The Tower" which extends up into the treetops and this allows views of canopy birds such as the Yellow-crowned Parakeet and Kaka.

How to get to the "Totara Walk": From Highway 3 drive to the park headquarters. Look for the "Totara Walk" signpost opposite the carpark. The walk is over flat contour and takes about 40 minutes.

Birds likely to be seen include -

New Zealand Pigeon	Kingfisher	Whitehead
New Zealand Falcon	Rifleman	Grey Warbler
Kaka	Pipit (before the park)	Bellbird
Yellow-crowned Parakeet	Fantail	Tui
Shining Cuckoo	Tomtit	Silvereye
Long-tailed Cuckoo	Robin	Kokako

Target birds: Falcon, Kaka, Yellow-crowned Parakeet, Rifleman and Kokako.

WHAKAMARU - ATIAMURI PINUS RADIATA FORESTS

General: These forest lie in the centre of the North Island south of Putaruru on Highway 1 and south of Rotorua on Highways 5 and 30. They are all plantation grown and generally of the pine species *Pinus radiata*. They are by-passed by many birders who feel they are not good for birds. The ones around Atiamuri Hydro Station on Highway 1, and between Atiamuri and Whakamaru on Highway 30, are often more productive than many of the central North Island indigenous forests.

How to get there: From Putaruru on Highway 1 travel until mature forests come into view on both sides of the roads. Stop where roadside parking allows. If travelling south from Rotorua on Highway 30, stop at the first mature forests. If travelling to Taupo on Highway 5, stop in the pine forests after the Reporoa turnoff.

Birds likely to be seen in the forest and their lakes include -

Little Shag	Shining Cuckoo	Fantail
White-faced Heron	(summer)	New Zealand Robin
Paradise Shelduck	Long-tailed Cuckoo	Tomtit
Grey Duck	(summer)	Blackbird (exotic)
Scaup	Morepork	Silvereye
Pukeko	Kingfisher	Tui
Australasian Coot	Whitehead	Bellbird
Eastern Rosella (exotic)	Grey Warbler	Chaffinch (exotic)

Target birds: New Zealand Robin, Tomtit, Whitehead.

WAIHAHA RIVER

General: This river, which is Blue Duck territory, is about 40 kms from Whakamaru towards Turangi on Highway 32. A track leads up-stream but it takes at least two hours to get into the Blue Duck territory. A small river is crossed after a 35 minutes walk, the track then climbing quite steeply over a saddle and back to the river. Once the river is again reached Blue Duck might be found. Make this an all day excursion. Blue Duck also live downstream from the bridge.

How to get there: After about 10 kms on past the Tihoi Trading Post, a main road shop and petrol station on Highway 32, the road drops steeply and crosses the Waihaha River over a small bridge. Stop after crossing the river and turn left into a car parking area. Don't leave valuables in your car.

Target bird: Blue Duck.

TONGARIRO

LAKE ROTOPOUNAMU

General: This lake lies in the forests at the south end of Lake Taupo. A walking track, which takes 1.5 hours to traverse and is of easy contour, goes right around it. This track is good for a variety of bush birds including the Rifleman. The lake is pleasant for swimming in summer at the south end.

How to get there: From Waihaha follow Highway 32 until it meets Highway 41. Travel south on Highway 41 until Tokaanu. After Tokaanu turn left (west) into Highway 47 and follow up the Te Ponanga Road and over the saddle. Lake Rotopounamu is signposted on the left as you descend towards Lake Rotoaira.

Target birds: Scaup, Kaka, Morepork, Rifleman, Whitehead.

LAKE TAUPO - FRETHEY DRIVE

General: Frethey Drive runs through the Waiotaka Reserve west of the Waimarino River. Its verges are a place to see Fernbirds and Bellbirds plus exotic finches. On the lake edge further along Frethey Drive are waterfowl including Dabchick and Scaup.

How to get there: From Turangi travel 7 kms towards Taupo on Highway 1. Turn left into Frethey Drive and stop almost immediately and search both sides of the road for Fernbird.

Target Birds: Spotless Crake, Fernbird, Redpoll, Bellbird.

TONGARIRI NATIONAL PARK - DESERT ROAD

General: Most of the roads which run east towards the Kaimanawa ranges, off the Desert Road south of Turangi on Highway 1, lead to the Tongariro River. All these localities have recorded Blue Duck with Rangipo Intake Road being the most reliable. These include -

- Access Road 10 which leads into the Waikato Falls.
- Tree Trunk Gorge Road which leads into the Pillars of Hercules gorge.
- Rangipo Intake Road which leads into the river.

Target bird: Blue Duck.

WHAKAPAPA RIVER - THE CHATEAU

General: The Whakapapa River flows under Highway 47 not far from The Chateau, Tongariro.

How to get there: From Highway 1, south of Turangi, turn right (west) into Highway 47. After about 37 kms, turn left (south) at the Whakapapa Village signpost. Follow up to the Chateau. Search the Whakapapa River near The Chateau.

Target bird: Blue Duck.

WHAKAPAPA RIVER - ACCESS ROAD

How to get there: From Highway 47, just east of the Whakapapa Village and The Chateau, turn right (north) down Access Road and travel to a carpark at the end. The water intake area above the dam and its buildings sometimes has Blue Ducks as do downstream areas. Before the carpark a track leads off on the right. This steeply descends over about 2 kms to a footbridge. This locality sometimes has birds.

Target bird: Blue Duck.

MAUNGANUI-ATEAO RIVER - RAETAHI

General: This river has several pairs of Blue Ducks in specific territories along its banks. Access to them is difficult but not impossible.

How to get there: From National Park on Highway 4 drive south towards Raetahi. North of Raetahi turn right (west) down Ohura Road. Travel for about 16 kms until a large steel bridge over the Maunganui Ateao River is encountered. Try for Blue Duck here. Try again further along wherever the Maunganui Ateao comes into view.

Target bird: Blue Duck.

LAKE KARIO - OHAKUNE

General: This lake, which is south of Ohakune, has many waterfowl including up to six Dabchicks. The forests are good for bush birds.

How to get there: Travel 14 kms south of Ohakune on Highway 49. It is signposted on the left.

Target birds: Dabchick, Scaup, Shoveler, Tomtit, Whitehead.

BAY OF PLENTY

MATAHUI POINT

General: Matahui Point is on the Tauranga Harbour just south of Katikati.

How to get there: From Katikati follow Highway 2 east for about 8 kms and then turn left down Matahui Road. Park at the end and walk to the point.

Birds likely to be seen include -

Cattle Egret	Spur-winged Plover
South Island Pied Oystercatcher	Pied Stilt
Variable Oystercatcher	Black Stilt

Banded Dotterel	Lesser Knot
New Zealand Dotterel	Wrybill
Black-fronted Dotterel	Turnstone
Pacific Golden Plover	Bar-tailed Godwit

Target birds: Mongolian Dotterel, Large Sand Dotterel, Bar-tailed Godwit, Hudsonian Godwit, Greenshank, Siberian Tattler.

MOUNT OTANEWAINUKU

General: This forested area is in the Tauranga district almost behind the city of Tauranga. It is a kiwi locality and good for bush birds including the New Zealand Falcon. A track leads to the summit through fine forests. Walk up the mountain in daylight hours and return at dusk listening for calling Brown Kiwi. Kiwi sometimes use the walking tracks as probing sites and for easy access to other parts of their territories.

How to get there: It is approached either through Oropi or up No 3 Road, Te Puke. If approached via Oropi, turn off Highway 29 at the Pyes Pa round-about and follow the Welcome Bay sign for 3 kms. Then turn right into Oropi Road and follow up through Oropi. Turn left into Seales Road and right into Mountain Road. The carpark and walking track are signposted.

Birds likely to be seen here include –

Kiwi	Robin
Kaka	Tomtit
Yellow-crowned Parakeet	Whitehead
Long-tailed Cuckoo	Grey Warbler
Shining Cuckoo	Bellbird
Morepork, Kingfisher	Tui
Fantail	Silvereye

Target birds: Brown Kiwi, Kaka, Yellow-crowned Parakeet, New Zealand Robin, Tomtit, Whitehead.

MOUNT MAUNGANUI

General: Mount Maunganui is the headland on the eastern edge of the Tauranga Harbour. It has a small breeding colony of Grey-faced Petrels on its higher altitudes. Another colony of birds breeds on the nearby Motuotau Island. Birds from these colonies circle the area after dark in winter and spring evenings and right to early summer when they can be heard coming into their nesting burrows.

How to get there: Follow Highway 2 from Tauranga. It is signposted. At Mount Maunganui travel right through the town to the camp ground which is located under the mountain. A walking track leads right around the mountain.

Target bird: Grey-faced Petrel.

KAITUNA RIVER-MOUTH

General: A lagoon at Kaituna River-mouth has both wading birds and waterfowl. The swampy areas nearby have recorded Banded Rail, Fernbird, Spotless Crake and Marsh Crake. Both Black Shag and Pied Shag nest in tall trees near the Kaituna river cutting.

How to get there: From Tauranga follow Highway 2. After Te Puke turn left into Maketu Road and then left into Kaituna River Road and then right down Ford Road. Tumu Road also leads into this lagoon from Highway 2.

Target birds: Grey Teal, Banded Rail, Fernbird, Spotless Crake.

MAKETU HARBOUR

General: Maketu Harbour is further along the eastern coast from Kaituna River-mouth. Wading birds, such as Bar-tailed Godwit and Lesser Knot can sometimes be seen from here but usually birds are in the distance.

How to get there: From Maketu take the Little Waihi sign and travel over the hill and then find Bledisloe Park. Look from here.

Target birds: Bar-tailed Godwits and Lesser Knots.

MATATA LAGOONS

General: This area is 69 kms east of Tauranga on the Bay of Plenty coast. Roads here are generally flat and skirt the coast, with pohutukawa trees on the inland cliffs. Matata town is a hotel, a few shops and a cluster of houses above them. In front are two shallow lagoons and an area of wetland which hosts large populations of waterfowl. These can be viewed from the verge on Highway 2 although vegetation obscures the eastern lagoon in some places. It is easier therefore to drive up a side road opposite the lagoon and scan the lake with a telescope. Look for Pollen Street and then take the first road to the left which leads to the cemetery. Look at the lake from here.

How to get there: Follow Highway 2 after Te Puke.

Target birds: Key birds here are White Heron and Royal Spoonbill in winter. Also Dabchick, Bittern, Shoveler, Scaup, Banded Rail, Spotless Crake, Marsh Crake and Fernbird, but the scrubby surrounds of the lagoons have a wide range of exotic species and the pohutukawa fringed roadside escarpments nearby have bush birds such as Tui and Bellbirds.

TARAWERA RIVER-MOUTH

How to get there: Travel further east from the Matata Lagoons for 2 kms and then turn left and drive down beside the Tarawera River to the coast.

Birds likely to be seen here include –

Pied Shag	Banded Rail
Little Shag	Marsh Crake
Little Black Shag	Spotless Crake
White-faced Heron	New Zealand Dotterel
Bittern	Banded Dotterel
	Fernbird

Target birds: Bittern, Spotless Crake and Marsh Crake.

AWAITI WETLANDS

General: This is a wetland with areas of open water which attract waterfowl and Dabchick.

How to get there: From Highway 2, east of the Matata wetlands and the Tarawera River, turn right into Grieg Road and follow until the Awaiti Wetlands come into view on the right.

Target birds: Bittern, Banded Rail, Spotless Crake, Marsh Crake.

RANGITAIKI RIVER - LAKE ANIWHENUA

General: This is a hydro dam lake on the Rangitaiki River and is good for waterfowl. Birds likely to be seen here are Scaup, Grey Teal, Grey Duck, Mallard, Black Swan and in winter there is often a White Heron.

How to get there: The Rangitaiki River flows under Highway 2 at Thornton about 23 kms west of Whakatane and about 10 kms east of Matata. At Thornton follow East Bank Road to Edgecumbe and Te Teko. Before Te Teko on Highway 30, turn left (south) into Galatea Road and travel about 8 kms to Lake Matahina. After Te Mahoe follow the signs to Galatea and at Kopuriki look for Lake Aniwhenua.

Target birds: White Heron, Scaup.

OHOPE SPIT

General: This is a breeding area for New Zealand Dotterel and Variable Oystercatcher. Also is a place from which to view the sea for Grey-faced Petrels and Fluttering Shearwaters.

How to get there: After Matata follow Highway 2 to Whakatane. From Whakatane follow the Ohope Beach signs. At Ohope follow right along the waterfront and past the camping ground out on to the spit.

Target birds: Variable Oystercatcher, New Zealand Dotterel.

ROTOMA AND PONGAKAWA DISTRICTS

General: By driving inland from Matata you come to the forests of the Lake Rotoma area which were once habitat for Kokako. However there are still good numbers of bush birds here which include Tomtits and Bellbirds. On nearby Lake Rotoehu there are large populations of waterfowl.

How to get there from Matata: Follow the road behind Matata township which says Manawahe. Past Manawahe turn left on to Matahi Road and follow on to Lake Rotoma. At Highway 30 turn right towards Rotorua and then right again. This leads into Lake Rotoehu. Manawahe Road, which leads from it, soon has forests on each side and it was here that Kokako were once easy to find.

How to get there from Rotorua: If approaching from Rotorua take Highway 30 past Lake Rotoiti. At the Pongakawa - Manawahe sign, after Hongis Track, follow along towards Lake Rotoehu and then turn right up Manawahe Road for 2 kms. Listen here for Kokako, Bellbirds and Whitehead.

Target birds: Kokako (slim chance) and Whiteheads.

PONGAKAWA - ROTOEHU ROAD

How to get there: Follow Manawahe Road up the hill to the Hamilton Road sign and turn left. Travel down to and into Pongakawa Road and along until Rotoehu Road is reached. Here turn right and travel a further 2 kms. Look for a small forestry road here on the left. This was a good place to see Kokako but they may now have gone. Bush birds are still plentiful though.

Target bird: Whitehead.

LAKE ROTOEHU

General: This lake, over the summer months, is full of Black Swans and Paradise Shelduck. It also has Black Shags, Little Shags, Little Black Shags and a range of other waterfowl.

How to get there: From Highway 30, turn east along Pongakawa Road. Travel along until Lake Rotoehu comes into view on your left.

Target birds: Large numbers of Black Swans and Paradise Shelduck.

ROTORUA

LAKE ROTORUA

General: Lake Rotorua provides very good bird-watching in behind the Rotorua Government Gardens. Here large flocks of Scaup rest in the calm waters with Black Swans, Mallards, Grey Ducks and Grey Teal. On a small island in the lake, large numbers of Black Shags, Little Black Shags, and Little Shags roost, often with Paradise Shelduck. Further round near the boat ramp several pairs of Dabchicks can always be seen along with Black-billed Gulls, Red-billed Gulls and Black-backed Gulls. Spotless Crakes and Fernbirds have been recorded from the swampy areas in the adjacent Motutara golf course. At the thermal area behind Tudor Towers and the Polynesian Pools, a colony of Black-billed Gulls nests with some Black-backed Gulls and Red-billed Gulls. This area also regularly records Banded Dotterels.

How to get there: Turn east off Fenton Street into Arawa Street and follow through to the gates which lead to the Tudor Towers bath-house. Follow on past Tudor Towers and you come to the lake.

Target birds: Dabchick, Little Black Shag, Little Shag, Scaup and Black-billed Gull.

ROTORUA - MOKOIA ISLAND

General: Mokoia Island is located in the centre of Lake Rotorua. It has always been part of the Rotorua tourist scene with launches travelling to it several times each day leaving from the lake front at the end of Fenton Street. As a place of birding interest it has only recently become important following the clearance of rats and predators from it and the subsequent introduction of Saddlebacks from Tiri Tiri Island. These birds have done well and can now easily be seen on the island.

The success of the Saddlebacks encouraged the Department of Conservation to introduce Stitchbirds, and birds from Little Barrier Island were taken there to form a nucleus stock. They are now breeding. Weka and North Island Robins have also been established.

Mokoia Island, along with Tiri Tiri Island and Kapiti Island, are the only places where Stitchbirds can be viewed away from Little Barrier Island. Mokoia Island is easier to get to than Tiri Tiri Island as launches leave for it daily. It is also a good place to see the Weka although this bird is not very confiding in this location. The journey to the island is scenic and also provides views of waterfowl and shags. At the island there is a grass area, bush walking tracks, and "Hinemoa Pool" for those who enjoy hot-water bathing.

How to get there: Fenton Street is the major motel and hotel street in Rotorua leading to Whakarewarewa in the south and Lake Rotorua in the north. To get to Mokoia Island follow it in a north direction until Lake Rotorua comes into sight. There is a large carpark there and wharf area.

Target birds: Weka, Robin, Stitchbird, Bellbird, Saddleback.

LAKE OKAREKA

General: This is a place to look for Dabchick, Little Shag, Little Black Shag, Black Swan, Paradise Shelduck, Mallard, Grey Duck, Shoveler, Scaup and Australasian Coot. It is a beautiful place and the nearby forests have good numbers of bush birds.

How to get there: From Rotorua, follow Highway 30 towards Rotorua Airport. At Lynmore turn right up Tarawera Road and follow signposts to Lake Okareka.

Target birds: Dabchick, Shoveler, Scaup, Australasian Coot.

MAMAKU - GALAXY ROAD

General: Galaxy Road leads into the Mamaku pine forests which are a good place to find Robin, Tomtit and Whiteheads. Also, the indigenous forest verge always has Bellbirds and Tui.

How to get there: From Rotorua follow Highway 5 north for 16 kms. After Oturoa Road on the right and Maraeroa Road on the left, watch for a small forestry road called Galaxy Road on the left.

Target birds: Robin, Tomtit, Whitehead, Tui, Bellbird

TAUPO

OPEPE RESERVE - LAKE TAUPO

General: This small forest reserve is situated on the Napier - Taupo road 14 kms from Taupo. The area is historical as here a party of soldiers was disturbed by Maori during the Maori Land Wars and many were killed. They are buried in the forest. A walkway has been constructed to the graves and a further one leads into the forest from near them. The contour of the walkway is flat to easy. The forest walk is noted for a very good population of Bellbirds and Tui which feed on fuchsia nectar and podocarp fruits. Large populations of Whiteheads are also found here. The forest is also noted for large podocarp trees which include rimu, totara, kahikatea and matai.

How to get there: Drive south from Taupo on Highway 1 and turn left on to Highway 5. Follow along for 9 kms until and area of forest comes into view. Birds likely to be seen in this forest include -

New Zealand Falcon	Grey Warbler
New Zealand Pigeon	Fantail
Kaka	Robin
Shining Cuckoo	Tomtit
Long-tailed Cuckoo	Blackbird
Morepork	Silvereye
Kingfisher	Bellbird
Rifleman	Tui
Whitehead	

PORONUI - KAIMANAWA FOREST PARK

General: Walking tracks here lead into very old beech forests, and bush birds, including Rifleman, are soon encountered. Expect the same species as for Opepe.
How to get there: From Opepe follow along Highway 5 for a further 11 kms and turn right (south) into Taharua Road. Follow along and into Clements Mill Road which leads into the Kaimanawa Forest Park.
Target birds: Rifleman, Robin, Tomtit, Whitehead.

LAKE ROTONGAIO

General: This lake has good numbers of waterfowl and is a place to see Bellbirds.
How to get there: From Taupo follow south along Highway 1 to Waitahanui. Where the road leaves the shoreline at Earthquake Gully, instead go straight ahead along the shore and to Lake Rotongaio.
Target birds: Waterfowl and bush birds.

WAIKAREMOANA

WHIRINAKI FOREST

General: Whirinaki is a fine podocarp forest with good numbers of bush birds including Kaka and Yellow-crowned Parakeets. Walking tracks lead into the forests.
How to get there: From Rotorua follow Highway 5 south for 22 kms. Turn left (east) on to Highway 38 which leads to Murupara and Waikaremoana. There are two ways to get into the forest.
Route 1: Turn off the Waikaremoana road at the Minginui signpost after Murupara, and follow down to Minginui Village. Follow walking tracks from here.
Route 2: Enter the forest by a side road which leads into the forest from Highway 38 about 5 kms east of the Minginui signpost.
Target birds: Kaka, Yellow-crowned Parakeet.

LAKE WAIKAREMOANA - HOPURUAHINE STREAM

General: This is a good locality in which to look for Blue Duck. Note that Blue Ducks usually show up in early morning or late afternoon. During the daytime they prefer to hide under the foliage of banks or in the nearby forests.

How to get there: After Minginui, unsealed windy roads follow on to Lake Waikaremoana. After Ruatahuna travel approximately 18 kms until you find Hopuruahine Stream. This stream crosses the road and is signposted. Stop here and walk down the stream and look for Blue Duck. Expect to walk for 1 km.

Target bird: Blue Duck.

LAKE WAIKAREMOANA - ANIWANIWA STREAM

General: This is a further place to try for Blue Ducks.

How to get there: Travel on to the Waikaremoana Park Headquarters, approximately 10 kms further on from the Hopuruahine Stream. Ask at the headquarters about nearby localities of Blue Duck. A short walk along the nearby Waikareiti Track gives a view into the Aniwaniwa Stream where you might see one. The bridge just before the headquarters, over the Aniwaniwa Stream, is another place to look.

Target birds: Blue Duck, Kaka, Yellow-crowned Parakeet, Rifleman.

LAKE WAIKAREMOANA - WAIKAREITI TRACK

General: The Waikareiti track leads up to Lake Waikareiti through some old forest which is very good for bush birds. It is an easy walk and it is a wide and well formed track. Early on it follows the Aniwaniwa Stream where Blue Ducks live. It then bears left into forests where Kaka and Yellow-crowned Parakeets are plentiful. A lush forests with many ferns is then encountered.

How to get there: When approaching the Waikaremoana Park headquarters on Highway 38, after Hopuaruahine Stream, look for the walking track on the left just before the Aniwaniwa Stream is reached.

Target birds: Kaka, Yellow-crowned Parakeet and Rifleman are here among others.

WHAKAKI LAGOON

General: Whakaki Lagoon, which is not far from the sea, is extensive and can be viewed from the main road. A telescope makes viewing easier. Huge flocks of Shoveler can be seen here along with large numbers of Little Black Shags, Black Swans, Paradise Shelduck and Mallards. Sometimes White Heron and Little Egret are also here.

How to get there: From Lake Waikaremoana follow Highway 38 to Wairoa. Then travel north on Highway 2 for about 12 kms until Whakaki Lagoon comes into sight on the right.

Target birds: Little Black Shags, Shoveler, White Heron, Little Egret.

GISBORNE - EAST COAST

TE PUIA SPRINGS

General: The lake at Te Puia Springs is good for waterfowl and can be viewed from Highway 35 just north of the village. Hot springs are found close to the village. Waterfowl, including Black Swan, Paradise Shelduck, Mallard, Grey Duck and Shoveler should be seen. A feature of the lake is the chorus of Bellbird song from lakeside trees.

How to get there: Te Puia Springs is about 10 kms north of Tokomaru Bay which is north of Gisborne.

Target birds: Shoveler, Bellbird.

HAWKES BAY

WHITE PINE BUSH

General: White Pine Bush has a half hour walking track which is sealed and is suitable for paraplegics. The track runs through tall forest. Bush birds are present, mainly New Zealand Pigeon, Grey Warbler, Fantail and Tui.

How to get there: From Napier follow Highway 2 north for about 30 km. White Pine Bush Reserve lies on the left (west) side of the road and is signposted.

LAKE TUTIRA

General: Lake Tutira has very good numbers of waterfowl including one of the largest numbers of Coot to be seen on any lake. Expect also to see Dabchicks, Black Swans and Mallards. Also in this area are Rooks, although continuing eradication programmes have kept the numbers to a minimum.

How to get there: From Napier follow Highway 2 north for about 33 km. Lake Tutira lies on the right (east) side of the road.

Target birds: Dabchick, Australasian Coot.

AHURIRI ESTUARY

General: This is a large tidal area just north of Napier which has good numbers of waders and sometimes rare migrants. It can be observed in two ways - from the Humber Street side of the inner harbour or from the walkway on the northern side of the inner harbour bridge on Meeanee Quay (Highway 2).

How to get there: This estuary is on Highway 2 just north of Napier and south of Napier Airport.

How to get to Humber Street: When driving north on Pandora Road (Highway 2) and before reaching the bridge across the inner harbour, turn left into Humber Street and follow to the end. There is ample parking here and also signs which indicate a walking track.

- **Track 1:** From the parking area a walking track leads out along a spit and this gives good views up the inner harbour and around Pandora Lagoon on the right, and back to the main road.
- **Track 2:** From the same parking area a further track leads west. This track follows around the inner harbour, across the old embankment bridge, across a boardwalk, and back to Highway 2 on the northern side of the inner harbour. From this track there are other lesser tracks leading further up the main outfall channel of the inner harbour. This walk in summer could produce such rarities as Mongolian Dotterel, Whimbrel, Hudsonian Godwit, Marsh Sandpiper, Terek Sandpiper and Little Tern. Resident species include Black Shag, Little Shag, Spotted Shag, White-faced Heron, Mallard, Pied Stilt, Black-backed Gull, Red-billed Gull and Kingfisher. Little Egret and Glossy Ibis have also been recorded here.

How to get to the Meeanee Quay walkway: Instead of turning down Humber Street cross the harbour bridge. Soon after, look for the walkway sign on the left (west). Park further along this road in the Westshore Hotel carpark, and walk back towards the bridge to the walkway.

Target Birds: Golden Plover, Banded Dotterel, Black-fronted Dotterel, Bar-tailed Godwit, Knot, Sharp-tailed Sandpiper, Red-necked Stint.

WESTSHORE WILDLIFE RESERVE - WATCHMAN ROAD

General: There are two lakes here both of which have good numbers of waterfowl. These can either be observed from the causeway between them or from a hide which is accessed along a small side road on the left as you turn into Watchman Road. In the winter the Shoveler here are a colourful sight and there are several pairs of Dabchick.

How to get there: From the Westshore carpark on Highway 2, drive a short distance further north and turn left into Watchman Road besides which is the Westshore Wildlife Reserve.

Target birds: Dabchick, Shoveler.

TUKITUKI RIVER

General: This is a place to look for Black-fronted Dotterels where birds can usually be seen fossicking around the wet puddles of the riverbed.

How to get there: From Napier follow Highway 2 south to Clive. After Clive cross the Tukituki River. Look up the river for dotterels from the bridge. Then follow right into Mill Road and right into Tukituki Road. Follow along near the river and turn right into Tennant Road. From the end of Tennant Road walk to the river.

Target Birds: Banded Dotterel, Black-fronted Dotterel.

MARAETOTARA - MOHI BUSH

General: This area of bush has a good range of bush birds including New Zealand Pigeon, Rifleman, Tomtit and Tui. There are good walking tracks through it.

How to get there: After crossing the Tukituki River on Mill Road turn right (south) into Tukituki Road. Follow south along Tukituki Road and then turn left into Wairamarama Road (sign says to Ocean Beach) just passed the Te Mata bridge where it crosses the Tukituki River. Follow along to Maraetotara Road which is on the right. Where Maretotara Road joins Waipoapoa Road at a T junction, turn right and follow along for 2.2 kms on a gravel road to Mohi Bush. Stop just before Tawa Road and turn left and drive in over a cattle stop to the bush.

How to get there - alternative route: Alternatively you can get to Mohi Bush from Havelock North by following Te Mata Road to the Te Mata bridge. The journey is 36 kms from Havelock North.

Target birds: Rifleman and Tomtit.

WAIRAMARAMA ROAD - ROADSIDE LAKE

How to get there: On Wairamarama Road, just before Maraetotara Road leads off to the right, a large roadside lake can be seen on the left. It is easily viewed from the road and even from the car. It has good numbers of waterfowl including Dabchick, Mute Swan and Shovelers. Black Shag and Little Shag can also be seen there.

Target birds: Dabchick, Mute Swan and Shovelers.

CAPE KIDNAPPERS

General: Cape Kidnappers, which is situated 30 kms east of Napier, is the largest mainland nesting colony of Australasian Gannets in New Zealand with nearly 20,000 birds. For many years it was the only mainland colony.

How to get there by walking: After the Tukituki River, travel to Clifton. From here walk the 8 kms along the beach and then climb the track to the promontory. The climb from the beach to the promontory takes about 40 minutes. Leave Clifton 3 hours after high tide and return from Cape Kidnappers 1.5 hours after low tide. The walk takes about 2.5 hours each way.

How to get there by commercial tour operators: The easiest way to get there is via commercial tour operators. These are -

- Gannet Beach Adventures Ltd: This operator visits the colony via tractor and trailer along the beach. Phone: +64 6 875 0898. Fax: +64 875 0849. Email: gannet.tractor.tours.napier@xtra.co.nz.
- Gannet Safaris Overland Ltd: This operator approaches the colony via Summerlee Station and takes visitors right to the edge of the nesting birds through Summerlee Station. It provides a dramatic final approach up a steep track with the gannets spread before you on arrival. Phone: +64 6 875 0888. Fax: +64 6 875 0893. Write: Summerlee Station, R D 2, Hastings. This tour, which is a 3 hour excursion, departs daily from October to April.

WAIRARAPA

NATIONAL WILDLIFE CENTRE - MOUNT BRUCE

General: This centre is open daily and contains native bush, wildlife ponds, caged native birds and a visitors' centre. It was originally set up as a place to breed rare and endangered bird species and is now opened to the public. Among those bred here since its inception are Brown Teal, Blue Duck, Shore Plover, Black Stilt, Takahe, Saddleback, and Kokako. The surrounding bush areas have native birds including Rifleman and Whiteheads.

How to get there: This centre is situated in the Wairarapa on Highway 2, 28 kms north of Masterton and 13 kms south of Ekatahuna. It is well signposted.

Target birds: Rifleman, Tomtit, Whitehead.

For further details: Phone: +64 6 377 0723. Fax: +64 6 377 2976. Email: jflack@doc.govt.nz   Web: www. mountbruce.doc.govt.nz

MOUNT HOLDSWORTH RESERVE

General: This reserve lies at the foothills of the Tararua Range west of Masterton. Walking tracks lead into the forest from the picnic area where Rifleman, Tomtit and Whitehead can be seen.

How to get there: From Masterton follow Highway 2 south, and cross the Waingawa River. Turn right (west) into Norfolk Road and follow up to the reserve.

Target birds: Rifleman, Tomtit and Whitehead.

LAKE WAIRARAPA

General: The lake domain has walking tracks which lead into swampy places where Bittern, Spotless Crakes, and Marsh Crake have been recorded. Look for waterfowl out on the shallow water which should include Black Swans and Mallards.

How to get there: From Featherston, which is south of Greytown on Highway 2, turn left (east) into Viles Road and then right into Murphy's Line. Follow down and turn right into Lake Domain Road and continue to the parking area.

Target birds: Bittern, Spotless Crake, Marsh Crake.

TARANAKI

PUKEITI RHODODENDRON GARDENS

General: These gardens lie south of New Plymouth on the verge of Mount Taranaki. They are surrounded by native forests which have walking tracks. New Zealand Pigeon, Tui and Bellbird are common. Look also for Rifleman, Tomtit and Whitehead and in summer, Shining Cuckoo and Long-tailed Cuckoo.

How to get there: From New Plymouth's Devon Street, follow Carrington Road for about 29 kms. The gardens are signposted.

Target species: Rifleman, Long-tailed Cuckoo (summer), Tomtit and Whitehead.

PUKEKURA PARK

General: This large park has many walking tracks from which birds can be seen. These birds include New Zealand Pigeon, Shining Cuckoo (summer), Morepork, Kingfisher, Welcome Swallow, Fantail, Grey Warbler, Bellbird, Tui and Silvereye. There are also many of the introduced birds including Hedge Sparrow, Greenfinch, Goldfinch, and Chaffinch. On the park lake are waterfowl.

How to get there: For the main park entrance, follow Liardet Street from Devon Street and go right to the end. Alternatively follow Carrington Road then turn left into Victoria Road. The park is on the left and tracks lead into it.

Target birds: New Zealand Pigeon and Bellbird.

BARRETT DOMAIN

General: This domain has a lake and wetland with good numbers of waterfowl. These include Dabchick, Canada Geese and Shoveler. Bush birds such as New Zealand Pigeon are also here in the forest verges.

How to get there: From Devon Street West turn left (west) into Cutfield Street and follow up to Tukapa Street. Turn right into Roto Street and follow to the end.

Target birds: Dabchick, Shoveler.

PARITUTU CENTENNIAL PARK

General: This park lies to the west of New Plymouth and overlooks Paritutu and the Sugar Loaf Islands. A visitor here at dusk, over the summer months, might hear Flesh-footed Shearwater, White-faced Storm Petrels and Diving Petrels coming into the breeding colonies on the Sugar Loaf Islands.

How to get there: From Devon Street West continue south into South Road and turn right (east) into Ngamotu Road and then left into Paritutu Road.

Target birds: Flesh-footed Shearwater, White-faced Storm Petrel and Diving Petrel.

WANGANUI - MANAWATU

VIRGINIA LAKE - WANGANUI

General: Virginia Lake near Wanganui was one of the first lakes to be colonised by Australasian Coot and many new colonies have spread from it. It also retains two pairs of Mute Swan.

How to get there: From Wanganui follow Highway 3 west towards New Plymouth. Virginia Lake is on the right before you leave the city.

Target birds: Mute Swan, Australiasian Coot.

PALMERSTON NORTH

General: There are two places of interest for birds in Palmerston North. One is the Centennial Lagoon where waterfowl can be seen and the other is the Esplanade where Black-fronted Dotterels are found.

How to get to Centennial Lagoon: First travel south along Fitzherbert Avenue towards Massey University and turn left before the Fitzherbert Bridge. Travel along Hardie Street to Jickle Street and then right and around to the Centennial Lagoon.

Target birds: Mute Swan, Coot.

How to get to the Esplanade: From Fitzherbert Ave travelling south, find Park Road on the right and turn west into it then left into Ruha Street. Then turn right into Dittmer Drive. Stop anywhere along Dittmer Drive and from the stopbank search the Manawatu River for Banded and Black-fronted Dotterel.

Target birds: Black-fronted Dotterel.

MANAWATU ESTUARY

General: This estuary is well known for its shorebirds and especially for its rarities such as Broad-billed Sandpiper, Bairds Sandpiper and Japanese Snipe. It also hosts flocks of Royal Spoonbills and waterfowl.

How to get there: From Highway 1 at Foxton, turn west into Foxton Beach Road. Follow in past the camp ground to the old sailing club and walk to the estuary.

Target birds: Royal Spoonbill, Sharp-tailed Sandpiper, Curlew Sandpiper and Terek Sandpipers.

WELLINGTON

KAPITI ISLAND

General: Kapiti Island, which is 2040 hectares in size, rising to 547 metres above sea level, lies off the west coast of the North Island opposite Paraparaumu Beach, about 55 kms north of Wellington and 10 kms from the mainland. It is bush covered and of rough terrain but is tracked to the summit. Visitors are allowed to walk along these tracks and also to a lagoon on the north end of the island.

The island is now free of bird predators such as possums (*Trichosurus vulpecula*) and the Norway rat (*Rattus norvegicus*) after extensive eradication programmes. Since then Takahe, Stitchbird and Saddleback have been released on the island and their numbers are increasing. A healthy population of over 1100 Little Spotted Kiwi is also found here and Weka are a common.

How to get there: Transport to the island is by boat from Paraparaumu Beach. From Highway 1 follow Kapiti Road (west) from Paraparaumu town to the beach. Visitors are required to wade through the sea to board. The same applies for landing at the island. To stop the ship rat (*Rattus rattus*) from getting on to the island, arriving boats must be vermin free and bags are inspected.

Birds likely to be seen on the island include -

Little Spotted Kiwi	Yellow-crowned Parakeet
Paradise Shelduck	Red-crowned Parakeet
Brown Teal	Shining Cuckoo (summer)
Grey Duck	Long-tailed Cuckoo (summer)
Harrier	Morepork
Weka	Kingfisher
Takahe	Whitehead
Pukeko	Grey Warbler
Variable Oystercatcher	Fantail
Pied Stilt	Tomtit
Black-backed Gull	Robin
Red-billed Gull	Silvereye
White-fronted Tern	Bellbird
Caspian Tern	Tui
New Zealand Pigeon	Stitchbird
Kaka	Saddleback
	Kokako

For further details: Contact Kapiti Island Alive, Kapiti Nature Lodge. Phone/fax: +64 6 364 8818. Write: P O Box 28, Otaki, New Zealand. Email: john.barrett@xtra.co.nz.

NGA MANU SANCTUARY

General: This small bird reserve, situated at the north end of Waikanae Beach 55 kms north of Wellington on the west coast, is comprised of waterfowl ponds and lakes as well as some caged birds and a kiwi house. Tracks lead into some tall native forest.

How to get there: Turn west off Highway 1 at Waikanae town and travel down Te Moana Road towards the beach. Turn right along Ngarara Road and travel for 3 kms until a signpost for Nga Manu is found. This reserve is open every day of the week.

Target birds: Spotless Crake, Brown Teal.

For further details: Phone/Fax: +64 4 293 4131. Write: P O Box 126, Waikanae. Email: ngamanu@clear.net.nz.

WAIKANAE ESTUARY

General: This estuary, which has shorebirds, Royal Spoonbill and waterfowl, is at the south end of Waikanae Beach.

How to get there from Waikanae: From Waikanae town on Highway 1, travel down Te Moana Road towards Waikanae Beach. Turn left into Waimea Road and follow through to Tutere Street. Turn south and follow to the end. Alternatively from Waimea Road, the estuary can be reached by turning left into Queens Road.

How to get there from Paraparaumu: Follow down Kapiti Road to the end and then turn right into Manly Street and follow to end where there is carparking.

Target birds: Little Shag, Little Black Shag, Royal Spoonbill, Variable Oystercatcher, Wrybill, Bar-tailed Godwit.

WAIKANAE - WAIMEHA LAGOON

General: This small lagoon is a good waterfowl habitat.

How to get there: From Waikanae town on Highway 1, travel down Te Moana Road. Turn left into Waimea Road and then left into Ngapaki Street. Travel to near the end. A small sign near the bend in the road, points left (south) into the Waimeha Lagoon and a hide.

Target birds: Dabchick, Shoveler, Scaup.

WELLINGTON - KARORI WILDLIFE SANCTUARY TRUST

General: This sanctuary, which comprises the forest surrounds of the old Karori Reservoir in Wellington, is 2.5 kms from the centre of the city. It has been developed by the Karori Sanctuary Wildlife Trust, a private community group, whose aim is to maintain a "mainland island" in the city devoid of predators. The Trust has fenced the 250 hectare area with a predator proof 8.5 km long fence. The fence was made to their design and keeps out 14 undesirable mammals including cats, possums, stoats, ferrets, weasels and rats. Introduction of endangered bird species has commenced with the Little Spotted Kiwi and Weka being put there. This work will continue.

How to get there: From the centre of Wellington travel up to Tinakori Road towards the suburb of Karori and then into Glenmore Street. After the Karori tunnel, turn left into Waiapu Street and follow to the end.

Target birds: Weka, New Zealand Pigeon, Tui.
For further details: Phone: +64 4 475 9300. Fax: +64 4 475 3791. Write: Karori Wildlife Sanctuary Trust, 31, Waiapu Street, Wellington.
Email: kwst@mail.netlink.co.nz. Web: http/www.sanctuary.org.nz

SOUTH ISLAND

MARLBOROUGH

QUEEN CHARLOTTE SOUND

General: Queen Charlotte Sound is of interest to birders. Two important species of birds are found here, the King Shag and the South Island Saddleback. King Shags can be seen near the entrance of the sound and at White Rocks just outside the entrance, while Saddlebacks are found on Motuara Island and Pickersgill Island. Bush birds can be seen on Blumine Island and these include Rifleman, Brown Creeper and Robin.

How to get there: Excursions to see these birds are run by Dolphin Watch Marlborough. Visitors to the South Island on the inter-island ferries arrive at Picton via Queen Charlotte Sound. Dolphin Watch Marlborough has its offices next to the railway station in Picton. It runs two excursions on the sound daily showing dolphins and the birds of the area.

Target birds: King Shag, South Island Saddleback.

For further details: Phone: +64 3 573 7906. Fax: +64 3 573 8040.
Write: Les and Zoe Battersby, P O Box 197.
Email: dolphin.Marlborough@xtra.co.nz.
Web: www.dolphinwatchmarlborough.co.nz.

MOUNT STOKES

General: Mount Stokes is located at the northern end of Queen Charlotte Sound north of Kenepuru Head. The Mount Stokes track leads in from Grahams Lookout. This is a place to see Yellowheads in the north of the South Island.

How to get there: From Picton follow Queen Charlotte Drive to Linkwater which is 20 kms from Picton. Turn right (north) up Kenepuru Road. Mount Stokes is 50 kms up this road and 25 kms north of Portage, which is a hotel, wharf and boat marina.

Target bird: Yellowheads and bush birds.

PELORUS SOUND - FROM HAVELOCK

General: An excursion on Pelorous Sound could give views of King Shags and seabirds.

How to get there: From Picton follow either Highway 1 to Blenheim and then Highway 6 to Havelock or travel there via Queen Charlotte Drive. At Havelock enquire at the information centre about the hiring of a boat for travel on Pelorus Sound. There are motels in Havelock.

Target bird: Westland Black Petrel and King Shag.

PELORUS SOUND - MAUD ISLAND

General: Maud Island is situated to the north-west of Pelorus Sound. It is predator-free so Takahe and Kakapo have been released there. Research work, including the establishment of a Fluttering Shearwater breeding colony on the island, has recently been undertaken with some success. The island has a resident manager who runs a few sheep near the homestead. Some of the work, such as supplementary feeding of Kakapo and weed control, is done by volunteers.

How to get there: To get to Maud Island, permission from the Department of Conservation is required. (See later for details.) A boat would then need to be chartered from Havelock.

Target birds: Takahe, New Zealand Pigeon, and Long-tailed Cuckoo.

For further details: Phone: +64 3 546 9335. Fax: +64 9 548 2805. Write: Department of Conservation, Private Bag 5, Nelson. Web: www.kakaporecovery.org.nz.

PELORUS BRIDGE

General: Pelorus Bridge is on Highway 6 where it crosses the Pelorus River between Havelock and Nelson, 20 kms west of Havelock. It is a good place to view Weka, Brown Creeper and other bush birds.

How to get there: From Havelock follow Highway 6 for 20 kms. Tracks lead into the lower hills of the Richmond Ranges. Look for Cirl Bunting in areas of pasture from here to Nelson.

Target birds: Weka, Tomtit, Brown Creeper and Cirl Bunting.

ST ARNAUD - MT ROBERTS - LAKE ROTOITI

General: This area is accessed off Highway 63 and is about 90 kms from Blenheim. It is rich in birdlife and in particular, Scaup, Kaka, Robins, Tomtits and Bellbirds. The Mount Roberts track, which leads up from Lake Rotoiti, is a good place for birds, whch are also very plentiful even around the lakeside cottages.

How to get there: Follow Highway 63 to St Arnaud. The lake is signposted.

Target birds: Kaka, Robin and Brown Creeper.

NELSON - DUN MOUNTAIN

General: This mountain is located behind Nelson and provides a one day walking excursion into forests which have good numbers of bush birds including Rifleman and Brown Creeper.

How to get there: From Trafalgar Square in the centre of Nelson, turn left into Nile Street East then into Tasman Street and Brook Street. The walking track up Mount Dun leads from the Brook River Valley. It is of gentle grade.

Target birds: New Zealand Pigeon, Rifleman, Robin, Tomtit, Brown Creeper, Bellbird, Tui.

NELSON - WAIMEA ESTUARY

General: The Waimea Estuary, which is south-west of Nelson, is accessed from Richmond.

How to get there: From Nelson follow Highway 6. At Richmond turn right (west) into Queen Street and follow to the estuary. Waders can be viewed from this point.

Target birds: Golden Plover, Bar-tailed Godwit and Sharp-tailed Sandpiper.

NELSON - RABBIT ISLAND

General: Waimea Estuary to the west of the bridge often has waders roosting near the in-shore shoreline. The Rabbit Island bridge provides a good vantage point for viewing them.

How to get there: From Richmond follow Highway 60 to Appleby. This crosses the Waimea River. After Appleby turn right (north) for Rabbit Island. After the bridge turn left into Tic Toc Road and look for estuary vantage points.

Target birds: White Heron, Royal Spoonbill, Golden Plover, Banded Dotterel, Bar-tailed Godwit.

MOTUEKA

General: Motueka is 33 kms along the coast from Richmond. It is an extensive estuary made up of the Moutere inlet and the Motueka sandspit, which encloses a large area of mudflat which is used by waders.

How to get to Moutere Inlet: From Highway 60, turn right (north) at the first round-about before entering the town and proceed across the causeway. Turn right into the road which leads to the fish factory and continue to the ramp. View from here.

How to get to Motueka Sandspit: From the causeway turn left into Beach Road and travel along until the sandspit comes into view. Birds roost near the western end.

Target birds: Royal Spoonbill, Banded Dotterel, Bar-tailed Godwit and Turnstone.

BLENHEIM - WAIRAU LAGOON

General: Wairau Lagoon lies to the east of Blenheim where the Wairau River flows into the sea. Numerous coastal birds can be found here including the Royal Spoonbill.

How to get to the northern side: At Tuamarina on Highway 1, 19 kms south of Picton, turn left (east) at Thomas Road just south of the Tuamarina and head east. Then follow Wairau Bar Road to the end.

How to get to the southern side: From Blenheim follow Highway 1 to Riverlands. After a further 6 kms turn left (east) into Redwood Pass Road and then left into Big Lagoon Road. A track which leads out to the boulder bank runs through private land but the lagoon can be viewed prior to this.

Target bird: Royal Spoonbill.

LAKE ELTERWATER

General: This small lake lies beside Highway 1 about 16 kms past Seddon and after Lake Grassmere. There are two places to view it from. One is a layby area towards the middle of the lake while the other is a grassy hill at the south end. Look for Hoary-headed Grebes here, which, although known to have bred in New Zealand, have not been seen for some years. Also look for the Chestnut-breasted Shelducks which were sighted here in March 2000 along with immature birds. Australian Little Grebes, which are resident on Far North Lakes and near Timaru, have also been recorded here. Use a telescope for viewing.

How to get there: Follow Highway 1 south of Blenheim and watch for it on the left after Seddon.

Target birds: Hoary-headed Grebe, Australian Little Grebe, Chestnut-breasted Shelduck.

KAIKOURA - PELAGIC BIRDING

General: Kaikoura is a seaside town about 135 kms south of Blenheim on Highway 1. It has become well known for its whale and dolphin watching expeditions. Birding expeditions are also part of the Kaikoura scene enhanced by the coastline being close to the edge of the continental shelf with its up-swellings of rich nutrients and sea-life from deep ocean trenches. The result is that seabirds are handier to the coast here than in most parts of New Zealand.

How to get there: Follow Highway 1 south from Blenheim.

Birds likely to be seen in these waters include -

Wandering Albatross	Broad-billed Prion
Northern Royal Albatross	Fairy Prion
Southern Royal Albatross	Grey Petrel
Black-browed Mollymawk	Black Petrel
Grey-headed Mollymawk	Westland Black Petrel
Yellow-nosed Mollymawk	White-chinned Petrel
Bullers Mollymawk	Flesh-footed Shearwater
Shy Mollymawk	Bullers Shearwater
Salvins Mollymawk	Pink-footed Shearwater
Chatham Island Mollymawk	Sooty Shearwater
Light-mantled Sooty Albatross	Huttons Shearwater
Southern Giant Petrel	Fluttering Shearwater
Northern Giant Petrel	Short-tailed Shearwater
Antarctic Fulmar	Wilsons Storm Petrel
Cape Pigeon	Grey-backed Storm Petrel
Grey-faced Petrel	White-faced Storm Petrel
White-headed Petrel	Common Diving Petrel
Mottled Petrel	

Other species: There are also shags, gulls and terns close to the shore. Near the town South Island Pied Oystercatcher, Variable Oystercatcher, Pied Stilt and Banded Dotterel can be found on the rock shelf to the south.

Best viewing months: May to September are considered the best months when it is not uncommon to see between 20 to 30 species of seabirds. Summer can also offer good numbers, although some species are nesting to the south at this time.

Target birds: Antarctic Fulmar, White-headed Petrel, Mottled Petrel, Grey Petrel, Pink-footed Shearwater, Huttons Shearwater.

For further details: Phone: +64 3 319 6777. Fax: + 64 3 319 6534. Write: "Ocean Wings Pelagic Birdwatching", 58 West End, Kaikoura, New Zealand. Email: info@oceanwings.co.nz.
Web: www.oceanwings.co.nz.

OARO - GOOSE BAY ROCK STACKS

General: These rock stacks lie just off the coast. They provide a spectacle of Spotted Shags, especially late in the day. View from Highway 1. If viewing in late afternoon look out to sea for seabirds and in particular for Huttons Shearwaters which might be circling before coming in to their nesting burrows after dark.

How to get there: From Kaikoura travel 10 kms south on Highway 1.

Target birds: Huttons Shearwater and Spotted Shags.

NORTH CANTERBURY

ST ANNES LAGOON

General: St Annes Lagoon is a bird-watcher's gem being rich in waterfowl and also very scenic. Important birds here are Bittern and Spotless Crake, crakes now having been found to be breeding in the wet areas around the lake. Australian Little Grebe and Cape Barren Geese have also been recorded here.

How to get there: St Annes Lagoon is situated 4 kms north of the town of Cheviot in North Canterbury on Highway 1. It is on the west side of the road and signposted.

Target birds: Australian Little Grebe, Australasian Bittern, Cape Barren Goose, Marsh Crake, Spotless Crake.

CANTERBURY

CHRISTCHURCH – HAGLEY PARK

General: The main features of this park are its large trees and the Avon River which flows through it. Birdlife is mainly of exotic species with the Little Owl being an important one. Grey Warblers, Fantails and Silvereyes will also be seen and sometimes. Bellbirds are possible. Mallards and gulls live along the Avon River.

How to get there: From Ferry Road turn into Moorhouse Road and follow in a southerly direction to Deans Ave. The park is located to the west of the main central area of Christchurch. It can be accessed from many roads including Moorhouse Ave, Lincoln Road and Riccarton Road.

Target bird: Little Owl.

CHRISTCHURCH - AVON-HEATHCOTE ESTUARY

General: This estuary receives the waters from the Avon River to the north and the Heathcote River to the south. It is a large estuary with the better birding sites being access via the New Brighton spit.

How to get there: From New Brighton Road find Rockinghorse Road which runs the full length of the New Brighton spit. At the end of this road walk through Stilt Lane to a high tide roost on the estuary side. While there also visit the ocean beach side of the spit.

Target birds: Royal Spoonbills, South Island Pied Oystercatchers, Banded Dotterels, Bar-tailed Godwits, Caspian Tern and White-fronted Terns.

CHRISTCHURCH – SUMNER

General: Sumner occupies the south head of Avon-Heathcote Estuary. The rocky promontories further south have nesting Spotted Shags.

How to get there: From Sumner follow Scarborough Road up the hill from the Sumner waterfront. Turn left at the top. A grass track leads to the cliff edge where birds can be seen nesting on cliff ledges.

LAKE ELLESMERE - EMBANKMENT ROAD

General: Lake Ellesmere at the end of Embankment Road contains large mudflats which always have a good number of wading birds. Vagrant species such as Little Whimbrel, Black-tailed Godwit and Greenshank have been seen from time to time in this general area.

How to get there: From Christchurch follow Highway 1 south. Access to the lake is via Embankment Road. From Highway 1 turn left (east) into Springs Road near Wigram Air Base. Follow down past Lincoln College to the end and turn left into Davidson Road and then right into Embankment Road. Follow to the end and then walk in through a gate to the lakeshore. Permission to enter is not required.

Target birds: Golden Plover, Wrybill, Turnstone, Curlew Sandpiper, Sharp-tailed Sandpiper and Red-necked Stint.

LAKE FORSYTH

General: Lake Forsyth is located on Highway 75 which leads to Akaroa. Large numbers of waterfowl can be seen here and especially large numbers of Canada Geese during the January moulting season. Crested Grebes are also regular visitors.

How to get there: After passing the north end of Lake Ellesmere and the Kaituna Lagoon on Highway 75, when travelling to Akaroa, watch for a large expanse of water on the right.

Target bird: Crested Grebe.

BANKS PENINSULA - HINEWAI RESERVE

General: This is a good location for bush birds and in particular for Brown Creeper.

How to get there: The Hinewai Reserve is a ten minute drive from Akaroa. Follow Long Bay Road which is about 4 kms before Akaroa. This road leads east. About 500 metres after the Summit Road junction follow along Long Bay Road to the reserve entrance on the right. Tracks lead into the reserve just before the Long Bay and Goughs Bay road junctions.

Target birds: Rifleman, Tomtit, Brown Creeper, Bellbird.

AKAROA HARBOUR

General: To see White-flippered Penguins and maybe Hectors Dolphin travel to Akaroa Harbour.

How to get there: Follow Highway 75 to Akaroa.

Target bird: White-flippered Penguins.

For further details: Phone: +64 3 328 9078. Fax: +64 3 328 8699. Email: info@blackcat.co.nz.

LAKE ELLESMERE - LAKESIDE

General: At Lakeside a small population of Mute Swan survives and there are good numbers of waterfowl. White Heron and Little Egret have also been recorded here in winter.

How to get there: From Highway 1 at Dunsandel turn left to Leeston then take the road to Lakeside. Before Lakeside turn left into Timberyard Road which leads to the Aquatic Centre.

Target birds: White Heron, Little Egret, Mute Swan.

TIMARU - WASHDYKE LAGOON

General: This is a good waterfowl lagoon which also has terns, Pied Stilts, South Island Pied Oystercatchers and an occasional Wrybill.

How to get to the northern end: From Highway 1, north of Timaru, turn east at the Washdyke Creek bridge. Follow until the lagoon comes into view.

How to get to the southern end: For the southern end, turn east into Bridge Street and soon after scan the lagoon from the road. Waterfowl will be seen although a telescope is usually required.

SOUTH CANTERBURY

WAIMATE - LAKE WAINONO

General: Lake Wainono is a coastal lagoon approximately 35 kms south of Timaru and 9 kms north of Waimate. It is known for its waterfowl and waders and for rarities which turn up from time to time.

How to get there: From Highway 1 at Studholm follow Foleys Road eastwards into Hannaton Road and turn right into Poingdestres Road. Stop at the gate and walk out to the shingle bank. Turn left along a track inside a stop-bank. Walk for 200 metres to the seaward end of the stopbanks.

Target birds: Cattle Egret, Wrybill, Little Tern, White-winged Black Tern.

WAITAKI RIVER-MOUTH

General: The Waitaki river-mouth is about 20 kms south of Waimate and about 14 kms north of Oamaru.

How to get there: At Glenavy on Highway 1, turn east into Fisheries Road and follow to end.

Target birds: Spotted Shag, Little Shag, Canada Goose.

OAMARU - PENQUIN LOCALITIES

General: These localities are found on the foreshore of Oamaru and are places where the Blue Penguin and the Yellow-eyed Penguin can be viewed without an excessive amount of travel. The Blue Penguin locality is a community project and is set up in an unused old quarry with the penguins nesting in artificial nestboxes. There is an admission charge to evening viewing.

How to get to the Blue Penguin locality: From Thames Street, the main road in Oamaru, or from Highway 1, turn eastwards towards the coast at the Wansbeck Street junction and then find Tyne Street and Waterfront Road. Follow this along to the end of the breakwater. The Blue Penguin colony is located at the base of the Breakwater at the end of Waterfront Road. While in Oamaru try to find Cirl Bunting on the racecourse north of the town past Redcastle Road.

For further details: Email: obpc@penguin.net.nz.
Web: www.penguin.net.nz.

How to get to the Yellow-eyed Penguin locality: From Highway 1 turn eastwards to the coast at Wansbeck Street and into Tyne Street. Then left into Bushy Beach Road and follow along until the end. The Yellow-eyed Penguin colony is on Bushy Beach. Note that Yellow-eyed Penguins will not come ashore if people are in sight. Also look for seabirds from this place.

Target birds: Yellow-eyed Penguins and Blue Penguins.

OAMARU - ALL DAY BAY

General: All Day Bay, about 13 kms south of Oamaru near Kakanui, has a waterfowl lagoon just opposite the beach carparking area.

How to get there: From Highway 1 turn left (east) at Maheno and follow to Kakanui and then turn south. There are many side roads leading to it from Highway 1 but the coastal road from Oamaru is probably the easiest.

Target birds: Royal Spoonbill, Grey Duck, Grey Teal and Shoveler.

SHAG POINT

General: Shag Point is 8 kms north of Palmerston, at the south end of Katiki Beach. It is a good place to try and see seabirds from the land and it is not too far from Highway 1. It is also a place to see Yellow-eyed Penguins. Look for the Yellow-eyed Penguin information board.

How to get there: Turn east from Highway 1 at the Shag Point sign and travel to end.

Target birds: Yellow-eyed Penguin, Sooty Shearwater and Stewart Island Shag.

INLAND CANTERBURY

ALFORD FOREST

General: This forest is inland from Ashburton. It has good walking tracks and good numbers of bush birds.

How to get there: Follow the Ashburton - Stavely road. It is signposted from Stavely.

Target birds: Rifleman, Tomtit, Bellbird.

LAKE CLEARWATER - LAKE CAMP

General: These lakes are found in a remote but attractive location and have Crested Grebes.

How to get there: From Stavely follow down to Mount Somers and turn right into Ashburton Gorge Road. Follow up to Lake Clearwater and to Lake Camp.

Target bird: Crested Grebe.

PEEL FOREST

General: This forest is north of Geraldine on the south side of the Rangitata River. It is similar to Alford Forest being an attractive beech forest.

How to get there: From Highway 1 follow the Arundel sign after crossing the Rangitata River.

Target birds: New Zealand Pigeon, Tomtit and Bellbird.

TEKAPO

General: Tekapo is situated approximately 100 kms west of Timaru. It is noted for two very good birding spots, Lake Alexandrina and Cass River. Lake Alexandrina is an easy place to see Crested Grebes and other waterfowl while the Cass River is a good place to see Wrybill and Black Stilt.

- **How to get to Lake Alexandrina:** From Timaru follow Highway 8 through the Burke Pass to Tekapo. Then drive south on Highway 8 and turn right at the Lake Alexandrina signpost. Further along this road a signpost on the left (south) directs you in over a rough road to the south end of the lake. Crested Grebe are frequently seen here along with other waterfowl.

Target bird: Crested Grebe.

- **How to get to the Cass River:** To get to the Cass River continue on to Lake McGregor and then after a further 10 kms the river is reached. Walk down from the bridge towards Lake Tekapo. Here Wrybill may be found in the spring months breeding among the river pebbles.

Target birds: Wrybill, Black Stilt.

Other birds: Of interest in this general area is the Chukor which is known from the rough country around the Mount John Observatory and towards Lake McGregor. Pipits and Hedge Sparrow are also common.

TWIZEL

General: At Twizel Black Stilts are bred in captivity.

How to get there: Twizel is located south of Lake Tekapo on Highway 8.

For further details about Black Stilts: Phone: +64 3 435 0802. Fax: +64 3 435 0852. Write: Department of Conservation, Wairepo Road, Twizel. Email: kakivisitorhide@doc.govt.nz,

TWIZEL – OHAU RIVER

General: This is a frequent place where Black Stilts might be seen. Search the river from the main road bridge. If birds cannot be seen from the bridge, walk downstream for about 1 km.

How to get there: Drive south from Twizel on Highway 8, for about 5 kms, to the Ohau River.

Target bird: Black Stilt.

LAKE BENMORE

General: This is another Black Stilt locality not far from Twizel.

How to get there: Drive south from Twizel on Highway 8 and turn left after the Ohau River bridge. This is the first road going south. This road leads into Lake Benmore. Drive in past B and C power stations. After C power station follow a left-hand track which leads to the lake edge. This sometimes has a pair of Black Stilts.

Target bird: Black Stilt.

AHURIRI RIVER

General: This locality is south of Twizel and is another Black Stilt locality.

How to get there: About 14 kms south of Clearburn, where Highway 8 crosses the Ahuriri River, is a place to look for a pair of Black Stilts and other waterfowl.

Target birds: Paradise Shelduck, Grey Duck, Banded Dotterel, Black Stilt.

LAKE HAYES - QUEENSTOWN

General: Lake Hayes is 14 kms from Queenstown towards Arrowtown. There are good waterfowl populations here including Australasian Coot and Scaup. Marsh Crake and Bittern have been recorded in the rush verges and Crested Grebe have been known to breed here.

How to get there: From Queenstown travel to Frankton and turn left on to the Lake Hayes road. The lake is signposted.

Target birds: Crested Grebe, Bittern and Marsh Crake.

OTAGO

HAWKSBURY LAGOON

General: Hawksbury Lagoon is 14 kms south of Palmerston at Waikouaiti. Waterfowl are found here and Chestnut-breasted Shelduck have been recorded. The embankments enclosing the lagoon are walkable.

How to get there: From Highway 1, follow Beach Road and then Scotia Street.

Target birds: White Heron, Little Egret, Chestnut-breasted Shelduck.

KARITANE POINT

General: Karitane Point is about 17 kms south of Palmerston. It is another locality where seabirds can sometimes be seen from the mainland.

How to get there: After the Waikouaiti River on Highway 1, turn east and continue to Karitane. From the Karitane Domain follow the walking tracks to the coast and look for seabirds.

Target Bird: Shy Mollymawk, Sooty Shearwater and Spotted Shag.

OTAGO HARBOUR

General: Boat excursions on the harbour can take birders out into good seabirding waters beyond the Taiaroa Heads. Here Royal Albatrosses and mollymawks can be viewed along with shearwaters and petrels. Yellow-eyed Penguins, Stewart Island Shags and Spotted Shags are also likely to be seen.

How to get there: Follow Highway 1 to Dunedin.

Target birds: Yellow-eyed Penguin, Royal Albatross, Shy Mollymawk, Southern Giant Petrel, White-chinned Petrel, Stewart Island Shag.

For further details: Phone: +64 3 477 4276. Fax: +64 3 477 4216. Write: Monarch Otago Harbour Cruises, P O Box 102, Dunedin.

Email: monarch@wildlife.co.nz.   Web: www.wildlife.co.nz.

DUNEDIN - ARAMOANA:

General: Aramoana is east of Port Chalmers on the north side of the Otago Harbour.

How to get there: From Dunedin follow Highway 88 to Port Chalmers. Then travel on until the beach is reached. Look for seabirds from the Aramoana Mole.

Target bird: White-chinned Petrel.

TAIAROA HEADS - PENGUIN LOCALITIES

General: There are several commercial operators in this area who take people to see Yellow-eyed Penguins and there are several commercial viewing places towards the end of the peninsula at which to see penguins. Commercial operators include -

- Wild South - which visits "Penguin Place Conservation Reserve" at Pipikaretu Beach. Here you get within close distance of the birds.
- Southlight - where you collect a key and enter a gate near the Taiaroa Heads. From here you drive to a viewing platform and watch the birds returning from the sea. Southlight does not require bookings. There is an entry charge. It is located just past Pakihau Road almost at the end of the peninsula and a short distance from the Royal Albatross colony at Taiaroa Heads. It is signposted.
- Wings of Kotuku - which tours to Sandfly Bay.
- Morning Magic - which tours to Sandfly Bay.

Penguin Place direct: Phone: +64 3 478 0286. Fax: +64 3 478 0257. Web: www.penguin.net.nz

How to get there: From Princes Street in Dunedin, follow south and into Anderson Bay Road and then turn left (north) into Portobello Road. This road runs along the southern side of the Otago Harbour to the Taiaroa Heads.

Target bird: Yellow-eyed Penguin.

For further details: Enquire at the Dunedin Visitors' Information Centre, 48 The Octagon, Dunedin. Phone: +64 3 474 3300. Fax: +64 3 474 3311.

PAPANUI INLET - HOOPERS INLET

General: These inlets, which are on the south side of Otago Peninsula, are good for birds. Birds regularly seen here are - White-faced Heron, Black Swan, Canada

Geese, Paradise Shelduck, Mallard, Grey Duck, Grey Teal, Shoveler, Pukeko, Golden Plover, Banded Dotterel and Turnstone. Rifleman and Brown Creeper are in the roadside verges.

How to get there: Travel along Portobello Road and at Weir Road detour to Papanui Inlet and to Hoopers Inlet.

Target birds: Golden Plovers and Turnstones.

SANDFLY BAY

General: The Sandfly Bay Yellow-eyed Penguin colony is located on the eastern side of the Otago Peninsula. This place suits those wanting to look for these birds away from the commercial places. It does involve some walking.

How to get there: From Princes Street in Dunedin follow south and into Anderson Bay Road and then turn left (north) into Portobello Road. This road runs along the southern side of the Otago Harbour to the Taiaroa Heads. From Portobello Road turn right (east) into Shore Street and then left into Sommerville Street. Turn right (east) into Every Street and follow along to Highcliff Road. Travel along here for approximately 12 kms until Sealpoint Road is met on the right. Follow to the end. Walk down for some distance over the sandhills to a hide.

Target bird: Yellow-eyed Penguin.

TAIAROA HEADS - ALBATROSS COLONY

General: Taiaroa Heads is located at the end of the Otago Peninsula on the southern shores of the harbour, 30 kms from Dunedin. The drive to it is mostly along the edge of the harbour where some shore-birds are also visible from the roadside. The Heads are a mainland breeding colony for a small number of Northern Royal Albatrosses. The nesting area has been fenced off for their protection and the area opened up in a controlled way for visitors. There is a visitors' centre, and some distance from this, up a steep track, is the observatory. From the observatory the albatrosses, and a large colony of Stewart Island Shags, with some Spotted Shags, can be observed.

How to get there: From Princes Street in Dunedin, follow south and into Anderson Bay Road and then turn left (north) into Portobello Road. This road runs along the southern side of the Otago Harbour to the Taiaroa Heads and to the Royal Albatross breeding colony.

Target species: Royal Albatross.

For further details: Phone: +64 3 478 0499. Fax: +64 3 478 0575.
Email: reservations@albatrosses.com.
Web: www.albatrosses.com.

BERWICK SWAMP - SINCLAIR WETLANDS

General: At Sinclair Wetlands there is an information centre and a place for viewing a large wetland and expanse of open water which has all the common species of waterfowl. Fernbirds live in the verges.

How to get there: From Highway 1 at Henley, south of Dunedin, turn west at the Berwick sign. At Berwick follow the signs to Sinclair Wetlands via Shaw Road and PrenticeRoad.

Target species: Fernbird.

SOUTHLAND

NUGGET POINT

General: This rugged coastal area is on the east coast, south of Dunedin. It is another place to look for Yellow-eyed Penguins. Also look for seabirds from the light-house at Nugget Point, especially Shy and Bullers Mollymawks and Sooty Shearwaters. There are also seals on the beach.

How to get there: Travel south from Balclutha on Highway 92. Turn left at the Otanomomo and Paretai sign-posts and follow on to Molyneux Bay and Kaka Point. Park before the Nugget Point light-house carpark, not at the light-house carpark. Walk into a hide above Roaring Bay.

Target birds: Yellow-eyed Penguin and Shy Mollymawk.

CATLINS FOREST PARK - BERESFORD RANGE

General: This park is located off Highway 92 south of Owaka, the scenic road to Invercargill. The major bird of interest here is the Yellowhead which can sometimes be seen after about a 15 minutes walk. Brown Creepers and other bush birds are also seen here.

How to get there: After Nugget Point travel on to Owaka and then south for approximately 12 kms. Turn right (west) up Puketiro Station Road and then left down Aurora Creek Road until the camping ground is seen. From the camping ground, walking tracks lead into the forest after crossing the river.

Target birds: Brown Creeper, Yellowhead.

CATLINS FOREST PARK - OWAKA VALLEY

General: Yellowheads can be found here in the riverflat areas of forest. Also look for Yellow-crowned Parakeet, Red-crowned Parakeet, Shining Cuckoo and Long-tailed Cuckoo.

How to get there: From Owaka on Highway 92, follow Owaka Valley Road towards Clinton and the Catlins State Forest Park. Turn left into Chloris Pass Road and drive to top of hill where good numbers of Brown Creeper live in roadside scrub. Next, at the bottom of the hill, turn left into the Wisp camp ground near the top of the Catlins River Walk.

Target Birds: Yellowhead, Brown Creeper.

CURIO BAY - SLOPE POINT

General: This area lies on the south coast of the South Island and east of Invercargill. It has a petrified forest on its shoreline which attracts a lot of visitors. It is also a very good place from which to view seabirds. Sooty Shearwaters in particular are very abundant off the coastline.

How to get there: From the Balclutha to Invercargill road, Highway 92, turn left (south) at Tokanui and take the Slope Point Road. It is signposted to the coast.

Target bird: Sooty Shearwater.

WAITUNA LAGOON

General: This is a shorebird lagoon which regularly records rarities.

How to get there: Travel east from Invercargill on the Fortrose road and after 14 kms turn right at Kapuka. Travel down Kapuka South Road and then left into Hodgson Road. At Kapuka South turn right down Waituna Lagoon Road until the inner beach is reached. Then travel west along by the shore to the end of the inland arm.

Target birds: Turnstone, Red-necked Stint, Terek Sandpiper.

AWARUA BAY

General: This is a good habitat for shorebirds and the swampy verges have Fernbirds.

How to get there: From Invercargill follow Highway 1, the road to Bluff, south and then turn into Tiwai Road. Before crossing the causeway to the Tiwai smelter turn left. The bay lies to the south of the road.

Target birds: Shore-birds, Fernbird.

GREENHILLS BUSH

General: This is an accessible area of forest about 4 kms from Highway 1 and about 10 kms before Bluff. It has Tomtits and Brown Creeper.

How to get there: From Invercargill follow south on Highway 1 to Bluff. At Greenhills, about 22 kms from Invercargill, turn right (west) into Omaui Road and follow along until an area of bush is found on the left.

Target birds: Rifleman, Tomtit, Brown Creeper.

STEWART ISLAND

General: Stewart Island is bush-covered with a small fishing and tourist-based population of about 500 people living in the town of Oban. The town is tidy with tar-sealed roads. It is attractive to birders for two main reasons. It provides an almost one hundred percent opportunity of seeing a Brown Kiwi via a commercial operator, and it offers very good seabirding from boats chartered from Oban. Bush bird populations are rich around Oban with Kaka, New Zealand Pigeon and Red-crowned Parakeets being very obvious. The island is also scenically attractive being almost all forested with the forests coming down to the coast. In Oban the houses sit attractively among the bush.

How to get to Stewart Island by plane: There are several flights daily from the Invercargill airport. Enquire from the office of Southern Air Ltd, at the airport. It pays to travel light as luggage may otherwise have to be left at the airport until you return. The flight to Stewart Island takes about 20 minutes. the plane landing on a tarmac airstrip with the passengers being transported by mini-bus to the township where there are hotels and other motel type accommodation.

How to get to Stewart Island by boat: The ferry leaves from Bluff Harbour, daily. If you wish to observe the seabirds in Foveaux Strait use the ferry but expect rough seas.

How to get to Mason Bay on Stewart Island: There is a walking track to Mason Bay. This leaves from Oban leading off the road to the airstrip. Enquire further about it from the Department of Conservation office situated near the South Seas Hotel. There is a long walk and a short walk depending on time. Brown Kiwi at Mason Bay are known for their crepuscular and even diurnal habits. Because they have existed there without disturbance for so long, they have developed some daylight feeding habits and it is not unusual to see them feeding in full daylight. The long twilight periods found on Stewart Island might also have encouraged birds to become daylight feeders although not all of Stewart Island's Brown Kiwi have this diurnal trait.

How to get to Ocean Beach on Stewart Island: Ocean Beach is on the peninsula on the south side of Paterson Inlet. It involves a boat excursion across Paterson Inlet to get to it. A commercial tourist operator visits this locality of an evening to find Brown Kiwi.

How to get to Ackers Point walking track: This track is on the southern arm of Half Moon Bay. Arrange to be taken by mini-bus to it and walk out to the point. Brown Kiwi have been recorded just before the lighthouse. After dark there will also be incoming Sooty Shearwaters along the track and Blue Penguins.

How to get to Ulva Island in Paterson Inlet: This attractive island has had Brown Kiwi liberated on it and more recently Saddlebacks. A visit usually produces good views of a range of birds.

Birds likely to be seen on Stewart Island include -

Brown Kiwi	Kaka
Weka	Kea
Banded Rail	Yellow-crowned Parakeet
Pigeon	Red-crowned Parakeet
Robin	Long-tailed Cuckoo
Brown Creeper	Shining Cuckoo
Grey Warbler	Morepork
Bellbird	Kingfisher
Tui	Rifleman
Silvereye	Fantail
Saddleback	Tomtit

For further details: Phone/Fax: +64 3 219 1210. Write: Thorfin Charters and Accommodation, P O Box 43, Stewart Island.
Email: thorfin@southnet.co.nz.   Web: www.thorfin.co.nz,

Or write: Department of Conservation, P.O. Box 743 Invercargill. Phone: +64 3 214 4589. Fax: +64 3 214 4486. Or enquire on arrival at their Stewart Island office which is near South Seas Hotel.

SOUTHLAND
(continued)

BUSHY POINT

General: This area of swampland is almost in Invercargill and is located at Otatara. It is swampland where Marsh Crake and Fernbirds have been recorded, while nearby forests have New Zealand Pigeon and bush birds.

How to get there: Find Stead Street and then turn left (east) into Marama Avenue South. Then turn right into Bryson Road and left into Grant Road. Drive to the end of Grant Road and enquire at the house of Ian and Jenny Gamble for permission to enter their boardwalk. This takes you right into the swamp without getting your feet wet. There is no charge to enter.

Target bird: Fernbird.

LAKE MURIHIKU

General: This small lake lies to the west of Invercargill not far from Bushy Point. The rush verges are known as habitat for Marsh Crake and for Fernbird.

How to get there: From Invercargill follow Longford Road west of the city. Turn left (south) into Otatara Road and then right (west) into Coggins Road. Lake Murihiku lies almost at the junction of Hughes and Coggins Road.

Target birds: Marsh Crake, Fernbird.

RIVERTON ROCKS

General: This is a place where seabirds can be seen from the mainland.

How to get there: From Invercargill follow Highway 99 west to Riverton. Turn left (south) at Riverton and follow the road to The Rocks. While in the area search the Riverton Estuary on Highway 99 for waders and waterfowl.

Target birds: Mollymawks, Shearwaters, Stewart Island Shag.

FIORDLAND

REDCLIFF WETLAND RESERVE

General: This is an area of protected wetland which contains waterfowl. Marsh Crake have been recorded here.

How to get there: From Manapouri drive east along Hillside Road and then right into Weir Road and into Blackmount Road. Travel for about 18 kms and look for sign.

Target bird: Marsh Crake.

EGLINTON VALLEY - CASCADE CREEK

General: This scenic area lies north of Te Anau town on Highway 94. It has fine beech forests which have a good range of South Island bush birds. A trip to Cascade Creek should include a stop on the Eglinton River for Blue Ducks and Black-fronted Terns. It should also include a visit to Milford Sound which is a further 45 minutes. Note that this is a high rainfall area and birding is almost impossible in the wet.

How to get there: From Te Anau follow Highway 94.

Areas which should be visited, and which are signposted in the Eglinton Valley are -

- **Mirror Lakes:** Look for Scaup, Grey Duck, Yellow-crowned Parakeet, Robin and Tomtit. Watch out for the signpost.
- **Ministry of Works depot before Knobbs Flat:** Watch out for a small cluster of buildings on right and take the dirt road into forests nearby. Look for Yellowheads.
- **Eglinton River near Knobbs Flat:** Look for Blue Duck and Black-fronted Terns here and in the forests for Yellowhead. Watch for Knobbs Flat signpost and then look for tracks to the river on the left. Blue Ducks are occasional visitors here.
- **Lake Gunn Walkway, starting at Cascade Creek:** Look for Brown Kiwi, Grey Duck, Scaup, New Zealand Falcon, Black-fronted Tern, Black-billed Gull, New Zealand Pigeon, Kaka, Kea, Yellow-crowned Parakeet, Shining Cuckoo, Long-tailed Cuckoo, Rifleman, Brown Creeper, Yellowhead, Grey Warbler, Fantail, Robin, Tomit, Silvereye, Bellbird and Tui. Watch for signpost.
- **The Divide:** Look for Kea and bush birds generally.
- **Hollyford River:** Look for Blue Duck anywhere on the river here but don't expect a quick sighting. They are usually very hard to find.
- **Homer Tunnel, Gertrude Valley:** Look for Rock Wren and Pipit. Gertrude Valley is found up a side-road on the right just before the Homer Tunnel entrance. Look for the Alpine Club building on the left. Follow the walking track from it over two bridges.
- **Milford Sound:** Look for Yellow-eyed Penguin, Fiordland Crested Penguin from the launch. Look for Yellowheads in the forests. Banded Dotterel are sometimes near the airstrip.

Where to stay: Note that there is no longer a hotel at Cascade Creek so birders should stay at Te Anau or Milford Sound.

Sandflies: Don't forget to take insect repellant into this area. Wear long trousers if you dislike this biting insect. (See "About New Zealand" at start of book.)

MILFORD SOUND

How to get there: Follow Highway 94 up the Eglinton Valley to the end.

Commercial launch trips: This is the best way to see the Fiordland Crested Penguin, Yellow-eyed Penguin and Blue Penguin. Some operators now make diversions if they sight a penguin on the rocks. An overnight commercial launch operator spends the night in Harrison Cove where noisy birds can be seen coming ashore at dusk. During the June to December breeding months, Fiordland Crested Penguins can often be seen either on the rocks, sheltering in cavities, or resting among the vegetation of the coastline. From late December onwards views of a Fiordland Crested Penguin on the rocks are unlikely. Instead viewers must look for them on the water.

Other birds around Milford Sound:

- The area is rich in Bellbird song which comes across the water to the boat.
- Brown Creeper and Tomtits sing in nearby forests.

- Yellowheads are occasionally recorded from nearby forests.

Launch bookings: These can be made at the lake-front office of Fiordland Travel Ltd at Te Anau. Phone: +64 3 442 7500. Fax: +64 3 442 7504. Write: Box 1, Te Anau. Or, tickets can be purchased at Milford Sound.

TE ANAU WILDLIFE PARK

General: This small bird park is located just south of Te Anau on the Manapouri road. It is worth a visit to see captive Takahe in an environment very close to their current habitat in the Murchison Mountains above the western shores of Lake Te Anau. The park also contains a waterfowl collection, which includes Brown Teal, and some caged birds, including Kea, Kaka and parakeets.

How to get there: Take the Manapouri road from Te Anau.

Target bird: Takahe in captivity.

HAAST - MAKARORA

General: Any forest in this area is worth a visit to see bush birds and maybe the New Zealand Falcon.

How to get there: From Wanaka follow Highway 6 north to Makarora. There are three places to visit -

- **Makarora:** At Makarora there is a visitors' centre with walking tracks nearby and behind it. Bush birds can be found here.
- **Davis Flat:** Follow north from Makarora for 14 kms and stop at Davis Flat campsite/picnic area. A walking track leads along the Haast River and over a foot bridge. Look for Yellowheads here.
- **Gates of Haast:** Follow north from Makarora for about 25 kms and you come to the Gates of Haast. Here there is an old bridal trail which leads west along the Burke River at the north end of the Mount Aspiring National Park. Look for bush birds, Yellowheads and New Zealand Falcon.

Target birds: New Zealand Falcon, Yellowhead.

WEST COAST

OKARITO AND WHITE HERON TOURS

General: The Okarito Lagoon is on the west coast of South Island, just south of Whataroa. The lagoon is scenically interesting but the White Herons, which have become synonymous with the name Okarito, are not often encountered around it. Instead they actually nest in the forest in a small colony on the banks of the Waitangi Roto River. Every November they return there from the various harbours and estuaries of New Zealand where they have been wintering and commence breeding. At the same time a few pairs of Royal Spoonbills also arrive to nest at the same place.

How to get to Okarito Lagoon: From Highway 6, approximately 15 kms south of Whataroa, follow west on Forks - Okarito Road.

How to get to the White Heron breeding colony: To see the White Heron breeding colony take a commercial tour in a jet boat. These tours are based in Whataroa. They go down the Waitangi Toana River and then up the Waitangi Roto River, where people disembark at a jetty and follow a short board-walk to a hide especially built for heron viewing.

For further details: Phone: +64 3 753 420. Fax: +64 753 4087. Write: White Heron Sanctuary Tours, P O Box 19, Whataroa.

Email: info@whiteherontours.co.nz.

Web: www.whiteherontours.co.nz.

LAKE KANIERE

General: This lake is 17 kms east of Hokitika and is approached through old forests which have bush birds. Great Spotted Kiwi are found in these forests. The lake itself has waterfowl and occasionally Crested Grebe.

How to get there: Follow the signposts from Hokitika.

Target bird: Crested Grebe.

LAKE BRUNNER

General: This is a good place to try and find the Great Spotted Kiwi in the bush areas around the Arnold River near the Lake Brunner camp ground. From the camp ground explore the river banks and any forested areas after dark. Marsh Crakes are also known from the wet verges.

How to get there: This can be accessed from the Arthurs Pass road, Highway 73 at Jackson, south of Greymouth or from Highway 7 at Stillwater, about 11 kms north of Greymouth. Follow in along the Arnold Valley.

Target bird: Great Spotted Kiwi.

LAKE PEARSON, LAKE GRASMERE, CASS

General: Lake Pearson and Lake Grasmere lie to the east of Arthurs Pass village. From Christchurch they make an easy day's excursion through the winding Porters Pass where the road climbs quickly. A visit to the lakes can be combined with a visit to Arthurs Pass Village to look for Rock Wrens and then a further excursion to the Otira River at Pegleg Creek to look for Blue Ducks. Enquiries about Rock Wrens and Blue Ducks can be made at the Department of Conservation office at Arthurs Pass.

How to get there: They can be reached either by driving south from Greymouth on Highway 6 and then following Highway 73 at Kumara Junction which is the road to Arthurs Pass, or they can be accessed by driving west from Christchurch on Highway 73, the Arthurs Pass road.

Places of interest:

- **Lake Pearson:** When travelling from Christchurch, Lake Pearson is the first lake arrived at and is on the left (east). It can be easily viewed from the road. Birds here include Crested Grebe, Little Shag, Canada Geese, Grey Duck and Scaup. Kea are sometimes seen and Bellbirds are common.
- **Lake Grasmere:** The second lake, has Crested Grebes and also Black Swans.

Target bird: Crested Grebe.

- **Cass:** There are further lakes in the area off the Craigieburn road, including Lake Sarah and Lake Hawdon. At Cass just past Lake Grasmere, turn in towards Lake Sarah. Cross the river and walk into dense beech forests. Yellowheads may be here.

Target bird: Yellowhead.

ARTHURS PASS - LAKE MISERY

General: On from Lake Grasmere is Arthurs Pass village. From the village travel to the top of the pass which is a distance of 5 kms. After the top of the Pass look for a pull-in area on the left (west) with an information board and map for Lake Misery. Follow the walking track for 30 minutes to a bridge over a stream and then walk for another 20 minutes to rock screes.

Target bird: Rock Wren.

ARTHURS PASS - OTIRA GORGE

General: At Arthurs Pass enquire at the Department of Conservation office about the whereabouts of Blue Duck in the area and how to access their locality. Then travel west over the Pass and find the confluence of the Otira River and Pegleg Creek. Walk up stream or down stream. Blue Ducks are regularly seen in this part of river.

Target bird: Blue Duck.

PUNAKAIKI

General: This area is known for its "pancake" like rocks. It is also a place to see Great Spotted Kiwi, Westland Black Petrel and Weka.

How to get there: Punakaiki is on Highway 6, 50 kms south of Westport or 40 kms north of Greymouth.

- **Target species - Great Spotted Kiwi:** There is access into the bush at Bullock Creek, 1 km north of the Punakaiki motor camp. Travel along this road for 6.2 kms to a locked gate. There is a rough camp-site here. Listen in this wider area at night.
- **Target species - Westland Black Petrels:** Look for incoming birds from the lookouts on thePunakaiki rocks or from along Highway 6 in the near vicinity. See below about commercial operations in the area.
- **Target species - Weka:** Look for this bird north of Charleston and in the Cape Foulwind area. They can often be seen on Virgins Flat Road and Wilsons Lead Road in that area.

For further details about Black Petrel viewing: Phone: +64 3 731 8826. Write: Paparoa Nature Tours, P.O. Box 1268, Christchurch.

NORTH - WEST

FAREWELL SPIT

General: This area is on the north-west tip of the South Island. It is known as a shore-bird locality and has good numbers of Bar-tailed Godwits and Lesser Knots. Some rare Arctic vagrants turn up here from time to time. There is also a colony of nesting Australasian Gannets and Caspian Terns.

How to get there: From Nelson follow Highway 60 to Motueka and then on to Collingwood.

For further details: Phone: +64 3 524 88257. Fax: +64 3 524 8939. Write: P.O. Box 15, Collingwood.

Email: enquiries@farewellspit.co.nz.

Web: http://farewellspit.co.nz,

VAGRANT SHOREBIRDS RECORDS

From time to time vagrant shorebirds arrive in New Zealand usually with the return of the godwits. Below is a list of such birds. Some locality records are added although some species have turned up in numerous places.

Red-capped Dotterel (*Charadrius ruficapillus*) – Canterbury, Manukau Harbour
Ringed Plover (*Charadrius hiaticula*) - Miranda
Grey Plover (*Pluvialis squatarola*) - Miranda
Japanese Snipe (*Gallinago hardwickii*) - Manukau Harbour, Manawatu Estuary
Great Knot (*Calidris tenuirostris*) - Manukau Harbour
Sanderling (*C. alba*) - Miranda, Lake Ellesmere, Farewell Spit
Dunlin (*C.alpina*) - Manukau Harbour, Miranda, Lake Ellesmere
Bairds Sandpiper (*C. bairdii*) - Miranda, Manukau Harbour, Manawatu Estuary
Western Sandpiper (*C. mauri*) - Miranda, Farewell Spit
Broad-billed Sandpiper (*Limicola falcinellus*) - Miranda, Manawatu Estuary
Ruff (*Philomachus pugnax*) - Manukau Harbour, Lake Ellesmere
Asiatic Dowitcher (*Limnodromus semipalmatus*) - Miranda
Little Whimbrel (*Numenius minutus*) - Miranda, Lake Ellesmere
Common Sandpiper (*Tringa hypoleucos*) - Lake Wainono
Greenshank (*T. nebularia*) - Manukau Harbour, Miranda
Lesser Yellowlegs (*T. flavipes*) - Manukau Harbour
Red-necked Phalarope (*Phalaropus lobatus*) - Manukau Harbour, Miranda
Grey Phalarope (*P. fulicarius*) - Manukau Harbour, Miranda

LAND-BASED SIGHTING PLACES FOR SEABIRDS

NORTH ISLAND

Northland - Mimiwhangata Coastal Park: This is a coastal park 40 kms north of Whangarei near Helena Bay. It is signposted. It has good populations of Brown Teal and New Zealand Dotterels. Coastal viewing from Okupe Beach in windy weather often allows views of seabirds and in particular Fluttering Shearwater and Bullers Shearwater.

North Auckland - Goat Island Marine Reserve: Turn east at Warkworth, north of Auckland, and follow the road to Leigh. 3 kms east of Leigh is the Goat Island Marine Reserve which is signposted. From the Goat Island Marine Reserve carpark follow a marked walking track behind the Marine Reserve buildings. This leads to a clifftop vantage point above the sea. Here seabirds come within telescope range. Usually Bullers Shearwater, Flesh-footed Shearwater and Fluttering Shearwater are seen.

North Auckland - Whangaparaoa: Often rafts of Fluttering Shearwaters are visible from the road-side at Tindalls Bay, Army Bay and Shakespear Regional Park near the end of the Peninsula. More regularly they are on the north side.

Coromandel - Colville: Regularly a good place to see Bullers Shearwater is from the road edge above the sea north of Amodeo Bay. This is about 12 kms north of the town of Coromandel.

Bay of Plenty - Matata Beach: Birds can be seen off-shore from the beach. Usually Grey-faced Petrels are observed.

SOUTH ISLAND

Nelson - Kaikoura: The coastal road in this area provides many chances for seabird viewing especially in rough weather. While here go on an "Ocean Wings" pelagic excursion from Kaikoura (see "Places"). Viewing from the coastal area south of Kaikoura, with a telescope, can often be very rewarding. Here, Albatrosses and Mollymawks come in close to the shore.

West Coast - Punakaiki: Search out to sea from the Punakaiki rocks area. Birds seen will probably be Westland Black Petrels and only after about 4 pm in the winter and spring months, when they gather off-shore prior to coming into the breeding burrows in the Paparoa Ranges.

South Canterbury - Oamaru: The cliff-tops at the end of Bushy Beach Road, near where Yellow-eyed Penguins are observed is a good viewing place, especially for Sooty Shearwaters over the spring months. (See "Places".)

South Canterbury - Shag Point: Shag Point is 8 kms north of Palmerston, at the south end of Katiki Beach. Turn east from Highway 1 and travel to the end. Sooty Shearwaters in the spring months are here and Stewart Island Shags.

Otago - Karitane Point: After the Waikouaiti River on Highway 1, turn east and follow to Karitane. From the Karitane Domain follow the walking tracks to the coast and look for seabirds.

Otago - Aramoana: This location is east of Port Chalmers on the north side of the Otago Harbour. Travel on until the beach is reached. Look for seabirds from the Aramoana Mole.

Otago Peninsula - Taiaroa Heads: Northern Royal Albatrosses will be seen here. Out to sea other species may be seen such as the Southern Royal Albatross, Bullers Mollymawk, Shy Mollymawk and Salvins Mollymawk.

Otago Peninsula - Sandfly Bay: This place can offer seabird viewing. When travelling towards Taiaroa, take a right turn at Portobello where signposting will lead you to Hoopers Inlet. Follow Highcliff Road from Portobello then Sealpoint Road and follow to the end.

South Otago - Nugget Point: Travel south from Balclutha turning left at the Otanomomo and Paretai signpost and then on to Molyneux Bay and Kaka Point. At the Yellow-eyed Penguin lookout above Roaring Bay, look for seabirds.

Curio Bay: This bay, at the end of the Slope Point road, is signposted from Tokanui, on the alternative Invercargill to Balclutha route, via the Catlins Forest Park. From a telescope above the coastline many seabirds can be seen. Usually these are Sooty Shearwaters.

Bluff Hill: Bluff is a small town south of Invercargill. Drive through Bluff to Stirling Point at the end of the road. Look for Shy Mollymawk, Sooty Shearwater and other seabirds.

Riverton: Riverton is a coastal town on the south coast of the South Island and west of Invercargill. From Invercargill follow Highway 99 and turn left at Riverton and follow the road to The Rocks. Mollymawks, shearwaters and Stewart Island Shags can often be seen from here in rough weather. While in the area search the Riverton Estuary on Highway 99 for waders and waterfowl.

Stewart Island: Set up your telescope on Ackers Point. Shy Mollymawk and sometimes Bullers Mollymawk will be seen in summer plus other seabirds including Sooty Shearwaters.

EXCURSIONS

A FAVOURITE EXCURSION
NORTH ISLAND

This excursion starts at Auckland

Key birds: Brown Kiwi, Brown Teal, Banded Rail, Takahe, Spotless Crake, Red-crowned Parakeet, Fernbird, Stitchbird, Saddleback and Kokako.
Tour pattern: Auckland to Tiri Tiri Island and then to the central North Island and back to Auckland.
Tour length: Eight days.

DAY ONE

Travel north of Auckland to Whangaparaoa Peninsula, go to Tiri Tiri Island and then return and visit local birding spots. From Gulf Harbour, just past Tindalls Bay, take the Fullers ferry. The boat trip takes 25 minutes.
Birds which might be seen during the boat trip: Blue Penguin, Bullers Shearwater, Flesh-footed Shearwater, Fluttering Shearwater, Pied Shag, Australasian Gannet, Arctic Skua, Black-backed Gull, Red-billed Gull, Caspian Tern, White-fronted Tern.
Birds which might be seen on the island: Little Spotted Kiwi (night), Brown Teal, Brown Quail, Takahe, Spotless Crake, Kaka, Red-crowned Parakeet, Long-tailed Cuckoo, Rifleman, Whitehead, Robin, Bellbird, Stitchbird, Saddleback and Kokako.
Shakespear Park - Whangaparaoa: After Tiri Tiri Island visit Shakespear Park beyond Gulf Harbour. Near the entrance on the left is a pond which has a collection of waterfowl. The bush walk beyond often has Bellbirds.
Weiti River - Whangaparaoa: Then visit the Wieti River. At the Whangaparaoa shopping centre turn down Wade River Road and follow to the Weiti River. At the first wharf look south over the water to a sandspit for shorebirds including New Zealand and Banded Dotterel.
Stay night in this area.

DAY TWO

Travel south from Whangaparaoa to Miranda via Clevedon. Turn off the southern Auckland motorway at Takanini and follow signs to Clevedon. Then follow signs to Kawakawa Bay.
Kawakawa Bay: Look for Variable Oystercatcher, South Island Pied Oystercatcher, Bar-tailed Godwit, Banded Dotterel, New Zealand Dotterel, Pied Stilt, Red-billed Gull, Black-backed Gull, Caspian Tern, White-fronted Tern. Look for Spotted Doves.

Turn inland at Kawakawa Bay and drive over the saddle through native forest. Observe straight-trunked kauri trees (*Agathis australis*), look for Kingfishers on power wires, and also look for bush birds.

At the Orere hall, head inland again towards Kaiaua. In this area expect

Californian Quail, Brown Quail, Pheasant, Pukeko, Eastern Rosella, Skylark, Greenfinch, Goldfinch, Chaffinch, Redpoll, Yellowhammer, House Sparrow, Starling, Myna and White-backed Magpie. Watch for Rooks from here to Miranda.

Waharau: After Matingarahi Beach, the road climbs along the cliff. From the road look down to the rocks on which Spotted Shag usually roost at half-tide. Here also see Pied Shag, Little Shag, Little Black Shag and Black Shag. Look for a Reef Heron on this stretch of coast. Look out to sea for Bullers Shearwater, Gannet and Arctic Skua.

Waharau Regional Park: This park is further along the coast. Here there are bush tracks. Expect New Zealand Pigeon, Fantail, Grey Warbler, Tui and Bellbird. Further into the park Tomtits may be seen.

Kaiaua: Stop at the bridge at Kaiaua just before the hotel and look for Banded Rail. South of the Kaiaua Hotel stop and look for Eastern Curlew.

Miranda: Visit "The Hide" and "The Stilt Ponds". Expect White-faced Heron, White Heron, Bittern, Royal Spoonbill, Cattle Egret, Black Swan, Canada Goose, Paradise Shelduck, Mallard, Grey Duck, Shoveler, Grey Teal, Harrier, Spur-winged Plover, Golden Plover, Wrybill, Whimbrel, Terek Sandpiper, Siberian Tattler, Turnstone, Lesser Knot, Sharp-tailed Sandpiper, Curlew Sandpiper, Red-necked Stint, hybrid and juvenile Black Stilt, Black-billed Gull, Little Tern, Welcome Swallow.

At Miranda consolidate on species already seen on route. Don't forget that Miranda has also recorded Grey Plover, Ring Plover, Large Sand Dotterel, Mongolian Dotterel, Black-tailed Godwit, Greenshank, Great Knot, Marsh Sandpiper, Bairds Sandpiper, Wandering Tattler, Pectoral Sandpiper and Broad-billed Sandpiper, so careful scrutiny is called for, preferably with a telescope.

Stay night at the Miranda Naturalists' Trust Centre.

DAY THREE

Travel on to Lake Patetonga. Expect here Australasian Bittern and Glossy Ibis. Observe waterfowl including Grey Teal and Shoveler. From here travel on to Tauranga and from Tauranga take the Te Puke sign and then follow the Matata sign. Find Kaituna which is near Maketu.

Kaituna: At Kaituna River-mouth look for waterfowl. Try for Spotless Crake.

Matata: Expect waterfowl including Dabchick and Scaup. Look for Marsh Crake, Black-fronted Dotterel, Fernbird and Hedge Sparrow. Grey-faced Petrels are sometimes seen off-shore.

Tarawera River-mouth: Explore Tarawera River-mouth travelling east. Look for Spotless Crake and Marsh Crake in marshy verges. Note that Greenshanks have been recorded here. Also look for White Heron and shags. On the river-mouth headlands look for New Zealand Dotterel.

Stay night at Matata.

DAY FOUR

Travel on to Rotorua heading inland up Manawahe Road. This climbs up into sheep farming areas and eventually into forested land surrounding Lake Rotoma. Look for Pipits here.

Lake Rotoma: Look for waterfowl and bush birds in the surrounding forests.

Lake Rotoehu: From Lake Rotoma travel on towards Rotorua and turn right into Lake Rotoehu Road. Look at the waterfowl on the lake before driving for 3 kms up Manawahe Road. Stop up here and look for bush birds. Whiteheads and Bellbirds are here. Kokako may still be here below the road. Travel on towards Rotorua and stop at Hongis Track and look for Tomtits.

Lake Okareka: Before Rotorua at Lynwood turn left up the road which goes into Blue Lake and Lake Okareka. Lake Okareka has good populations of waterfowl including Dabchick and Australasian Coot.

Stay night at Rotorua.

DAY FIVE

Travel on to Rotorua.

Rotorua Centennial Gardens: Find Arawa Street and travel to the lake-front. See a wide range of waterfowl. Black-billed Gulls nest in a thermal area before the lake.

Mokoia Island: Take the ferry to Mokoia Island in Lake Rotorua. Here see Weka, Robin, Stitchbirds and Saddlebacks.

Stay night at Rotorua.

DAY SIX

Leave Rotorua and head south on Highway 5, the Taupo road. At Rainbow Mountain, head east to Murapara and to Te Whaiti, Ruatahuna and the Urewera National Park.

Hopuaruahine Stream: Stop here and look for Blue Duck. If the Blue Duck is missed here travel on to the Waikaremoana Park Headquarters and enquire about the whereabouts of Blue Ducks. Travel back to Highway 5 and turn left to Taupo.

Stay night at Taupo.

DAY SEVEN

Follow Highway 1 and travel north from Taupo. After Wairakei travel on to the Atiamuri power station and turn left into the Whakamaru road. Stop on this road and look for Tomtits, Robins and Whiteheads among the pine forests. At Whakamaru, cross the dam and head for Mangakino, turning down Highway 30 which says Barryville and Pureora.

Pureora: At the Pureora Forest Park Headquarters sign, turn left and drive into the park. Here make enquiries about locations for Kokako. Look for New Zealand Falcon, Kaka, Yellow-crowned Parakeets, Long-tailed Cuckoo, Morepork and Rifleman. Visit Bismarck Road and "The Tower", and do the bush walk near the Information Centre. Travel on to Te Kuiti.

Stay night at Te Kuiti.

DAY EIGHT

Return to Auckland via Otorohanga.

Otorohanga Kiwi House: This is sign-posted at the north end of Otorohanga town.

This tour gives an opportunity of seeing 103 species.

A FAVOURITE EXCURSION
SOUTH ISLAND

This excursion starts at Wellington

Key birds: Great Spotted Kiwi, Brown Kiwi, Mollymawk species, Westland Black Petrel, Huttons Shearwater, King Shag, Blue Duck, Falcon, Chukor, Weka, Marsh Crake, Black Stilt, Kea, Rock Wren, Rifleman, Brown Creeper, Yellowhead, Cirl Bunting and Saddleback.

Tour pattern: Leave Wellington on the Cook Strait ferry for Picton. From Picton take a boat trip on Queen Charlotte Sound. Travel on to Nelson, Westport, Lake Brunner, Arthurs Pass, Lake Kaniere, Franz Josef and Fox Glaciers and through the Haast Pass to Wanaka. From Wanaka travel to Omarama and then to Oamaru. Travel to Christchurch or Dunedin for the onward flight.

Tour length: Eight days.

DAY ONE

Take the Cook Strait ferry, a trip which takes three hours and gives a chance of seabirds and shags.

Wellington wharves: Black Shag and Spotted Shag.

Cook Strait: From the Cook Strait ferry Giant Petrel, Cape Pigeon and Black-backed Gull are regularly seen. The following are occasionally seen. Blue Penguin, Fairy Prion, Sooty Shearwater, Huttons Shearwater, Fluttering Shearwater, White-faced Storm Petrel, Arctic Skua, Red-billed Gull, Caspian Tern and White-fronted Tern.

Queen Charlotte Sound: The following species are regularly seen in the sound - Pied Shag, Little Shag and Little Black Shag. King Shag is possible near the entrance.

Picton: At Picton take the 2.45 pm boat excursion on the sound. This is run by "Dolphin Watch Marlborough". On this trip King Shags are sometimes seen. Birds which might be added to the list are - Flesh-footed Shearwater, Diving Petrel, Australasian Gannet, White-faced Heron, Reef Heron, Black Swan, Paradise Shelduck, Mallard, Harrier, New Zealand Pigeon, Shining Cuckoo, Kingfisher, Rifleman, Welcome Swallow, Fantail, Tomtit, Robin, Brown Creeper, Grey Warbler, Bellbird, Tui, Silvereye and Saddleback.

Stay night in Picton.

DAY TWO

From Picton travel on the windy road to Havelock via Pelorus Sound and Grove.

Estuary birds: Birds regularly seen are - Pukeko, Variable Oystercatcher, South Island Pied Oystercatcher, Spur-winged Plover and Banded Dotterel. Expect a Banded Rail among coastal verges.

Native bush birds: Birds regularly seen here are - Long-tailed Cuckoo, Shining Cuckoo, Fantail (look for Black Fantail here too), Tomtit, (note yellow breast), Brown Creeper, Grey Warbler, Bellbird, Tui, and Silvereye. The following may also be seen - Yellow-crowned Parakeet and Rifleman,

Exotic species: Regularly seen here are - Californian Quail, Pheasant, Skylark,

Song Thrush, Blackbird, Hedge Sparrow, Greenfinch, Goldfinch, Chaffinch, Redpoll, Yellowhammer, House Sparrow, Starling and Magpie.

Travel on through Havelock to Pelorus Bridge and look for Weka and bush birds. There are good walking tracks here and good numbers of birds. Note that at Linkwater, after Pelorus Bridge, you could drive up Kenepuru Road to Grahams Lookout (45 kms) and try and find the Yellowhead. This diversion would add a day to this tour. Travel on to Nelson and to Motueka.

Motueka Estuary: Expect to see here - Royal Spoonbill, Grey Duck, Golden Plover, Bar-tailed Godwit, Lesser Knot, Ruddy Turnstone, Pied Stilt, Black-fronted Tern. Look for Cirl Bunting on pastures. Travel back to Richmond and follow Highway 6 to Westport.
Stay night at Westport.

DAY THREE

From Westport travel to Punakaiki and look for Westland Black Petrels and Great Spotted Kiwi.

Westland Black Petrel: Look from the coast road. They are winter breeders so they are not always on the nesting site.

Great Spotted Kiwi: Try Bullock Creek Road in the evening. Alternatively travel on to Greymouth and then to Lake Brunner. Camp at Lake Brunner and look for Great Spotted Kiwi here near the Moana Camping Ground.
Stay night at Punakaiki or Greymouth.

DAY FOUR

Past Greymouth follow Highway 73 at Kumara and turn inland for Arthurs Pass. Look for Blue Duck at Otira Gorge, and for Rock Wren at Arthurs Pass. Enquire at the Department of Conservation office about where to find Yellowheads in the Hawdon Valley. Look for Crested Grebe on Lake Pearson and Lake Grasmere and Kea in the hills.
Stay night at Arthurs Pass.

DAY FIVE

Travel back towards Kumara and at Jackson turn right for Lake Brunner if you want to try again for Great Spotted Kiwi.
Stay at the Lake Brunner camping ground.

DAY SIX

Travel to Hokitika. A few kilometres from Hokitika, at Kaniere, turn inland to Lake Kaniere. Follow in for about 10 kms. Likely new birds here are Bittern, Cattle Egret, Shoveler, Scaup, Falcon, Marsh Crake, Spotless Crake, Kaka, Fernbird and Pipit. Yellow-crowned Parakeets may be seen here along with other bush birds already seen.

White Heron Tours: At Whataroa take the two hour White Heron Sanctuary Tour. Return to Highway 6 and travel on to Lake Moeraki stopping at Franz Josef and Fox Glaciers. See Kea here and look for Rock Wrens above the tree-line at the glaciers. Enquire at Wilderness Lodge Lake Moeraki where to find Fiordland Crested Penguins.

Stay night at Wilderness Lodge Lake Moeraki.
Email: lakemoeraki@wildernesslodge.co.nz.

DAY SEVEN

Travel through the Haast Pass. At the Gates of Haast follow a track into the bush and look for Yellowheads. At Davis Flat 14 kms north of Makarora try for Yellowheads and New Zealand Falcon. At Makarora look for New Zealand Falcon. Travel on to Wanaka and from there follow Highway 6 and then turn left into Highway 8a to Tarras. At Tarras turn left, and follow Highway 8 north to Omarama.
Stay night at Omarama.

DAY EIGHT

Travel north on the Twizel road to the Ahuriri Bridge. Look for Black Stilts. Travel on to Twizel. Before Lake Tekapo divert to Lake Alexandrina and look for Crested Grebe. Then travel further up this road to the Cass River delta and look for Black Stilt and maybe Wrybill if it is the nesting season. Look for Chukor near Lake Tekapo. Add Rook in this area.
Stay night at Christchurch.

Comments about this tour: Great Spotted Kiwi are difficult to find but the chances of hearing them are good. Black Stilts are extremely rare (down to about 34 birds) and so might be missed. This tour only gives Blue Ducks one chance. If the weather is good Rock Wrens may be spotted at Arthurs Pass. There are several chances for seeing Yellowheads.

This tour gives an opportunity of seeing 100 species:

ANOTHER FAVOURITE EXCURSION
SOUTH ISLAND

This excursion starts at Dunedin

Key Birds: Brown Kiwi, Yellow-eyed Penguin, Fiordland Crested Penguin, Albatross species, Stewart Island Shag, Blue Shag, Blue Duck, Falcon, Weka, Marsh Crake, New Zealand Dotterel, Kaka, Kea, Rifleman, Rock Wren, Robin, Fernbird, Brown Creeper and Yellow-head.
Tour pattern: Leave Dunedin for Taiaroa Heads, Invercargill, Stewart Island, Eglinton Valley and Fiordland. Return to Dunedin.
Tour length: Seven days.

DAY ONE

From Dunedin travel to Taiaroa Heads on Otago Peninsula.
Harbour birds: Birds regularly seen along the coast are - Australasian Gannet, Black Shag, Little Shag, South Island Pied Oystercatcher, Variable Oystercatcher, Bar-tailed Godwit, Pied Stilt, Red-billed Gull, Black-backed Gull, Caspian Tern and White-fronted Tern.

Taiaroa Heads: At Taiaroa see Royal Albatross, Stewart Island Shag and Spotted Shag. Also expect Skylark, Pipit, Song Thrush, Blackbird, Hedge Sparrow, Yellowhammer and Redpoll.

Papanui Inlet: Travel back towards Dunedin and at Weir Road detour to Papanui Inlet and to Hoopers Inlet. Birds regularly seen here are - White-faced Heron, Black Swan, Canada Geese, Paradise Shelduck, Mallard, Grey Duck, Grey Teal, Shoveler, Pukeko, Golden Plover, Banded Dotterel, and Turnstone.

Sandfly Bay: Travel back towards Dunedin and at Portobello turn left and follow Highcliff Road and then Sealpoint Road. From the end of the road walk down to a hide and observe Yellow-eyed Penguins.

Other birds: Other birds seen around Dunedin are - Harrier, Californian Quail, Eastern Rosella, Kingfisher, Rifleman, Fantail, Grey Warbler, Bellbird, Silvereye, Greenfinch, Chaffinch, Goldfinch, Redpoll, Sparrow, Starling and Magpie.

Stay night at Dunedin.

DAY TWO

Leave Dunedin for Invercargill via the south coast.

Nugget Point: At Balclutha follow the signpost which says Owaka and soon after turn left and take the Kaka Point road which leads to Nugget Point. Stop at the Roaring Bay carpark and walk to a hide to see Yellow-eyed Penguins. At the lighthouse look for seabirds such as Shy Mollymawk, Bullers Mollymawk, Giant Petrel and Sooty Shearwater.

Catlins Forest: Travel back towards Owaka. At Puketiro Station Road turn left and then right down Aurora Creek Road. Stop at the camping ground here and walk into the forest. Birds regularly seen here are - New Zealand Pigeon, Shining Cuckoo, Long-tailed Cuckoo, Rifleman, Fantail, Tomtit, Brown Creeper, Yellowhead, Grey Warbler, Silvereye, Bellbird and Tui. Expect also New Zealand Falcon, Kaka and Yellow-crowned Parakeet. Travel on towards Invercargill. Stop at Curio Bay and Waituna Lagoon.

Curio Bay: At Tokanui turn left for Slope Point and Curio Bay. Look for seabirds off-shore such as Sooty Shearwater.

Waituna Lagoon: From Curio Bay drive on to Invercargill. At Kapuka, turn left and then left again and then right to the Waituna Lagoon. At the east end of the beach look for Marsh Crake and Fernbird. Other shorebirds known from here are - Spur-winged Plover, Black-fronted Dotterel, Eastern Curlew, Turnstone, Lesser Knot, Sharp-tailed Sandpiper, Curlew Sandpiper and Red-necked Stint.

Invercargill: At Invercargill drive to Lake Murihiku and look for Marsh Crake and waterfowl. Also drive to Bushy Point for Fernbirds.

Stay night at Invercargill.

DAY THREE

Travel to Stewart Island either by boat and look for seabirds on the way, or by plane. The boat leaves the wharf at Bluff Harbour and the plane from Invercargill Airport.

By boat to Stewart Island: Expect to see a lot of birds if the weather is rough. Birds regularly seen are - Blue Penguin, Shy Mollymawk, Bullers Mollymawk, Cape Pigeon, Cooks Petrel, Broad-billed Prion, Fairy Prion, White-faced Storm Petrel and Diving Petrel. Expect Wandering Albatross, Black-browed

Mollymawk, Grey-headed Mollymawk, Salvins Mollymawk and Southern Skua.
On Stewart Island: Upon arrival at Stewart Island the bush birds will be evident. Expect to see New Zealand Pigeon, Kaka, Red-crowned Parakeet, Yellow-crowned Parakeet, Shining Cuckoo, Long-tailed Cuckoo, Morepork (evening), Fantail, Tomtit, Grey Warbler, Hedge Sparrow, Tui, Bellbird, Silvereye and Redpoll.
Kiwi tour: Take the commercial kiwi excursion in the evening to Ocean Beach.
Stay night at Stewart Island.

DAY FOUR

Arrange a boat trip into deep water and then back to Ulva Island in Paterson Inlet. Look for Blue Shag in Paterson Inlet.
Ulva Island: On Ulva Island see Weka, Pigeon, Kaka, Yellow-crowned Parakeet, Red-crowned Parakeet, Fantail, Tomtit, Brown Creeper, Grey Warbler, Bellbird, Tui and Saddleback. There is also a breeding colony of Pied Shag and Little Shag here.
Stay night on Stewart Island.

DAY FIVE

Leave Stewart Island by plane for Invercargill. Travel to Te Anau.
Riverbed birds: Look for Black-fronted Dotterel and Black-fronted Tern on the Oreti River. Black-billed Gulls will be common throughout this area as will Paradise Shelduck and South Island Pied Oystercatchers. Watch for Little Owl in areas which have dense roadside hedges.
Redcliff Wetland Reserve: If you want to try again for Marsh Crake and Spotless Crake visit Redcliff Wetland. Expect also Bittern and Coot here.
Te Anau: Travel on to Te Anau. Visit the Te Anau Wildlife Reserve and see captive Takahe and other birdlife. Look for New Zealand Falcon in this area.
Stay night at Te Anau.

DAY SIX

Travel up the Eglinton Valley.
Mirror Lakes: See Scaup and Robin.
Cascade Creek: Do the Lake Gunn walk and look for bush birds. Look for New Zealand Falcon, Kaka, Kea, Yellow-crowned Parakeets and Yellowheads.
Hollyford River: Once over the Divide, look for Blue Ducks.
Homer Tunnel: Drive to the Homer Tunnel and look for Rock Wren to the right of the tunnel entrance or up Gertrude Valley prior to the tunnel. Pipit, Chaffinch and Redpoll might also be seen here and Yellowhead in beech trees lower down.
Milford Sound: Drive to Milford Sound. Tomtits are common everywhere. Sometimes Yellowheads might be heard in the forests nearby.
Boat trip on Milford Sound: On Milford Sound look for Fiordland Crested Penguins. Also watch for Yellow-eyed Penguins and Blue Penguins. You may also see dolphins here. Bellbirds sing from the forests verges.
Stay night at Te Anau.

DAY SEVEN

Return to Dunedin. This tour gives an opportunity of seeing 94 species.

LOCALITY GUIDE BIRD LIST

In the order of "Checklist of the Birds of New Zealand" (Turbott 1990)

Brown Kiwi
Little Spotted Kiwi
Great Spotted Kiwi
Crested Grebe
Dabchick
Hoary-headed Grebe
Australian Grebe
Wandering Albatross
Southern Royal Albatross
Northern Royal Albatross
Black-browed Mollymawk
Shy Mollymawk
Salvins Mollymawk
Chatham Island Mollymawk
Grey-headed Mollymawk
Yellow-nosed Mollymawk
Bullers Mollymawk
Light-mantled Sooty Albatross
Flesh-footed Shearwater
Bullers Shearwater
Sooty Shearwater
Fluttering Shearwater
Huttons Shearwater
Little Shearwater
Common Diving Petrel
Black Petrel
Westland Black Petrel
White-chinned Petrel
Cape Pigeon
Southern Giant Petrel
Northern Giant Petrel
Fairy Prion
Broad-billed Prion
Pycrofts Petrel
Cooks Petrel
Black-winged Petrel
Chatham Islands Petrel
Mottled Petrel
Grey-faced Petrel
Taiko
White-faced Storm Petrel
Yellow-eyed Penguin
Blue Penguin
White-flippered Penguin
Fiordland Crested Penguin
Australasian Gannet
Black Shag
Pied Shag

Little Black Shag
Little Shag
King Shag
Stewart Island Shag
Spotted Shag
Blue Shag
Pitt Island Shag
White-faced Heron
White Heron
Little Egret
Reef Heron
Cattle Egret
Nankeen Night Heron
Australasian Bittern
Glossy Ibis
Royal Spoonbill
Mute Swan
Black Swan
Canada Goose
Paradise Shelduck
Chestnut-breasted Shelduck
Blue Duck
Mallard
Grey Duck
Grey Teal
Brown Teal
Chestnut Teal
Shoveler
Scaup
Harrier
New Zealand Falcon
Nankeen Kestrel
Californian Quail
Bob-white Quail
Red-legged Partridge
Chukor
Grey Partridge
Brown Quail
Pheasant
Peafowl
Guinea Fowl
Banded Rail
Weka
Spotless Crake
Marsh Crake
Pukeko
Takahe
Australasian Coot

South Island Pied Oystercatcher
Variable Oystercatcher
Pied Stilt
Black Stilt
New Zealand Dotterel
Banded Dotterel
Black-fronted Dotterel
Large Sand Dotterel
Mongolian Dotterel
Shore Plover
Wrybill
Pacific Golden Plover
Spur-winged Plover
Ruddy Turnstone
Stewart Island Snipe
Lesser Knot
Great Knot
Curlew Sandpiper
Sharp-tailed Sandpiper
Pectoral Sandpiper
Red-necked Stint
Eastern Curlew
Asiatic Whimbrel
Little Whimbrel
Asiatic Black-tailed Godwit
Bar-tailed Godwit
Wandering Tattler
Siberian Tattler
Marsh Sandpiper
Terek Sandpiper
Southern Skua
Arctic Skua
Pomarine Skua
Black-backed Gull
Red-billed Gull
Black-billed Gull
White-winged Black Tern
Black-fronted Tern
Caspian Tern
White-fronted Tern
Antarctic Tern
Fairy Tern
Eastern Little Tern
Grey Ternlet
New Zealand Pigeon
Rock Pigeon
Barbary Dove
Spotted Dove
Sulphur-crested Cockatoo
Galah
Kakapo

Kaka
Kea
Crimson Rosella
Eastern Rosella
Red-crowned Parakeet
Yellow-crowned Parakeet
Shining Cuckoo
Long-tailed Cuckoo
Morepork
Little Owl
Kookaburra
Kingfisher
Rifleman
Rock Wren
Skylark
Welcome Swallow
Pipit
Hedge Sparrow
Blackbird
Song Thrush
Fernbird
Whitehead
Yellowhead
Brown Creeper
Grey Warbler
Chatham Island Warbler
Fantail
North Island Tomtit
South Island Tomtit
Snares Island Tomtit
New Zealand Robin
Black Robin
Silvereye
Stitchbird
Bellbird
Tui
Yellowhammer
Cirl Bunting
Chaffinch
Greenfinch
Goldfinch
Redpoll
House Sparrow
Starling
Myna
Kokako
North Island Saddleback
South Island Saddleback
Magpie
Rook

USEFUL BOOKS

P.C.Bull, P.D.Gaze and C.J.R.Robertson 1985: *The Atlas of Bird Distribution in New Zealand*. The Ornithological Society of New Zealand.

W.L.Buller 1872: *A History of the Birds of New Zealand*. John Van Voorst, London.

W.L.Buller 1887-1888: *A History of the Birds of New Zealand: Second Edition*. (Two volumes). Published by the author, London.

W.L.Buller 1905: *Supplement to the 'Birds of New Zealand'* (Two volumes). Published by the author.

David Butler, Peter Gaze and Jenny Hawkin 1990: *Birds of the Nelson Region and where to find them*. David Bulter Associated Ltd, Wellington.

B.A.Ellis 1987: *The New Zealand Birdwatchers' Book*. Reed Methuen, Auckland.

R.A.Falla, R.B.Sibson, and E.G.Turbott 1979: *The New Guide to the Birds of New Zealand. Collins*, Auckland and London.

C.A.Fleming 1982: *George Edward Lodge - The Unpublished New Zealand Bird Paintings*. Nova Pacifica, Wellington.

H.Guthrie-Smith 1925: *Bird Life on Island and Shore*. William Blackwood and Sons, Edinburgh.

P.C.Harper and F.C.Kinsky 1978: *Southern Albatrosses and Petrels*. Price Milburn, Wellington.

P.Harrison 1983: *Seabirds - An Identication Guide*. Crom Helm Ltd and A.H. and A.W. Reed.

Barrie Heather and Hugh Robertson. 1996: *The Field Guide to the Birds of New Zealand*.Viking, Auckland, New Zealand.

H.R.McKenzie 1972: *In Search Of Birds in New Zealand*. A.H.and A.W.Reed, Auckland.

P.Moncrief 1925: *New Zealand Birds and How to Identify Them*. Whitcombe and Tombes, Auckland.

G.Moon 1979: *The Birds Around Us*. Heinemann, Auckland.

W.R.B.Oliver 1930: *New Zealand Birds*. Fine Arts (NZ), Wellington.

W.R.B.Oliver 1955: *New Zealand Birds - Second Edition*. A.H.and A.W.Reed, Wellington.

Reader's Digest 1984: *Complete Book of New Zealand Birds*. Reed Methuen, Sydney.

S.Rowe and A.Plant 1988: *Beach Patrollers' Guide to Stormcast Seabirds (PROCELLARIIFORMES) found in New Zealand*.

E.F.Stead 1932: *The Life Histories of New Zealand Birds*. The Search Publishing Company, London.

The Checklist Committee 1970: *Annotated Checklist of the Birds of New Zealand*. Ornithological Society of New Zealand.

The Checklist Committee 1990: *Checklist of the Birds of New Zealand*. Ornithological Society of New Zealand.

INDEX